FUNDAMENTALS OF

Fourth Edition

BANKING

The New England Banking Institute

SIMON & SCHUSTER
CUSTOM PUBLISHING

Printed in the United States of America

10 9 8 7 6 5 4 3 2

Please visit our website at www.sscp.com

ISBN 0–536–00016–6

BA 98733

SIMON & SCHUSTER CUSTOM PUBLISHING
160 Gould Street/Needham Heights, MA 02494
Simon & Schuster Education Group

FOURTH EDITION CONTRIBUTING AUTHORS

James J. Basl
Cambridgeport Bank

John S. Burnett
Cape Cod Bank and Trust Company

Terri Donahoe
American Eagle Federal Credit Union

Cheryl A. Gross
Bank Boston

Joseph P. Madaio
Eastern Bank

Robert J. Morton
Bay State Savings Bank

Sandra L. Owen
Wellington Group, Inc.

David A. Pimenta
Bank Boston

Claudia Rioles
Citizens Trust Company

Stephen I. Sall
Cambridge Trust Company

Lawrence J. Sands
Bank Boston

Michael J. Tallo
Everett Savings Bank

Patricia D. Urbano
Family Bank

Donald R. Washburn
MassBank for Savings

Claudia C. Durning
State Street Bank and Trust

STUDENT ASSISTANT
Brian P. Chisholm
Bank Boston

MANAGING EDITOR
Deborah J. Pepper
The New England Banking Institute

DEDICATION

To THOMAS F. MCLAUGHLIN, JR., AND
JAMES T. CHAMBERLAIN

. . . for their vision and leadership.

CONTENTS

THE NEW ENGLAND BANKING INSTITUTE: A PROFILE

The New England Banking Institute (NEBI), a not-for-profit college and educational organization, serves all segments of the banking and financial services industry throughout the region. Founded in Boston in 1909, the Institute has achieved national attention as the only bank-sponsored educational organization in the country to be recognized as an accredited, degree-granting college. This unique status provides NEBI's membership with an educational resource of extraordinary excellence and esteem recently cited as a model for business and higher education collaboration.

Organized into three distinctive service divisions, college programs, training and management development and customized problems. NEBI offers a wide variety of programs for all levels of bank and financial services personnel. In a typical year, the Institute will deliver over 600 programs at over 40 different locations, and will enroll more than 10,000 bankers in its programs. Perhaps most important, NEBI has an impressive, highly credited faculty of 485 bankers and other professionals including college professors from area universities, attorneys, accountants, and a variety of industry consultants.

The New England Banking Institute offers a well-rounded education that includes business and liberal arts in addition to its banking and financial services curriculum. A primary objective is to help people acquire the skills and knowledge necessary to promote individual career development, and to serve as an educational resource for the regions's banking industry.

NEBI offers an Associates Degree in Business Administration in Banking Studies as well as certificates in specific banking concentrations in Connecticut, Massachusetts, and Rhode Island. Plans are now underway to expand NEBI's offerings to serve the New Hampshire market.

In the Fall of 1990, the New England Banking Institute and Bentley College, working together in a unique partnership, began offering a Bachelor's Degree that focuses on banking. Since 1990 NEBI has introduced similar partnerships with Assumption College, University of Hartford, and Providence College. The goal of these programs is to produce graduates who have cross-functional skills, and who understand all aspects of bank and financial management. Employees with this type of high quality broad-based education will be invaluable in this changing environment.

PREFACE

This fourth edition of Fundamentals of Banking is a revision of the text originally written in 1989 and revised again in 1991 and 1994. This text gives a broad based and practical overview of the various elements impacting banking today, with a flavor of changes currently taking shape and a best guess at those changes yet to come. An attempt has been made to be more inclusive of non-bank banks participating in "traditional" banking. As you read please take into account that the term "bank" has an ever-growing and broader definition and that our use has that context in mind. Reference to various regulations are made and many specific examples using Massachusetts state law are used in the text. State-by-state regulations vary so be mindful of these differences specific to your area as you read.

In addition we hope we have provided in this text an excellent resource for you as you tackle your career in banking and financial services. Since 1909 NEBI has focused on training and educational excellence. In all three of our service divisions our goal is to give you immediately applicable and relevant information which you can then translate on-the-job and use.

On behalf of the Institute, I would like to thank the contributing authors of this text for volunteering their time and energy and especially for their responsiveness to this project and its unyielding deadlines. I would also like to thank the many supporters of The New England Banking Institute, our members, boards, committees, advisory groups, and partners in higher education.

It is appropriate to provide special recognition to our faculty and to our students who each contribute to the success of our fine organization and who continually challenge us to maintain and achieve the standard of excellence we have come to be known for and help us to reach even beyond excellence in the face of change.

The foundation of The New England Banking Institute is built upon a unique need and a unique response to that need from the banking industry that has created and supported us. We hope this text provides you with the knowledge you seek and becomes a light for your educational and professional journey. In the meantime, we look forward to walking and if we're honest, at times running, along side you. This is an exciting time in a dynamic industry and we are enthusiastic about sharing the future with you.

Deborah J. Pepper
Senior Vice President and
Corporate Director of Academic Affairs

1

INTRODUCTION
Stephen Sall

SECTION I

INTRODUCTION

This chapter will briefly discuss what a bank actually is. It will describe the products and services that banks have to offer, and it will answer the question, "Just why do people go to a bank?"

It will then go on to describe the various members of the banking industry, including commercial banks, thrift institutions, and credit unions (which in some respects are banks and in others are not).

LEARNING OBJECTIVES

After reading this chapter, you should have an understanding of the following:

1. What are the various products and services offered by banks?
2. What is meant by the term financial intermediary?
3. What are the different types of financial institutions in the U.S. today? How are they similar to and different from one another?
4. What is involved in correspondent banking?
5. What is the difference between a bank and a credit union? What are the reasons underlying the current controversy between banks and credit unions?

1

WHAT IS A BANK?

What is a bank? What functions do banks perform? According to *Webster's New World* Dictionary, a *bank* is "... an establishment for receiving, keeping, lending or sometimes issuing money and making easier the exchange of funds by checks, notes, etc. ... banks make a profit by lending money at interest...."[1] This is certainly a good start, but it needs further development. Why exactly do people come to banks? What specific services do banks perform? What do banks have to offer? At this point, a list might be helpful:

Banks offer the following products/services:

1. A place to safely *deposit* one's money.
2. A way to efficiently pay one's bills; a *payments mechanism*.
3. A place to borrow funds: the *lending* of money for commercial loans, consumer loans, and mortgage loans.
4. A place to go for trust services.
5. A way to finance international trade.
6. A place to store one's valuables: safe deposit services.
7. A place to obtain brokerage services (as long as certain specific conditions are met).
8. Life insurance (SBLI). (Traditionally only offered through thrifts, but now also available through commercial banks, should they choose to do so.)

As can be seen from the above list, many of the various functions and services can be divided into the three essential functions of banking. In fact, any bank, no matter which type, will perform (to varying extents, of course) each of these three functions.

> A bank is an institution that receives, lends, and pays out funds.

1. *Deposit Function*—The deposit function is simply obtaining the raw materials of banking. Corporations, consumers, and governments deposit funds in banks to pay debts and/or to earn interest on excess funds. Banks provide many deposit vehicles (which will be described in Chapter 5) in which individuals can deposit funds for various periods of time, ranging from demand deposits which can be withdrawn with no prior notice—to long-term certificates of deposit.

2. *Lending Function*—The lending function converts the raw material (deposits) into an earning asset through the process of intermediation (which will be described below). The income derived from the lending function is used to pay interest to the depositor and cover the bank's operating expenses (with, hopefully, some left over as profit). Many types of loan vehicles are available (and are discussed in Chapters 10 through 12), ranging from 30-day loans to businesses to 30-year mortgages to individual consumers.

3. *Payment Function*—Every day, millions of checks flow through the economy. An efficient system must be present so that those who accept a check will be assured that they will be either paid or notified of non-payment in a timely manner. Those who wish to issue checks need such a system to ensure that their checks will be accepted.

Without a payment system in place, businesses in Los Angeles, example, would not accept checks from customers in Boston. Customers from Boston, on the other hand, are not about to send cash through the mail. The use and acceptance of checks not only avoids such risks but also provides the writer with a receipt of payment.

The banking system provides this payment function not only for paper checks but also through electronic systems, such as Automated Clearinghouses (ACH) and ATM networks (discussed in Chapter 7).

Intermediation

*Banks act as **intermediaries** (middlemen) between depositors and borrowers.*

When performing deposit and lending functions, banks can be said to be intermediaries. An ***intermediary*** is a middleman. Specifically, banks function as financial intermediaries. They are the middlemen between depositors (those with an excess of funds) and borrowers (those with a need for funds). Money comes into the bank as deposits (bank liabilities) and leaves the bank as loans and investments (bank assets).

These deposit and lending functions could exist without a bank, but the following example may help to explain how inefficient such a system would be without a financial intermediary and how critical such institutions are to the smooth functioning of the economy.

Imagine that you want to buy a new car. You need $15,000. Without the existence of a bank, you would have to find individuals who have funds available and negotiate a contract with each one. Those individuals with funds to invest would have to search out those who need funds, negotiate a contract, and hope that they will be paid. Obviously, this process is time consuming for both parties and exposes each one to a number of risks. By the use of an intermediary, the process is greatly simplified.

Are banks the only financial intermediaries? Certainly not. Life insurance companies take in money as premium payments and in turn place it in real estate and other long-term investments. Money Market Mutual *what is this?* Funds take in money as deposits (or shares) and in turn place it in high-denomination, high-yielding, short-term investments.

***Disintermediation** is the net withdrawal of funds from the banking system.*

When the process breaks down, disintermediation is said to occur—a condition where money is withdrawn rather than being deposited. ***Disintermediation*** indicates money being withdrawn from the banking system. It has in fact happened in the not-so-distant past and was one of the reasons for the large-scale deregulation of the banking industry that took place in the early 1980s (which will be discussed in great detail in the next chapter).

TYPES OF BANKS

Within the U.S. banking industry, there are three major categories of banks:

1. Commercial Banks.
2. Thrift Institutions.
3. Credit Unions.

Thrifts and commercial banks have been differentiated traditionally by the types of financial products and services they provide for their customers and by the nature of their relationships with other banks.

Commercial Banks

Commercial banks traditionally have concentrated on providing services to businesses, such as corporate demand deposit accounts and commercial loans. Although the majority of their business has been historically with the business sector, they also have participated heavily in the retail (consumer) market, offering such products as personal checking accounts and consumer loans.

Commercial banks supplement their basic lending and payment functions with a wide variety of cash management products and services (many of which are discussed in Chapter 13). They also handle foreign currency exchange, domestic and international money transfers, and municipal services (services to state and local governments).

In addition, many of the larger commercial banks also provide an array of correspondent services to smaller commercial banks and to thrift institutions.

Correspondent Banking

In the financial community, the term *correspondent services* is used to denote a bank's purchasing of certain banking services from another organization. A *correspondent bank* is a bank that performs a service for another, typically smaller bank. Smaller banks use the services of a correspondent bank for one of two reasons. Either they simply don't have the ability (in terms of staffing, equipment, etc.) to perform the service on their own, or it is less expensive to pay the correspondent than to perform the service on their own.

Most correspondent services are provided by large commercial banks, central banks (such as the Federal Reserve System, which is discussed in Chapter 4), and outside service bureaus. The processing of checks (encoding, sorting, and presentment) is an example of a correspondent service. Other types of correspondent services include:

1. On-line computer services to handle daily tellers' transaction postings (as well as mortgage, consumer, or other loan payments).

2. Supply coin and currency.

3. Domestic and international wire transfer services.

4. Collection services for foreign checks, E-bonds, and food stamps.

5. Direct Deposits (Automated Clearinghouse Transactions; these are discussed in great detail in Chapter 7).

6. Loan participations (buying and selling commercial loan packages).

7. Credit card agent services.

8. Safekeeping of securities.

9. Providing training.

Traditionally, these services are paid for in either "soft" or "hard" dollars as follows:

1. **Compensating Balances**—Also referred to as *soft dollar* payment. In this type of payment, a bank will agree to leave on deposit, in an interest free account, a predetermined daily collected balance of X dollars. Rather than directly paying the correspondent bank for the service(s), the bank is sacrificing the income that it could have earned had these funds been invested elsewhere (an *implicit,* or *opportunity* cost).

2. *Hard Dollar Fees*—Rather than agreeing to keep a specified balance on deposit in its account, the user bank agrees to have its account charged monthly for whatever fees were incurred. It is billed for the actual costs of the services that have been provided (an *explicit* cost).

Margin notes:

Smaller banks often buy *correspondent services* from larger, *correspondent banks*.

Banks can pay for correspondent services by maintaining deposit accounts with larger, correspondent banks. These accounts are considered soft-dollar payment.

The income a bank could have earned, but forgoes in soft-dollar payments, is an implicit cost of doing business.

Correspondent banks may simply bill smaller banks for services, and these are explicit costs.

Better Copy

Thrift Institutions

Thrift institutions comprise mutual savings banks (MSB's), savings and loan associations (S&L's), and cooperative banks.

Unlike commercial banks, thrifts traditionally have been the bank of the consumer, at one time even calling themselves "people banks." Their basic role has been to link savers and borrowers. They offer a variety of savings account programs and continue to be very active within the residential mortgage market.

Throughout most of the U.S., the thrift industry consists mainly of Savings & Loan Associations (S & L's). Here in Massachusetts, however, the thrift industry is dominated by Mutual Savings Banks (MSB's) and Cooperative Banks. While S & L's can be found in all fifty states, Mutual Savings Banks and Cooperative Banks developed only in specific areas. Mutual Savings Banks are located mainly in the northeastern and northwestern states (including Alaska). Cooperative Banks are unique to New England. The great majority of Cooperative Banks, in fact, are located here in Massachusetts, with just a few in the neighboring states of New Hampshire and Rhode Island.

In 1979, more than 75 percent of residential mortgages in the U.S. were held by the savings and loan associations and mutual savings banks. The primary source of funds for these mortgage loans was traditionally provided by savings deposits.

These distinctions between commercial banks and thrifts, however, were diminished considerably when the banking industry was deregulated nationally as a result of the Depository Institutions Deregulation and Monetary Control Act of 1980 and the Garn-St. Germain Act of 1982 and locally by the Brennan Bill of 1982. In a nutshell, these laws eliminated most of the legal distinctions between commercial banks and thrifts by allowing all banks to offer almost any type of financial service. (Each of these laws is discussed in greater detail in the following chapter on Bank History.)

Although thrifts as a group now have the power to provide virtually any service that commercial banks can provide, they have used their new powers in widely varying degrees. While many members of the S & L industry have jumped right into the provision of numerous commercial services, the Mutual Savings Banks and Cooperative Banks, for the most part, have been more conservative in taking advantage of their new-found powers.

Although the playing field between commercial banks and thrifts has in fact been leveled, there do continue to be differences. Although many thrifts have certainly chosen to take advantage of their new powers, a good number remain for the most part consumer-oriented institutions.

To recapitulate, the thrift industry is made up of three types of institutions: Savings & Loans, Mutual Savings Banks, and Cooperative Banks. Although they are typically grouped together as thrifts, there are differences between them. The next section will discuss the development of each institution and how they vary from each other.

Savings and Loan Associations

Early S&L's tended to be limited (or closed) to small groups of potential house builders.

Until very recently, S & L's have been mainly involved in the financing of home mortgages. The origins of S & L's date back to the building and loan societies of the 1830s, which were modeled on the English building societies. The first such institution in the U.S. was the Oxford Provident Building Association of Philadelphia, which was organized in 1831. The association's original 40 members agreed to save a specified amount each week and pool these funds for home loans for each other.

In 1836, the Brooklyn Building & Mutual Loan Association became the second such institution in the country; the third opened for business in South Carolina in 1843. The early associations did not charge any interest on loans and held drawings to determine the order in which members received loans. The funds that could be generated by such "closed systems" were, however, quite limited.

In fact, the original such institutions grew slowly because they were organized as limited life funds. These funds were originally intended to be terminated when all the members had purchased their homes.

In the 1880s, a new, more flexible financial organization was introduced. Known as the "Dayton Plan" (because it originated in Ohio), this kind of financial institution encouraged savings accounts from the general public. In addition, depositors were allowed to withdraw their funds after meeting certain time conditions; it was no longer necessary to wait until all the members had financed their homes. These institutions became known as Savings & Loan Associations and grew very rapidly. In fact, by the turn of the century, there were approximately 5,000 such institutions operating throughout the U.S., located in every state then in the country.

When the Home Owners' Loan Act was passed in 1933, federal charters for S & L's became available for the first time, thus creating a "dual" federal and state regulatory system as in the case of commercial banking. Federally chartered S & L's must belong to the Federal Savings & Loan Insurance Corporation (FSLIC) and must become members of the Federal Home Loan Bank System.

S & L's grew and prospered through the 1950s and 1960s, mainly due to stable interest rates and the fact that the government was playing a very active role in the encouragement of home ownership. In fact, from 1960 to 1970, the total assets of all S & L's more than doubled, from $71 billion to $176 billion.

During the early 1980s, as will be described in the following chapter on bank history, the S & L's, along with the rest of the thrift industry, were granted greatly expanded powers. By the end of 1988, total S & L assets had reached $1.2 trillion, with over 3,500 such institutions operating approximately 25,000 branches. Many of these S & L's, however, used their new powers very aggressively—to a point where a good number of them failed or found themselves in a precarious financial condition.

Cooperative Banks

Similar to S & L's, Cooperative Banks were developed with the specific purpose of financing home ownership. While the S & L's developed across the country, Cooperative Banks, as previously mentioned, are unique to New England, located mainly in Massachusetts, but also to a small degree in both New Hampshire and Rhode Island.

Unlike S & L's, however, a Cooperative Bank refers to its customers as shareholders, not as depositors. One becomes a shareholder simply by opening an account. The shareholders themselves are said to be the owners of the institution. The shareholders elect directors, who in turn elect operating officers and vote on major operating issues of the bank and financial institution. These shares are not negotiable, meaning they cannot be transferred.

Cooperative Banks are restricted in some lending functions. Unlike other institutions, which can lend to anyone, Cooperative Banks can lend only to their shareholders. In terms of their powers, they are very similar to Mutual Savings Banks, which will be described below.

The *Dayton Plan* encouraged S&L's to open themselves to the general public for deposits and loans.

S&L's have become progressively deregulated in the 1980s.

Cooperative banks are owned by their shareholders (depositors) and can lend only to those shareholders.

Cooperative Banks can now also be stock institutions. They can convert their ownership from a mutual (being owned by the depositors) to a stock institution by a vote of the existing shareholders. Such a conversion allows the institution to raise capital by issuing shares of stock.

Mutual Savings Banks

Mutual savings banks are owned by their depositors, but do not generally finance mortgages. They encourage general thrift.

Mutual Savings Banks can trace their roots back to the Reverend Henry Duncan of Scotland in 1810. Duncan stressed the idea among his parishioners that they should set aside some portion of their income for the future. His idea was well received, and by 1820 over 300 such institutions had developed in Scotland, England, Wales, and Ireland.

The first such savings bank chartered in the United States was the Provident Institution for Savings in Boston in 1816. The first to actually open its doors was the Philadelphia Savings Fund Society (PSFS), now known under the name Meritor. These institutions catered to individuals who could save small sums on a regular basis. Commercial banks at that time did not seek nor want to do business with individual consumers. Mutual Savings Banks, unlike Cooperative Banks and S & L's, were developed not for the specific purpose of financing home ownership, but simply to encourage thrift. Rather than concentrating on financing residential mortgages, a large portion of their deposits were invested in government securities. For many years Mutual Savings Banks had the ability to make a wider variety of investments than the Cooperative Banks and S & L's. They were, for instance, able to grant unsecured personal loans considerably earlier than either of the others.

Similar to Cooperative Banks, Mutual Savings Banks were typically chartered as mutual institutions. They were owned by the depositors, who in turn elected a board of "corporators" and a president. All of the profits of the bank belonged to the depositors. Many Mutual Savings Banks (as was the case with Cooperative Banks) have chosen to convert their ownership from mutual to stock format. Again, such a conversion allows a bank to raise capital, in the form of stock, to supplement its deposits in an effort to grow and prosper in a deregulated and competitive environment.

INTRODUCTION
Terri Donahoe

SECTION II

INTRODUCTION

This section is intended to describe the unique nature of credit unions. We have chosen to include greater detail at the request of students and members who are from the credit union segment of the industry. To that end, we'll explore such concepts as the difference between members and customers, the definition of financial cooperatives, what common bond requirements mean to a credit union's *field of membership (FOM)*, the credit union organizational structure, federal and state charters, and various legislation affecting credit unions.

A variety of credit union products and services will also be examined to illustrate that larger credit unions can offer a full menu of products to meet their members' needs.

This chapter will also explore the history of the credit union movement from the mid-nineteenth century to present day, as well examine three controversial issues that serve as a continual bone of contention between credit unions and the banking industry.

LEARNING OBJECTIVES

After reading this chapter, you should have an understanding of the following:

1. What is meant by the term "financial cooperative"
2. The basic differences between a credit union and other financial institutions
3. The various products and services offered by credit unions
4. The history of the credit union movement to present day
5. The reasons for present day controversy between credit unions and banks

WHAT IS A CREDIT UNION?

A Credit Union is a
financial cooperative
which is owned and
operated by the people
it serves.

A Credit Union is a financial cooperative which is owned and operated by the people it serves. A cooperative is a type of business which is owned and run by its members on a not-for-profit basis. Because of the cooperative nature of credit unions, the people who belong to one are called **members** rather than customers. A cooperative exists to serve its members, not to generate a profit for shareholders or stockholders, as do other financial institutions. It is the members of the credit union who benefit from any profit the credit union generates by virtue of new or improved products and services, lower rates on loans, higher rates on savings, and minimal or no fees for services. It is this aspect of Credit Unions—their cooperative nature—which contributes toward their unique nature. It also illustrates the greatest difference between a credit union and a bank or savings and loan.

In short, the people who use credit union financial services—its members—are the same people who have a voice in running the credit union. Members can exercise their democratic rights in a variety of ways: by participating in yearly membership meetings where they can vote for Board of Director representation; by running for a Board position or for some other com-

mittee position, or by volunteering as credit union employees. Many smaller credit unions are operated entirely by volunteers. Others employ a mix of volunteer and paid staff; while still others are operated entirely by a paid, professional staff.

The motto of all credit unions is "Not for Profit, Not for Charity, But for Service."[11] This philosophy nicely summarizes the ultimate focus of all credit unions—that of providing service to its membership.

To belong to a credit union, you must fit the field of membership requirements. That means you must meet the *common bond* requirements of the credit union. The common bond is the tie that links credit union members together. People who are eligible to join credit unions are people who have something in common such as an employer, a geographic area or a religion, club, or trade association, etc. Common bonds are typically classified as occupation-based, community-based, or associational-based.

An *occupational-based* common bond might include all people who work for the same employer. Some credit unions have expanded to include several different employer groups which makes it possible for several groups from different small companies to band together to gain access to credit union membership. Otherwise it might be difficult for smaller companies to generate enough resources to take advantage of credit union services. The majority of credit unions today are occupational based. The largest of all is the Navy Credit Union with assets of $3.171 billion and almost 900,000 members.[12]

A credit union which is *community-based* serves members of a particular community (city, county, or part of the state). To become a member of a community based credit union, an individual would simply have to live or work in a particular community. The Norwich Municipal Federal Credit Union is an example of a community-based credit union because it serves people who live or work in the Norwich, CT community.

Associational-based credit unions serve people who belong to the same association or group such as a labor union, religious group, professional organization, or other organizational group. "Student groups, parent-teacher organizations, alumni associations, and students in a trade school or other curriculum—and church groups constitute associational common bonds."[13]

> The common bond is the tie that links credit union members together.

HOW DOES A CREDIT UNION GET STARTED?

Starting a credit union requires a charter. Before the Federal Credit Union Act of 1934, which created a federal regulating body to oversee credit unions, all credit unions were created under state charters. After 1934, individuals or groups seeking to start a credit union could apply for either a state or a federal charter. In fact, if the name of the credit union contains the word *federal*, it is an indication that its charter was granted by a federal chartering agency. Choosing to apply for a state or federal charter is a function of which laws are more or less strict with regards to running the credit union. Some state laws are more lenient than federal laws and vice versa.

National Credit Union Administration

The federal chartering agency is the National Credit Union Administration or NCUA. The NCUA grants charters to establish federal credit unions and creates the various bylaws by which a credit union is run. As of December 1996, there were over 11,000 federal credit unions. Periodically, all credit unions are audited by their regulating body (state or federal) to ensure compliance with the bylaws of its charter. Any changes in the credit union's original charter (to expand the field of membership, for example, or to change its name) requires approval by the NCUA.

Democratic Principles

As a democratic organization, all credit unions hold annual meetings whereby its membership is invited to vote for representation on the Board of Directors, as well as to voice opinions and ask questions concerning the operation of the credit union. Each member has one vote, regardless of the amount of funds he or she has on deposit.

Organizational Structure

The Board of Directors of a credit union are elected from the general membership by the members. Theirs is usually a volunteer position which is charged with setting the strategic direction of the credit union and ensuring that the members' interests are kept at the forefront of all decision making. This focus on the member is what keeps fees and other miscellaneous costs minimal or non-existent. While specific duties will vary depending on the size of the credit union, other Board responsibilities may include approving membership applications, setting loan policies, determining security needs, appointing committees, and supervising credit union investments.

The individual responsible for the day-to-day operations of the credit union may be called the Manager, Chairperson, or President/CEO, depending on the size of the credit union. This position is generally a paid position. In addition, there may be a vice chairperson or vice president, again depending on the size of the credit union. A Treasurer or Financial Officer is responsible for the financial operation of the credit union which includes investing members' funds in safe investment vehicles, such as short term certificates to generate income for the credit union. It's noteworthy that credit unions tend to be more restricted than banks in terms of the investments they can make with members' funds.

Staff positions within a credit union vary widely depending on the credit union's size. In smaller credit unions a teller may also lend money to members; a loan officer may also perform loan processing work; a member services representative may also perform teller functions. In large credit unions, employees serve in a more specialized capacity. Some credit unions do not handle cash at all; others are completely full service financial institutions offering a variety of products from debit cards and Trust accounts to residential mortgages.

HISTORY OF THE CREDIT UNION MOVEMENT

Credit Unions were formed around the middle 1800s in Europe. In those days, obtaining a loan from a bank required that you had sufficient collateral to support the loan. The society of the time consisted of the wealthy and the working class poor; there was no middle class. Consequently, banks were not a viable option for most people. While there were other lending avenues that could be explored, these other sources of loans often demanded exorbitant interest rates, and working class people were often thrown into debtors' prison for failure to repay. It was within this economic context that credit unions were born. They began as "a self-help organization for the working classes."[14] They have variously been described as being a "workingman's bank"[15] or "an institution for little people"[16] who were ill-served by other types of financial institutions.

The Cooperative Spirit

"One of the most successful early cooperatives began, (not as a financial co-operative but) as a store in Rochdale, England. Formed by a group of workers, it was called the Rochdale Society of Equitable Pioneers. This cooperative store sold shares to its members to raise capital to buy goods at lower than retail prices and then sold the goods at a savings to members. Members were entitled to a share of the society's earnings at the end of the year. The Rochdale principals included open membership to any person of goodwill, democratic control whereby members each had one vote, limited interest on share capital, and the return of earnings above expenses to members in proportion to their patronage."[17] It is this cooperative principle that Hermann Schultze-Delitzsch built on a few years later in Germany.

Hermann Schultze-Delitzsch

Hermann Schultze-Delitzsch, a prominent German political figure, was instrumental in fostering the growth of such cooperatives, which he called "people's banks."[18] These "people's banks" operated under the principal of mutual self help rather than charity. Instead of relying on contributions from the wealthy to fund his cooperative, Schultze-Delitzsch charged each member of the "bank" a fee. This fee bought a share of the ownership. When necessary, members could take advantage of those pooled resources. Today we call those pooled resources "savings" and the act of taking advantage of those resources, "loans."

Friedrich William Raiffeisen

While Schultze-Delitzsch worked primarily with the urban poor, Friedrich William Raiffeisen, a former mayor, was instrumental in helping the poor farmers of Germany. Raiffeisen's approach initially differed from Schultze-Delitzsch's in that he depended on donations from the wealthy to keep his cooperative funded. He later adopted Schultze-Delitzsch's philosophy of mutual self help and formed the first credit union in 1864. Membership was based on whatever assets the farmers had, as well as on their moral character. If another farmer would write you a letter a reference, you were accepted for membership.

Interestingly enough, while the financial cooperatives organized in Europe were essentially divided between urban and rural groups, in North America, it was a different story.

Alphonse Desjardins

In North America, the credit union movement began around the turn of the century. A man by the name of Alphonse Desjardins, a journalist, became a champion of the poor and working class in Canada. As such, he worked hard to establish the first credit union in North America in 1901—La Caisse Populaire de Levis *(which is just across the St. Lawrence River from Quebec City)*.

Edward Filene

Further South, Edward Filene of Filene's Department Stores helped spread the credit union movement throughout the United States. Filene, together with Roy Bergengren, a Massachusetts lawyer, and others worked to establish legislation which would permit the operation of credit unions in the United States. Filene's and Bergengren's work not only contributed greatly to the development of individual credit unions, but also to the development of a unified organization for credit unions—credit union leagues.

The Growth Continues

The first credit union in the United States was St. Mary's Parish in Manchester, New Hampshire, founded by Alphonse Desjardins in 1909. St. Mary's is still in operation today as a progressive $350 million community credit union.

Interestingly enough, the Great Depression of the 1930s was a time of positive growth for credit unions. As more and more banks and savings and loans failed, people looked for alternative ways to ensure the safety and growth of their money.

The first credit union in the United States was St. Mary's Parish in Manchester, New Hampshire, founded by Alphonse Desjardins in 1909.

The Federal Credit Union Act of 1934

Throughout the 1920s and early 1930s, the credit union movement remained a fairly unorganized effort. Prominent men worked hard to establish credit unions, however, a more organized effort and legislative support was needed. Due to the earlier work of Filene and others, on January 3, 1934, the Federal Credit Union Act was passed by Congress. This Act established a means to "make more available to people of small means credit for provident purposes through a national system of cooperative credit, thereby helping to stabilize the credit structure of the United States."[19] The Federal Credit Union Act defined what a federal credit union was and provided those seeking to start credit unions an alternative to state charters. Most importantly, the Act gave the credit union movement the legislative backing of the United States and established criteria for the formation of federal credit unions. It also required all federal credit unions to set aside a portion of their earnings to cover bad debt and to purchase bond coverage to protect against loses from theft. The federal agency designed to grant federal credit unions charters was called the Farm Credit Administration. In 1970, the chartering agency changed to the National Credit Union Administration, or NCUA, as it is known today.

The Federal Credit Union Act established a means to make more available to people of small means credit for provident purposes.

Credit Union National Association

Now federally sanctioned, credit unions needed an organizing body. That body became known as CUNA or the Credit Union National Association, established in August of 1934. CUNA is a not-for-profit organization which provides training and educational programs, magazines and newsletters, research, legislative representation, public relations, new product development, and many other support programs for credit unions throughout the United States.

CREDIT UNION PRODUCTS AND SERVICES

Like other financial institutions, credit unions offer a variety of savings, loan, and convenience products and services. Usually, credit unions offer higher rates on savings products and lower rates on loans products. The fees for such products and services are also minimal, since the focus of the credit union is not on making a profit for shareholders, but on providing the best product value to its membership. The number and variety of products and services depends on the size of the credit union. Each credit union determines its product offerings based on its members needs and the resources available.

Savings Products

The primary account is the share savings account. This type of account is similar to savings accounts at other financial institutions. It is an interest bearing account with the interest added to the account either quarterly or monthly, as determined by the Board of Directors. A member must open the share savings account with a minimum deposit which can range from $5.00 to $25.00 or greater. Again, this depends on the policy established by the Board of Directors. This minimum deposit represents the member's *share* in the credit union.

In addition, a credit union may offer some kind of **Living Trust account,** where a member can essentially change account ownership from that of a person to that of a entity—the Trust—to protect the member's assets upon his or her death.

Share Draft Accounts or **Share Checking Accounts** are comparable to checking accounts at other financial institutions. A share draft is a piece of paper which essentially functions just like a check. Many share draft accounts also earn dividends. Share drafts typically come with carbon-less copies, reducing the need for the credit union to return canceled checks to the member. This helps minimize cost, and the savings is passed on to the member in the form of reduced service charges. Members can also obtain a copy of the check if one is needed. Often, no minimum balance requirements are needed to open a share draft account, and there are usually no per check processing charges.

Certificate Accounts (Share Certificates) are timed deposit accounts. A member may open a certificate account and choose a term, a specific length of time, during which he or she may not access the funds without penalty *(usually a loss of dividends)*. Usually, there is a higher opening balance the member must meet to open this kind of account, $1000 for example. The benefit is the higher dividend rates these funds can earn.

Credit Unions also offer **Money Market Accounts** which are generally tiered accounts. The higher the average balance, the higher the dividend rate is. Money markets are not timed deposits; therefore, the member may access these funds at any time without penalty.

Individual Retirement Accounts (IRAs) are intended to help members save for their retirement years. These are tax deferred accounts. Typically, when a member begins to withdraw from this account he or she is in a lower tax bracket, consequently, the member pays less taxes on the dividends these funds earn. A member must be a wage earner to qualify for an IRA and may choose to fund it through payroll deduction.

Christmas Club, Vacation Club, Special Purpose Club Accounts are "generic" types of share accounts designed to help members save for a specific purpose. Such club accounts earn dividends and usually require no minimum balance.

LOAN PRODUCTS

Credit Unions are offering an increasing variety of loan products for its members. **Auto loans,** for example, account for much of a credit union's loan to share ratio, one measure of its financial health. Generally, the higher the loan to share ratio, the more financially sound the credit union. Credit Unions do the highest volume of their lending through car, boat, mini van, or other vehicle loans. As stated earlier, rates tend to be lower on such loans than in other financial institutions. Some credit unions offer **car leasing** opportunities, as well. Loans are typically granted based on collateral and the character of the member. Many members who might have difficulty getting a loan elsewhere may be able to get one at the credit union, not because lending standards are less stringent, but because the members are generally *known* to credit union lenders. Many credit unions also offer **credit life** and **credit disability insurance** as well, to protect the borrower from defaulting on the loan. Such insurance is free of charge in some credit unions; others charge a minimal premium which is typically added to the member's monthly loan payments.

Personal or *signature* **loans** are also provided at many credit unions. Such loans are made with no collateral other than the signature of the member. Such loans are used for almost any purpose.

Business loans are offered by community credit unions for the purpose of starting a business or other business-related purpose.

Home equity loans are also available at many credit unions, where the member uses the equity in his or her home as collateral for a loan. Home equity loans are often used for debt consolidation, weddings, home improvements, education, and new car purchases. Depending on the credit union, a member may have the choice of a home equity fixed rate, where the rate stays the same for the life of the loan, or a home equity credit line, where the member can write out checks to draw on the established credit line as needed. Credit Union lending personnel usually advise the member as to which option is best for him or her.

Residential real estate loans are long term loans for up to 30 years where the house serves as the collateral. Depending on the size of the credit union, it may offer a variety of residential mortgage products ranging from balloon mortgages and jumbo mortgages to bi-monthly mortgages.

Credit Unions may also offer **credit cards, overdraft protection, automatic debt repayment, safety deposit boxes, member education and financial counseling services.**

CONVENIENCE PRODUCTS

Technology is slowly changing the way most people do their financial business. Armed with an **ATM or debit card, automated telephone access, a home computer, 1-800 numbers, payroll deduction, direct deposit, automatic loan payment transfers** and various other **electronic fund transfers,** a credit union member may not ever have to set foot in the building in order to enjoy a full range of financial products and services and quick and efficient service.

Finally, credit unions can offer an array of other financial products and services including: money orders, travelers cheques *(single and double signature),* notary public services, night depositories, wire transfers, and *NADA Used Car Guides.* Credit unions have expanded their product and service greatly since the 1980s and are now able to provide a full range of financial products and services to its members. The distinction between larger credit unions and banks, especially small community banks has become more and more blurred.

CREDIT UNION LEGISLATION

National Credit Union Administration

In 1970, the National Credit Union Administration or NCUA was created. The NCUA is the regulatory agency for federal credit unions. This 1970 Act required that members' deposits be insured through the National Credit Union Share Insurance Fund for up to $100,000.00. State chartered credit unions may obtain insurance through the NCUA or obtain state share insurance.

The credit union insurance fund provides the same levels of protection that the FDIC provides bank depositors. However, the credit union fund is structured differently. It is built to ensure that tax payers will not be responsible to bail out credit unions should one fail.

Revision of the Federal Credit Union Act

In 1977, the Federal Credit Union Act was revised. This new legislation gave credit unions a good deal more flexibility in the types of products and services they could offer. In particular, the Act allowed credit unions to offer residential mortgages and pre-authorized lines of credit. Prior to this legislation, credit unions could only offer small, short term loans to its members.

The end result of this legislation was that credit unions began to compete more seriously with other financial institutions in terms of the number and variety of financial products and services they could offer. In the early days of credit unions, the basic offerings were savings and loans, and that was all!

> In 1977, the Federal Credit Union Act was revised and gave credit unions a good deal more flexibility in the types of products and services they could offer.

Depository Institutions Deregulation and Monetary Control Act

The Depository Institutions Deregulation and Monetary Control Act of 1980 further blurred the differences between credit unions and banks by allowing share draft checking accounts (*they previously were not allowed to offer checking accounts*) and by allowing credit unions to grant loans at higher rates than what was previously acceptable. This meant that credit unions could extend more loans to more members.

In 1982, NCUA deregulated rates on share savings, share draft/checking, and certificate accounts. Such rates would no longer be set by NCUA; instead they would be determined by each credit union's Board of Directors. In light of some corresponding deregulation set by the Depository Institutions Deregulation Commission, which allowed banks greater autonomy in the types of accounts they offered and in setting rates, the competition grew.

The Birth of SEGs

Another major change occurred in 1982 and concerned credit union field of membership requirements. It was a time of record credit union failures. In response to these failures, the NCUA revised its chartering policy to permit credit unions to offer their services to multiple groups with *unlike* common bonds. Such *select employer groups* (SEGs), as these unlike groups were known, required approval by the NCUA, since they did not fit under the original charter. The result was that smaller employers who didn't have the resources to start their own credit union had an opportunity to offer its employees the benefits of credit union membership, and the number of credit union failures markedly declined.

CONTROVERSY

As long as credit unions remained small organizations with strict common bond requirements, "they were hardly noticed . . . they were below the sight lines of many banks."[20] Lately, however, common bond requirements have become more relaxed and credit union growth has become much more aggressive. Over the years, three main issues seem to surface as triggers for disputes between credit unions and banks.

Tax Exempt Status

One of the biggest points of contention between credit unions and other financial institutions is the credit union's tax exempt status. Since a credit union is a *cooperative,* meaning it's owned and operated by the people it serves, the profits a credit union generates do not benefit the organization but rather its members. Since the credit union derives no income, it is not subject to federal income taxes. Other financial institutions view this as special treatment and consider credit unions to have an unfair financial advantage over them. Numerous movements have been afoot in the legislature to remove this tax exempt status, but so far none have been successful, In the mid 1980s, Congress, not the banks, attempted to remove the tax exempt status in order to raise money to reduce the national deficit. Credit Union lobbyists were successful in fending off this attempt at taxation, however, and the tax exempt status remains.

Merging the NCUA

Another controversy arose in 1986 regarding the role of the National Credit Union Administration (NCUA). The NCUA is the regulating body for federal credit unions. One of the NCUA's responsibilities is to oversee the National Share Insurance Fund *(which insures members' deposits for up to $100, 000).* The FDIC *(Federal Deposit Insurance Corporation)* and the FSLIC *(Federal Savings and Loan Corporation)* also insure customers' deposits for up to $100,000 for the banking industry. During the late eighties, many banks and savings and loans failed, which put a severe drain on FDIC and FSLIC funds. Legislation was proposed to combine all three agencies to strengthen the dwindling funds. Credit Unions fought strongly against integrating the NCUA with these other two agencies because the NCUA insurance fund was strong and extremely sound. The debate on this issue has not been completely resolved, but at the present time, the NCUA remains a separate entity.

Common Bond Definitions

"The most recent controversy began in 1989 and is ongoing to date. From 1934 to 1982, occupational-based credit unions limited their members to employees sharing a single common bond *(working for a single employer).* However, in 1982, NCUA expanded and changed its interpretation of the single common bond to include multiple occupational groups." Interpretative Ruling and Policy Statement (IRPS) 82-1, 47 Fed. Reg. 16775 (4/20/82).[21] In 1989, several banks filed a series of lawsuits against a North Carolina federal credit union attacking its multiple common bond field of membership. The District Court for Washington DC ruled in favor of the credit union and the NCUA permitting the credit union to continue its multiple common bond policy.

However, in July of 1996, in The First National Bank and Trust Co., et al. v. NCUA, the U.S. Court of Appeals for the District of Columbia Circuit reversed the Decision made in 1989 and "invalidated certain select group additions to the field of membership of the same North Carolina credit union."[22] The Court ruled that groups with *unlike* common bonds could not be joined to form a single credit union and thereby reversed the 1989 lower court's ruling.

Prior to October 1996, common bond lawsuits were restricted to the case in North Carolina. However, in October, three banking associations filed a broader lawsuit which focused on NCUA's multiple group policy itself. The bankers wish to have NCUA's policy declared invalid and stop future federal credit union expansions through select employer groups. In other words, all federal credit unions were prohibited from adding employer groups that were unrelated to the group described in their original charter. Such restrictions may have tremendous ramifications for future credit union growth.

While community-based credit unions are not affected by these recent court decisions, this October 1996 court order adversely affects over 158,000 select groups in 3,586 multiple group federal credit unions throughout the United States. The possible effects of this most recent controversy remain unclear, although one real possibility is that employees of small employers may be deprived of the opportunity to join a federal credit union with the advantages credit union membership brings.

CREDIT UNION ORGANIZATIONS

What began as an unorganized, loose collection of financial cooperatives in the late 1800s has now established itself as a worldwide organizational presence.

The entire credit union organizational structure begins with the individual member. It is the member for whom the system exists.

Each state has its own non-profit trade association called a *league*. When your credit union joins the league, it automatically becomes part of a *chapter*. A chapter is simply a geographic location within the state. In larger states, chapters may meet more often and be the primary contact for a credit union. The function of the credit union league is to help individual credit unions resolve problems, offer educational and informational resources, and work for the credit union's legislative interests at the state level. Because leagues are not-for-profit, they are limited in the kinds of services they can offer credit unions. As a result *league service corporations* were formed. These are profit-oriented organizations designed to help credit unions meet specific needs such as data processing, marketing, insurance services, and so on.

A *corporate credit union* is a credit union's credit union. As such it can offer its member credit unions the opportunity to take advantage of economies of scale and diversification in managing their funds, rather than investing in or borrowing from for-profit institutions.

On the national level, there is *CUNA & Affiliates.* The *Credit Union National Association* (CUNA) is a not-for-profit trade association that provides programs and services such as educational and training materials, workshops and management schools, magazines and newsletters, legislative support and new product development—on the national level. *CUNA Mutual Group* offers different types of insurance and financial services to credit unions throughout the world.

Finally, the *World Council of Credit Unions* is an international organization of credit unions and financial cooperatives. It supports the growth of credit unions in almost ninety countries.

CONCLUSION

Banks today provide a myriad of products and services. The majority of them however, can be said to fall under one of the three basic banking functions. We described these functions as being the taking of deposits, the lending out of these deposits and the provision of a payment system.

There are today three major categories of banks in the U.S.—commercial banks, thrifts and credit unions. The thrift industry is further divided into Savings & Loan Associations, Cooperative Banks and Mutual Savings Banks.

Although both commercial banks and thrifts now have essentially similar powers, the thrifts have taken advantage of their new powers to varying degrees. Cooperative Banks and Mutual Savings Banks, as a rule, still tend to concentrate on consumer products and services (with of course, some exceptions). Many S & L's, on the other hand, have diversified to the extent that they resemble commercial banks in many ways.

Credit unions can, in some respects, be similar to commercial banks and thrifts, but in other respects are quite different. The fact that they are defined to be non-profit institutions and therefore not subject to either federal or state taxation is one of the most important and most controversial differences.

Credit unions are member-owned and operated financial cooperatives in which members share a common bond. Credit Unions can be divided into three main types: occupation-based, community-based, and associational-based. In order to start a credit union, you must obtain a charter from either the state or the federal chartering agency, the NCUA. Many positions in smaller credit unions are held by volunteers, in larger credit unions, they are paid positions. Board of Directors are elected by the membership to represent them, and these are usually volunteer positions.

The credit union movement was born out of economic adversity in Europe during the middle of the nineteenth century. The movement spread to the United States around the turn of the century, spurned on by men like Edward Filene and Roy Bergengren. Initially, credit unions offered only savings and small loans, but with the passage of numerous legislation, credit unions have expanded their products and services to include many of the same offerings as banks.

The Federal Credit Union Act of 1934 is perhaps the most significant of all credit union legislation, since it established a federal system for the establishment of credit unions. From this Act in 1934 to the current complex hierarchy of national and international organizations, credit unions continue to provide a financial alternative to banking for a growing body of individuals.

STUDY QUESTIONS

1. Explain how the process of intermediation works. Is such a process necessary for the smooth functioning of the economy? Why?/Why not? What would happen to the banking system if a prolonged period of disintermediation were allowed to continue unchecked?

2. Of all the differences between Credit Unions and other types of banks, which is the most controversial? What are your feelings on this issue?

3. Debate the differences and similarities between a credit union and a bank. Do you think there are more similarities or more differences? How does your answer support or refute the current common bond controversy ?

4. Why do you think credit unions prospered during harsh economic times?

5. List some benefits of credit union membership.

6. Were there any credit union products and services that surprised you? Why?

7. Briefly describe how credit unions got started. Explain how the underlying concept of people helping people is still evident in the modern credit union.

NOTES

1. *Webster's New World Dictionary of the American Language*, The World Publishing Company, New York, 1968, p. 115.
2. *The Common Bond*, Credit Unions: Working Man's Private Bank, The Credit Union League of Massachusetts, July 1988, p. 6.
3. *ABA Banking Journal*, Fighting the Threat from Credit Unions, American Bankers Association, April 1989, p. 37.
4. *Massachusetts Banker*, Credit Unions: It's Time for Another Look, Massachusetts Bankers Association, April 1988, p. 1.
5. *Ibid.*
6. *The Common Bond.*
7. *Massachusetts Banker*, p. 1.
8. *The Common Bond*, p. 6.
9. *Ibid.*
10. *Massachusetts Banker*, p. 1.
11. *Credit Union Orientation Staff Training And Recognition Program*, 2nd edition, Credit Union National Association, 1990, p. 3.
12. *ABA Banking Journal*, Fighting the Threat from Credit Unions, American Bankers Association, April, 1989, p. 37.
13. *Chartering and Field of Membership Manual*, National Credit Union Administration, 1994, p. 4.
14. *Massachusetts Banker*, Credit Unions: It's Time for Another Look, Massachusetts Bankers Association, April, 1988, p. 1.
15. *The Common Bond*, Credit Unions: Working Man's Private Bank, The Credit Union League of Massachusetts, July 1988, p. 6.
16. *Massachusetts Banker*, p. 1.
17. *Credit Union Orientation Staff Training and Recognition Program*, p. 31.
18. *Ibid*, p. 32
19. *Ibid*, p. 40.
20. *Massachusetts Banker*, p. 1.
21. Interpretative Ruling and Policy Statement (IRPS) 82–1, 47 Fed. Reg. 16775 (4120/82).
22. CUNA News Release, August 1996.

BIBLIOGRAPHY

"Credit Unions: It's Time for Another Look," *Massachusetts Banker*, Massachusetts Bankers Association, April 1988.

"Credit Unions: Working Man's Private Bank," *The Common Bond*, The Credit Union League of Massachusetts, July 1988.

"Fighting the Threat from Credit Unions," *ABA Banking Journal*, American Bankers Association, April 1989.

"The Case for FOM Diversity" *The Federal Credit Union*, November/December 1996.

Chartering and Field of Membership Manual, National Credit Union Administration, July 1994.

Credit Union Orientation Staff Training and Recognition Program, 2nd edition, Credit Union National Association, 1990.

Credit Union Teller Handbook, 2nd edition, CUNA & Affiliates, 1996.

Credit Unions: The Consumers' Choice, CUNA & Affiliates, Washington, 1996.

2

History of American Banking
Sandra L. Owen

Introduction

This chapter describes the history of the American banking system from the early Colonial days to its present environment. It is necessarily brief, for a complete chronicle of the evolution of this nation's financial services industry is, in a large part, the history of the nation itself and would require volumes to document properly.

For the student who has a passion for American history, perhaps this chapter will serve as a catalyst for additional research; however, every student should gain a better understanding of the principles of today's banking institutions after examining this chapter.

Learning Objectives

After reading this chapter, you should have an understanding of the following:

1. The relationship between the founding and maturing of the United States as a Country and the formation and evolution of its banking system.
2. The principal provisions of major regulatory banking acts.
3. Economic impact on the banking system as a whole.
4. The concept of regulation versus deregulation.

THE ROOTS OF BANKING

The history of American banking is, in many ways, the history of America.

The development of the banking industry in the United States closely resembles the general maturing of the country from its infancy to its present maturity. The history of this nation's economic, political, and even social development is intertwined with the evolution of the banking industry. As with all institutions that have survived and prospered over decades, American banks have had to adjust constantly to meet the changing needs of commerce, governments, and consumers over vastly different time periods so that the modern banks of today barely resemble the early banks of Colonial America. Nevertheless, basic, recognizable roots and principles in today's financial institutions can be traced back to the early days of this nation, and historians may justly point out that even those genes may be found in civilizations before the discovery of America.

Ancient Banking

Banks as we define them did not exist until the 1600s, when the concepts of interest and credit became culturally—and morally—acceptable.

If the simplistic definition of banking is the function of accepting deposits from customers and the lending of money to borrowers, then technically banks did not exist before the seventeenth century because there was little need for credit prior to the Renaissance. Before the Renaissance, the world economy was primarily agricultural with little incentive for territorial expansion and virtually no demand for industrial expansion. Thus the need for credit was nil, and barter (the exchange of goods for goods) was the common method of purchase. Most societies of the period frowned upon credit in principle; scholars, rulers, and religious leaders believed that the collecting of interest was immoral because the only borrowers were those in distress who would be taken advantage of by the wealthy money lenders.

However, during the new light of the Renaissance, when the growth of trade and commerce led to business expansion, credit was deemed morally acceptable with the rationale that, if additional profits could be made by borrowing money, then a portion of that profit could be returned to the lender as interest.

The Early Goldsmiths

Specie is money in kind—gold and silver coins.

Historians generally trace the origins of today's banks to the early goldsmiths. Goldsmiths were artisans who used precious metals to create art, utensils, and decorative coins. Goldsmiths maintained retail shops and had the safest vaults of the day. In most ancient societies, money consisted of specie *gold and silver—coins.* People who accumulated a surplus of these coins had two basic choices in protecting their wealth from thieves. They could hide or bury their surplus coins, or they could "deposit" their valuable specie with goldsmiths for storage in the artisans' vaults.

Goldsmiths' receipts of deposit of gold and silver were a crude form of the first paper currency.

When goldsmiths accepted gold and silver coins from depositors, they issued paper receipts evidencing the deposit. Initially, these receipts were issued to the actual names of the depositors who brought the gold and silver to the goldsmiths for safekeeping. However, as the goldsmiths' reputation became more trusted in the community, their paper receipts became a substitute for the actual coins, and people began to accept these receipts for the sale of goods and services. These receipts became an early form of paper currency.

A bank's reputation for strength and integrity is its most valuable asset.

The goldsmiths soon discovered that as long as they protected their impeccable reputation by consistently redeeming paper receipts for specie, they were seldom presented with withdrawal requests and they always seemed to have a surplus of specie in their vaults. As long as the public had "faith" in the paper receipts of the goldsmiths and as long as sellers accepted these receipts for face value, there was little demand for the withdrawal of precious gold and silver coins. Consequently, the goldsmiths concluded that they could safely consummate loans to borrowers using their paper receipts as the loan proceeds as long as these notes or receipts were accepted as a medium of exchange. Technically, these paper receipts were still redeemable for specie, but as long as all the depositors did not demand withdrawals on the same day, the goldsmiths could issue more receipts than the total value of specie they maintained in their vaults. The key to this phenomenon then was as it is today, to prevent all depositors from withdrawing their deposits at the same time. This assurance is the reason a bank's reputation for strength and integrity is its most cherished asset.

BANKING IN THE NEW COUNTRY

The Colonial Period

One must remember that our American ancestors were immigrants who originally journeyed from their respective homelands to build a new life in America. The majority fled their native countries to live in freedom from persecution, tyranny, and religious and social oppression. Freedom of speech and religion and the right to assemble were guarded virtues that caused the early colonists to take up arms to protest any infringement upon those well-earned rights. The early settlers did not trust government, for they were an independent lot.

These well-protected individual rights extended to the establishment of banks so that new banks could open almost as easily as one could establish a bakery or tavern without government permission. The craze for independence and freedom included the right to create and issue paper money.

In 1777, the Continental Congress attempted to finance the Revolutionary War by issuing currency. At that time, Congress issued forty-two separate currencies. In addition, individual states and private banks also issued bank notes and all of this currency was supposedly backed by specie. Specie, however, was scarce as the colonies experienced a trade imbalance with more imported goods for which other nations would only accept specie as payment.

Public faith in the many bank notes dwindled and the value (purchasing power) of most currencies was discounted by as much as 50 percent. Inflation became rampant. In Virginia, a pair of shoes cost $5,000 and a man's suit sold for more than $1 million.

Clearly the Colonies were faced with a financial crisis when all faith was lost in the majority of paper bank notes and citizens reverted to a barter system or using basic specie, of which there was a critical shortage. "Not worth a Continental" was a common phrase used to describe the credibility of the paper money of the day.

Colonial freedom extended to banking and the individual issuance of currency, which in turn led to rapid inflation because of a lack of faith in that currency.

The First Bank of the United States—1791–1811

The First Bank of the United States (1791) was founded by Congress to stabilize the nation's monetary system and regulate state-chartered banks.

Alexander Hamilton was appointed Secretary of the Treasury under the nation's new Constitution. He believed that the federal government must take responsibility for stabilizing the nation's monetary system and proposed a new federal bank that would have the backing of the federal government. Congress approved his proposal, and the First Bank of the United States opened in Philadelphia in 1791. Its charter was granted for a twenty-year period at which time it could be renewed by Congressional approval. In addition to the main office in Philadelphia, eight branches were established throughout the Colonies. The new bank was established under close scrutiny of the Congress and had strict capitalization requirements. It could issue paper currency only up to the amount of its capital and acted as a "policeman" over the state-chartered banks by accepting bank notes from the state-chartered banks and demanding redemption in specie.

While the creation of the First Bank of the United States stabilized the monetary system and gained public confidence, its existence was loudly protested by the state banks, who yearned for a return of the days when their issuance of bank notes was unchallenged by the central bank. They pointed out the fact that there was no provision in the Constitution that allowed the federal government to create and operate a bank. On the other hand, neither was there any provision forbidding it to do so, which would in time be pointed out by the Supreme Court (in the 1818 case of McCullogh vs. Maryland):

> (Chief Justice) Marshall, turning to the old problem of Congress' right to establish a national bank, a question still sharply debated in many states, agreed with the Hamiltonian contention that Congress possessed implied powers to carry out its enumerated responsibilities as well as powers that were "necessary and proper" to accomplish a legitimate end within the scope of the Constitution.[1]

The issue became a national, emotional topic that led to fierce debate and even duels between those who favored a strong central bank and those who resisted any encroachment by the federal government on individual rights. The issue of the power of the federal government versus that of the individual states was not adequately dealt with by the U.S. Constitution. There were those who felt that the U.S. was a "loose confederation of sovereign states" and others who felt it was first and foremost a single unified country.

The "state's rights" issue would come up again and again throughout the early and middle 1800s, involving such issues as banking, tariffs, and, of course, slavery. This question was not settled for good until 1865, when the forces of the Confederacy finally surrendered. From then on, it was quite clear that the powers of the individual states were subordinate to that of the federal government.

The famous duel between Alexander Hamilton and Aaron Burr on August 11, 1804, centered on the issue of the First Bank of the United States. Hamilton died the next day, and seven years later, when the charter of the First Bank of the United States matured, it too died when Congress failed to renew its charter.

After the First Bank of the United States was legally abolished, state banks proliferated, with several new independent state banks being chartered.

In 1802, there were 75 chartered banks. By 1812, there were 208 banks—all issuing bank notes in exchange for deposits in specie. To compound the problem, counterfeiting was common, causing the public's faith in paper currency to once again dwindle so that money, as a measure of monetary acceptance, had little value. Hard currency—in the form of gold and silver—specie was scarce, but it was the only true standard of purchasing power. Financial chaos returned to the nation's monetary system.

The First Bank of the United States did not have its charter renewed in 1811.

The Second Bank of the United States—1816–1836

The Second Bank of the United States was established in 1816.

Amid the chaos, the Federalists emerged and won a twenty-year charter for the Second Bank of the United States in 1816. Much as the First Bank of the United States did, the new institution provided stability to the nation's monetary system because it had the direct support and backing of the federal government.

In 1823, Nicholas Biddle was elected to run the bank. He expanded the bank by establishing twenty-nine branches and promoting new lending. Biddle also recognized the importance of controlling the nation's money supply by thwarting inflation by tightening the amount of money in circulation and by printing more money in recessions. Biddle's belief in a strong central bank for maintaining the health of the economy was fiercely opposed by antagonists of the Federalist style. This opposition was more than a philosophical debate, for the opponents of the Second Bank of the United States regarded a centralized banking system as a monster whose overthrow was essential to the preservation of human rights and human progress.

Among the prominent politicians of the day stood Andrew Jackson, a devoted disciple of Jeffersonian beliefs who distrusted both a controlling federal government and any central bank. "The Bank of the United States," snorted President Andrew Jackson, "[was a] monster, a hydra-headed monster equipped with horns, hoofs, and tail and so dangerous that it impaired the morals of our people, corrupted our statesmen and threatened our liberty."[1] The eventual fate of the Second Bank of the United States was sealed when Andrew Jackson was elected President.

> Such a fearsome beast must not roam the country at will, he declared, at least not while Andrew Jackson sat in the White House. There was only one thing for him to do, kill the brute, and the sooner the better. The bank is trying to kill me (said Jackson) . . . but I will kill it (first).[2]

The Second Bank effectively failed in 1836 because of President Andrew Jackson's opposition.

With strong encouragement from the President, its charter was not renewed in 1836. In fact, by withdrawing the government's deposits from the bank, Jackson had actually sealed the bank's fate before the expiration of the charter.

The period between 1836 and 1863 has been described by some historians as the darkest period in the financial history of our nation. By 1836 there were 567 banks, which maintained a total of 146 branches. By definition, all were state-chartered banks that issued their own individual bank notes. Total collective deposits were $115 million, yet there were $140 million of bank notes in circulation.

American banks of the period operated along the same lines as their antecedents, receiving deposits and making loans. Loans, however, were usually no more than 30 days in maturity, with 60 days being the exception and those loans were reserved for the most credit-worthy borrowers.

This reluctance to provide credit on longer terms and to encourage only the affluent to use the banks of the day led to the founding of building and loan associations (now called savings and loan associations) and mutual life insurance companies. These building and loan associations (as mentioned in Chapter 1) were cooperative ventures in which individuals pooled their funds in order to provide mortgage loans for home ownership.

While the nation's banking system grew rapidly with many new state banks, the stability of many banks was very weak during this period. Ironically, it was during this period that the economy of the country began to change from an agricultural to an industrial-based system. The new industrial revolution bred a strong manufacturing emphasis, and the population began to shift from rural to urban areas where large cities emerged around large manufacturing plants.

The coming of the industrial revolution required a strong banking system that would do away with worthless notes issued by bankrupt or wildcat banks.

Never before in our history was a sound banking system more necessary to seal the growth of the nation, yet the industry was fragmented and weak and most banks were distrusted by the public and private sectors. By 1860 there were approximately 7,000 different bank notes in circulation, including more than 1,600 from bankrupt banks. These figures do not include an estimated additional 5,000 counterfeit bank notes. With the exception of those bank notes issued by a few well-managed conservative banks, paper money (bank notes) issued by most banks was received with great suspicion.

History to this point in time revealed that the component necessary for a sound banking system was monetary stability. The following major banking acts were enacted by Congress throughout our history in response to an economic crisis of the period.

ECONOMIC EVENTS THAT PARALLEL ACTS OF BANKING REGULATION OR DEREGULATION

Environment	Act
Civil War, lack of faith in the banking system. No regulation	National Bank Act 1863–1864
Pyramiding of reserves, inflexible currency	Federal Reserve Act 1913
Laws limiting domestic bank branching	McFadden Act 1927
The Great Depression Stock Market crash	The Glass-Steagall Act (1933)
Limitations on the growth of group banks	Bank Holding Company Act of 1956
Disintermediation and general decline in Fed membership	Monetary Control Act 1980
Thrift crisis	FIRREA 1989
Recession, multiple bank failures, strain on the bank insurance system	FDIC Improvement Act 1991
Re-engineering of the banking system as a whole	Interstate Banking Bill (1994)

The National Banking Act—1863–1864

Two primary factors spawned the passage of the National Banking Act. The first was the obvious need to provide some degree of stability to the nation's monetary system and the second, more subtle reason was the federal government's need to raise capital in order to finance the Civil War.

The passage of the act was also made considerably easier by the fact that the most stubborn states rights advocates, who surely would have objected to such an increase of federal authority, were no longer in the Union, the states of the Confederacy having seceded in late 1860 and early 1861. Had the Southern states still been in the Union, it is doubtful whether such legislation could have been passed.

On December 9, 1861, Salmon P. Chase, Secretary of the United States Treasury, delivered his "Report on the State of Finances" to Congress. The

The National Banking Act (1864) was a masterful compromise between pro-centralists and states' rights backers.

major portion of his report described what two years later would become the National Currency Act. However, Congress rejected Chase's plan in deference to the emotional objections to a central national bank as well as to the massive political pressure of the state-chartered banks, who feverishly demanded the right to print their own bank notes. However, as the Civil War expenses continued to mount in Washington, Congress finally enacted the National Currency Act in 1863 in a desperate effort to raise money to support the massive Union Army. A year later the act was amended and became the National Banking Act of 1864. This act was the first major banking legislation passed in more than thirty years. The passage of the bill was a masterful piece of compromise legislation that appeased both those who favored a strong central bank and those who insisted on protecting the rights of state-chartered banks to operate independent of any centralized federal control. There were four major provisions in the National Banking Act:

The Act created National Banks that were privately owned, but federally regulated—especially as to reserve requirements.

1. ***Creation of a National Bank***—The federal government was given authority to charter national banks. These banks would be privately owned—not owned or managed by the federal government. There were strict rules regarding capitalization of these banks. Under the rules, a group of five or more "distinguished" citizens could form a national bank provided they could raise capital of $50,000 if the bank was to be located in a city of less than 10,000 population. Initial capitalization of $100,000 was necessary if the bank was to be located in larger communities. The stockholders of "national" banks could be held personally liable if the bank failed due to negligence.

   There were limits placed upon the total amount of loans a national bank could grant based upon the size of its capital and deposits.

   All national banks would be required to have the word "national" in their legal title. State banks could convert to national banks, but they were not forced to do so.

The *Comptroller of the Currency* examined and chartered new national banks.

2. ***Creation of the Comptroller of the Currency***—The Office of the Comptroller of the Currency was established as a division of the Treasury. This new office was to review charter applications for new national banks and to examine national banks on a regular basis in an effort to assess their soundness.

   The first Comptroller of the Currency was Hugh McCullock, the former President of the Bank of Indiana. Ironically, Mr. McCullock was originally an opponent of all proposals to establish the National Banking Act.

A single, standard national bank note was created.

3. ***Creation of a National Bank Note***—A standard, uniform bank note was established, and national banks were required to issue only these notes. The notes (paper currency) could only be issued up to the amount of government bonds purchased by the national banks. With this requirement, not only was the public assured of a standard paper currency, but the federal government now had a solid mechanism for raising money to finance the Civil War, for if a national bank wanted to issue money, it could only do so by lending funds to Washington. National bank notes were finally standardized in design, color, and dimension (the only difference being that the name of the issuing bank was printed on the note).

New national banks had to meet federally established *reserve requirements*, which were kept at progressively larger banks.

4. ***Reserve Requirements***—The National Banking Act required all national banks to maintain substantial reserves against their total deposits as an added measure of safety. Because the Federal Reserve System had yet to be established, reserves were kept at correspondent banks. Smaller rural banks kept reserve balances at medium-sized banks and they, in turn,

kept reserve balances at large city banks. This resulted in a *pyramiding* of balances throughout the nation, with the apex of the pyramid winding up at the very large New York City banks.

While the National Banking Act revolutionized the American banking system, American bankers at the time did not rush to gain national charters. If was not until five months after the enactment of the bill that the first national bank was chartered, the First National Bank of Philadelphia. In the first year following the enactment of the bill, only 134 institutions were chartered as national banks and, of those, only one was a conversion of a state bank.

State chartered banks continued to exist and continued to issue their own bank notes. One year after the passage of the National Banking Act, in 1865, Congress passed a bill that placed a 10 percent tax on all bank notes issued by state banks. With the passage of this unprecedented tax on state bank notes, many state-chartered banks converted to national banks. Such conversions substantially reduced the problems associated with multiple bank notes. However, many state banks continued not only to exist, but also to prosper. Because the passage of the National Banking Act never required the elimination of state banks, it created a dual banking system in which national and state banks coexist. The dual banking system continues to exist today as both nationally chartered and state chartered banks operate in today's society.

> Even today, we continue to have a dual (national and state) banking system.

Weaknesses of the National Banking Act

While the passage of the National Banking Act in 1864 served to stabilize the nation's banking system and restored the public's confidence in paper currency, over time the historic legislation revealed three major weaknesses:

1. ***Lack of an Adequate Check Collection System***—The post-Civil War period may best be described as an expansionary economy. A wave of new immigrants flocked to major industrial cities such as New York, Boston, and Chicago. The population mushroomed in these industrial centers.

> The growth of the American economy meant more checks, but the National Banking Act had created no mechanism to deal with this growth.

   The country was becoming an industrial and financial giant, finally having weaned itself from European dependence.

   The nation's banking system grew to keep pace with the industrial expansion and population explosion. One year after the passage of the National Banking Act in 1864, the number of commercial banks stood at 2,000. By 1910, the total number of America's national banks was 20,000. Of those banks, 7,000 carried national charters.

   Unlike earlier years, when the use of checking accounts was reserved for the privileged few, the use of checks as a payment mechanism was becoming popular among both businesses and common citizens.

   The country was now populated from the Atlantic to the Pacific, and the process of routing checks to the drawee banks was both awkward and painfully slow. There was no efficient mechanism for the routing and collection of checks.

2. ***Inflexible Currency***—The economic expansion of the period demanded the support of an increased money supply. The nation's money supply grew at a meager 1.3 percent collective pace from 1867 to 1879. During the last two decades of the nineteenth century, the money supply increased by 6 percent, and from 1897 to 1914 the amount of money in circulation expanded by 7.5 percent. Still, the money supply failed to keep pace with the needs of this economic expansion, and the restrictions imposed on new bank note issuance by the National Banking Act inhibited the supply of currency necessary to support an expanded economy.

> The national money supply failed to match the growing economy of the late 1800s.

One will recall that a major provision of the National Banking Act restricted the amount of new bank notes created by national banks to the amount of federal government bonds purchased.

After the Civil War, the federal government's financial position improved immensely with new taxes from a growing economy, and the government was intent on not incurring additional debt. Consequently, the problem of pumping more money into the nation's economy was exacerbated as Washington was intent on reducing its Civil War debt rather than incurring more debt.

3. *Pyramiding of Reserves*—One of the features of the National Banking Act was the requirement that all national banks maintain a percentage of their deposits as reserves in other banks in order to promote public confidence and prevent bank failures due to unexpected withdrawal requests.

The pyramiding of reserves created havoc with the monetary and stock markets, as large amounts had to be called in on loans on a very short basis. A stock panic resulted in 1907.

As deposits grew, the amount of reserves grew, and the apex of this pyramid focused on large New York City banks that made the city the financial capital of the nation. Reserve deposits were interest-bearing deposits, and the giant New York banks were forced to "invest" their substantial balances in high-yielding loans and investments to offset the large amount of interest paid to correspondent banks. Much of this concentrated money was lent to underwriters and brokers who, in turn, invested in the stock market. When the banks reduced their reserve balances, the action had a rippling effect that forced the New York banks to "call" their broker loans in order to satisfy the demands of their smaller correspondent banks. The "calling" of broker loans, in turn, created chaos in the stock market as large blocks of stocks were sold quickly in order to raise money for repayment of the loans. This type of action would create a panic in the stock market and, in fact, did in 1907.

The Federal Reserve System—1913

Chapter 4 is devoted to a detailed description of the Federal Reserve System. Consequently, its mention here is deliberately brief and is intended only to continue a description of the historical sequence of American banking progression.

While banking was becoming increasingly dynamic at the turn of the century, the nation's currency supply remained relatively rigid, and the liquidity of the country's banks was minimal. The panic of 1907 prompted one economist to describe it as "the most extensive and prolonged breakdown of the country's credit mechanism since the establishment of the national banking system." Clearly, additional reforms were necessary in order to, once again, restore faith in the banking system.

The panic of 1907 and the three weaknesses of the National Banking Act led to the creation of the Federal Reserve System in 1913.

When Woodrow Wilson was elected President in 1912, he turned his attention to currency reform. Legislation was drafted that would address the three weaknesses of the National Banking Act. In 1913, The Federal Reserve Act was passed. Once again, the creation of the Federal Reserve System was a masterful piece of compromise legislation that satisfied the demands of those who favored a strong central bank and those who advocated local, independent control. Unlike the First and Second Banks of the United States, the Federal Reserve Bank would not deal directly with the public—thus avoiding the alleged impropriety of the government being engaged in a profit-making venture.

Twelve Federal Reserve Banks were established in various geographic sections of the country. Member banks were required to maintain reserves with the local Federal Reserve Bank, thus solving the problem of pyramiding large cash deposits at the New York banks.

The Federal Reserve Banks were also charged with the responsibility of routing and clearing checks between the various districts of the entire nation. This system of check collection proved to be less costly and more efficient than banks dealing directly with each other.

Finally, the problem of an inflexible currency was solved by allowing the Federal Reserve Banks to issue their own currency, which was not backed by government bonds. The new currency was called "Federal Reserve Notes," and it is the paper money we use today.

It is important to note that while the Federal Reserve System is charged with the responsibility of monitoring the nation's money supply in order to combat recession and inflation and, therefore, is somewhat responsive to Congress, it is an independent unit of the federal government and is quite independent of politics.

The Federal Reserve Banks are owned by their member banks, and six of the nine directors of each Federal Reserve Bank are elected by its members. The remaining three directors of each Federal Reserve District are appointed by the Board of Governors of the Federal Reserve System.

The Glass-Steagall Act—1933

As the prosperity of the 1920s gave way to the depression of the 1930s, the faith in our banking system dwindled to perhaps its lowest point since the enactment of the National Banking Act.

The depression of 1929 threw 25 percent of the nation's working population into unemployment. As businesses declared bankruptcy, they defaulted on their bank loans and fired their workers. Banks, in turn, were forced to write off their uncollectable loans while honoring unusually heavy withdrawal requests—a double-edged sword that spelled failure for many banking institutions of the day. From 1930 through 1933 more than 9,000 banks failed and more than $7 billion in deposits disappeared. Because there was no insurance on deposits, when a bank declared bankruptcy a depositor's money was lost.

The **Great Depression** of 1929 led to the failure of many banks and President Roosevelt's declaration of a national bank holiday in 1933.

When President-elect Franklin Delano Roosevelt arrived in Washington on March 2, 1933, the public's lack of confidence in the banking system had turned to panic, and banks throughout the country were failing. "Banking holidays" were being declared by state governors across the nation in an attempt to stem the tide of public panic as depositors lined up to withdraw their deposits. When Roosevelt declared a nationwide bank holiday on March 5, 1933, he was merely formalizing what already had come to pass. The nation's banks were closed.

Roosevelt blamed the bankers for the depression. Bankers, he said, had lied to the nation and "were now pleading tearfully for restored confidence." What was needed now, he said, "was strict supervision of all banking and credit and investments.

On June 16, 1933, the Glass-Steagall Act was passed by Congress and was signed into law.

In 1933, the **Glass-Steagall Act** responded to banking breakdown with three major provisions.

This major banking bill carried the following provisions:

1. *The Creation of the Federal Deposit Insurance Corporation (FDIC)*—All bank deposits would be insured up to $2,500. After July 1, 1934, all deposits up to $40,000 would be fully insured. After the initial funding by the Treasury Department, member banks would be required to support the insurance fund by paying a portion of their deposits as annual premiums. All banks that were members of the Federal Reserve were required to join FDIC, and non-member banks could join if they wished.

The **Federal Deposit Insurance Corporation** (FDIC) was created to insure all deposits up to $40,000.

Commercial banks were forbidden to engage in investment banking or stock market activities.

2. ***The Separation of Commercial Banking from Investment Banking***—Prior to the Glass-Steagall Act, banks were permitted to engage in speculative underwriting of securities, to advance loans to brokers, and to buy and sell stocks for customers. The underwriting of securities involves the purchase of the securities from the issuing corporation and their resale to the general public. The underwriter could be described as a middleman. The underwriter earns a profit by selling the securities to the public at a higher price than he purchased them from the issuer. Securities underwriting is a very risky (but also possibly very profitable) activity, as there is no assurance that the securities will in fact be able to be resold at a high enough price to enable the underwriter to earn a profit. Margin requirements were liberal as banks advanced loans for the purchase of stock with little down payment from the borrowers. When the banks "demanded" payment, frequently the borrowers were forced to sell their stocks in order to raise money to repay the bank debt. This action created artificial swings in the stock market and panic selling. Indirectly, the banks were influencing the stock market prices.

The new legislation strictly prohibited commercial banks from engaging in any security transactions. Loans to brokers were forbidden, and banks could not underwrite new stock issues.

It was felt that allowing the same institution to be involved in both commercial lending and securities underwriting caused serious conflicts of interest. Such an institution would have a great interest in making sure that the securities that were being underwritten were able to be sold profitably. This concern might induce such a bank to make commercial loans to the same companies whose securities they were underwriting (that otherwise might have been judged to be too risky).

There were also conflicts of interest involving the banks' trust business. Such institutions, at times, induced their trust customers to purchase the securities that were being underwritten, when it may not have been in their (the customers') best interest to do so.

> Banks, acting as managers of new security issues, often sold unsold (or unsellable) quantities of securities to trust funds under their management. As a result, the banks earned a hefty return at the expense of these trust funds, many of which often sold the securities later at a substantial loss.[3]

The Act forbade banks from paying interest on checking accounts (demand deposit accounts).

3. ***The Prohibition of the Interest Payment on Demand Deposit Accounts***—Because checking account deposits are available for withdrawal "on demand"—that is, without notice to the bank—the Act of 1933 forbade the payment of interest on checking accounts in an additional effort to force conservative management of the banking system.

Prior to 1933, banks routinely paid interest on checking account deposits, which served to encourage bank managers to seek out speculative investments and loans that yielded above average income returns in order to offset the heavy interest expense of demand deposits.

4. ***The Setting of an Interest Rate Ceiling on Savings and Time Accounts***—The Glass-Steagall Act specified maximum interest rate caps on all savings and time deposits. Banks could not pay interest rates above the maximum allowed by law. This provision was incorporated into the Federal Reserve Regulations as Regulation Q and, as with all other provisions of the Act, was strictly enforced by bank examiners.

Regulation Q set legal interest rate ceilings on all savings and time deposits.

With the Glass-Steagall legislation in place, President Roosevelt broadcast his first radio address to the American public, stating:

> "I want to talk for a few minutes with the people of the United States about banking," he began. "I can assure you," he added, "that it is safer to keep your money in a reopened bank than under the mattress."

While President Roosevelt's dramatic actions served to stem the panic in relatively short order, the new banking laws dramatically changed the many structures of banking for decades. Many of Glass-Steagall's restrictions are still law today, more than a half century later.

The public's confidence in the banking system was slowly restored, and the number of bank failures dropped drastically. The economy slowly recovered from the Great Depression, but, ironically, full economic recovery was not evident until World War II. The conservative lending and investment practices of the 1930s and 1940s left banks in a highly liquid position and eager to meet the new demands of a post-war nation. After the war, consumers wanted automobiles and home appliances, and the banks, flush with cash, were prepared to provide loans to encourage the public's optimistic view of the future. Businesses, too, were ready to expand after years of stagnation, and the banks were eager to provide the necessary financing. By the mid-1950s commercial banking was flourishing; still highly regulated and, backed by public confidence, there was a strong demand for its product, particularly loans. This strong loan demand—coupled with regulated, low-cost deposits—virtually guaranteed handsome profits for America's banks.

Over the next two decades, the banking industry became complacent as it watched non-bank competitors erode its traditional customer base. Corporate treasurers, no longer content to leave large deposits in non-interest bearing demand deposit accounts, sought other investments. The commercial paper market (through which credit-worthy corporations can borrow directly from the public, avoiding the need for bank financing) provided an attractive vehicle for both corporate investment and financing. Restricted by the maximum interest rate caps of Glass-Steagall, bankers watched as billions of dollars left the industry attracted by the high interest rates paid by a new investment instrument, first introduced in 1977 by Merrill Lynch, called the Cash Management Account. The account, unrestricted by interest ceilings of Glass-Steagall because Merrill Lynch was not a bank, paid market interest rates, which at the time were three times higher than the maximum rates banks could pay.

As deposits dwindled, banks searched for ways to raise funds to satisfy a continuing strong demand for loans. The search for additional deposits resulted in many banks withdrawing their membership in the Federal Reserve, thus releasing large, non-interest earning reserve balances. Because all national banks are required to be members of the Federal Reserve, many banks canceled their national charters and obtained state charters, for which Federal Reserve membership is an option, not a requirement. The many membership withdrawals from the Federal Reserve left the Fed in a precarious position to influence monetary policy, one of its principal functions, because its jurisdiction was limited to its membership of banks.

Clearly the financial markets were changing and, just as in the past, a reexamination of banking laws was needed to respond to the new economic, political, and social forces. It was in this environment that the Depository Institutions Deregulation and Monetary Control Act of 1980 was signed into law.

World War II effectively ended the Great Depression.

Over the 1960s and 1970s, banks lost deposits to new financial instruments such as *Cash Management Accounts*, offered by brokerage houses and other institutions.

The McFadden Act of 1927

The National Banking Act of 1863 prohibited banks with a national charter from establishing branches. In 1916, the American Bankers Association announced its opposition to branch banking in any form. However, in 1922 the Comptroller of the Currency, concerned that national banks were at a competitive disadvantage in states where state chartered banks were permitted to branch, permitted national banks to branch within a bank's home office city.

In 1927 Congress passed the McFadden Act. This legislation authorized national banks to establish branches in states where state banks were allowed to branch and thus granted the states the power to dictate branching for national as well as state chartered banks.

Part of the reasoning behind the passage of this Act stemmed from the financial problems encountered by banks in the early 1930s. Small banks were very much concerned about their future since over a third of the banks that failed from 1930 to 1933 were small rural banks. The Act attempted to ensure the survival of small banks by limiting banking competition from out-of-state banking institutions. Although a great deal of emotion surrounds the issue of interstate banking, a ban on branching across state lines cannot be supported. Banks compete with an increasing variety of financial institutions, many of which are not restricted by state boundaries. Restrictions on national banking are inconsistent with the concept of free enterprise which is the principle of a free market economy. Interstate banking has been considered by every commission that has researched our banking system in recent years. There now appears to be a consensus that there is excess in the banking industry which, ultimately, is detrimental to the economy and our citizens. As you will see later in the chapter, a national banking bill was passed in 1994 which reverses the provisions of the McFadden Act.

The Bank Holding Company Act of 1956

The Bank Holding Company Act of 1956 defines a holding company as one that controls two or more banks by owning 25% of the voting shares or controls in any manner the election of a majority of the directors of two or more banks. In the early 1950s, the number of bank holding companies was rapidly increasing and Congress was concerned by the lack of regulatory controls on such organizations. The separation between banking and non-banking activities dictated by the Glass-Steagall Act of 1933 did not apply to bank holding companies. Bank regulators wanted to bring banking companies under federal supervision and to prevent them from controlling both banks and non-banking organizations. The regulators warned that holding companies provided clear conflict of interest issues whereby a bank may make unwise loans to a non-banking affiliate or might pressure its credit customers to do business with its non-bank subsidiaries.

The resulting law, the Bank Holding Company Act of 1956, required all bank holding companies to register with the Federal Reserve Board who was charged with the responsibility of regulating the activities of bank holding companies.

The Act required banking organizations to divest themselves of all non-banking subsidiaries and specified that interstate banking regulations such as the McFadden Act applied to bank holding companies.

The success of bank holding companies stems in large part from the services provided to its subsidiary banks. Such services include auditing, marketing, investment advice, operations, accounting, etc. These services provide for specialization and cost savings by economics of scale and free local bank personnel to concentrate on implementing banking services.

The Monetary Control Act of 1980

The Monetary Control Act of 1980 made seven major changes in the national banking system.

The Depository Institutions Deregulation and Monetary Control Act, commonly called the Monetary Control Act, represents a significant draft of bank legislation and, in a historical perspective, ranks equivalent to the National Banking, the Federal Reserve, and the Glass-Steagall Acts. The Monetary Control Act of 1980 incorporated a wide variety of changes in the way financial institutions operate. The Monetary Control Act of 1980:

- *Increased FDIC Insurance to $100,000*—The maximum coverage provided by FDIC prior to 1980 was $40,000. The new coverage of $100,000 represented a 60 percent increase and resulted in insuring approximately 70 percent of aggregate total bank deposits.

- *Required Non-Member Banks to Keep Reserves*—All financial institutions offering transaction accounts (checking, NOW, share draft) were required to maintain reserves at the Federal Reserve Bank. This requirement applies to member and non-member banks alike. The reserve requirement for transaction accounts was set at 3 percent up to $25 million and 12 percent for all deposits above $25 million. This provision allowed the Federal Reserve once again to regulate the nation's money supply because all depository institutions, including credit unions, are subject to the reserve requirement.

- *Eliminated Deposit Interest Rate Ceilings*—The Monetary Control Act of 1980 called for the gradual elimination of all interest rate ceilings on Savings and Time deposits. For the first time since the Glass-Steagall Act of 1933, banks were free to pay market interest rates to attract new deposits. This new provision gave banks the tool to prevent disintermediation, a process by which funds are withdrawn from lower yielding investments and placed into higher interest earning accounts outside the banking system. Armed with this new power, banks could more justly compete with their nonbank competition within the financial services industry.

- *Expanded the Powers of Savings & Loan Institutes (S & L's) and Credit Unions*—The new act gave the Savings Banks and Credit Unions new powers. Because it was now required that these institutions maintain reserves based upon their transaction account balances, it was reasonable that they be allowed to offer new services.

  Consequently, the act authorized Credit Unions to make real estate loans and Federal Mutual Savings Banks to make commercial loans. Permission to issue credit cards and to offer trust services was also part of the expanded powers given to the S & L's under the act.

- *Established Fees for Federal Reserve Services*—The new act directed the Federal Reserve to implement charges for the service it provided banks. Heretofore, the Fed provided coin and currency, check clearing, wire transfer, and collection services free of charge to its members. As a result of the Monetary Control Act, these services would be performed for fees, and the services of the Federal Reserve would be available to all institutions—not just to its member banks.

- *Expanded Loan Services to Non-Member Banks*—The act allowed non-member Federal Reserve banks to utilize the discount window of the Fed. Now all depository institutions required to maintain reserves could also use the Fed to obtain loans.

- *Authorized Nationwide NOW Accounts*—Negotiable Order of Withdrawal (NOW) accounts were originated by a savings bank in Massachusetts. For several years these accounts were limited to banks in Massachusetts and then New England. Initially, there was much controversy surrounding the accounts because it violated the Glass-Steagall provision requiring the non-payment of interest on Demand Deposit accounts. However, the courts determined that NOW accounts were Savings accounts and therefore could earn interest.

  The Monetary Control Act dictated that NOW accounts could be offered on a national scale and, for all intents and purposes, the country had an interest-bearing transaction account product for the first time since 1933.

Implications of the Monetary Control Act

The Monetary Control Act brought banks into the competitive free market.

With the passage of the Monetary Control Act, the banking industry was forced to change its methods of conducting business. Rather than relying on what was essentially a subsidy by the federal government for restricting the amount of interest that legally could be paid on deposits, banks were now forced to compete in an arena of free market forces. Payment to the Fed for services rendered added to the notion that banks were to operate much like any other profit-motivated corporation in a free enterprise system. Banks were forced to pay attention to all expenses and were challenged to offer efficient products and services at the lowest cost to its customers. Clearly, the Monetary Control Act of 1980 changed the way banks conduct their business.

Garn-St. Germain Act—1982

The *Garn-St. Germain Act* (1982) had ten provisions to allow banks to create money market accounts.

President Ronald Reagan signed the Garn-St. Germain Bill on October 15, 1982. The act allowed banks to create a Money Market Deposit Account in order to compete with the Cash Management accounts being offered by the security brokers. The Money Market account originally contained the following provisions:

1. A minimum balance of $2,500 was required.

2. There would be no interest rate ceiling for balances in excess of $2,500, but the maximum interest rate paid for balances under $2,500 would be the prevailing NOW account rate.

3. The new account would be available to all depositors, both consumers and corporate customers.

4. Money Market accounts were insured up to a maximum of $ 100,000.

5. There would be no restrictions on the size or frequency of withdrawals as long as the withdrawals were made in person or by mail.

6. Transfers to other accounts were limited to six per month, and no more than three checks per month were permitted.

7. Specific interest rates could be guaranteed for no longer than one month.

8. Banks could require a seven-day notice of intent to withdraw from the account.

9. Loans to meet the minimum balance requirements were prohibited.

10. Balances of consumer Money Market accounts were exempted from reserve requirements, and balances of non-personal accounts were subject to a 3 percent reserve requirement.

In addition to the creation of the Money Market Account, the Garn-St. Germain Act allowed federal insurance agencies to approve interindustry or interstate mergers or purchases of failed institutions and allowed thrift institutions to convert from mutual to stock charters. The act also further expanded the types of investments that could be made by S & L's, giving them a great degree of freedom in this area.

In addition to being deregulated on a federal level, banking was also deregulated on a local level here in Massachusetts.

The Brennan Bill

The *Brennan Bill* (Massachusetts, 1982) mirrored the Garn-St. Germain Act in three areas.

In 1982, the Brennan Bill was enacted by the Commonwealth of Massachusetts. Similar to the Monetary Control Act and the Garn-St. Germain Bill on a national level, the Brennan Bill went a long way toward "leveling the playing field" on a regional level for Massachusetts-chartered commercial banks and thrifts. The bill reformed the commonwealth's banking laws in three major ways:

1. It equalized the powers between state-chartered thrifts and commercial banks.

2. It equalized the rate of taxation (by the state) on commercial banks and thrifts. Previously, the thrifts had been taxed by the state at a higher rate than commercial banks.

3. It relaxed the state branching regulations; however, not to the extent in which they exist today.

Incidentally, it is the state—regardless of whether a bank has a national or a state charter—that has the power to set the branching regulations for banks located within its borders.

The Thrift Crisis

One of the most highly debated and chronicled aspects of the evolution of the banking system is the Thrift Crisis or more commonly called the Savings and Loan Crisis. While no single factor can be blamed for this crisis, most analysts agree that three contributing factors can be identified as having major impact.

- Inexperience in dealing with deregulated powers and products
- Sudden, unpredicted economic downturn resulting in narrowing spreads
- A level of fraud and mismanagement.

Inexperience

Deregulation of the thrifts often led to poor commercial loan practices.

Although the deregulation of the banking industry was certainly well intentioned, especially as it related to the Savings and Loans (S&L's), it did play a role in what today is known as the "Thrift Crisis." As part of the S&L's problems were caused by the fact that their lending powers were strictly limited to residential mortgages, it was felt that allowing them to diversify their investments would aid them in returning to profitability.

It was the expectation of those who enacted the legislation that the S&L's would take advantage of their newfound powers on a gradual basis (i.e. taking the time to learn the commercial lending business before diving into it). Keep in mind that commercial lending, especially real estate development, is infinitely more complex and risky than residential mortgage lending. A great many of the S&L's didn't act as it was hoped and expected, they jumped headfirst into commercial lending without a thorough knowledge of the business. As a result a great many loans were made which never should have been granted in the first place, and probably wouldn't have been had the S&L's taken the time to learn the business beforehand.

During this same period, many S&L's also chose to convert from mutual to stock organizations. As a result, they found themselves with considerable cash balances available to invest and with stockholders who expected dividends. This in turn also influenced S&L's to accept a higher level of risk than was prudent.

Not only did the S&L's accept a much higher level of risk than was appropriate in the area of commercial lending, but a small number of them chose to invest very heavily in high risk securities, commonly known as junk bonds.

One especially great weakness of the deregulatory laws was that they didn't mandate any increased supervision or examination. One would think that if an industry is being given new powers, it would be closely supervised to ensure that these new powers were being exercised prudently. But due to the political landscape of the 1980's, this was not the case at all.

First of all, the executive branch believed very strongly in deregulation in general, not only as it related to banking (and running on such a platform, received the strong endorsement of the public). There were many who felt very strongly that the government had become too pervasive, that its role in the economy had become too significant. The less government interference, the better, it was thought.

Political pressures helped maintain thrift deregulation.

The Congress had other reasons for not interfering in the thrift industry. The reasons are a direct result of the method by which we finance political campaigns in this country. It has become necessary to raise immense sums of money in order to run a credible campaign for public office. Among the most generous of campaign contributors has been the thrift industry. Its certainly realistic to expect that if one is receiving considerable campaign contributions from a particular interest group that one will become sympathetic to its concerns. This is exactly what happened; because of the support which many congressmen were receiving from the industry, they became very reluctant to enact any sort of legislation which the industry would have considered objectionable.

Some thrifts grew imprudent became of deposit insurance guarantees of a federal "bailout."

Another aspect of deregulation which played a significant role in the crisis was the increase in the levels of deposit insurance (a part of the Monetary Control Act of 1980) from $40,000 to $100,000. Although the role of deposit insurance is to encourage safety, the increase in its level actually had the opposite effect in many cases. How could this possibly be true? Because, in a way, it actually encouraged many of the thrifts to take on higher levels of risk in their investments. If the institution itself were to fail as a result of these investments, the federal government would in a sense "pick up the tab". The depositors would be taken care of, so why not take the added risk? This was especially likely to happen in situations in which a given institution may have been very close to failure already. What would now be the temptation? To accept a very high level of risk, in the hope that it would work out for the best. And if it didn't, the depositors would still be protected.

This increased level of deposit insurance also caused complacency among depositors. Instead of being concerned with what a given institution may have been doing with their deposits, with the level of risk they were accepting, their only concern was to look for the institution paying the highest rates. Why? It didn't matter if the institution failed or not, they would still be insured. Instead of looking for conservative, well managed institutions in which to place their deposits, the public simply looked for the highest rates.

Economic Downturn

In the late 70s, interest rates increased significantly based on market conditions resulting in a period of disintermediation for banks. Deregulation of the industry in the early 1980s permitted the S&L's to offer a variety of new loan products. This rapid loan growth had to be supported by a corresponding increase in the deposit base, and with interest rate ceilings now lifted, the fierce competition for deposits led to rate wars. Since most S&L's granted fixed-rate loans at that time, the spread or difference between the rate of return on loans and investments and cost of deposits narrowed. With rapidly increasing rates paid for deposit dollars and a slow increase in rates charged for loans actual negative spreads existed.

As the general health of the economy declined, increasing unemployment, and severely decreased real estate values exacerbated the decline of the health of all banks.

Fraud and Mismanagement

The volatile environment and inexperience handling new powers and products resulted in what some call a "window of opportunity" for management to creatively attempt to solve the vast problems presented and also to select fraudulent practices for personal or professional gain. There are well documented trial cases from the Congressional level to the branch network of practices including making fraudulent loans or approving loans that lending criteria would reveal would probably not be repaid.

Many S&L's invested heavily in junk bonds or securities of companies that were too young or too heavily in debt to receive investment-grade status. As high-risk, high-yield obligations, banks gambled and lost when their investments plummeted after purchase resulting in significant loss when the bonds were sold.

While the S&L's (thrifts) led the way, all banks began to experience difficulty in the late 1980s due to deteriorating loan portfolios that resulted from depressed real estate values in many parts of the country.

There are several incidents involving specific institutions in which fraud clearly played a major role in the development of the crisis. There are in fact several cases in which the federal government has indicted thrift owners and actually filed multi-million dollar lawsuits in an attempt to recover some of the losses. It should be stressed, however, that on the whole the role of fraud in causing the crisis itself pales in comparison to that of deregulation, mismanagement and lack of proper supervision and examination.

In addition, the fact that the economy had softened, especially in certain parts of the country, certainly played a role, but again not a major one. One keeps coming back to the same factors just mentioned above.

FIRREA—Financial Institutions Reform, Recovery, and Enforcement Act

In 1989, Congress essentially re-regulated the thrifts. Eight major reforms followed.

Finally, by February 1989 the crisis had become so serious and obvious that President Bush sent to Congress a package of proposed reforms intended to both bail out the Federal Savings and Loan Deposit Insurance Corporation (FSLIC), which had by now become hopelessly insolvent and to essentially re-regulate the thrift industry. After seven months of often heated and contentious negotiations and in the end, compromise, between the House, the Senate and the President, in August 1989, the Financial Institutions Reform, Recovery and Enforcement Act of 1989 (more commonly known as the "Bailout Bill" or FIRREA) was passed and signed into law.

The primary purpose of this act was to reform and consolidate the federal deposit insurance system and once again as we have seen, regulation resulted from the need to build the public's confidence in the nation's banking system.

This act contained a number of reforms, the most important of which are as follows:

1. Capital requirements were strengthened.

2. S&L's were now forbidden to invest in junk bonds. Those S&L's who currently had such investments in their portfolios were told to gradually divest.

3. The Federal Home Loan Bank Board (FHLBB), which had been the regulatory body overseeing the thrift industry, was disbanded. In its place the Office of Thrift Supervision (OTS) was established. Unlike the FHLBB, the OTS is not an independent entity, it is a part of the Treasury Department.

   The reason for this change was that it was clear that the U.S. Treasury, unlike the FHLBB, was a strong, independent government agency, which would be far less likely to be intimidated by political pressure.

4. Fifty billion dollars was appropriated to bail out the FSLIC. In fact, the FSLIC itself was replaced by a new agency, the Savings Association Insurance Fund (SAIF). Only twenty billion was to be borrowed by a newly created agency, the Resolution Funding Corporation (RFC).

5. Another new agency, the Resolution Trust Corporation (RTC) was created. Its job was to shut down and dispose of the assets of insolvent S&L's.

6. The jail terms for defrauding a financial institution were quadrupled.

7. S&L's were told to refocus their lending activities back toward home mortgages and other housing related loans.

8. It was made easier for commercial banks to acquire S&L's.

While well intended, this act fell short in several projections. Original estimates of the cost to close insolvent thrifts necessitated not $50 billion but over $16 billion. The RTC found itself with high portfolios of junk bonds to liquidate at a great loss and billions of dollars of assets to liquidate such as real estate. The ability to break original contracts between failed institutions and CD customers afforded by FIRREA to reduce interest expenses resulted in further deposit deterioration in the banking system.

To many, the thrift crisis was the direct result of deregulation of the industry. However, many would argue that economic deregulation was necessary for the survival of the industry. What was not understood was the difference between economic deregulation and safety-and-soundness control. In the airline industry, economic dereguation was accomplished by eliminating the Civil Aeronautics board, but the important issue of safety was not only protected but enhanced by increasing the powers of the Federal Aeronautics Administration. If the amount of regulatory examination and supervision had increased as the thrifts became accustomed to their new found powers perhaps this expensive calamity could have been avoided.

Federal Deposit Insurance Corporation Improvement Act of 1991

Following FIRREA, Congress passed the Federal Deposit Insurance Corporation Improvement Act of 1991 (FDICIA) to recapitalize the Bank Insurance

Fund (BIF) by allowing FDIC to borrow an additional $30 billion from the Treasury. As a result of FDICIA, banks were required to meet new safety and soundness standards. Some of the major reforms dictated by FDICIA were:

- Revised bank regulation (domestic and foreign) requiring on-site examinations and annual audit requirements.
- Revised bank accounting standards.
- State chartered banks were prohibited from engaging in activities that are prohibited for national banks.
- Assessments became required to test credit exposure to correspondent banks.
- Financial institutions were subject to the thruth-in-savings law which also limited brokered deposit activity.

We see again a shift toward regulation often referred to as micro-management of the banking industry based on crisis. Hotly debated today are the issues of less bank management and expanded powers versus risk avoidance regulation.

Interstate Banking

On September 13, 1994, the U.S. Senate approved landmark legislation abolishing decades old barriers that restrict banks from operating branches across state lines. President Clinton hailed the Senate passage by saying; "this act will help American banks better the needs of our people, our communities, and our economy." The new legislation repeals legal barriers to branching dating back to 1927 when the McFadden Act was passed.

There is a distinction between interstate branching and interstate banking and the new bill deals with both. Interstate banking took effect one year after the bill was signed into law. Bank holding companies could buy banks in any state commencing October, 1995.

Effective July 1997, banks could merge with banks in any other state, provided the state has not declined to participate in branching. These branching powers permit interstate banking organizations such as Bank of America to consolidate their affiliates into a single bank.

Banks can establish branches in states where they do not own a deposit taking institution.

CONCLUSION

The banking industry in the United States is unique among its counterparts throughout the world. No bank is owned and operated by the Federal government; instead, today there are a shrinking number of commercial banks, savings and loan associations and mutual savings banks. The number of banks and branch offices has declined drastically since 1991, as a result of the Thrift Crisis and general decline in economic conditions.

Vigorous debate continues over the nature of the national banking system.

The history of our banking system was based on a fierce insistence on individual freedom by our forefathers. The threads of that ideology can be found today in our institutions. Nevertheless, history has taught us that banks, because of their unique ability to affect the overall economy by influencing the money supply, cannot be entirely independent of government monitoring. Undoubtedly, the degree of government intervention and regulation will be debated as vigorously in the future as it has been in the past through every piece of bank legislation from the chartering of the First and Second banks of The United States to the passage of Interstate Banking.

Certainly, a recognized change is the rate of speed at which the banking industry is changing as a whole. As a matter of fact, this industry has changed more in the last two decades than in its entire history. As we move from a manufacturing economy to a service economy, technology plays a major role. Future trends will be defined by customer demand, bank regulation, risk analysis, and internal and external forces. Hopefully, we will learn from our history that continued fine tuning to meet modern society's needs is not only good but necessary to the survival not only of banks but also of the nation's economic well-being. To that extent, the summary of this chapter should not be construed as the end, but more appropriately, the beginning of a new and exciting rapidly evolving era of American banking.

NOTES

1. Robert V. Remini, *Andrew Jackson & the Bank War*, Norton & Company, New York City, 1967, p. 31.
2. *Ibid*, p. 15.
3. *Ibid*, p. 15–16.
4. David R. Kamerschen, *Money & Banking*, Ninth Edition, Southwestern Publishing Co., Cincinnati, OH., 1988, p. 88.

STUDY AND REVIEW QUESTIONS

1. What is meant by the term dual banking system?
2. How would a period of disintermediation effect banks?
3. How many Federal Reserve Banks exist today and why do we need that number?
4. What conditions led to the Glass-Steagall Act?
5. Was the Monetary Control Act of 1980 an act of regulation or deregulation and why?
6. What provisions of the National Bank Act exist today?
7. How would the Federal Reserve Act of 1913 solve the problems of pyramiding of reserves and the inability to collect on checks?
8. Proponents of Interstate Banking argue that this will be good for the economy because?
9. What acts of regulation resulted from economic downturns?
10. Select one act of regulation and one of deregulation and explain.

EXERCISES

1. Group Discussion: Assign each group significant dates in banking history e.g. 1625, 1929, 1950, 1977, 1992. Ask them to discuss what they envision the banking climate to be like. Consider number of banks, types of banks, employees, products and services, and forms of technology.

2. Take an imaginary walk down any Main Street, USA. What do we see for banks? What are their names? How are they alike and how are they different?

3. Discuss how the Thrift Crisis effected your particular institution. Since the Thrift Crisis what proactive steps has your bank taken to reposition itself for the future?

4. The future with Interstate Banking and Branching available may change the shape of the banking industry. How do you think the industry will be impacted? Will the number of banks change? How will products and services be effected?

BIBLIOGRAPHY

American Banker, March 18, 1986.

Bank Systems & Equipment, March 1986.

Bowden, Elbert & Judith Holbert, *Revolution in Banking*, Reston Publishing Co., 1984.

Carrubba, Paul A., *Principles of Banking*, Fifth Edition, American Bankers' Association, 1994.

Kamerschen, David R., *Money & Banking*, 9th Edition, Southwestern Publishing Co., Cincinnati, 1988.

The New York Times, June 2, 1985.

Norwest World, October 1994.

Public Affairs Insight, Bank of Boston, July 25, 1986.

Reed, Edward W. / Gill, Edward K., *Commercial Banking*, Fourth Edition, Prentice Hall, Inc., 1989.

Remini, Robert V., *Andrew Jackson & the Bank War*, Norton & Company, New York City, 1967.

3

MONEY
Robert J. Morton

INTRODUCTION

In this chapter, the development of a need for the exchange of goods and services, which in turn lead to the development of what we call money, is discussed. The first method of exchange was a barter system, which has both the positive and negative aspects that bear examination. However, as will soon become obvious, the overwhelming negative aspects of barter necessitated the development of a more efficient method of exchange, namely money.

What is money? In order for something to be classified as money, it must serve three major functions. In addition, it must possess a number of other characteristics in order for it to truly function effectively.

How is money created? What is the function of the banking system in the creation of money? How can the supply of money be measured? What is considered money, and why? The Federal Reserve System measures the money supply in three ways. What are these classifications and what are the differences between them?

Finally, what is inflation and how does it effect monetary policy and interest rates.

LEARNING OBJECTIVES

After reading this chapter, you should have an understanding of the following:

1. Why did a need for exchange develop?
2. What are the two major deficiencies of a barter system?
3. What are the three functions of money? What other characteristics must money possess?

4. How do banks create money?

5. What is the expansion multiplier and how is it calculated?

6. What are the three classifications of money? How do they differ from each other?

7. The FEDS fight against inflation.

8. The effects on interest rates as the result of monetary policy.

DEVELOPMENT OF A NEED FOR EXCHANGE

As economics have become more advanced, individuals have tended to become increasingly specialized. As we look back to earlier times, individuals were, in many cases, self-sufficient. They were able to produce on their own much if not all that they needed. Hence, there was very little need for exchange.

However, as individuals began to specialize in the production of a single good or service, a need developed to exchange their single good or service for all the other goods and services that they needed.

The earliest form of exchange was a barter system, a system in which goods and services were exchanged for each other. If one is going to specialize, if one is no longer going to be self-sufficient, a way to acquire other needed goods and services is necessary. A barter system provides just such a method. For example, if someone produces wheat, he would go around to all those individuals who produce the other goods and services that he needs and attempt to trade his wheat for their products.

Such a system is, however, extremely inefficient. Specifically, it can be said to have two major deficiencies.

First, in order to get the goods and services wanted under such a system, one must locate someone who both produces what one wants and wants what one is producing. One must go through this process for every single product not produced on one's own but for which one has a need. Thus, each and every barter transaction requires what is known as a "coincidence of wants."[1] What may very well happen is that one will end up using as much time trying to locate prospective traders as in the actual production of the good or service in which one is specializing.

Second, there are likely to be great disparities between the values of various goods and services. Such disparities may in fact require that certain types of goods be divisible into very small units in order to be easily traded. However, such goods are often impossible to be divided into such small units, leading directly to the issue of "indivisibility."[2] Examples of such goods would be big-ticket items, such as autos, machinery, "even a suit of clothes."[3] Such items are not only quite valuable, but they cannot be traded for in pieces.

An example of this problem is given by Wonnacott & Wonnacott in their textbook *Economics*. They cite the situation of the farmer. How can a farmer trade his products, be they wheat, beef, or whatever else for such big-ticket items? There are obviously tremendous differences in value between his products and these types of items. There is no possible way that their producers could have a need for the amount of cattle or wheat that would be necessary for the farmer to exchange in order to match the value of their products. Furthermore, the farmer could not resolve this problem by exchanging for pieces of such items from various producers, giving each of them a certain amount of wheat or of beef. One simply cannot divide an auto into pieces! It is "indivisible." A better method had to be developed.

The earliest form of exchange was *barter*: goods and services traded for other goods and services.

Barter is inefficient relying on a *coincidence of wants* and the *divisibility of goods*.

Such differences truly require that a better system be developed for the exchange of products and services. Such a system came to be known, as you have probably guessed by now, as money. How is money an improvement over the barter system? What is money? What functions must it perform?

Money is something that "can be used to buy and sell any and all goods and services; it represents general purchasing power."[4]

Things are often defined by what they do, by their functions. Well, what does money do? What, in fact, are its functions? Money is often described as having three major functions, as follows:

Money is an entity user to buy and sell goods and services. It has three functions.

1. A *Medium of Exchange*—It's used to purchase goods and services.[5]

2. A *Standard of Value*—It is used as a means for quoting and comparing prices.

3. A *Store of Value*—It is used as a way of holding wealth; "[it] can be used to purchase goods and services whenever the need arises."[6] Is it a perfect method of holding wealth? No; during periods of inflation, money will tend to lose its value; it will tend to depreciate.

QUALITIES OF MONEY

In addition, to truly function effectively, money must also possess certain qualities.

Money must be uniformly interchangable, or fungible.

First, whatever is decided to be used as money must be uniform; it must all be the same. If one particular dollar bill, for instance, is regarded as being better than others, problems are going to arise. If one is concerned about the genuineness or quality of particular units of currency, the system will not function effectively. The currency has to have the confidence of the public. If people are going to refuse to accept the currency, the system will grind to a halt.

After having read the previous chapter, this possible scenario should not sound too far-fetched. Prior to the enactment of the National Banking Act of 1864, this country did not have a single, uniform national currency. What it had instead were thousand of varieties of state bank notes, in which the public had varying degrees of confidence, and many of which were prone to rampant counterfeiting.

Money must have a reasonably valuable purchasing power, conveniently held.

Second, the decided-upon money "should be sufficiently valuable that a reasonably large purchasing power can be carried conveniently."[7] What is meant by this? You may have seen pictures of people in pre-World War II Germany carrying currency in wheelbarrows in order to have enough to make common everyday types of purchases. Is this an efficient system?

Another example can be provided by the currency of the Confederate States during the latter part of the Civil War. "A common saying late in the (Civil) war was that you (could) take your money to market in a basket and bring back what you buy in your pocketbook."[8]

Money must be easily divisible.

Third, as we saw in the discussion of barter systems, whatever is chosen as money must be easily divisible.

CREATION OF MONEY BY THE BANKING SYSTEM

In the first chapter, it was mentioned that one of the functions of banks is the creation of money. Just how does this process work? How do banks create money?

FED reserve requirements and excess reserves "create" money.

The ability of the banking system to create money is dependent upon two factors, both of which are affected by the policy of the FED—namely, the reserve requirement and the level of excess reserves within the system.

Multiple deposit expansion is the re-loaning of current loans.

The FED and its powers will be discussed in great detail in the following chapter, but first, how do banks create money? ***They do it by the process of multiple deposit expansion.*** Multiple deposit expansion is like a snowball effect whereby the same funds are loaned and reloaned over and over again by the banking system.

Before going into the details, keep in mind that the process may be described as a model. A model is an illustration that makes one or more unrealistic assumptions in order to simplify the explanation of a given process. This model assumes that banks loan out all of their excess reserves. Everyone knows that this really is not the case. Banks, for example, have to adhere to reserve requirements and also invest in government securities.

A *model* is an illustration simplifying the explanation of a process.

Now for the details. An original deposit of $10,000, by being deposited and loaned out and then deposited again and loaned out again and again, is able to support loans several times its own amount, depending on the size of the reserve requirement.

As the reserve requirement decreases, the amount of lending that a given initial deposit will be able to support increases, so there is an ***inverse relationship.***

As reserve requirements decrease, loans increase, in an *inverse relationship*.

Suppose a bank receives a new deposit of $10,000 (for now, imagine that the money came from an old desk drawer). The bank will then loan out the funds subject to its reserve requirement (if its reserve requirement is 10 percent, as in Case A below, it will loan out 90 percent or $9,000). What happens to this $9,000? The customer who receives the loan will spend it, the proceeds being deposited in the bank of the recipient. This bank will, in turn, loan out 90 percent of the $9,000, or $8,100, and so on and so on.

What if the reserve requirement was 5 percent instead, as in Case B? The first bank could then loan out 95 percent of the initial deposit, or $9,500. The next bank would receive the $9,500 and loan out $9,025, and so on.

	Case A	Case B	Case C
Reserve Requirement	.10	.05	.15
Initial deposit	$10,000	$10,000	$8,500
second	9,000	9,500	10,000
third	8,100	9,025	7,225
fourth	7,290	8,574	6,141
fifth	6,561	8,145	5,220
sixth	5,905	7,738	4,436
Multiplier	10	20	6.67
Maximum Possible Expansion	$100,000	$200,000	$66,700

Lastly, what if the requirement were 15 percent, as in Case C? The first bank could only loan out $8,500. The next bank would receive the $8,500 and in turn loan out $7,225.

If we were to follow this expansion process to its conclusion, where would it end? What would be the maximum amount of new money that could be created by a given initial deposit? As was mentioned above, it is determined by the reserve requirement. Specifically, it is determined by the ***Expansion Multiplier.*** The expansion multiplier is the reciprocal of the reserve requirement. For example, if the reserve requirement is .10, the multiplier would be 1/.10 or 10. The maximum possible expansion of the money supply in case A would then be 10 X $10,000, or $100,000; in case B it would be 20 X $10,000 or $200,000, and in Case C, it would be 6.67 X $10,000 or $66,700.

The *Expansion Multiplier* is the reciprocal of the reserve requirement.

Do you see the relationship between the reserve requirement and the expansion multiplier? Do you see that it is indirect? As the reserve requirement increases, the value of the multiplier decreases. What therefore happens to the maximum possible expansion of the money supply as the reserve requirement is increased? It too decreases! This relationship is also indirect.

THE MONEY SUPPLY

The Federal Reserve (FED) measures money as M1, M2, and M3.

The Federal Reserve System (FED) uses a three-tiered system to measure the money supply where different types of cash (coin versus currency) and bank deposit products (demand deposit accounts versus certificates of deposit) are grouped. The measurements are known as M1, M2, and M3.

M1 represents funds that can be used in transactions.

M1 = currency + coin + demand deposit accounts + NOW accounts + travelers' checks

M2 = M1 + non-checkable savings deposits + MMDA accounts + small time deposits (less than $100,000)

M3 = M2 (which includes M1) + large time deposits ($100,000 and over) + certificate of deposits held by businesses

M2 is M1, plus small time deposits (CD's, etc.).

M3 is M1, M2, and large time deposits (CD's, etc.).

The FED has created these classifications to recognize the relative liquidity of different types of cash and bank deposits products. For example, a demand deposit account is considered very liquid when compared to a $20,000 one year certificate of deposit. The main importance of the categories is due to the differences in relative liquidity, how liquidity effects the expansion multiplier and therefore effects the money supply. The FED not only measures these classifications, it also analyzes the flow of money between the classifications in an attempt to determine trends in the money supply. All this just to control inflation.

CONTROLLING INFLATION VIA THE MONEY SUPPLY

Inflation: Rise in prices of goods and services, as happens when spending increases relative to the supply of goods on the market—in other words, too much money chasing too few goods

So why does the FED measure the supply of money? One important reason is to control inflation. Inflation is defined as the continuing rise in the average level of prices and the erosion of purchasing power. What this means is that a dollar today is worth more than a dollar a year from now and consequently a dollar will purchase more goods and services today than it will a year from now.

Inflation is a complicated and much debated subject. For the purposes of this text the important concept to understand is that inflation is the result of growth in the economy and some inflation is good. Therefore if our economy is growing, some inflation will occur. As long as general wages are increasing at a greater rate than inflation, we all benefit in that our purchasing power increases and we experience a true increase in wealth. However, if there is excessive growth, excessive inflation will occur faster than the increases in general wages. Think of this way, if you receive a 5% annual raise and moderate inflation is running at 3%, how much additional purchasing power did you realize? The answer is 2%. However, if excessive inflation is running at about 9% the effect on your purchasing power is a negative 4%. So even though you received a 5% increase in actual dollars, you are actually worse off because your purchasing power has been eroded due to excessive inflation.

One way of defining excessive growth is when aggregate demand is significantly greater than aggregate supply. What effects demand? One major influence is consumer confidence which is defined as the aggregate consumer attitude on purchasing power. People make purchasing decisions based upon

Consumer Confidence:
Aggregate consumer
attitude on purchasing
power. People make
purchasing decisions
based upon how well
off they are today and
how well off they
believe they will be in
the future.

how well off they are today and how well off they feel they will be in the future. When people feel secure in their employment and that the income levels will rise over time they will tend to have a strong consumer confidence. The result is increased purchases and an increase in the demand for aggregate goods and services.

What are other factors that influence consumer confidence? Employment and expected future income increases have already been discussed. What about the cost of money? If money is cheap, the influence to spend is greater than if money is expensive. How do we determine the cost of money? The answer is interest rates. Remember earlier in the text on the discussion on intermediation between those with an excess of funds and those with a need of funds? Interest is the compensation for those with an excess of funds for saving money while interest is the expense for those with a need for funds who borrow money to consume today what they will pay for in the future.

THE EFFECTS ON INTEREST RATES

Recession: Downturn
in economic activity,
defined by many
economists as at least
two consecutive
quarters of decline in a
country's Gross
National Product.

Business Cycle:
Recurrence of periods
of expansion
(RECOVERY) and
contraction (RECES-
SION) in economic
activity with effects on
inflation, growth, and
employment.

Our economy goes through periods of expansion (recovery) and decline (recession) which is commonly referred to as the business cycle. As mentioned earlier, excessive inflation occurs as the result of excessive growth whereby aggregate demand is significantly greater than aggregate supply. In other words, too much money (demand for goods and services) chasing too few goods (supply of goods and services). During periods of high inflation and excessive growth, they FED will implement contractionary monetary policy by increasing rates and decreasing the money supply (A more in-depth analysis of the mechanics on Monetary policy is discussed in Chapter 4). This in turn will dampen consumer demand which will in turn slow the economic growth. Based upon this you can begin to appreciate the events within our economy during the years 1990–94. During the early 1990s the U.S. economy was experiencing a recession whereby soft demand for goods and services caused a decline in sales for businesses who in turn laid people off, or decreased annual increases in compensation, or even went out of business. The rising unemployment, lower raises and large layoffs drove consumer confidence even lower. The FED responded by implementing expansionary monetary policy and lowered its FED fund rate. Banks in turn lowered their prime rate from a high of 11.5% (February 1989–June 1989) to a low of 6% (July 1992 –March 1994). In late 1993, early 1994, the FED believed that the recovery was gaining too much momentum and became concerned with rising inflation so they began implementing contractionary monetary policy. As a result the FED has periodically increased its FED funds to banks who have in turn raised their prime lending rate. Prime increased from its low of 6% in March 1994 to 8.5% in November 1994 and has been relatively stable through December 1996 with a current prime rate of 8.25% at the time of this publication.

UNDERSTANDING TRENDS IN INTEREST RATES

A customer comes into the bank and says they are interested in a five year equity loan. Assuming your bank has a variable rate option tied to prime or a fixed rate option, which one would you recommend? If you know that the economy is growing rapidly and the FED is exercising contractionary monetary policy, interest rates are probably rising and therefore, all things being equal, it might make sense to lock in today's lower rate. Conversely, if the economy is experiencing a recession and interest rates are expected to fall, it might make sense to go with the variable option and take advantage of lower expected rates.

CONCLUSION

As economics advanced and individuals became more specialized, a method had to be devised for the exchange of goods and services. The earliest method was a barter system, simply the trading of goods and services for one another. Although such systems certainly were a step in the right direction, they suffered from two major deficiencies. They required a "coincidence of wants" and, because many commodities are not easily divisible, didn't allow for goods of varying values to be conveniently and easily traded.

Money can be described by its three functions; a medium of exchange, a standard of value, and a store of value. In addition, whatever is picked to be money must be uniform, "sufficiently valuable," and easily divisible.

The banking system, through a process known as multiple deposit expansion, is able to create money. The amount of money that the system is capable of creating is dependent upon the reserve requirement and the level of excess reserves within the banking system. The expansion multiplier can be used to show the maximum possible expansion which a given reserve requirement will support.

Money can be measured in a number of ways, depending on how strictly one adheres to the medium of exchange function. The FED uses three measurements, M1, M2, and M3, M1 being the narrowest.

Lastly, one of the main responsibilities of the FED is to control inflation. Depending on where the economy is in the business cycle will dictate whether the FED is exercising contractionary or expansionary monetary policy.

One important note, the FED can influence the economy and interest rates but it cannot control them. The economy and the business cycle are too great of a force to be controlled by any individual, group or government.

STUDY AND REVIEW QUESTIONS

1. What is the importance of financial intermediation and the role of money within our economy?
2. What are the characteristics of money?
3. How does the expansion multiplier increase the money supply? How does it decease the money supply?
4. Why is controlling inflation important?
5. How does inflation, monetary policy, and interest rates interact?

BIBLIOGRAPHY

The Federal Reserve Bank of Boston, *Putting it Simply . . . The Federal Reserve*, September 1986.

The Federal Reserve Bank of New York, *What's all this about the M's?* December 1988.

The Federal Reserve Bank of Richmond, *Money*, October 1986.

Wonnacott, Paul & Ronald, *Economics*, 3rd Edition, McGraw-Hill, 1986.

THE FEDERAL RESERVE SYSTEM
Michael J. Tallo

INTRODUCTION

This chapter will outline the development of the Federal Reserve System and define its responsibilities. The Federal Reserve's role in creating and carrying out monetary policy will be discussed, and monetary policy will be compared to fiscal policy, the government's other major economic policy tool.

The chapter will close with a discussion of the various state and local government agencies that are responsible for the chartering and examination of banks.

LEARNING OBJECTIVES

After reading this chapter, you should have an understanding of the following:

1. How the Federal Reserve Act of 1913 improved upon the weaknesses of the National Banking Act of 1864.

2. The organization of the Federal Reserve System.

3. List the responsibilities of the Federal Reserve System.

4. Describe the Federal Reserve System's involvement in monetary policy, and identify the three major tools of monetary policy.

5. Compare monetary policy to fiscal policy, and define Keynesian Economics.

6. Explain how the bank chartering process works.

7. Explain what is involved in a bank examination.

THE FEDERAL RESERVE ACT OF 1913

The Federal Reserve System (called the FED) was created in 1913 by the Glass-Owen Bill. Named after Representative Carter Glass of Virginia and Senator Robert Owen of Oklahoma, it is better known as the Federal Reserve Act of 1913. The act was a political compromise between those who felt that a central banking authority was needed and those who feared such a concentration of power.

The Federal Reserve (FED) was created in 1913 to rectify weaknesses in the National Banking Act of 1864.

Woodrow Wilson had fought hard during his first year as president for reforms in the nation's banking system. The 1913 bill has been called a "Christmas present for President Wilson," who signed it into law on December 23 of that year. Its opponents, however, called it a "Christmas present for the money trust"[1] (the money trust being the term used to describe the most powerful members of the financial community at the time).

A centralized check collection system was created by the establishment of twelve FED districts.

Although it represented a major step forward, the National Banking Act of 1864 (Chapter 2) contained three weaknesses that the Federal Reserve Act specifically addressed: the lack of a centralized check collection system, an inflexible currency, and the pyramiding of reserves.

The lack of a centralized check collection system was resolved by creating twelve Federal Reserve districts. A check written on a distant bank could now be sent to the local FED branch for collection. That branch would then send it to the FED branch serving the bank against which the check was drawn. The check would next be sent, by the FED, to the drawee bank. Although the checks still followed a long and indirect route back to the drawee banks, individual banks no longer had to send checks back and forth among themselves.

Inflexible currency was the loosened-up by the FED's issuance of Federal Reserve Notes.

The inflexible currency problem was corrected by giving the FED the power to issue Federal Reserve Notes. Unlike National Bank Notes, these notes were not tied to U.S. government bonds. As has been mentioned, under the National Banking Act, banks could only issue new currency (National Bank Notes) up to the amount of government bonds that they had purchased. While this requirement helped finance the Civil War, after the war the Federal government wanted to reduce its debt. It then discouraged banks from buying additional bonds, thus restricting the amount of bank notes in circulation. The problem was compounded by the fact that the country's economy was expanding, and additional currency (bank notes) was needed to support this expansion. With the advent of Federal Reserve Notes, banks no longer had to purchase more bonds in order to increase the amount of currency in circulation. By the mid 1930s, national banks had ceased issuing their own notes.

Pyramided reserves were spread out among the twelve FED districts.

The problem of pyramiding reserves was also resolved by establishing the twelve FED districts. The individual FED branches were responsible for holding the reserves of member banks within their districts. In this way, the reserves were spread across the country rather than concentrated in the major New York banks. Member banks could also borrow from their local FED branches, subject to certain requirements.

The United States was far behind Europe in the development of centralized banking. The Bank of England, for example, was established in 1693. Even after its creation, the Federal Reserve System was much less powerful than European central banks. It took many years before the FED gained the power to control the money supply or to monitor and regulate credit. In 1913 the country recognized that a centralized banking authority was necessary, but the FED, as we know it today, did not evolve until the 1930s. The shock of the Great Depression finally caused Americans to accept the idea of a central bank with powers similar to those of the European banks.

ORGANIZATION OF THE FEDERAL RESERVE SYSTEM

The President appoints each FED governor every two years, one at a time, for a fourteen-year period.

The chairman serves a four-year term.

The Federal Reserve System is run by its seven-member Board of Governors. Each governor is appointed by the President, subject to Senate approval, for a single fourteen-year term. The terms are staggered so that only one expires every two years. This staggering prevents a President from packing the board with his political allies. A President can, however, take advantage of the resignation or death of a member to make additional appointments.

The chairman of the Board of Governors serves a four-year term. He, too, is appointed by the president with Senate approval. He may be selected from the appointed members or from outside the board altogether. The chairman can serve up to three and a half terms, or a total of fourteen years—the same as any other member. If not reappointed as chairman, he may serve the rest of his fourteen years as a regular member, but none have chosen to do so to date.

The first chairman was Charles S. Hamlin, who served from 1914 until 1918. The longest serving chairman was William McChesney Martin, whose tenure ran from 1951-1970 under five presidents (Truman, Eisenhower, Kennedy, Johnson, and Nixon). Martin served a total of nineteen years because he began his first term as a replacement appointee, and a replacement appointee serving out the remainder of a departed member's may then be reappointed to serve his own complete fourteen-year term.

As mentioned above, the FED is broken up into twelve districts. It is traditional for the board to contain no more than one member from any of the districts. The district headquarters are located in the following cities:

District

1.	Boston	5.	Richmond	9.	Minneapolis
2.	New York	6.	Atlanta	10.	Kansas City
3.	Philadelphia	7.	Chicago	11.	Dallas
4.	Cleveland	8.	St. Louis	12.	San Francisco

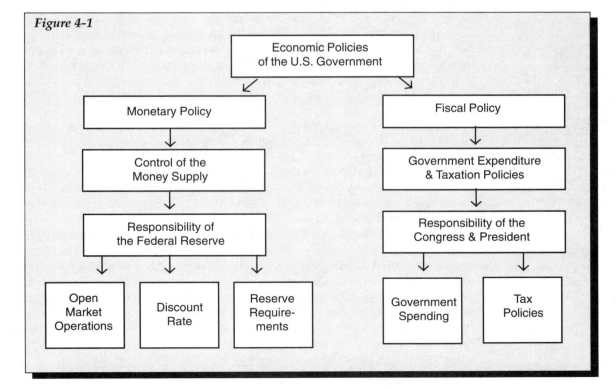

Figure 4-1

RESPONSIBILITIES OF THE FED[2]

1. *To issue paper currency (Federal Reserve Notes).* The largest denomination now printed is the $100 bill. No larger bills have been printed since 1969. Previously, denominations of $500 (William McKinley), $1,000 (Grover Cleveland), $5,000 (James Madison), and $10,000 (Salmon Chase, Treasury Secretary under Abraham Lincoln), and $100,000 (Woodrow Wilson) were produced. Because of the widespread use of checking accounts, electronic fund transfers, and wire transfers, larger bills are not in great demand. If you look at any Federal Reserve note, you will see the seal of the branch that issued it, along with its alphabetic code (Boston's is "A").

2. *To act as a "banker's bank."* The FED is responsible for functions such as check clearing and setting the discount rate, which will be described later.

3. *To supervise, inspect, and regulate, to varying extents, all banks.* The extent of these activities vary according to the type of bank.

4. *To act as the federal government's bank.* As the central bank of the U.S., the Fed maintains the bank account of the national government. Other central banks worldwide include the Bundesbank (West Germany), the Bank of England, and the Bank of Canada.

5. *To conduct monetary policy.* This is a very important role, which the FED did not acquire until the 1935 Banking Act. Monetary policy is the process by which the FED tries to control the nation's money supply and the level of interest rates. [*See* Figure 4-1 (Economic Policies of the U.S. Government).]

HOW THE FED CONDUCTS MONETARY POLICY

> The FED controls the money supply by setting member reserve requirements.

> Reducing the money supply is a *contractionary* policy.

> *Expansionary* policy requires increasing the money supply.

> The FED's open market operations are the buying and selling of government securities.

> The FED buys securities from primary dealers.

The FED conducts, or carries out, monetary policy by controlling the quantity of reserves held by the banking system. As discussed in Chapter 3, in periods of high inflation, the FED seeks to reduce the money supply and slow the economy. This process is known as *contractionary monetary policy*. In periods of recession, the FED seeks to expand the supply of money. This is called *expansionary monetary policy*. The FED has three tools available to conduct monetary policy: open market operations, changing the discount rate, and changing the level of required reserves. [*See* Figure 4-2 (Tools of Monetary Policy).]

Open market operations is by far the most common of the three tools. [*See* Figure 4-3 (Open Market Operations).] It involves the buying and selling of U.S. government securities. This buying and selling is done by the Federal Open Market Committee (FOMC). The complete Board of Governors and president of the New York FED serve as permanent FOMC members. The remaining four seats are filled, on an alternating basis, by the other eleven regional FED presidents.

If the FED wants to increase the nation's money supply (expansionary monetary policy), it buys U.S. government securities, primarily from a group of dealers known as "the primary dealers." It is very prestigious for a dealer to be on the FED's list. In order to be on the list, one has to meet a series of strict requirements. Among the most important is that they must agree to buy and sell securities to the FED upon their request (in line with the dealer's financial capacity to do so). These purchases inject money into the banking system and increase the reserves of the system. In turn, the nation's money supply increases by several times the amount of the purchase.

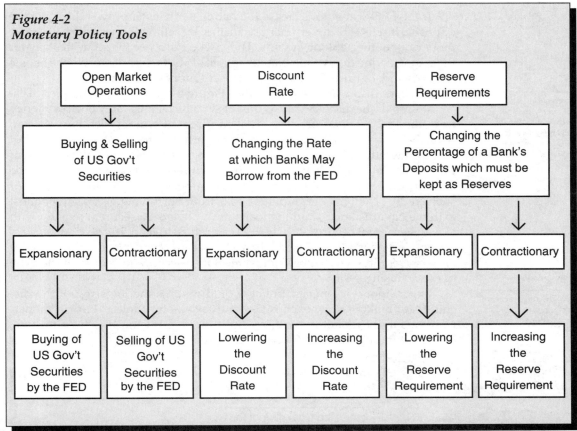

Figure 4-2
Monetary Policy Tools

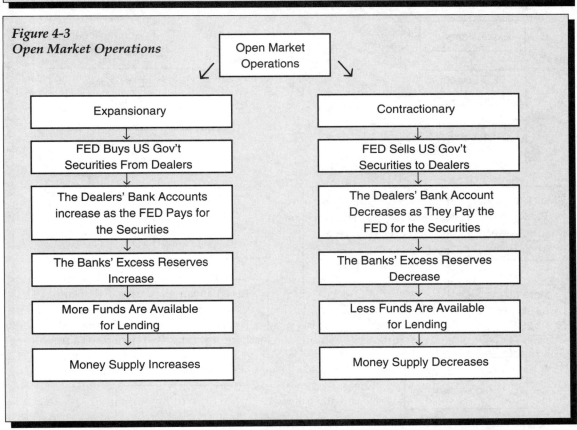

Figure 4-3
Open Market Operations

If the FED wants to decrease the nation's money supply, it does just the opposite: it sells U.S. government securities. By selling the securities, it draws money out of the banking system. Those who purchase the securities pay for them by drawing down their bank accounts. This process decreases the bank's reserves and, in turn, decreases the nation's money supply.

Changes in the discount rate. [*See* Figure 4-4 (The changing of the Discount Rate).] The discount rate is the rate at which banks may borrow money from the FED. This procedure is called discount window lending. As you read above, open market operations are tightly controlled by the FOMC, but discount window lending is subject in large part to the internal decisions of the individual banks. Although the discount rate itself is determined by the FED, it is the individual banks who determine whether or not to apply for such credit. The FED discourages banks from borrowing except in the most extreme circumstances, and the loans must always be secured, usually with U.S. government securities. The FED can refuse to lend, if it so desires. Discount window lending is used when a bank cannot meet its cash position, or "reserve requirement." A bank must meet its reserve requirement at the close of every business day.

> By changing the *discount rate* (the borrowing price for FED members) the FED can control the money supply.

Expansionary monetary policy would involve the lowering of the discount rate, making it *less* expensive—and easier—for banks to borrow money. Contractionary monetary policy would involve raising the discount rate, making it more expensive for banks to borrow.

> *Low* discount rates are expanionsary, *high*, contractionary.

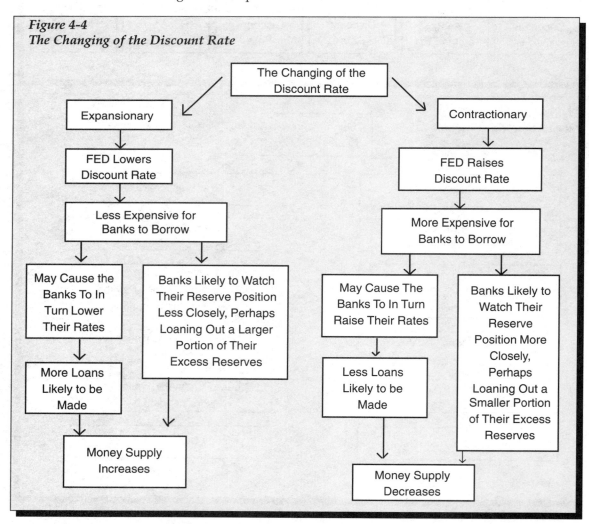

Figure 4-4
The Changing of the Discount Rate

Changes in the level of required reserves lower or raise the percentage of a bank's deposits that must be kept as reserves. (*See* Figure 4-5 (The Changing of Reserve Requirements).] Such changes have a very powerful effect on the amount of money that banks may create. Although the FED has the power to change the level of required reserves, it rarely, if ever, uses such drastic measures.

Lowering reserve requirements is expansionary, *raising,* contractionary.

Expansionary monetary policy would lower the level of required reserves and create excess reserves that banks could then loan out. The nation's money supply would increase several times the actual amount of the extra reserves.

Contractionary monetary policy would raise the level of required reserves and create a shortfall of reserves among banks. They, in turn, would cut back on their lending activity.

FISCAL POLICY

Fiscal policy relates to U.S. government taxing and spending.

Monetary policy is only one of the U.S. government's economic policy tools. The other tool is *fiscal policy*. Monetary policy is the responsibility of the Fed, but who shapes and controls fiscal policy?

Fiscal policy includes government spending and taxation. [*See* Figure 4-6 (Tools of Fiscal Policy).] For that reason it is the responsibility of the legislative and executive branches of government—the Congress and the President.

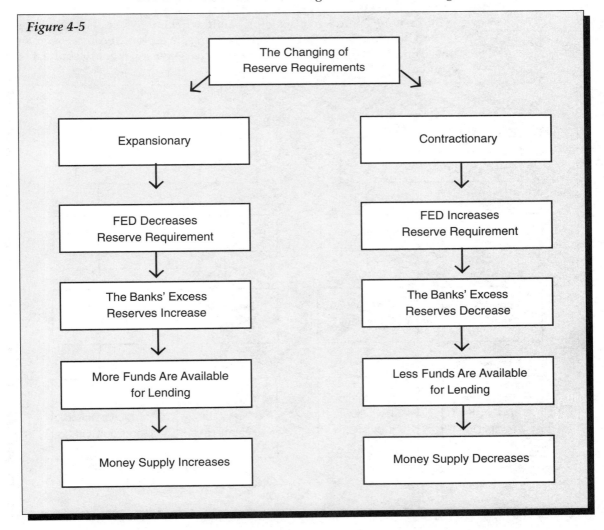

Figure 4-5

The Changing of Reserve Requirements

Expansionary	Contractionary
FED Decreases Reserve Requirement	FED Increases Reserve Requirement
The Banks' Excess Reserves Increase	The Banks' Excess Reserves Decrease
More Funds Are Available for Lending	Less Funds Are Available for Lending
Money Supply Increases	Money Supply Decreases

Anything involving these two branches of government is likely to be highly political, that is the main problem with fiscal policy.

To understand fiscal policy, it is necessary to understand the basics of Keynesian economics (named after British economist John Maynard Keynes). In a nutshell, Keynesian economists believe that the government should play an active role in shaping the economy: it should help to stimulate the economy during periods of downturn and work to "cool it off" during periods of high inflation.

In Keynesian theory, during economic downturns, the government should conduct an expansionary fiscal policy. During such times, it should run a deficit, it should spend more than it takes in thereby stimulating the economy. To accomplish this, the government may cut taxes, increase spending, or do both. The total demand for goods and services nationwide (aggregate demand) will then increase. For obvious reasons, politicians generally favor following such a policy.

During upturns (periods of increased inflation), the opposite should be done, a contractionary fiscal policy should be conducted. The government should either increase taxes, cut spending, or do both. These measures will cause aggregate demand to decrease. In contrast to expansionary fiscal policy, politicians find contractionary fiscal policy especially difficult to follow.

Expansionary fiscal policy is very popular politically and is the type of policy that has been carried out most often in the past. The Kennedy tax cuts of the early 1960s are a good example. Contractionary fiscal policy is unpopular and, therefore, very rarely used. Of course, taxes have been raised many times, but this is almost always done to increase revenue, not to contract the economy.

> The British economist John Maynard Keynes promulgated fiscal policy theories.

> Cutting taxes and increasing spending is *expansionary fiscal policy*. Raising taxes and lowering spending is *contractionary fiscal policy*.

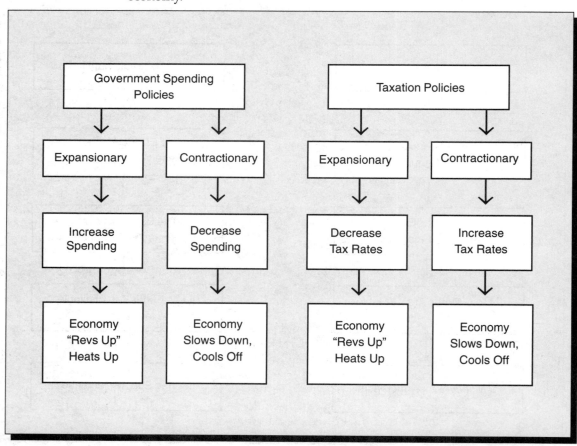

The FED's strength is its a-political nature.

The Federal Reserve System and, therefore, monetary policy, is less affected by politics. Because of its organization—with members appointed for one fourteen-year term—the FED can make painful economic policy decisions that politicians fear to make. Or, as former chairman William MeChesney Martin said, "The Federal Reserve's job is to take away the punch bowl just when the party gets going."[2]

BANK REGULATION

Bank Chartering

The *dual banking system* allows for either state or federal bank charters.

The first area of bank regulation is the process by which a charter is obtained. As previously discussed (in Chapter 2), the United States operates under the "dual banking" system. *A dual banking system* is defined as the process by which one can obtain a charter to operate from *either* the federal or state authorities. The concept of states' rights is prevalent throughout most of the banking legislation enacted since the 1880s. It is interesting to note that the major banking legislation passed in 1863, 1913, and 1933 was done to correct weaknesses in the system, but each act included compromises to allow state-chartered banking to continue, as well as to preserve some portions that contributed to the weaknesses.

Bank chartering is important to assure public faith in the system and guarantee the safety of the flow of funds so important to the economy today. The chartering process is necessary to assure that qualified and knowledgeable people are operating the bank, as well as showing that there is a need for a bank and describing its prospect for long-term viability.

Banks are chartered by the *Comptroller of the Currency*, thrifts by the *Federal Home Loan Bank Board*.

At the federal level, application would be made to either the Comptroller of the Currency or the Federal Home Loan Bank, depending on whether the charter applicant wants to open a commercial bank or a savings and loan institution. The application to open a national bank would be reviewed by the Federal Reserve and the FDIC, as national banks must belong to both organizations. The savings and loan application would be reviewed by the FSLIC as well as the Federal Home Loan Bank.

State bank charters require proof of *need* and *expertise in management*.

The application process at the state level differs from state to state. Suffice it to say that the chartering process requires that there is a need for a new bank and proof that knowledgeable people are involved, both in establishing the bank and in operating it. The application would be approved by a board consisting of elected officials and representatives of the states's bank examination authority. If the bank required FDIC insurance or membership in the Federal Reserve system, these agencies would also review the application.

Bank Examination

The primary regulator for a bank is dependent on two factors:

1. What type of charter was obtained, and
2. Who is the insurer of the depositor's funds.

National banks must answer to the *FED*, the *FDIC*, and the *Comptroller of the Currency*.

A national bank would have the Comptroller of the Currency as its primary examiner. The Federal Reserve would also have regulatory authority, as all national banks are required to be members of the system. Also, the FDIC would have an interest in the operation of the bank because it insures the deposits of the bank. All of these agencies would not conduct an annual examination; rather, they would share reports and periodically conduct a formal examination as they deem necessary.

A bank that obtained its charter from state authorities would be examined by that state's bank examination department. If the bank chose to become a member of the Federal Reserve System, the Federal Reserve would become the primary examiner, working closely or jointly with the state banking department. If the bank had its deposits insured by the FDIC, they would also conduct periodic audits.

If a state chartered bank was not a member of the Federal Reserve System but had its deposits insured by the FDIC, then the examinations would be conducted by the FDIC working closely with the state banking authorities. Banks that are not members of the Federal Reserve and not insured by the FDIC would have to answer only to the state banking authorities.

Federal savings banks, chartered by the Federal Home Loan Bank system and insured by the FSLIC, would have their periodic exams conducted by those agencies.

Banks that issue stock shares must also answer to the Securities and Exchange Commission (SEC).

In addition to bank regulators, banks that issue stock are subject to examination and regulation by the Securities and Exchange Commission. This body requires banks to file reports so that stockholders have adequate information available to evaluate their decision to buy or sell the stock. The Department of Justice and Treasury Department also have a role in bank mergers, currency transactions, and the Bank Secrecy Act to ensure that a bank is following the laws and regulations defined in the various acts.

Purpose of a Bank Examination

Examinations determine the safety and soundness of banks.

The primary purpose of a bank examination is to determine the safety and soundness of the bank. Examiners would evaluate the assets, liabilities, surplus, income, and expenses of the bank. They would evaluate the accounting and reporting systems used and the bank's compliance with the laws and regulations that apply. An examination would also evaluate the adequacy of the bank's capital and surplus, as this would measure the bank's ability to absorb losses and adverse economic conditions. Bank management is evaluated to determine if the managers are qualified and effective in their positions. Also, the bank's policies are evaluated and procedures are tested to ensure that they are followed.

An examination report would contain a balance sheet and income statement, prepared in accordance with regulatory accounting principles. Various ratios would be calculated and compared to industry standards, as well as to prior years, in order to reveal positive or negative trends. The report would also identify weaknesses and recommendations to correct those problem areas. The purpose of an examination is not to find fraud and embezzlement (though occasionally an examination will discover a loss) but to point out areas where procedures are not being followed or areas where controls are weak and embezzlement could occur.

Weak banks may find themselves on a regulator's "watch list". These banks generally have a low capital to asset ratio or a large number of non-performing assets. These banks will find themselves subject to more frequent examinations and in some cases periodic reports to regulators as to a plan to restore capital and improve financial health of the institution.

In addition to "on-site" examinations, banks submit reports on a monthly or quarterly basis, depending on the requirements of the various regulators. These reports help regulators monitor a bank's performance between formal examinations. Many of these reports also become available to the general public. While many bank customers may not understand them, there are firms in the country that analyze these reports and rank banks according to their findings. These reports are also available to the public and are used by banks as another management tool.

Bank Audits

Banks must also be audited by independent accounting firms.

In addition to the regulatory exams, banks are required to have an independent Certified Public Accountant perform an audit of the books and records of the bank. While the regulators are concerned with a bank's adherence to laws and regulations, this audit is directed more to the financial records of the bank. The CPA firm will prepare a balance sheet, income statement, and statement of cash flows in accordance with generally accepted accounting principles. These principles may differ from the regulatory accounting principles, and in some cases the differences can be significant.

The CPA firm is hired by the bank and must be totally independent. The firm will review the financial records to ensure that assets, liabilites, income and expenses are properly reported. The audit will also test to ensure that internal controls are being followed. Again, an audit is not performed to discover fraud and embezzlement, but to assure that sufficient controls are in place and followed to minimize its occurence.

The public accounting firms also provide other management services such as tax return preparation and computer consulting. These additional areas help the bank to automate systems and utilize technology so that the work force is more efficient. Tax advice can help a bank plan a strategy to minimize its tax liability, as well as helping the bank stay current in an ever changing environment.

CONCLUSION

The a-political FED is a powerful player in the nation's economic health.

The Federal Reserve Act of 1913 overcame the lack of a centralized check collection system, the inflexible currency and the pyramiding of reserves that were inherent weaknesses in the National Banking Act of 1864. Its responsibilities include issuing paper money, acting as a "banker's bank," regulating all banks, acting as the federal government's bank, and conducting monetary policy. The Fed has developed into a powerful institution that can increase or decrease the nation's money supply to combat inflation or other monetary problems. It was set up purposely to operate outside the political arena, which enables it to make often painful economic decisions. All these factors combine to make the Federal Reserve Act one of the most important piece of banking legislation ever passed by the U.S. Congress.

NOTES

1. Gerald Dunne, The Federal Reserve Bank of St. Louis, *A Christmas Present for The President—A Short History of the Creation of the Federal Reserve System.* p. 26.

2. Paul Wonnacot and David Wonnacot, *Economics*, 3rd ed. (McGraw Hill Book Company). p. 232-233.

STUDY AND REVIEW QUESTIONS

1. What are the major functions of the Federal reserve System?

2. Please discuss the similarities and differences between Monetary Policy and Fiscal Policy. Which is more effective in controlling the money supply?

3. Please describe the mechanics of contractionary monetary policy. How will this impact interest rates? Why?

4. What is the significance of a dual banking system?

5. Why are bank examinations important?

BIBLIOGRAPHY

Dunne, Gerald, *A Christmas Present for the President—A Short History of the Creation of the Federal Reserve System*, The Federal Reserve Bank of St. Louis, *Who We Are and What We Do.*

The Federal Reserve Bank of Cleveland, *Your Federal Reserve Bank.*

The Federal Reserve Bank of Philadelphia, *"The Man Who Made the Fed," "Glass Insulation," "The Hats the Federal Reserve Wears."*

Pather, James, The Federal Reserve Bank of Richmond, *The Origins of the Fed—A Short History of the Federal Reserve Act of 1913 on its 75th Anniversary.*

The Federal Reserve Bank of Boston, *"Fedpoints," "Putting It Simply: The Federal Reserve," "Historical Beginning: The Federal Reserve."*

The Board of Governors of the Federal Reserve System, *The Federal Reserve System—Purposes and Functions.*

Kamerschen, David. *Money and Banking.* (Southwestern Publishing Company), Chapters 7–9.

Wonnacot, Paul and David Wonnacot. *Economics.* 3rd Ed. McGraw Hill Book Company, Chapters 11–14.

5

ACCOUNT OWNERSHIP AND TITLE
Claudia Rioles

INTRODUCTION

This chapter discusses what is involved in the opening of a deposit account, emphasizing the fact that both the depositor and the bank are agreeing to be bound by certain conditions.

The chapter then goes on to describe the various types of deposit accounts that are available and the many different forms (or, more properly, "titles") in which they may be opened. Lastly, it discusses the actual mechanics of opening up a new deposit account.

LEARNING OBJECTIVES

After reading this chapter, you should have an understanding of the following:

1. The nature of the contractual relationship that exists between the depositor and the depository (the bank).

2. The differences between the various types of deposit accounts that all banks offer, specifically:
   Checking accounts (demand deposit accounts)
   NOW accounts
   Super NOW's
   Savings accounts
   Time accounts (Certificates of Deposit)
   MMDAs (Money Market Deposit Accounts)

3. The differences between the various titles under which the above types of accounts may be opened, specifically:
   Individual
   Power of attorney

> Joint
> Trustee
> Uniform Transfer to Minors Act
> Estates of deceased persons
> Trusts under a will
> Trusts under a trust
> Guardianship
> Conservator
> Corporate
> IOLTA

4.   The steps involved in the opening of various types of accounts.

THE ACCOUNT AGREEMENT/CONTRACT

A deposit account represents a binding contract between depositor and depository.

Every deposit account is backed by an agreement or contract between the depositor and the depository whereby the depositor commits a sum of money or periodic sums to the depository for varying periods of time (from one day to years) and the depository promises to safeguard these funds, to make them available in accordance with the terms and conditions and in the time frames as agreed upon between the parties and, depending upon the type of account, to pay interest on the deposited funds in the manner set forth in the agreement.

The key words here are "as agreed upon between the parties" because they convey the meaning of a binding agreement or contract. Both sides make promises based on the initial delivery of money from the depositor to the depository. The depositor gives and entrusts his money; the depository accepts the trust and promises to safeguard the funds. The depository sets forth the rules and conditions under which it, to protect itself and to minimize inconvenience when paying out those funds, will act and require the depositor to act. By signing the appropriate signature card, the depositor accepts those rules and conditions with the understanding that the depository will provide the financial services he or she expects. Depending upon the type of account, the depository promises to pay interest on the funds at interest rates and at intervals that are acceptable to the depositor.

Contracts are carefully spelled out and watched over by government regulators.

As in any contractual relationship, in order to avoid future conflicts and contentions that might arise, it is imperative that both sides be aware of, and understand, all aspects of the deposit agreement. Because the depository is the author of the agreement, the people who represent the depository must be familiar with its terms. In recent years, government regulators, intent on providing depositors with a full understanding of these deposit agreements, have required depositories to provide extensive written disclosure statements that spell out in detail the provisions—that is, how interest is calculated and at what intervals it is paid, minimum balances required to avoid charges, when and what fees and charges can be imposed, and so forth.

TYPES OF DEPOSIT ACCOUNTS

Prior to embarking upon a detailed discussion of how to open new accounts and what necessary generic forms are needed for each new account, perhaps it would be worthwhile to review briefly the major types of deposit instruments. While many banks advertise their deposit product lines under various and sundry "trade" names, this section will attempt to describe the various legal types of deposits that most banks currently offer the consumer and commercial customer.

Demand Deposit Accounts

Demand Deposit accounts are commonly called checking accounts, and, by law, cannot pay interest.

Demand Deposit accounts, otherwise known as checking accounts, represent deposits that are withdrawable by check at the demand of the depositor. Funds on deposit may also be withdrawn by debit cards at an automated teller machine. Banking regulations prohibit banks from paying interest on demand deposits and from requiring owners of such accounts to give the banks any prior notice of intent to withdraw. Demand deposit accounts may be opened for individuals, partnerships, corporations, trusts, unincorporated associations, or governments.

NOW Accounts

Negotiable Order of Withdrawal (NOW) accounts are technically savings accounts on which checks may be written and interest paid.

Negotiable Order of Withdrawal accounts are savings accounts through which an account holder may withdraw funds by writing negotiable orders of withdrawals payable to third parties.

Because NOW accounts are legally savings accounts, interest is paid on balances, yet the depositor enjoys check writing privileges.

Funds on deposit may also be withdrawn by debit card at an Automated Teller Machine (ATM) or Point of Sale terminal (POS) (supermarket, gas station, etc.).

NOW accounts are available to individuals, proprietorships, as well as to certain non-profit corporate entities. NOW accounts are not available to profit-making business entities such as typical corporations.

SUPER NOW Accounts

Super NOW's are MMDA's with unlimited check-writing privileges. They are unavailable to corporations.

The Super NOW Account was authorized by the Depository Institutions Deregulation Committee in December, 1982. Essentially, the Super Now account has the same characteristics of the MMDA account with the following two important exceptions:

1. There is no limit on the number of third party checks that may be written against a Super NOW account.
2. Super NOW accounts are not available to corporations.

Savings Accounts

Savings accounts bear interest without specific maturity dates. There are no ceilings on such interest.

Savings accounts are interest-bearing deposits that do not have a specific maturity date. Although banks may legally require an advance notice of withdrawal of no more than seven days, banks rarely exercise this right because to do so might be interpreted by the public as trouble and could begin a panic run on the bank. Prior to the passage of the Monetary Control Act of 1980, banks were restricted as to the maximum amount of interest that could be paid on a savings account. Today, however, banks are free to pay whatever rates they choose on savings accounts. Traditionally, savings accounts were represented by passbooks, but with the technology of today, "statement" savings accounts are popular both as stand alone accounts and companion accounts to a demand deposit, which may be reported on a single statement. In many cases, total savings balances are counted toward fee waivers against the primary check-writing account. Funds on deposit in statement savings accounts may also be withdrawn by a debit card at an Automated Teller Machine (ATM) or Point of Sale terminal (POS).

Certificates of Deposit

Time deposit accounts (commonly, *CD's*) bear interest at specified maturity dates.

Time accounts are interest-bearing deposits that have a specified maturity date. No interest may be paid on the deposit after the maturity date, and funds may not be withdrawn before the maturity date without the depositor's incurring a substantial penalty.

Time deposits are usually single instrument deposits; additional deposits to an existing account are forbidden. Time deposits are represented by a certificate or receipt; thus the most common form of time deposit is a Certificate of Deposit. Time deposits are available to all customers.

Money Market Deposit Account—MMDA

Money Market Deposit accounts earn competitive interest rates and allow limited check writing privileges. There is no specified maturity date.

Money Market Deposit Accounts (MMDA) are the third type of account on which checks may be written. Authorized by the Garn-St. Germain Act of 1982, primarily to compete with the cash management accounts offered by security firms, these accounts pay a rate of interest normally higher than NOW accounts, but usually with a higher minium balance requirement.

Many banks tier rates on MMDA's, paying premium rates on higher balances. Although MMDA's enjoy the benefit of higher interest rates, they are restricted in that:

— No more than three third party checks may be written in one month period.

— Banks *may* impose a seven day notice of intent to withdraw funds.

However, unlimited withdrawals may be made in person or by mail and funds may also be withdrawn via debit card.

Figure 5-1
Deposit Account Chart

Type of Account	Interest Bearing	Check Writing	Minimum Balance	Fees	Penalty for Early Withdrawal
DDA	No	Yes	Depends on bank	Depends on bank	No
NOW	Yes	Yes	Depends on bank	Depends on bank	No
SUPER NOW	Yes	Yes	$2,500	Depends on bank	No
MMDA	Yes	Yes	$2,500 to earn MMDA interest rate. (May be as low as $1000) Below the minimum balance earnes NOW rate	Depends on bank	No
Savings	Yes	No	Usually $10 to earn interest, may be higher	No	No
CD (various lengths)	Yes	No	Depends on length of CD and on bank	No	Yes

Some banks combine money market accounts with DDA/NOW/Super NOW statements. In many cases, total balances are counted toward fee waiver against the primary check writing account. Transfers may be allowed via packaged account services in person, through an ATM or over the telephone at some depositories.

TITLES AND OWNERSHIP OF ACCOUNTS

Unless otherwise stated, all of the following titles may apply to any of the various types of accounts that have been discussed in the preceding section.

Individual

Individual account ownership is limited to the one person who signs the title card to the account.

The title of this type of account is in the name of one person. In such an account, ownership rests with the person whose name appears in the title. The basic provision in the individual account agreement stipulates that the depository will honor withdrawal requests only by the individual depositor upon his signed instructions or orders.

In most jurisdictions, anyone able to sign his name is eligible for an individual account and may be accepted by the depository to open such an account. In the event of the death of an individual depositor, only the executor or administrator of the deceased's estate may have access to the account. In certain jurisdictions, the law may permit a depository to pay the funds of a deceased depositor to the next of kin if the balance on the account is under a specified amount. Internal Revenue regulations require the depository to obtain the social security number of the person whose name appears on the account.

Power of Attorney

Power of attorney accounts grant an account owner's named agent certain specified rights in the account.

An *attorney-in-fact* is a depositor-owner's agent.

This kind of account is used in most cases as a modification of an individual account, although it can be used with certain other titles. In this kind of account, the depositor/owner designates another party as his attorney-in-fact (agent) through a signed document called a Power of Attorney (P/A). Under the P/A, the agent is given access to the account primarily to be able to make withdrawals. In some depositories, the agent's name will appear with the depositor/owner's name in the title and will be identified as agent, or *attorney-in-fact* plus the words "under P/A, dated __/__/__." Other depositories will not show the agent's name in the title but will flag the account to indicate that a P/A does exist.

P/A documents can vary from a single sentence authorizing an agent to make withdrawals (some depositories provide such a form to be signed by the owner and the agent) to an extensive document that spells out the powers entrusted to the agent. Some P/A's will contain a catch-all statement that authorizes the agent "to do anything I (the depositor/owner) could do if I were present."

Rescission by the owner-depositor is the cancellation of power of attorney.

By giving the agent access to the account by the P/A, some control is given up by the owner, but there is no surrender of ownership. The owner actually maintains complete control because he unilaterally can rescind the P/A at any time. The depository must always be alert to any notice or rescission so that access to the account by the agent can be cut off. If the notice of rescission is received by the depository that subsequently fails to prevent a withdrawal by the terminated agent, the depository may be liable to the depositor.

A P/A is also terminated by the death of the depositor/owner, as well as by his mental disability or incapacity. In recent times, laws have been enacted in most of the states permitting P/A's to be extended to cover periods of mental disability or incapacity of the depositor/owner. These are referred to as Durable P/A's. The Durable P/A must contain wording to the effect that the P/A will not terminate in the event of the mental disability or incapacity of the depositor/owner. P/A accounts are really accommodations extended to depositors, but the depository must be aware constantly that the authority given under the P/A can be terminated at any time by the depositor/owner. In the event of the death of the depositor/owner of a P/A account, the P/A terminates, the account becomes an individual account, and access to the account is the same as stated above under Individual Accounts. Internal Revenue regulations require the depository to obtain the social security number of the depositor/owner, but not the agent's.

Joint

Joint accounts can be owned by two or more people.

In this kind of account the title is in the name of two persons; some depositories will allow one or two additional names. Title on a standard joint account gives access to the account to all the parties named by language appended to the title. The names can be connected by the word "or" and/or the names can be followed by the phrase "payable to either or the survivor." In instances where there are more than two names, the phrase would read "payable to any one or the survivor." The agreement/contract, to which the parties assent on a joint account, usually provides that the depository will honor a withdrawal request by any one of the parties and that the action of any one is binding on all, thus providing some protection for the bank if there is a disagreement between or among the joint owners. Ownership on a joint account is not always obvious except between or among the parties whose names appear in the title. For example, an owner of an account, instead of appointing an agent through a Power of Attorney, to have access to the account, may make the account joint by adding another party. This other party then serves as a convenient joint owner, but most times, the bank may not know it. Another owner may add a name or a joint owner to avoid having his funds tied up in the event of his death. Courts, when asked to determine who owns a joint account, will come down many times to a 50-50 split because even the parties to the account will not agree on who owns what. Even the social security number supplied by the depositors on a joint account cannot be said to identify the owner. Most times, it only tells the depository and the Internal Revenue Service which party is going to report the earnings on his tax return.

There are usually no restrictions on who can open and be a party to a joint account. The parties are expected to be able to sign their names and understand the meaning and consequences of two (or more) people having independent access to the account.

In the event of the death of one of the parties, title, control, and access remain with the other party or survivor.

In the event that all parties to a joint account are deceased, only the executor or administrator of the estate of the last person to die may have access to the account. As in the case of an individual account, the depository may be permitted by law to pay the next-of-kin of the last person to die if the balance on the account does not exceed the amount prescribed in the statute.

Internal Revenue regulations require the depository to obtain the social security number of any person whose name appears on the account.

Figure 5-2
Signature Card with Typical Bank Deposit Contract

(Front)

(Name of Bank)	Account Number		Type

ACCOUNT NAMES		TIN	SOCIAL SECURITY NO.
1.			
2.			
3.			

CHEX OK by	Opened by	Contact Off.	Approx. Off.	Branch	Mother's maiden name	DATE

❐ Subject to   ❐ Not subject to backup witholding per IRS code, Section 3405 (a) (1) (c).

I have read, understand and agree to the information on the back of this card. Under the penalties of perjury, we certify that the taxpayer information provided on this form is true, correct and complete.

CLIENT SIGNATURE	IDENTIFICATION (2)
1.	
2.	
3.	

SIGNATURE CARD

(Back)

Agreements for each account signer.
I agree that all transactions between the Bank and signers of this form shall be governed by_____(BANK'S NAME)_____*Terms and Agreements*, which I have received.

For clients opening interest-earning accounts.
I have received for my information a copy of "Payer's Request for Taxpayer identification Number" (IRS Form W-9).
Certification for clients applying for a taxpayer identification number or tax-exempt clients. (Please check appropriate box and sign.

❐ I have applied for (or I will apply for) a taxpayer identification number from the appropriate Internal Revenue or Social Security Administration Office. I understand that if I do not provide a taxpayer identification number to the Bank within 60 days, the Bank is required to withhold 20% of all reportable payments thereafter made to me until I provide a number.

❐ I am tax-exempt because I am not a citizen nor a resident of the United States. I am a citizen of _____
and hold passport no. _____

Under penalty of perjury. I certify that the taxpayer information provided on this form is true, correct and complete.

Client Signature _____

Trustee

Trustee accounts are owned by one person on behalf of another (the *beneficiary*).

In this type of account, title is in the name(s) of one or two trustees (self-appointed or voluntary) on behalf of another person, referred to as the beneficiary. The trustee, or trustees in the case of joint trustees, controls the account as long as the trustee(s) wish. In jurisdictions where these accounts are regulated by law, the beneficiary succeeds to the ownership and control of the account if the trustee(s) die. These accounts have been the subject of many interpretations over the years, both by the courts, who have been asked to determine ownership, and by the public, who have tried to make these accounts accomplish many things, including serving as a substitute for a will.

These accounts originally were established to allow very young children who were unable to write to have their money put into a depository. In most cases, a parent or parents served as the trustee(s) and had complete control over the accounts. However, parents and others began to use these accounts in which to deposit their own funds. Also, these kinds of accounts became an easy way for people to manage and thus control the funds of a person who, because of age and infirmity or some disability or incapacity, was not able to manage his own money. Thus, people began to use these accounts to do many things, including the avoidance of paying income taxes on the earnings. Before the days of the requirement that every account be identified with a social security number, many trustees failed to report the interest earned on these accounts to state and federal tax authorities. In many instances, the paying of taxes was avoided because of difficulty in locating the accounts except for spot checking. When the social security number requirement was first applied and the regulations indicated that the social security number of the owner should be supplied, many trustees evidently supplied the number of the

Figure 5-3
Trust Account

I hereby agree to abide and be governed by the Regulations and By-Laws of the _____ or any amendment thereof.

Sign here ☞
Trustee for:

DETAIL WITH RESPECT TO TRUSTEE	DETAIL WITH RESPECT TO BENEFICIARY
Address	
Bithplace	
Date of Birth	
Father's Name	
Mother's Name	
Name of Husband or Wife	

Statement by Trustee: It is understood that this money belongs to the beneficiary.

Relationship of beneficiary to trustee

Signed _____ Trustee

Orig. Dep.	Trans. From	Date

This account I hold in trust, to hold and dispose of as I see fit during my lifetime, but on my death to pay to the Beneficiary the full amount then standing to the credit of this account.

DATE _____

SIGNED _____

Trustee

beneficiary. Though this may have been the intent of the originators of the voluntary trustee account concept, the Internal Revenue Service must have recognized that volumes of dollars were moving into these accounts, so the Service changed its approach by establishing a new guideline, which basically said that if you control an account as a trustee does on this kind of an account, you own it; therefore you must supply the social security number of the trustee or, if there are two, the number of one of them. This requirement, however, upset the original intent of the account and the intent of the trustees who really meant to follow that concept. However, recent IRS rulings that require taxpayers to identify the social security number of their dependents on their tax returns and require dependents to pay a tax based on the same rate as their parents, have cut further into the manipulative ways these accounts have been used. They still serve a good use for depositing the holiday and birthday gifts of money received by children too young to set up their own accounts.

Internal Revenue regulations require the depository to obtain the social security number of the trustee or, if two trustees exist, the number of one of them.

These accounts are not generally opened as transaction accounts (checking & NOW) as their titles do not lend themselves to wide acceptance as negotiable instruments.

Uniform Transfer to Minors Account

A *Uniform Transfer to Minors Account* cedes property or gifts to persons under 21 years of age. An intermediary *custodian* usually controls the account until majority age is reached.

Under the Massachusetts Transfer to Minors Act (formerly Uniform Gifts to Minors Account), anyone may make a gift or transfer property to a minor (anyone who has not attained age 21) with the property being subject to the control and management of an adult or financial institution (known as custodian) until the minor attains age 21. If the requirements of law are met, a completed, irrevocable gift or transfer will result when the property is transferred to the custodian.

Figure 5-4
Minors

	UNIFROM TRANSFERS TO MINORS ACCOUNT	ACCT. NO.
████████	as custodian for	

(minor) under the
Massachusetts Uniform Transfers to Minors Act., (G.L. CH. 201A)

Custodian's Address	Are you a citizen of the U.S.?
Minor's Address	
Minor's Date of Birth	
Minor's Birthplace	

Subject to the By-Laws of the _____ and its Rules and Regulations in effect from time to time. I acknowledge that I hold the above described account as custodian for said minor pursuant and subject to the Massachusetts Uniform Gifts to Minors Act._____

CUSTODIAN

This account establishes under law ownership of the account in a named minor child and control of the acouunt in a named custodian. These accounts are further identified by placing the name of the state in the title, so a title may read: John Jones, as Custodian for Mary Jones under the Massachusetts Uniform Transfers to Minors Act. These accounts are regulated by specific statutes setting forth how custodians are appointed; how and when certain transfers are made; the powers and responsibilities of the custodian in managing and maintaining records on custodial property; the accountability of the custodian to, for example, the minor's guardian, an "adult member of the minor's family"; the party who transferred the property to the custodian's care and even to the minor upon reaching age fourteen; and the point upon reaching maturity: when the custodian must convey the property over to the minor. Upon the death of the minor, while the property is still held by the custodian, the funds are payable to the executor or administrator of the minor's estate.

Because of the legal technicalities applicable to Uniform Transfer to Minors Act accounts (the information presented in this description of these accounts has been extracted from Massachusetts General Law, Chapter 201A), depositories and their employees should be cautious, in discussing these accounts, that they do not get into the area of legal interpretation and advice. A prospective depositor, who evidences more than very superficial knowledge about these accounts, should not create any hesitation in the bank employee to open this kind of account. On the other hand, if insufficient understanding of the provisions of the statute is evidenced by the prospective depositor, it may be in everyone's best interest to refer such a person to his lawyer or accountant.

The Internal Revenue Service regulations require the depository to obtain the social security number of the beneficiary (minor). The Internal Revenue Service will recognize the ownership of the property by the minor and provided the minor is or will be age 14 prior to the end of the applicable tax year, earnings on the property will be taxed to the minor and not the person making the gift. If the minor does not reach age 14 prior to the close of the applicable tax year, the earnings may be taxed in whole or in part, for federal income tax purposes at the highest marginal tax rate of the minor's parents.

Estates of Deceased Persons

Executors or court-appointed administrators of the estates of deceased persons may settle such estate obligations and report to the court all matters relevant to the estate.

In this kind of account, person(s) are identified in the title as executor(s) or administrator(s) of the estate of a deceased person. While ownership rests with the estate, control and access are the fiduciary responsibilities of either the executor(s) or administrator(s) specified in the title. Both are court appointees who have identical responsibilities and accountabilities: gathering and accounting for all the assets and property of the deceased; determining all of his liabilities and debts, including taxes; settling all the deceased's obligations; and making disbursements of any net assets after making a final accounting to the court.

Executors are usually named in wills. When they cannot or will not serve or there is no will, then court appointed administrators step in.

The designation *executor* or *administrator* merely reflects the type of fiduciary appointment. Where he or she was appointed to be an executor, one has to have been specifically named in a will and be able to serve after the will has been presented to a state court having jurisdiction over such matters, with the court approving and certifying the appointment of the person so named. An administrator is also certified and approved for appointment by the court. However, his or her appointment comes about either when an executor named in a will is unable or is unwilling to serve or there was no will.

The depository should request a copy of the court decree certifying the appointment. Some depositories keep a copy on file; others record pertinent data: the court's name, docket number, and dates of the appointment and of the certificate decree. This information allows the depository, if necessary, to verify the information.

If an executor or administrator, once certified by the court, resigns or dies, the court makes another appointment, always with the designation of administrator.

Internal Revenue regulations require the depository to obtain the social security number of the deceased person.

These accounts are generally not opened as Certificates of Deposit, because the primary responsibility of an executor or administrator is to settle the financial affairs of the deceased. Such a responsibility involves paying bills and other obligations, so he or she is apt to keep the assets in more liquid types of accounts.

Trustee(s) Under a Will

A will may designate certain assets to the control of a *trustee*, who deals with these assets after an executor or administrator settles the terms of the will.

This is an account on which person(s) are identified in the title as trustee(s) under the will of a deceased person. Under the terms of the will, certain property and/or assets of the deceased person are placed in a trust to be administered by persons designated in the will to be the trustees. The trust comes about when the executor or an administrator, in settling the estate, transfers the designated property and/or assets to the trustees. These trusts can be set up to exist for various periods of time depending upon the intent of the deceased. Some are designated to terminate on the happening of a specific event; others may come to an end with the expiration of all the assets assigned to the trust.

As in the case of an executor or administrator, a depository may need to verify the appointment of trustees under a will by requesting a certified copy of the will. Usually, a will has a provision for any succession of a trustee; thus, a depository needs to be aware of how this succession comes about. There may be other reasons to verify the will. For example, there may be a need to know, in the case of multiple trustees, if one trustee can act alone or if all trustees must participate in every action. If this information is not clearly set forth in the will, the trustees may need to provide an assent statement on any assignment relative to their authority, if the will does not forbid such action. A depository should be expected to require the appropriate documentation, a will, or other guarantee to help it avoid any possible conflicts.

The Internal Revenue regulations require the depository to obtain the tax identification number (not a social security number) of the trust.

Trustee(s) Under a Trust*

A *trustee under a trust* account (a "living trust" or "indenture") is similar to a trustee under a will account, except that the donor/grantor is still living at the time of the trust establishment.

In this kind of account, trustee(s) are designated in a trust instrument executed (signed) by a grantor/donor during his lifetime to administer the property or assets placed in trust. These accounts are handled by the depository in the same manner as the Trustee Under a Will account. A beneficiary is usually named in such a trust. It can be the grantor/donor himself who remains the beneficiary of the income during his lifetime, and then another person or sometimes a charity or non-profit organization becomes the beneficiary, depending upon the provisions of the trust investment. For the same kind of reasons set forth in the section on Trustee Under a Will, the depository may want to see a certified copy of the trust to satisfy itself regarding the authority of the

* (sometimes referred to as a living trust, an indenture, or a declaration of trust.)

persons representing themselves as trustees in order to establish an account in the name of the trust.

Probably the most common reasons for establishing a trust is the need for professional and/or specialized investment management. Living trusts are more ususally created for this reason as well as the following:

1. To alleviate concern an individual may have over his or her potential incapacity

2. To eliminate the necessity of probate

3. To obtain tax savings

4. To hold property as a separate estate

Because ownership rests with the trust and because trustees who control and have access to an account in the name of the trust can come and go, the depository may at some point be faced with determining who can have access to the account—if, for instance, all the trustees who have been recorded on bank records as having access have died or whose whereabouts are unknown.

The Internal Revenue regulations require the depository to obtain the social security number of the grantor if the grantor or his/her spouse is a trustee of the grantor trust. If neither the grantor nor his/her spouse is the trustee, then a separate trust ID number must be submitted to the IRS.

Guardianship

Guardianships can be set up for persons who are legally incapacitated to execute their affairs.

In this kind of account, a person(s) is named in the title as the guardian(s) of another person, the ward. Ownership rests with the ward, but control and access are the fiduciary responsibility of the guardian(s). The guardian(s) is an appointee of a state court, which issues a certificate stating that the appointment is in effect and sometimes gives the reason for the guardianship: for example, a minor child, an infirm person, or a mentally incompetent person. The depository should always request a copy of the certificate, verify the names of the guardians(s) and the ward, and at least record the name of the court, the docket number, the date of the appointment, and the date of the certificate.

Guardianships are usually established for individuals who are considered legally incapacitated and who:

1. Own property not otherwise protected

2. Have business affairs that are jeopardized by their incapacity

3. Need funds for support or education and protection is necessary to provide these funds

4. Require funds for the individual's support or for the support of the individual's dependents.

Most common instances of legal incapacity are minors and adults who are incapacitated by medical causes or senility. Other forms of adult incapacity would include mental illness, addiction to drugs or alcohol, confinement, detention by a foreign power or disappearance. Guardianship may be voluntary, as well.

If the guardian resigns or dies, the court must appoint a new guardian: if the ward dies, the funds are payable only to his estate.

It is possible for a guardianship to be removed. The most common instance is when a minor reaches maturity. Most depositories prefer to have the guardian sign off at that point rather than unilaterally recognizing the minor's reaching that stage. Though quite rare, other guardianships have been lifted by the courts. Usually the court will issue a decree that is acceptable to a depository.

Internal Revenue regulations require the depository to obtain the social security number of the ward.

Conservator

Conservatorship accounts protect wards. A conservator has control over only the *ward's* finances.

This is an account on which a person(s) is named in the title as the conservator(s) of another person, the ward. Everything said about a guardian in the previous section is applicable to a conservator. What differentiates a guardian from conservator under the law is that the former has legal control of the ward's person and his property; the latter has legal control of the ward's property, not his person. Because the depository deals only with the ward's property, these accounts are handled by the depository in an identical fashion to those of a guardianship; only the titles of the fiduciary will be different.

Non-Personal Account

A *non-personal account* is owned by an organization.

This is an account on which title and ownership rests in the name of a partnership, proprietorship, corporation, governmental unit, other organizations that range from formally incorporated educational, religious, social, and charitable associations to relatively informal groups, such as a Saturday night bridge club. In every one of these cases, the depository will require documentary evidence that the organization, business, or group (1) voted or decided to open an account in the depository, (2) voted or agreed that certain person(s) whose names will be provided to the depository have been authorized to make withdrawals from the account, and (3) voted or agreed to keep the depository free from any liability due to any misuse of the account by any authorized or unauthorized member of the business, organization, or group. In many cases the depository will provide the very formal form that requires certifications to be signed and corporate seals to be affixed. Substituted documentation conveying the same information is usually acceptable to the depository. Periodically, as authorized signers change, a new certificate must be filed with the depository.

Internal Revenue regulations require the depository to obtain the tax identification number of the business, organization, or group named in the title of the account.

Corporations may not open NOW accounts, as federal laws do not permit such accounts to be offered to profit-making organizations and businesses.

Interest on Lawyers Trust Accounts (IOLTA)

IOLTA's are interest-bearing accounts for client funds temporarily held by lawyers in trust. The interest is paid by the financial institution to a "public interest" charity, designated by the lawyer or law firm.

On May 23, 1985, the Supreme Judicial Court approved a rule establishing a voluntary Interest on Lawyers Trust Accounts (IOLTA) program. On September 26, 1989, the Court revised its rule to convert the program to a comprehensive program in which all lawyers holding clients' funds are required to enroll, effective January 1, 1990.

The IOLTA program's purpose is to provide funds for civil legal services to the poor and for improvements in the administration of justice.

The program generates funds for these public purposes by requiring lawyers to place client funds traditionally held in aggregated non-interest bearing accounts into aggreggated interest-bearing accounts. Only funds which

Figure 5-5
Business Accounts

ORIGINAL: CMI	85227-6	COPY: BRANCH FILE

Account Title   Account & Type

Plan Code   Maturity Date   Rate   ☐ Temporary Card

1.	SSN
2.	SSN
3.	SSN

Opened
By: CSR   Branch   Date   Amount

- Each individual listed acknowledges receipt of the Disclosure for Personal Accounts. ☐
- Each Signatory authorizes
  to obtain credit information from any source, including but not limited to, a check protection service.

Name 1   ☐ Tel.
Street   Alt Tel.
City ☐   State   Zip
Employment ☐   D.O.B.
Identification   Mother's Maiden
Name 2   ☐ Tel.
Street   Alt Tel.
City ☐   State   Zip
Employment ☐   D.O.B.
Identification   Mother's Maiden
Name 3   ☐ Tel.
Street   Alt Tel.
City ☐   State   Zip
Employment ☐   D.O.B.
Identification   Mother's Maiden

Savings Interest Payment Options:

Mailing Address:

Special Instructions / Customer Account Title:

are nominal in amount or held for too short a period of time to generate interest returnable to an individual client will be placed in IOLTA accounts. The interest from the accounts will then be remitted by the financial institution to one of three designated charitable entities selected by the lawyer or law firm: the Boston Bar Foundation, Massachusetts Bar Foundation, or the Massachusetts Legal Assistance Corporation.

Partipation in the IOLTA program by financial institutions remains voluntary under the court's revised order.

The title of the account should contain the words, Attorney IOLTA Account.

OPENING A NEW ACCOUNT

In order to open a new account, banks generally require that a signature card and/or an application be filled out. Such documents usually ask the depositor to provide his residential address (and mailing address, if different), telephone number, place of business, date of birth, social security number, and mother's maiden name (a widely used back-up identification aid). As stated earlier, by signing such a document, the depositor is agreeing to the terms and conditions of the account (See Figures 5-2 through 5-5 for examples of signature cards for specific types of accounts).

At this point, a bank employee should make sure that the depositor understands the terms and conditions that apply to the account(s) being opened. He or she should be made aware of any fees and charges and the nominal and effective interest rates, if applicable. If there are disclosure statements required by either federal or state law, they too should be explained.

If the account being opened is a fiduciary account (estates of deceased persons, guardians, conservators, trustees under wills, or trusts) the bank should ask for court appointment certificates or copies of the will or trust as appropriate. Check and confirm the names on any of these documents to be certain there are no discrepancies on the titles of these accounts on back records.

Before opening any of the various types of business accounts, the depositor will need to have a certificate regarding the authorization for opening and managing the account.

In some instances, because additional signatures have to be obtained, application and signature forms or the business account certification forms have to be given out to be completed and signed and returned to the depository at as early a date as possible. The bank should point out that the account may not be used until the required documents are returned.

If the account being opened is a checking, NOW, or money market account, the bank should explain the check collection schedule and the availability of funds as prescribed by federal regulations.

If the account is a certificate of deposit, the bank should point out the maturity date and tell the depositor that he will get a notice of maturity thirty days in advance of the maturity date (required by statute in Massachusetts). The bank needs to explain the penalties incurred when premature withdrawals are made.

The opening of a new account provides an excellent opportunity for bank employees to cross-sell other bank services. It is often said that bankers have thought of themselves as being order-takers rather than salespeople. With the end of deregulation (as described in the first two chapters) and increased competition among banking institutions, the time for being merely order-takers has clearly passed.

CONCLUSION

The opening of a deposit account consists of more than simply taking the customer's check and/or cash and handing him back a sheaf of forms. It is important that the depositor understand the nature of the conditions governing the use of the account. It is also necessary for both the customer and the bank representative to understand the differences between the various types of accounts and the various titles under which they may be approved.

It should also be understood that the opening of a new deposit account provides the bank with a golden marketing opportunity to cross-sell other bank services.

STUDY AND REVIEW QUESTIONS

1. Explain the differences between a DDA and NOW account.

2. Explain the differences between a MMDA and TIME account.

3. What is the difference between a Trustee (voluntary savings trust) and UTMA account?

4. In what instances should a social security number or tax ID number be used when an account is established under the title of a Trustee Under a Trust (Living Trust)?

5. Is opening a a new account a privilege or an obligation?

6. How might you advise your customer who wishes to deposit $15,000 in the bank and has the following needs:

    a. Needs $10,000 in one month.

    b. Has no immediate plan for the other $5,000 and wishes to maximize interest.

    c. Would like payroll check directly deposited into an account for bill paying.

    What account(s) would you recommend and why?

7. How might you advise a customer inquiring and considering an IRA account?

EXERCISES

1. Bring to class your banks new account opening package for a corporate account. Be sure kit includes Truth-In-Savings Disclosure and Corporate Resolution. In class we will preview account opening procedures, discussing required forms and form language.

2. John Q. Public comes into the bank with $50,000 to open an account. He would like to earn high rates of interest, have the ability to write checks and use a debit card. What do we need from Mr. Public to open his account(s)? What account(s) would you recommend and why?

3. Match the following account titles with the appropriate ownership.

    Mary Johnston in trust for Stephen Johnston   _____

    Michael Maxwell or Josephine Maxwell   _____

    Francis Smith custodian for Linda Smith   _____

    Eileen McCarthy executrix for Thomas Gafney   _____

    A. Power of attorney

    B. Single

    C. Trustee

    D. Joint

    E. Estate

    F. Uniform Transfer to Minors Act.

4. Bring to class a copy of your bank's power of attorney form and your policy with regard to accepting power of attorney forms. Is your bank's form a *Durable Power* or not? What would the difference be?

Checks and Their Characteristics
John S. Burnett

In spite of the leaps of technology into debit cards, "smart" cards and ACH (Automated Clearing-house) and, cyber-payments, there can be no doubt that the "old fashioned" paper check still has a lot of life in it.

Introduction

This chapter discusses the characteristics of checks. What is a check? How is it negotiated? How may it be endorsed? It will then go on to discuss certified checks and "cashiers' or treasurer's" checks. How do they differ from regular checks? Lastly, we will discuss Regulation CC and how it has affected the ways in which checks are handled.

Learning Objectives

After reading this chapter, you should have an understanding of the following:

1. How checks evolved historically to their present level of broad acceptance as a method of payment.
2. How checks are used in the payments system.
3. The responsibilities and liabilities of the parties to a check.
4. Negotiation and endorsement of checks.
5. Special types of checks.
6. Stop payment orders.
7. The objectives of Regulation CC.

THE EVOLUTION OF CHECKS

Checks evolved historically as written instructions to cashiers or goldsmiths to pay funds to third parties.

Some historians credit the Romans with using check-like instruments as early as 400–300 B.C. Others say that the Dutch were the first to use checks; around 1500 A.D., they began depositing their cash and other valuables with *cashiers*, for a fee rather than risk storing it at home. As part of the cashiers' service, they would collect and cancel debts in response to the depositors' written orders—a procedure that is not too dissimilar from the checking accounts of today.

During the seventeenth century, people in England started depositing their wealth with goldsmiths, who also charged a fee for protecting their depositors' money. "Goldsmiths' Notes," issued as receipts for the deposits, were simply hand-written promises to repay the depositor upon request. Eventually, goldsmiths came to accept written instructions from the depositors to pay a sum of money to another person or to the bearer of the letter out of the money on deposit. The use of these written instructions to transfer the ownership of deposit money is very much like the operation of our checking accounts today.

THE GROWTH OF CHECK USAGE IN THE U.S.

The use of checks in the United States started with the chartering of banks and "deposit banking" following the Revolutionary War. The use of checks grew slowly but steadily until the period of the Civil War found that checkbook money payments exceeded the volume of payments made with currency.

Individual checking accounts grew rapidly in number after World War II.

Prior to 1946 most checking accounts were maintained by commercial and industrial companies and governments. Very few individuals used checks to pay their bills. During the late 1940s, with the rise of the consumer as an economic force after World War II, commercial banks recognized the potential increase in deposits available by selling checking accounts to individuals. The banks started a very successful sales effort that continues today and that started a thirty-year period of explosive growth in the use of checks.

Check volume is huge and must be dealt with through electronic means.

During this period, check volume grew at the rate of 7% a year. This rate of growth compounded meant a doubling in check volume every ten years. Check volume growth of this magnitude caused staffing problems for bank management because proving deposits and collecting checks is very labor intensive. To ease the problem of hiring, housing, and training clerical staff to handle the increased volume, the commercial segment of the banking industry did a couple of things. First, in the late 50s and early 60s the industry, together with check printers and equipment manufacturers, developed the technique of magnetic ink character recognition (MICR). The successful implementation of MICR systems increased the speed with which checks were processed from 600-800 per hour to 1000-1200 checks per minute, once the check amount was encoded in magnetic ink. The second effort was, and continues to be, to encourage the use of electronic funds transfer (EFT) as the successor to checks in the payments system. The EFT system utilizes 38 automated clearing houses (ACH) strategically located around the country. The U.S. Government has been the leader in using the ACH system, with slower but steady growth by commerce, industry, and individuals. During the past few years, the increase in check volume has slowed to 3–4 percent per year, and the banking system is processing more than forty billion checks each year.

It is generally agreed that checks account for about 90 percent of all payments made in our economy, leaving only 10 percent of the payments being made with coin and currency. This figure is impressive testimony to the acceptance of checks as the preferred method of payment and of their importance to the money supply.

What Is a Check?

The word "draft" has the same origin as the word "draw." Both are used here in the sense of pulling (money) from an account. You can compare this with the term "draft (pulling) horse."

The Uniform Commercial Code, in Section 3–104, defines a check as "a draft drawn on a bank and payable on demand." To understand this definition, one must understand what a draft is, as well as the concept of being payable on demand.

Drafts (sometimes referred to as "bills of exchange") are commonly used in commerce. In international trade, drafts are a leading form of payment instruction. A draft is a written order from one party (the drawer), addressed to (or drawn on) a second party (the drawee), to pay money to a third party (the payee).

A draft can order payment made on a future date (a "time draft") or when presented to the drawee (a "demand draft"). If a draft is drawn on a bank or institution and payable on demand, it is called a check.

Typical Check Format

```
Any Bank & Trust Company  (Drawee)
Anytown, USA
                                           (Date) _____

Pay to the Order of _____ (Payee) _____    $ XX.XX
(Amount written in words) _____

                                    (Drawer/Maker) _____
```

Although each of the three parties to a draft or check holds a separate legal position, it is possible that one party can be in more than one of these positions. For instance, it is not unusual for a person to make a check payable to him or herself, and, as we will see when we discuss Official Checks, a bank often issues checks drawn on itself.

Although strictly speaking, the term "maker" refers to the person who signs a promissory note, the same term is often applied to the drawer of a check.

Negotiation

Once the drawer issues and delivers a check, the payee acquires a claim on funds in the drawer's account. The payee, as the original holder, may present it to the drawee bank or institution for payment, or may choose to transfer ownership to another party. The new holder of the check has all of the same rights as the payee, and can continue transferring ownership (and rights), or present the check for payment to the drawee bank or institution.

The transfer of ownership and rights in a check is called "negotiation" and is usually accomplished by endorsement (see below) and delivery. However, if the check is payable to "bearer" or "cash," negotiation may be completed without endorsement.

Proper negotiation requires two events—*delivery* of the check to the transferee and **intent to transfer ownership.** The intent is usually evidenced by an endorsement. If either of these events does not take place (as would be the case when a lost or stolen check is presented for payment), legal negotiation has not occurred.

ENDORSEMENTS

The purpose of an endorsement (also spelled *indorsement*) is normally to transfer title or ownership of a negotiable instrument, including a check. When a check is deposited in a bank, the depositor's endorsement gives the bank the authority to act as the depositor's agent in obtaining payment from the drawee bank.

There are four basic types of endorsements with which bank employees deal regularly. Each of these serves to facilitate the negotiation of a check in a particular way:

1. A *general* or *blank* endorsement, which consists of the payee's signature alone, on the back of the check. This has the effect of making the check a *bearer* instrument.

2. A *special* endorsement identifies by name the party to whom the check is being transferred. The usual format for such an endorsement is "Pay to the order of John Smith (signature of owner of check)."

3. A *restrictive* endorsement restricts the way that the transferee may use the check. The most frequent form of *restrictive* endorsement is used when depositing a check, and is in the form, "For deposit only, (signature of owner of check)."

4. A *qualified* endorsement is rarely seen, but is used by an owner of a check to avoid liability should the check not be paid (see *Warranties of an endorser* later in this chapter). The usual wording seen in such an endorsement is "without recourse." Because the endorser wishes to escape potential liability, this type of endorsement should be viewed as an exception. One legitimate use of a qualified endorsement is seen when handling casualty insurance payments that are payable jointly to the owner of property (a car, for example), and the lienholder or mortgagee. Often, the lienholder in such a case will give a qualified endorsement in order to allow negotiation (transfer ownership in the check or draft), but escapes liability in the unlikely event the check or draft is dishonored.

It should be noted that each form of endorsement requires a signature of the endorser. An endorsement reading "For deposit only" without a signature is not complete. You should remember, however, that a signature doesn't always have to be manually applied. It can be part of a rubber stamp, and in block letters, for example. Some insurance and annuity checks on the other hand, require the payee's manual endorsement to demonstrate the payee was alive on the date of the payment.

WARRANTIES OF AN ENDORSER

Most people endorse checks without a thought as to the legal ramifications of their signatures. Under the UCC, an endorser of a check who receives value for it (cash or credit to an account, for example):

1. warrants (guarantees) that he or she has good title to the check

2. warrants that all of the signatures on the check are genuine and authorized (even if the endorser didn't deal with the person signing)

3. warrants that the check has not been altered in any material way (amount, payee, etc.)

4. warrants that he or she has no knowledge of bankruptcy proceedings affecting the check.

Of particular importance is a general promise to make payment on the check (or other negotiable instrument) if the drawer or drawee does not make payment, so long as the check is properly presented for payment.

These warranties, plus a desire to demonstrate to whom money has been paid out, are often given as the reason that banks normally require their tellers to obtain endorsements even on bearer checks when encashing them for customers and others, even though an endorsement might not otherwise be required to complete negotiation to the bank.

HOLDER IN DUE COURSE

Each person who receives a check under conventional circumstances is known as a "holder" of the check. It is basic to the law of negotiable instruments that each holder who negotiates an instrument to another party transfers those rights to the instrument that the original holder (the payee) has. For example, the payee has the right to present a check for payment to the drawee bank or institution. If the payee endorses the check to another party, the new holder now has the right to present the check, and the original payee no longer holds that right.

The UCC creates a special status for particular holders known as *holder in due course*. The purpose of this special status is to make intermediary holders (those between the payee and the drawee, for example) more willing to accept the transfers of negotiable instruments, thereby making checks (and other negotiable instruments) more welcome in commerce.

Under certain conditions, a *holder in due course* enjoys rights that are superior to those of the original payee. To become a holder in due course, a holder:

1. must give value in exchange for receiving the instrument. Value can be credit to an account, cash, property, a month's rent, services, etc.

2. must receive the instrument in good faith. This means that the holder can't be accepting the transfer in order to use holder in due course status fraudulently or otherwise in bad faith.

3. must receive the instrument under proper conditions of delivery and negotiation. This means that one cannot be a holder in due course by theft or when finding a check on the street. It also means that the prior owner must have meant to make the transfer.

4. must receive the instrument without notice that it is overdue or has been previously dishonored.

5. must receive the instrument without notice of any claim against the instrument or defense against it. If the transferee knows, for example, that the payee on a check has committed a fraud to obtain the check, the transferee knows of a claim or defense against the check, and cannot attain holder in due course status.

Earlier, we said that a holder in due course may have rights superior to those of the original payee of a check. If used car dealer Slick sells a car to Abbott, knowing that the car won't pass inspection to be registered, and ac-

The Federal Trade Commission has issued a ruling that limits the application of the UCC's holder in due course rule. The FCC's rule protects signers of promissory notes that are negotiated by sellers to lenders when there is a business relationship between the seller and the lender.

cepts Abbott's check in payment, Slick may then negotiate the check. If he transfers the check to Barnes, his fuel oil dealer, to obtain a delivery of oil, it is likely that Barnes will be a holder in due course. If Barnes passes all of the tests to be a holder in due course, he may be able to force Abbott to pay him the amount of the check even if Abbott stops payment at this bank.

STOP PAYMENT ORDER

An order not to pay a check to a payee is *stop-payment* order.

Just as the maker of a check has the authority to issue a check, ordering his bank or financial institution to pay money out of his account, so does he have the authority to countermand or cancel that order before the check has been presented to the drawee bank for payment. When the depositor tells his bank or financial institution not to pay a check that he issued, he has *stopped payment*.

Stop payment orders may become a liability of the bank if handled improperly, because if the institution pays the check on which a stop order has been placed, the depositor is entitled to a reimbursement and the bank will suffer the loss. In such cases, the rights of the depositor are transferred to the bank: for example, any merchandise purchased by the "Stopped" check is transferred to the drawee bank.

A *stale dated check* is presented to the drawee bank six months after the check date.

Stop payment orders are valid for a period of six months. There has been some confusion between stop payment orders and stale dated checks. A *stale dated check* is a check that is presented to the drawee bank six months *after* the date of the check. A bank may refuse to honor a stale dated check; however, it is under no legal obligation to either "pay" or "refuse to pay" the check. (If a bank were under legal obligation to refuse payment on a stale dated check, many legitimate checks written on January 1 each year would have to be returned without payment by the drawee bank.)

Consequently, a depositor who relies upon his bank or financial institution to refuse payment on a previously "stopped" check because of a stale date does so at his own peril. The only certain way to guarantee that the check will not be paid is to renew the stop payment order.

Verbal stop payment orders may be accepted by the depositor's bank, however, verbal instructions are valid only for a period of fourteen days. Written instructions confirming the verbal stop payment order must be received within the fourteen-day period to consummate the order for a six-month period. (*See* Figure 6-1 below for an example of such a written order.)

The courts generally allow a bank a certain amount of time to notify all of its departments and branches that a "stop payment" has been received and that the item should not be paid. If a bank had multiple branches and received a stop payment order at 10:00 A.M. and the "stopped" check was cashed at one of the bank's branches at 10:02 A.M., the courts would probably rule that the bank did not have sufficient time to notify all of its branches of the stop payment and, consequently, the depositor would have no claim against his bank for reimbursement. Generally speaking, most courts allow a bank twenty-four hours to implement a stop payment. However, there is no clear ruling regarding this time factor, and each case must stand on its own merits. Clearly, if a stop payment request was accepted by a Customer Service Representative at Branch A and the same employee approved the same check for encashment five minutes after receiving the stop, the courts would find for the customer, and the bank would be ordered to reimburse the customer for his or her damages (not always the same as the check amount).

Figure 6-1
Stop Payment Order

MAKER   AMOUNT   DATE

_____
MAKER MUST NOT WRITE ABOVE THIS LINE

.... 19......

Please stop payment on Check No. .... Dated .... Amt. ....

Payable to ....

  Reason ....

This confirmation is our record of your Stop Payment order and represents our understanding of the order. If it is incorrect in any particular, please advise us immediately as the Bank will NOT be responsible for stopping payment on any item unless accurately described in this Stop Payment Confirmation. ORAL Stop Payment orders are effective for 14 calendar days only. If you wish to stop payment for a longer period, you must sign a written Stop Payment Order, copy of which is enclosed for your convenience. A written Stop Payment Order signed by a depositor will not be effective after 6 MONTHS, but may be renewed in writing. (CODE 4-403)

Maker   Acct.
Sign Here ....   # ....
          DO NOT FAIL TO NOTIFY US IF CHECK IS FOUND, OR DESTROYED, OR IF NEW CHECK IS USSED

STOP PAYMENT RECORD
MAKER WILL PLEASE FILL OUT THE REVERSE SIDE OF THIS CARD AND
RETURN TO THE BANK AT ONCE.

_____
BELOW THIS LINE FOR BANK'S USE ONLY

                                              A.M.
REC'D _____ 19 ____ AT ____ P.M.   BY _____
                                              A.M.
REC'D _____ 19 ____ AT ____ P.M.   BY _____
                                              A.M.
REC'D _____ 19 ____ AT ____ P.M.   BY _____
                                              A.M.
REC'D _____ 19 ____ AT ____ P.M.   BY _____

DIDSPOSITION _____

CERTIFIED CHECKS

A *certified check* substitutes the bank's credit for the check maker's.

When a bank *certifies* a check, it is effectively replacing the credit standing of the maker with the credit standing of the bank by "certifying" that:

1. the check is genuine.

2. there are sufficient funds in the bank to pay the check.

3. the bank has accepted responsibility for payment of the check.

In order to certify a check, the maker presents it to an authorized representative of the bank who will determine that there is a sufficient collected balance in the maker's account, deduct the amount from the maker's account, and credit the amount to the bank's certified check account. The bank will mark the check with the word *certified* together with the date and an authorized signature and return it to the maker. At that point, the bank has assumed responsibility for payment of the check from the maker.

Payment of a certified check is guaranteed by the drawee bank or financial institution. Banks are under no legal obligation to certify checks and, in fact, many banks will *not* certify checks for the payee. When a check is presented for certification, the bank will verify the maker's signature and satisfy itself that there is a sufficient and collected balance to cover the amount of the check. If so, the funds are withdrawn from the customer's account immediately and transferred to the bank's certified checks account.

The bank will stamp the check *certified* and an officer or appropriate person will sign the check, which serves to transfer the obligation of payment from the customer to the bank. The bank will also punch holes in the MICR-imprinted account number of the customer to prevent the check from being subtracted from the customer's account upon presentment because the funds were withdrawn from the customer's account at the instant of certification.

Stop Payments on Certified Checks

Because certified checks become the legal obligation of the drawee bank to pay the sum specified on the checks, it is difficult to place a stop payment on a certified check. If a bank refuses to honor payment of a certified check, it may be held liable for the amount of the check plus all damages suffered by the payee. Under no circumstances should a bank accept a stop payment order on a certified check if the reason given by the maker is breach of contract. However, just as ordinary checks may be lost, so too may certified checks be lost in transit, and because the funds have already been withdrawn from the maker's account, some mechanism must be found to protect both the bank and the customer in placing a stop order on a certified item.

Typically, banks will ask that the maker sign an *affidavit of indemnity* that confirms the circumstances surrounding the reason of the stop request and, more importantly, serves to make the maker liable if the bank should be sued for not honoring the check. In addition, many banks will require that the depositor purchase an indemnity bond naming the bank as the payee to insure that the depositor has sufficient resources to back his guarantee of protecting the bank against claims for not paying the certified check.

OFFICIAL CHECKS

An *affidavit of indemnity* transfers a bank's liability for a certified check on which payment has been stopped back to the check maker.

Cashier's checks and treasurer's checks are checks drawn on the bank itself. Traditionally, national banks named the chief financial officer of the bank a *cashier*, while state banks referred to the heads of their financial departments as *treasurers*; thus cashier's checks are those issued by a national bank while treasurer's checks are issued by state banks. Both are official checks issued by banks and are signed by officers who have been granted specific signing authority by their boards of directors.

Because the drawer and drawee are the same, it is a legal obligation of the banks to pay the face amount of official bank checks upon presentation. This type of instrument may be purchased by a customer who wishes to guarantee payment but is not intent upon receiving the canceled instrument back for his permanent records.

Cashier's checks are similar to certified checks in that the bank's credit standing supports the validity of the check and, for that reason, the same precautions must be taken when considering stop payment requests by a purchaser of an official bank check.

PERSONAL MONEY ORDERS

A *cashier* (national bank) check is drawn on the bank itself. State banks issue a *treasurer's* check.

Personal money orders, like cashier's and treasurer's checks, may be purchased from banks. However, unlike official bank checks, personal money orders are not signed by designated officers. Personal money orders are sold as blank checks and are signed by the purchaser as the maker of the check.

Most courts have ruled that personal money orders are not official bank checks and that the purchase transaction between the buyer of a money order and the bank is the equivalent of a one-check checking account opened by the bank for the purchaser of the money order. Therefore, a stop payment order may be accepted from the purchaser without jeopardizing the reputation of the bank because the stop payment order is similar to a checking account customer's placing a stop on one of the checks issued from the depositor's account.

REGULATION CC

In 1987, Congress passed the "Competitive Equality in Banking Act of 1987" (CEBA). Title 6 of CEBA was a reaction of congress to the practice of a few financial institutions to impose unreasonably long delays on the availability of deposits made by checks. The title is called the "Expedited Funds Availability Act" (EFAA).

Personal money orders, though bought from a bank, are *not* like cashier's checks. They are "one-check checking account" instruments.

The thrust of EFAA is three-fold. First, it sets limits on the duration of holds placed on deposits by check. Secondly, it requires financial institutions to pay interest on interest-bearing transaction accounts beginning no later than the day when the financial institution receives provisional credit and use of the funds. Finally, EFAA requires that financial institutions inform their customers of their funds availability policies.

In Massachusetts, the legislature adopted the federal act and regulation, but expanding their applicability to include all of the state in the definition of "local check."

The Federal Reserve Board issued Regulation CC to implement EFAA. Regulation CC sets limits on delays in availability based on the nature of the checks being deposited to checking, NOW and other transaction accounts. It applies both to consumer and business accounts. For example, on-us and U.S. Treasury checks are generally given next day availability, which means that these funds must be available on the business day following the day they are deposited. Checks drawn on other local banks are generally limited to a two business day delay in availability. Checks on non-local banks can be delayed up to five business days. However these limits may change as the industry continues to evolve.

There are exceptions in the rules for large check deposits; for accounts open for less than 30 days; for depositors who are chronically overdrawn; for checks being redeposited, etc.

In addition to setting limits on delays in availability, Regulation CC set standards for check endorsements to better identify the bank accepting a check for deposit, and clarified the UCC to require that dishonored checks be returned directly and expeditiously to the bank of first deposit (the "depositary" bank).

CONCLUSION

Checks are still by far the most common method of making payments in the U.S. today. A check is a negotiable instrument involving three parties, the drawer, the drawee, and the payee.

Checks may be endorsed in one of five ways—blank, special, restrictive, conditional, and qualified (the first three being the only generally acceptable).

Regulation CC has been in effect since September 1, 1988. It has specified how long various types of checks may be held by banks, cleaned up the endorsement process, and mandated that bad checks must be returned through the collection system as quickly as possible.

Regulation CC will certainly help to increase the efficiency of the check collection system. However, the fact remains that a system in which billions of pieces of paper are moving across the country each year is by nature inefficient. There are clearly more efficient ways to make payments in this day and age. The following chapter on bank operations will address this issue directly.

STUDY AND REVIEW QUESTIONS

1. Name the two factors required in proper negotiation of a check.
2. Why do you suppose the UCC imposes warranties on an endorsement?
3. Should a bank accept a stop payment order on a certified check when the drawer of the check is claiming that the payee shipped defective merchandise? Why or why not?
4. Why is status as a holder in due course important to someone holding a check?
5. Regulation CC often requires banks to make funds available to depositors before the banks learn a check has been dishonored. Discuss ways in which the banking system might improve on this situation.

7

BANK OPERATIONS
James J. Basl

INTRODUCTION

This chapter will describe the back office functions of a typical depository institution. It will also discuss the computer processing systems that support the operation of the institution.

LEARNING OBJECTIVES

When you have completed this chapter, you should have an understanding of the following:

1. Describe how a depository institution participates in the payment mechanism for paper-based payments like checks.

2. Describe how a depository institution delivers electronic services.

3. Describe the basic back office functions associated with deposits and with loans.

Bank operations refers to the delivery of customer services.

4. Understand the basic computer processing environment.

In general, *bank operations* refers to the part of the depository institution that delivers the services provided the customers of the institution. In some institutions, this is traditionally only the deposit and payment services. For other institutions, it also includes the services associated with loans. The particular bank operation, structure, and responsibilities depend on the size, the type of services provided, and the market orientation of the depository institution. For the purposes of this text, bank operations will refer to all the back office functions.

A *payment mechanism* is the means by which value is exchanged between buyer and seller.

Historically, bank operations grew out of the need of a depository institution to provide various payment services. As the volume of paper-based payments grew, the personnel required to implement the various mechanized functions began to take on the air of a factory operation. Hence, bank operations was born.

The *payment mechanism* includes the various means by which a nation exchanges value. A depository institution is an active participant in the exchange of value between buyer and seller. The institution provides the deposit account which can be accessed by a check, and then provides, along with related organizations, much of the process of making the final exchange of value. This final exchange of value is accomplished when the check travels from the seller until the funds are removed from the buyer's deposit account. Because this is a major function of any bank operations area, this chapter will explore this function first.

BANK OPERATIONS AND THE PAPER PAYMENT MECHANISM

Float is the time delay between the writng of a check and the reduction of account funds.

Within the Uniform Commercial Code, the basic tenets of negotiable instruments are defined along with the responsibilities of both banks and the depositor. This basic legal framework, coupled with the various regulations written by the federal or state governments or by the Federal Reserve, provides the legal definition of the various facets of the processing required by the payments mechanism. Several of the texts listed in the Bibliography specifically address these areas.

Despite the attempts of many institutions and the banking system as a whole to reduce the volume of paper payments, paper payments—or checks—are still the dominant type of payment in this country (*See* Figure 7-1). The convenience of being able to control the timing of the issuance of a check as payment and the ability to do this without any special equipment make the

---

Figure 7-1
Total Number and Total Volume of Check Items Handled By the Federal Reserve Banks 1940–1995 (Millions)

Year	Number of Pieces Handled*	Amount Handled
1940	1,184	280,436
1945	1,852	688,109
1950	2,321	921,523
1955	3,494	1,056,680
1960	4,097	1,264,364
1965	5,322	1,773,178
1970	7,964	3,549,268
1975	12,430	4,615,405
1980	16,538	8,642,759
1990	19,304	13,153,694
1993	19,681	14,622,961
1994	17,149	12,607,350
1995	16,128	12,082,954

*Multiple checks handled as one item are counted as one piece.
Sources: Banking and Monetary Statistics 1941–1970, and *Annual Reports* of the Federal Reserve Board of Governors

1994 Payment System Activity

Instruments	Volume of Transactions (in millions)	Value of Transactions (in billions)
Cheques issued[1]	61,670.0	71,500.0
Payments by Card		
Debit[2]	1,046.0	44.9
Credit[3]	13,681.6	730.8
Paperless credit transfers:		
CHIPS	45.6	295,443.8
Fedwire[4]	72.0	211,201.5
Federal Reserve ACH[5]	1,525.7	3,284.8
Direct Debits:		
Federal Reserve ACH[6]	847.0	5,084.7
Total	**78,887.9**	**587,290.5**

[1]Includes personal cheques, commercial and government cheques, commercial and postal money orders and travellers' cheques. Data for volume of cheques not processed by the Federal Reserve are estimated.

[2]Estimates are based on June data and include on-line POS debits and ACH/POS debits. *Source:* POS News (Faulkner & Gray, New York).

[3]Includes all type of credit card transactions (i.e. bank, oil company, telephone, retail store, travel and entertainment, etc.) Bank cards include VISA and MasterCard credit cards only (excluding debit cards). *Source:* The Nilson Report (Oxnard, CA).

[4]Fedwire funds transfer volume only.

[5]Does not include commercial "on-us" items increase total ACH volume (debits + credits) by at least 13%.

[6]Does not include commercial "on-us" debit items. Excludes debit items with no value such as notifications of changes in customer information.

Source: Payment Systems in The Group of Ten Countries, Prepared by the Committee on Payment and Settlement Systems of the central banks of the Group of Ten countries. Basle Switzerland: Bank for International Settlements 1993.

---

check a very difficult payment mechanism to replace. Also, the writer of the check has the advantage of using the *float*—a time delay between the writing of the check and the actual reduction of the funds in the account. In many cases the depositor will be earning interest on these funds until they are taken from the account.

In order to apply mechanization to the processing of checks in the early 1960s, the banks developed a standard coding on the checks. This coding was translated to Magnetic Ink Character Recognition (MICR). A standardized format was developed and printed on the check in ink that could be magnetized. The numbers and the special symbols in the MICR format were required to be in a certain form and position on the bottom of the check (*See* Figure 7-2).

The key fields on a check are as follows:

- *Routing and Transit*—This field identifies the Federal Reserve District where the bank is located and the bank on which the check is drawn. (In Figure 7-2, this is composed of the check routing symbol, institutional identifier, and the check digit.)

MICR (magnetic ink character recognition) numbers appear on all checks.

- *Account Number*—This field identifies the number assigned to the account holder by the identified Depository Institution.

- *Process Control*—This field is generally the check number on personal checks, but it also could contain a numeric designator controlling the processing of the item—for example, a Transaction Code.

- *Amount*—This field identifies the amount of the value being exchanged.

- *Serial Number or Auxiliary ON-US*—This field identifies the serial number of a business check and is to the left of the Routing and Transit number. (Not shown in Figure 7-2.)

Figure 7-2

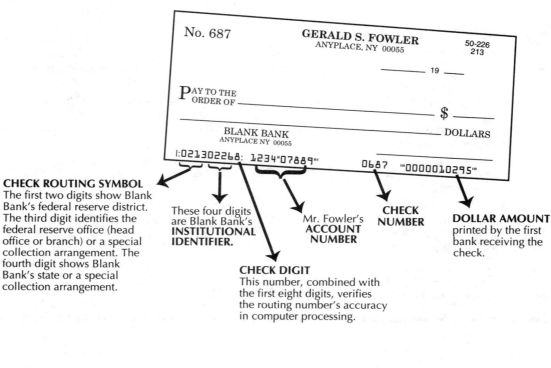

CHECK ROUTING SYMBOL
The first two digits show Blank Bank's federal reserve district. The third digit identifies the federal reserve office (head office or branch) or a special collection arrangement. The fourth digit shows Blank Bank's state or a special collection arrangement.

These four digits are Blank Bank's **INSTITUTIONAL IDENTIFIER.**

CHECK DIGIT
This number, combined with the first eight digits, verifies the routing number's accuracy in computer processing.

Mr. Fowler's **ACCOUNT NUMBER**

CHECK NUMBER

DOLLAR AMOUNT printed by the first bank receiving the check.

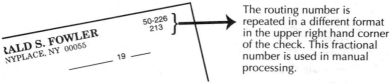

The routing number is repeated in a different format in the upper right hand corner of the check. This fractional number is used in manual processing.

These fields control the processing of the item and identify the account from which the designated value will be removed. With this standardization, the banking industry is able to process easily the volumes of paper that form the basis of the financial world.

The basic function of the paper payment mechanism is to move the paper representing the value exchanged from the point of acceptance to the point where the value can be obtained—for example, from a merchant to the bank where the writer of the check has an account. This process can cover great distances and be separated by time periods of various lengths. Also, the actual flow of the value through the process must be controlled in order to protect all participants in the process. Once the item is received by a financial institution, it is the goal of that institution to move quickly enough to insure that the item is passed to the final institution as expeditiously as possible.

To see how this is accomplished, we will follow two items through the payment mechanism. Both items are received by a merchant in Chicago and are included in the merchant's deposit at The First Loop National Bank. The two items are included in the work that is received by a teller at the main office branch of the bank. The items are then forwarded to the processing center. There the amount is encoded (printed) in the correct position of the MICR line. Then the items are processed on a reader/sorter—a large electromechanical device that magnetizes the magnetic ink on the check, reads the item, and decides how to process the item. The first item is determined to be ON-US, or belonging to an account holder of the First Loop National Bank. This item will be passed directly to the computer system for processing.

The second item is determined to belong to Second ILLINI Bank in Springfield, Illinois. This item is NOT ON-US. The First Loop National Bank has several options to physically move the item to the Second ILLINI Bank. They are as follows:

- *Use the Federal Reserve System*—In this case, the First Loop National Bank would prepare a *cash letter,* a bundle of checks with a listing of those checks, and send it to the Federal Reserve Office in Chicago. The Federal Reserve of Chicago would then put the packet with those from other banks and process the work. The end result would be a new cash letter of items drawn on the Second ILLINI Bank. This cash letter would be presented to the Second ILLINI Bank and they would process it to post the items to the respective accounts.

- *Use a Correspondent Bank*—During the course of the development of the financial structure of the United States, a class of institutions developed that would represent other financial institutions in particular areas. These institutions were called correspondents and provide various services for the respondent institutions. One of these services is processing checks. In this case the First Loop National Bank would again prepare a cash letter and would send it to the MegaBalances Trust Co. There the cash letter would be processed with other incoming work. The item for Second ILLINI Bank would either be selected as an item to be passed to a processing system, if MegaBalances Trust Co. was providing data processing services to Second ILLINI Bank or it would be put into an outgoing cash letter.

    This new cash letter could be routed in several ways, it could be sent directly to Second ILLINI Bank and handled as same day settlement, it could be routed through the local clearinghouse, or it could be sent to the Federal Reserve Bank in Chicago. The direct presentment or the clearinghouse, an organization of banks that meet to exchange cash letters, are the two most probable ways of routing the cash letter.

At each institution along the way from the merchant to the Second ILLINI Bank, the check would be reprocessed through a reader/sorter. The only exception to this would be if it passed through a clearinghouse, where normally cash letters are only exchanged and not reprocessed. The reason for this is that at most clearinghouses cash letters are exchanged for each member organization. When the item finally reached the Second ILLINI Bank, it would again be reprocessed. At this point the item is ON-US to that bank, which creates an electronic image of the transaction for processing in the computer.

These routing options can be followed in Figures 7-3 and 7-4.

Following a similar path in each case, the value that was exchanged will move through various settlement points.

In the first case with the ON-US item, the settlement to create the exchange of value comes directly from the payee of the check to the payor of the check. This moves through general ledger of the First Loop National Bank.

In the second case, various options can be followed, but here are two possibilities:

1. If the First Loop National Bank used the Federal Reserve of Chicago, the Reserve Account of the bank would be credited according to the availability schedule of the Federal Reserve. On presentment of the cash letter containing the item to the Second ILLINI Bank, that bank's reserve acount would be charged for the item. Thus, the value exchanged would move through the accounts of the Federal Reserve.

2. If the First Loop National Bank used a correspondent like MegaBalances Trust Co., it would receive credit for the item based on that bank's availability schedule. Depending on how MegaBalances Trust Co. routed the item, it would receive credit from the next organization in the path. Ultimately the funds would move from the payee's account and offset the charge received by the Second ILLINI Bank.

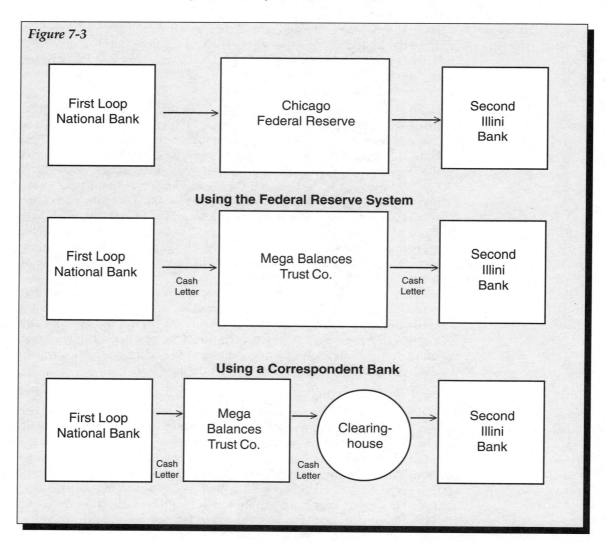

Figure 7-3

Availability allows credit to an institution, which can then use the funds.

The routing of the NOT ON-US item would be chosen so that the first bank received the best availability and spent the least amount to process the item. *Availability* means that an institution receives credit for the item and can use the funds for lending or investment purposes. The costs are the direct charges associated with the routing of the item and can be incurred either at the Federal Reserve or at the correspondent. At a clearinghouse a member usually pays only an annual fee.

Figure 7-4

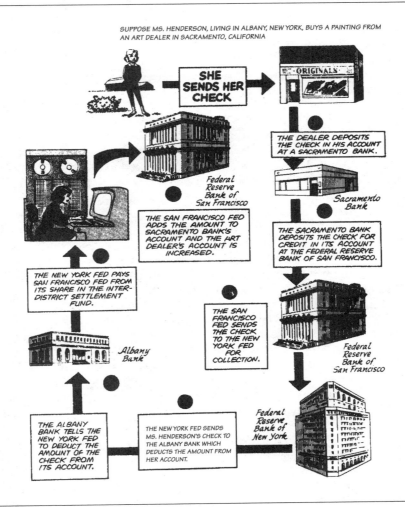

SUPPOSE MS. HENDERSON, LIVING IN ALBANY, NEW YORK, BUYS A PAINTING FROM AN ART DEALER IN SACRAMENTO, CALIFORNIA

The process described above explains how a depository institution participates in the paper payment mechanism. It supplies the account for the check issuer and then provides the routing of the item so it is finally posted to the account of the payee.

BANK OPERATIONS AND THE ELECTRONIC PAYMENT MECHANISM

The financial services industry has attempted to reduce the volume of paper payments. As we have seen, the processing of paper items is very labor intensive and requires the rehandling of the items at each point on the way to final posting. Very early on, the industry instituted wire transfers for sending via

Mechanized electronic
payment systems
include wire transfers
(for large amounts)and
ATM's (automatic
teller machines) and
ACH's automated
clearing houses) for
small, or retail
amounts.

electronic means messages indicating that funds were moving through the
Federal Reserve System for credit to a particular individual or company. This
service is still very active and accounts for most if not all of the large dollar
transactions passing through electronic means (See Figure 7-1). The volume
is still comparatively slight for even the heaviest wire organizations in the
money center institutions. From a retail standpoint, several attempts have
been made to deliver various electronic payment mechanisms. To date, the
only ones that have had any real success are Automatic Teller Machines
(ATM's) and Automated Clearinghouses (ACH's).

The following sections discuss how these various electronic payment
mechanisms function.

Automated Clearinghouses (ACH's)

ACH's mimic the
"paper trail" payment
mechanism
electronically.

As a step toward an electronic exchange mechanism, the financial institutions
and the Federal Reserve System came together to develop a process for exchanging electronic images. The result was the Automated Clearinghouse or
the ACH system, which permits a financial institution to originate an electronic debit or credit and have it passed to the receiving institution. The processing of this system is modeled on the paper mechanism in that "electronic
cash letters" are passed to a local clearinghouse and then routed on to their
destination. One of the most common transactions generated by a private
organization and passed through the ACH processing environment is a
payroll deposit. Let's follow this type of transaction.

A company in Richmond, Virginia, processes its payroll and wants to
deposit the pay for an employee in Camden, Maine, in that employee's bank
account. The company takes the collection of electronic transactions on a computer tape to its bank, Belle Isle National Bank. In the processing of the transactions, Belle Isle National will separate the transactions belonging to its account holders from the transactions going to other institutions. The transactions for all other institutions will be grouped and from these a tape is produced once a day to go to the local ACH organization. This organization will
process the transaction, probably at the Richmond Federal Reserve. (Only the
New York City ACH does its own processing at the time of this writing.)

The Richmond Federal Reserve receives tape from other local institutions,
groups them together, and then creates new tapes. Each local institution will
receive back a tape of its own transactions. Tapes are similarly created for the
other Federal Reserve District Offices—in this case, the Boston Federal Reserve. These tapes will be transported to the appropriate destination, where
the transactions will be grouped with the particular local items and tapes
produced for each institution. In this case the Boston Federal Reserve would
take the Richmond item and group it with any items generated in New England or anywhere else in the country. Then, a tape would be produced for
the First Lobster Savings Bank. This tape would be presented to the bank for
processing the transaction and would be held until the effective date and then
made available to the customer. (See Figure 7-5). The largest user of the ACH
system is the government.

Private use of ACH's is
growing in such ways
as corporate trade
payments.

Private use is increasing, especially now that some companies are using
the ACH system for corporate trade payments. In other words, they are
paying selected vendors for merchandise by sending electronic credits with
the invoice identified in the descriptive data. Another area for particular
growth is the use by some oil companies to process electronic cash transactions from customers at gas stations (See figure 7-5).

Figure 7-5
Automated Clearinghouse

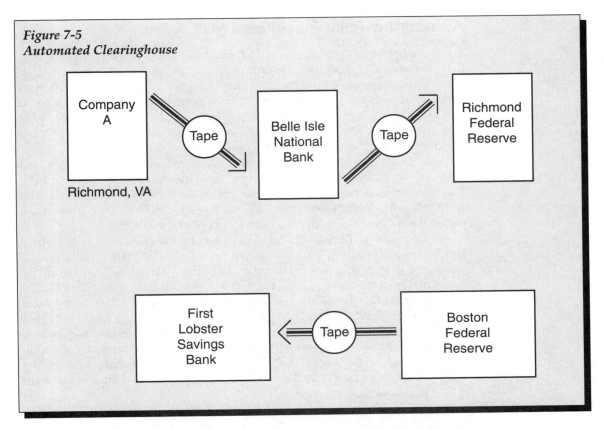

Figure 7-6
Automated Teller Machines

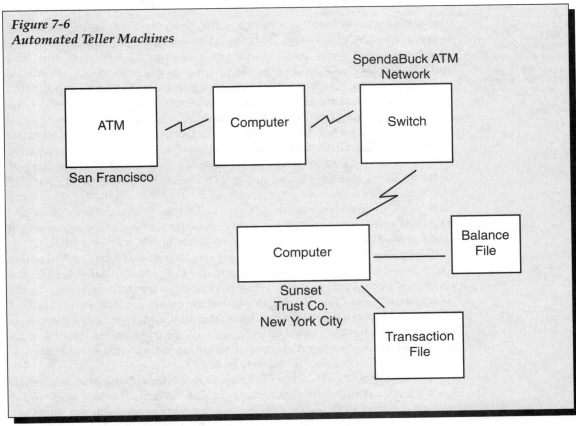

Automated Teller Machines (ATM's)

In order to provide the customers of a financial institution with greater access to their funds and to reduce the number of people involved in this process, many institutions have implemented an ATM program. By using this electro-mechanical device to perform selected transactions that are usually performed in a branch by a bank employee, the institution both extends the hours for performing these selected transactions and reduces the involvement of bank personnel in the transaction. In this case the customer is provided with a special card, a debit card, to access a deposit account through the ATM. Along with this card the customer is given a personal identification number or PIN. This number is used to validate the usage of the card by the customer. The ATM networks can be restricted to one bank's customers, or it can be a national network. The following is an example of the latter:

A customer of the Sunset Trust Co. in San Francisco is in New York City and requires more cash for his vacation spending. The individual locates a bank in New York City that is a member of the SpendaBuck ATM network. By inserting the debit card to access his deposit account and keying his PIN, the customer activates the ATM. His request for cash is passed to the Sunset Trust Co. and authorized. The response to give the customer more funds is passed back through the network of computers and phone lines connecting the two financial institutions. The funds are passed to the customer, and he goes off to continue his fun (See Figure 7-6). The transaction is recorded at the Sunset Trust Co. and later passed to the proper system, posted, and later a statement is sent to the customer.

Bank-Issued National Credit or Debit Cards

Bank-issued credit cards (VISA, MasterCard) work through the electronic or paper-based clearance of accounts at merchant servicing

One of the most pervasive payment mechanisms is the use of credit cards like Visa and MasterCard. The plastic cards are issued by banks and provide the customers with a credit line to use for purchases or cash advances. Both Visa and MasterCard have built networks to support the authorization, verification that the transaction can be completed successfully, and to support the routing of transactions. These networks link together the merchant servicers, banks or other organizations that facilitate the merchant use of the credit card, and the cardholder servicers, banks or other organizations that process the cardholder's accounts. In addition to the use of these networks for credit card transactions, many banks have begun to issue plastic cards to access deposit accounts like a checking account, debit cards, with the Visa or MasterCard emblems. Debit cards are as acceptable to the merchant, who usually has no idea whether a deposit account or a credit line is being used. Only the merchant's customer knows what account is being accessed and chooses which card to use. The transaction flow is the same for either type of card.

The processing of the transaction is becoming more electronic but still is paper based for some merchants. Particularly in the authorization phase, the process is done through on-line registers or separate terminals tied to the merchant servicer. Often during the authorization the transaction is captured by the merchant servicer to be routed to the cardholder servicer for processing. If the merchant is still relying on paper based transactions then the merchant servicer will convert the paper to an electronic image and route the transaction to the cardholder for processing.

For example, the customer of Prairie Dog National Bank in Plano, Texas, has a VISA card and wants to charge a meal in Hawaii. The customer would present the card to the waiter and assuming there is an on-line connection, the restaurant personnel would authorize the transaction. At the same time, an electronic record of the transaction would be created. This electronic record along with the restaurant's other charge card receipts for the day would be passed from the merchant servicer through the VISA servicing network to the cardholder servicer for Plano National Bank. Transactions for other cardholder servicers would be routed to them at the same time. The cardholder servicer would post the transaction to the cardholder's account. A transaction to credit the merchant's deposit account would be generated by the merchant servicer and passed to that account through automated clearinghouse processing. The VISA network would arrange for settlement between the merchant servicer and the cardholder servicer.

If the restaurant in Hawaii used paper based processing, it would have delivered the paper sales drafts to the merchant servicer. There they would have been converted to electronic images prior to being passed into the VISA servicing network. Otherwise, the processing is the same.

The capture of the transaction while it is being generated at the merchant is referred to as Point of Sale or POS. Either a debit card or a credit card may be used in this POS environment. Since the example assumed on-line capture, it was a POS transaction. The merchant does not receive credit at the same time as the generation of the transaction nor is the cardholder immediately charged. The transaction processing is quicker but is still delayed by the processing cycles of the merchant servicer, the VISA processing network, and the cardholder servicer.

Other Forms of Electronic Funds Transfer

The prior three methods of electronic funds transfer or electronic payment processing present the possible foundation for building a future "cashless" society. The principle behind each is that paper documents do not have to move to the final destination physically; rather, an electronic image is passed to the point of final settlement. By varying the device used to convert the transaction to an electronic image, a new service can be developed from these foundations. For example:

POS (point of sale) transactions are both authorized and captured or transacted by the merchant on electronic devices.

A debit card resembles a bank credit card but deducts funds from a deposit account.

- *Point of Sale*—Point of Sale (POS) was already discussed for the processing of National Debit or Credit Cards, but it also is applicable to the use of debit cards issued exclusively for the networks of ATM's. A merchant again generates the electronic image at the time of the purchase. The ATM network organization will sell the concept to the merchant and provide the link from the merchant's POS devices to the ATM network. A transaction is then processed just as it would be through the ATM environment. Merchants receive credits to their deposit accounts by transactions generated at the network switch and sent through the automated clearinghouse environment. Gasoline retailers and supermarkets have adopted this electronic payment method in many areas. The goal of the ATM network organizations is to make it appealing to more merchants. Customers have been increasingly receptive to this because of the convenience.

- *HomeBanking*—Exchanges of value from the home, for example, the payment of bills to vendors, have traditionally been accomplished by the writing of checks. The replacement of this activity with electronic transactions is becoming more of a reality. Telephones were the first devices used to generate transactions and as home computers have decreased in cost, they have become the preferred device. Many banks are beginning to offer this proprietary connection to the systems of the bank for accessing account information and generation transactions.

- *Internet Banking* —Starting in 1995 the Internet suddenly became a new vehicle for connecting people and organizations. Quite simply the Internet is a network of computers storing various forms of information that can be accessed through home computers. These home computers have the capability of connecting to the network and accessing the information. The information is delivered directly to the personal computer and can take a variety of forms, text, graphics, sound, or video. The presentation given the user of the Internet is very easy to navigate and very visually oriented. The use of the Internet started as more of an advertising presentation but as the security aspects evolved it became a vehicle for commerce. In this more secure environment some banks have begun to allow their customers access to individual account information and the generation of payment transactions. The connection is not proprietary and anyone anywhere can become a customer of the bank simply by having a connection to the Internet.

  Whether the basic transaction flow begins with a telephone, a home computer, or a connection to the Internet, the transaction begins by indicating what account to charge and what vendors are being paid or credited.

  Once the transactions are collected at the service provider, either the bank or a contracted organization, they can be passed into a processing environment. The automated clearinghouse/environment will accept both the debit to the bill payer's account and the credit to the vendor's account. Standard transaction formats include the descriptive information with the credit that would allow the vendor to credit the proper account in the vendor's processing systems. The transactions would be moved through the same processing points as described earlier for such transactions as payroll credits or insurance premium debits. While this is the possibility, in the current situation there is growing implementation of this full processing mode. In some cases the organization that collects the transactions actually writes a check to the vendor being paid grouping all payments collected in a processing day on one check and only posts the debit electronically. As banks improve the ability to pass the descriptive data with the credit to the vendor electronically this electronic payment mechanism will grow in usage.

Each of the electronic transfer mechanisms has had a slow initial introductory stage prior to becoming well established in the marketplace. The customers of financial institutions are often very reluctant to give up the audit trail, the freedom of timing, and the float delay that the use of checks gives them in paper payment processing. In some regions Point of Sale has a rapid growth and it will be only a matter of time before HomeBanking should become very prevalent in a full implementation of electronic transfer.

Wire Transfer of Funds

Probably the most successful electronic funds transfer mechanism has been in the area of wire transfer of funds by corporate customers. This technique has been around for quite awhile and is widely used for transactions of considerable dollar value. There are three major networks for wire transfer:

- *FEDWIRE*—This network is maintained by the Federal Reserve System and is used primarily to send messages between domestic banks. These messages indicate that balances in reserve accounts are being debited and credited. These transactions represent the movement of funds from one institution's customer account to another institution's customer account.

- *CHIPS*—(Clearinghouse Interbank Payment System): This network is maintained by the New York City Clearinghouse for the primary use of New York City banks and their overseas branches. Again, messages are settled through the New York City Clearinghouse.

- *SWIFT*—(Society for Worldwide Interbank Financial Telecommunication): This network is a private system developed for international and domestic institutions that require messages to be sent for international customers. The funds are transferred through correspondent banks.

FUNCTIONS OF THE BANK'S BACK OFFICE AREAS

Back office bank functions fall into ten basic categories for deposit accounts and six for loan services.

The back office areas of a financial institution are involved in the delivery of the service on the various products, both loans and deposits, that are offered by the institution. The actual structure and assignment of responsibilities will vary from institution to institution, but in general the following functions will be found:

For Deposit Accounts

1. *New Account Opening*—One area in the institution will have the responsibility for ensuring that new accounts are correctly set up on the computer system so that the proper service can be delivered. While some of this could be done in a branch at the time of the actual set-up of the account, a back office will probably ensure that the correct codes are used for the account. Also, certain documents such as a signature card have to be on file, and if these documents are filed in a central location, this area will ensure that all are correctly executed.

2. *Answering Inquiries*—This particular function can be done in many areas depending on the type of computer system used. In most cases, though, there is a particular area or areas that will respond to both phone and written inquiries. The various types of inquiries will often have responses available in a computer system or in reports. Often though the final resolution of the inquiry will require some additional research. The answer to the inquiry may indicate that maintenance be performed to the account or that adjusting transactions be made to the account.

3. *Filing Checks or Other Transaction Documents*—A bank has two main options for filing checks: by account number or by bulk filing. In the former the checks are passed multiple times through the reader sorter to put them into account number order, and then they are filed by account number. In the latter the items are passed through the reader sorter to pull out any exception items (items that must be looked at by someone) and to separate the checks into statement cycles. The checks are then put on shelves in date order for each cycle.

4. *Rendering Statements*—Each customer's transaction account receives a monthly statement. Savings accounts may receive a monthly statement or one less frequently. In many cases, certificates of deposit receive an annual statement. The period of time between which a customer receives a statement is referred to as a cycle. Generally, the cycles are identified by a number or a date. If the customer's documents are being returned, for example checks, then the documents must be put with the printed statement and mailed to the customer.

If the checks have been filed by account number, then they will be put with the statement and mailed to the customer. If bulk filing has been used, the documents are sorted into the same order as the statements and then put with the statements to be mailed. In large organizations much of the statement rendering has been automated with special equipment.

When the customer's documents are not returned, this is referred to as truncation. Some institutions will truncate only certain documents, for example, deposit tickets, or documents will be truncated for certain accounts, for example, money market accounts. At other institutions even the checks will be truncated. For check truncation good quality microfilm records are required to provide document copies when a customer requests them. Some institutions have now started using image technology to capture a picture of the check for statement rendering with check truncation. In this case additional pages with the pictures of several checks per page are included with the statement to the customer.

5. *Control Settlements*—The computer systems must be settled and various general ledger accounts reconciled on a daily basis to assure that the bank's records accurately reflect the money held for customers.

6. *Stop Payment Processing*—When a customer requests that a particular item not be paid against an account, this is referred to as a stop payment. Once this request has been made, the activity on the account must be monitored so that this item is not paid. The computer systems used to process the accounts will make this review easier, but someone has to make the final decision on an item. If the item matches the information given by the customer, then the item will be sent back to the bank of original deposit or returned. Return items are grouped together and sent out as a return cash letter.

7. *Overdraft or Nonsufficient Funds Processing*—in some cases, checks for a customer will be posted when there are not enough funds to pay the item, which creates an overdraft or an NSF item, depending on the institution's terminology. In these cases, someone must determine if the item should remain posted or if it should be sent back to the bank of original deposit, or returned. In either case the bank will usually assess the account a charge for the processing of this type of item.

8. *Large Balance Activity and Kiting*—Some customers will have large balance activity or will move money between institutions in an attempt to defraud an institution. Monitoring various reports of exception type activity will help detect this type of fraud and may prevent a loss to the institution.

9. *Interest Payment*—Interest is paid on some deposit accounts. In these cases various control procedures must be followed to assure that the interest payment is handled correctly. Some of these payments are actually checks sent to the customer.

10. *Retirement Account Control*—Certain types of deposit accounts are used for retirement purposes and are controlled by a unique set of regulations. These regulations strictly define certain procedures that must be followed by the bank. The processing of retirement accounts requires reports in certain formats and the production of these reports must be controlled to assure compliance to the regulations.

For Loans

1. *New Account Opening*—One area of the institution will have the responsibility for ensuring that the new accounts are correctly set up on the computer system so that the proper service can be delivered. The actual set up of the account can be done in a Loan Origination area, but a back office will probably ensure that the correct codes are used for the account.

2. *Answering Inquiries*—This particular function can be done in many areas, depending on the type of computer system used. In most cases, a particular area or areas will respond to both phone and written inquiries, a function that will often demand some research and could require maintenance to the account as well as correcting transactions.

3. *Document Control and Filing*—In most cases certain documents require retention in the loan department files. These documents define the contract between the institution and the borrower, describe and define the institution's interest in any collateral used to secure the loan, and document the evaluation of the borrower. These files have to be controlled and protected to ensure that the institution can always prove its position in the relationship with the borrower. This process often requires the filming of certain documents and the permanent retention of the same documents in a secure location. Also, certain procedures are often in place to provide assurance that all the proper documents are received either at the booking of the loan or subsequently.

4. *Control of Insurance*—The institution will often require the borrower to maintain insurance on the property used as collateral for the loan. The accounts in this category must be monitored for cancelled policies and the presence of the proper insurance documents. Other types of insurance, such as life insurance, are often sold to the borrowers by the bank. The collection of premiums and their payment to the insurance company must be controlled.

5. *Escrow Processing for Mortgages*—Mortgage loans often are set up so that the payment includes a portion that will be held in escrow so that certain payments—real estate taxes and various insurances—can be made on behalf of the borrower. When required, these payments will be made and the escrow reduced. Periodically, the portion of the payment being applied to escrow will be evaluated and either increased or decreased so that the borrower's requirements will be met. This process is referred to as escrow analysis.

6. *Secondary Market Reporting*—In the financial world one can "sell" a loan to an investor. When this happens, the institution usually "services" the loan for the investor for a fee. Based on the relationship with the investor, certain funds will be remitted to the investor on a periodic basis. This reporting and servicing has to be controlled by certain procedures to assure accuracy.

THE BASIC COMPUTER PROCESSING ENVIRONMENT FOR FINANCIAL INSTITUTIONS

Few services rendered by financial institutions today are not computerized. Yes, there are those institutions which, because of size or volume of activity, can still perform a particular manual service for a particular customer or group of customers. However, the basic functions of deposit and loan servicing and related services have been automated in most banks for quite some time. Financial institutions, as compared to other organizations, have a relatively complex computer processing environment. The mechanism to produce the services for the customer requires computer processing as do the support functions that are related to the delivery of the services. Also, the management information required for making the decisions to run a financial institution in today's ever-changing environment must be derived from the computer environment. These data processing requirements are interwoven such that a change in one often requires changes in the other. Other organizations tend to have data processing environments which are less interwoven. Because of these extensive requirements, the ways financial service firms satisfy their needs can vary.

There are three major ways that data processing can be provided to a financial services firm:

- *Service Bureau*—In this case, the services are purchased from an outside company, which generally provides services to a number of institutions at the same time. The computer equipment (hardware) and the computer programs (software) will be owned by the service bureau, and the financial institution will contract for certain services to be performed.

- *Facilities Management*—In this case, the hardware and software may be owned by the financial institution or by an outside company. The people and the management of the data processing function are provided by the personnel from an outside company.

- *In-house Processing*—In this case, the hardware and the software are owned by the financial institution and the personnel are employees of the bank. The financial institution's management is directly responsible for the management of the computer resources.

Opinions vary greatly as to which of these options provides the type of data processing support required in today's environment. The financial institution must evaluate the cost of the option, what it is receiving for its investment, and its ability to effectively administer the resource within its particular management environment and corporate culture.

In addition to these three methods of providing data processing services there are two major processing environments:

- *Batch Processing with Some Online Real Time*—The data processing environment originally required that all transactions be converted to electronic images and then posted to the collection of accounts representing a particular service delivered to customers. For example, all transactions for savings accounts were applied to the collection of all the institution's savings accounts. This method is called batch processing; a batch or group of transactions was processed at one time. In most cases, the batch was all the transactions from a day's processing. With the reduction of the cost of hardware and the increased flexibility of software, this method has been modified in many institutions to include some online real time transactions. Online real time transactions are processed as the transaction is converted to an electronic image. In this case, a name and address change is keyed into the computer, and the electronic record would be changed immediately. The amount of online real time activity varies greatly by institution. The primary source of monetary transactions in this case is from an item processing environment with a reader sorter. Most, if not all, of the monetary transactions are passed from the teller line or other input points through the reader sorter for conversion into electronic images. This collection of images becomes a batch of transactions for processing and posting to the various accounts.

In many cases there will be a data processing method that resembles Online Real Time processing. This is called *memo posting* and consists of an online record to a file that is a copy of the live data. Often the copy has less data about each account and the file is set up to allow quick access. The file is available to the terminal networks in branches or to the networks which support ATM or POS authorization. Any transaction which is memo posted is also recorded and passed with the other transactions in the batch processing mode for the posting to the account. Memo posting will be used in addition to the batch processing environment to permit the financial institution to keep a record of transactions as they occur in the institution. This is the way that a batch processing organization simulates the full online real time processing environment for financial transactions.

> Memo posting is an intermediate process between online and batch processing.

- *Full Online Real Time Processing*—In this processing environment, most transactions are converted to electronic images and processed as they are converted. The major exception might be a large group of transactions from an external source like the Federal Reserve System. Customer transactions in the branch are input to the computer and processed while the customer is present. This type of processing is quite common in some areas where thrift institutions have a large base of passbook customers and has been extended to all types of accounts offered by these institutions.

Again, there is much debate in the industry as to which is the best processing for a financial institution. The batch processing environment has long been the stereotype of a commercial bank or a similar institution. The online real time environment has been the stereotype of the thrift industry. These past characterizations are breaking down as the financial services industry moves in a direction where the distinctions between the institutions is more in name and not in the types of services delivered. Each institution has to define its requirements from the services offered its own processing requirements, and the level of service to be delivered to the customer. The options available also depend on the processing options that have been chosen.

An Example of the Data Processing Environment in a Typical Bank

The following discussion gives an overview of a typical financial institution method of delivering the basic deposit and loan services. The batch processing environment with an in-house processing option has been chosen for the model. The major differences from online will be pointed out. The differences from other processing options would only involve the location of equipment and the type of communication resources available (See Figure 7-7).

The primary contact with the customer of a financial institution is at the branch—in the teller line for financial transactions or in the customer service area (Platform) for new accounts or servicing of existing accounts. It has become fairly common for a financial institution to have access to information stored in a computer through a terminal (a Cathode ray tube device, or a CRT). This device allows the branch personnel to answer inquiries and to determine the type of account relationships the customer has with the bank. At the teller line, the financial institution may have installed some online

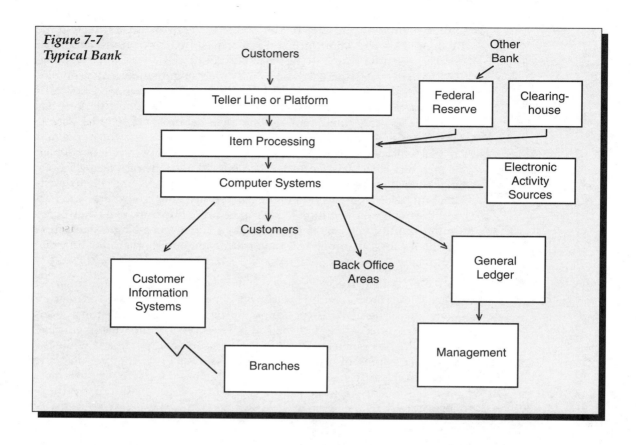

**Figure 7-7
Typical Bank**

device for transaction control and authorization, or it might have installed only offline teller machines for control of the work being processed and the cash control of the teller's drawer.

In either case, the branch is the point where control over the processing of the transaction is established. Thus, the branch personnel must be knowledgeable in processing transactions correctly, in explaining and selling the various services of the financial institution, in trying to resolve any problems in the servicing of the account, and in presenting a pleasant and professional image for the financial institution.

If the transactions have not been processed in an online environment, they will be grouped so that debits and credits are together. This means that if the customer made a deposit to an account with a check, the debit would be the check and the deposit would be the credit. For multiple transactions, the customer's debits would equal the customer's credits. Sometimes these debits or credits will be general ledger transactions, such as cash-ins or cash-outs. Batches of work will be sent at various times during the day to the processing area.

Once the transaction batches are sent to the operations area, they are encoded and balanced to determine if debits equal credits. They are then batched again and prepared for processing on a reader sorter. This encoding and batching could take place on a single pocket proof machine or on a multipocket proof machine. What kind of machine is used is determined by the financial institution's philosophy for establishing control and the overall processing environment. Sometimes (particularly for a service bureau-type environment), a multipocket proof machine will be used so that NOT ON-US items can be outsorted and cash letters formed to send to a collection point. The processing flow of the service bureau may also require that certain transactions be kept separate from others. Somewhere, though, it is most likely that the transactions are converted to electronic images on a reader/sorter. Various proofs are done to insure that all the work is processed and correctly converted to an electronic image.

These electronic images are then passed to the correct application or processing system. For example, electronic images of checks would be passed to the checking or the NOW system. Loan payments would be passed to the respective loan system. Once passed to the respective processing system, the transactions would be posted or rejected if the criteria for posting were not met. This processing of transactions results in the production of the various reports used to provide service to the customers of the financial institutions. From this processing comes any customer notices or statements used to communicate with the customer concerning an account.

At the completion of this processing, certain information concerning an account would be made available for access through some sort of computer terminal (or CRT). This information can include balance and descriptive data about an account and the history of transactions posted to the accounts. The complete customer relationship may be available if the financial institution has chosen to use a Central Information System for its customers.

In recent years, this kind of system has become very popular not only to aid the delivery of service by the organization but also to support various cross-selling programs and marketing analysis of the customer base.

The dollar impact of the various transactions is passed to the General Ledger, either electronically or manually, based upon various reports produced by the processing systems. The general ledger provides the financial picture of the institution so that management may evaluate the success of the institution's strategy.

Transactions that originate with the customer base flow through the processing environment and are returned to the customer in the form of notices or statements. This transaction activity is mirrored in the entries made to the General Ledger and is provided for the servicing of the customers in several different forms for the employees of the organization.

- *For Online Processing*—If the financial institution has chosen to use the Online Real Time Mode of processing, then the branch is equipped with terminal devices. These terminal devices allow the branch personnel to access the customer's accounts and to post transactions. The transactions are converted to electronic images and passed to the application and posted to the appropriate account. If NOT ON-US items are deposited by a customer these are usually outsorted at the branch and deposited in a correspondent bank. The correspondent bank passes the items through the clearing process until they are posted.

    After the processing for the day is completed with the settling of the branches, the system will be processed to handle any interest accrual and reporting such as statements or various control reports. All the transactions that are posted during the day are reflected in general ledger transactions which are passed for posting. If the systems permit it, the application systems for deposits and loans can be integrated with a Customer Information System. This Online environment would also support the maintenance of the accounts. Other than the method of transaction capture and the timing of the posting (as the transaction happens), the processing environments are very similar.

Margin notes:

All data are converted to electronic images and sorted as on-us and not-on-us transactions.

After batch processing, customer data is stored for retrieval by CRT's (computer terminals).

All transactions are mirrored in the general ledger.

CONCLUSION

Bank Operations includes all of the above processes in one way or another. The financial institution delivers services to acquire the raw material of its profit—money in the form of deposits. It is Bank Operations that makes the delivery of the services a success. But Bank Operations does not operate in a vacuum. The understanding of the selling environment by Bank Operations personnel and the understanding of Bank Operations by the rest of the organization make this success easier to achieve and in turn go a long way toward helping to make a successful organization.

STUDY AND REVIEW QUESTIONS

1. Describe the payment mechanism of the United States.
2. What is the standard coding used to process checks?
3. What is availability of funds for a financial institution?
4. What are four methods of routing checks for collection?
5. What are five methods of processing transactions electronically?
6. What type of account is accessed by a debit card?
7. What are five back office functions in the Deposit Operations function?
8. What are five back office functions in the Loan Operations function?
9. What are three ways that data processing can be provided to a financial services firm?
10. What are two options for processing the transactions in a financial services firm?
11. Diagram how your check drawn on your bank, mailed to a Colorado mail-order house clears through the Federal Reserve system.
12. How does your local bank process checks and electronic transactions?

BIBLIOGRAPHY

The following sources can give the reader more detailed information on the various aspects of Bank Operations:

1. *Bank Systems & Technology*. Monthly magazine by Gralla Publications.
2. Burt, Harry V. et al., *Bank Operations*. Needham Heights, MA: Ginn Press, 1990.
3. Friedman, David H., *Deposit Operations*. Washington DC: American Bankers Association, 1987.
4. Lipis, Allen H. et al., *Electronic Banking*. New York: John Wiley and Sons, 1985.
5. Mayer, Martin, *The Bankers*. Chapters 6 and 7. New York: Ballantine Books, 1974.
6. Mayer, Martin, *The Money Bazaars*. Chapter 4, 5, 6, and 12. New York: Mentor Books, 1985.

INFORMATION TECHNOLOGY IN BANKING
Claudia C. Durning

INTRODUCTION

Technology is an essential part of the bank business and can be used to maximize competitive edge, win new business and improve customer retention. [1]

This chapter discusses information technology, it's affect on the banking industry and banking operations, and it's importance to bank management and consumers.

LEARNING OBJECTIVES

After reading this chapter you should be able to:

1. Define information technology.
2. Describe why information technology is important to bank management and consumers.
3. Describe the affect information technology has on banking.
4. Define and describe image processing, SmartCards, EDI, and electronic banking and their role in banking operations.

Information Technology is the developing and improving of computer systems, as tools, to terminate the paper chase and provide product or service differentiation in the marketplace.

Technology is a tool enabling organizations to manage their businesses more efficiently and effectively. Information Technology is the developing and improving of computer systems, as tools, to terminate the paper chase and provide product or service differentiation in the marketplace. [2]

OVERVIEW

It's hard to imagine that most routine banking once had to be done within the walls of a financial institution's branch office. That meant getting to a certain location by a certain time, no matter what the weather, traffic, or other circumstances. ATMs changed all that by making cash access and other services instantly available in almost any neighborhood day or night. Image processing improved back-office banking operations and eased convenience into consumer homes. VISA Check cards, BankBoston Check Xpress ATM cards, and SmartCards added to that convenience by bringing purchasing power to millions of supermarkets, gas stations, and other merchant locations around the world. And now electronic banking is revolutionizing convenience again by making an array of new services accessible 24 hours a day, 365 days a year, through personal computers (PCs), screen phones, touch-tone phones, personal intelligent communicators (PICs), Internet access, and other devices that are making account access easier and faster than ever before.[3]

The banking industry is undergoing a metamorphosis.[4] Banks are being forced by corporate customers and individual consumers who demand real-time information on accounts, competitors, and regulatory changes to speed up the process of transferring information and checks. This makes information technology a top priority for banks. In today's environment, banks are using information technology in the delivery of products and services to gain a competitive edge.

ATMs

Automatic Teller Machines (ATMs) changed routine banking from making cash access and other services available only within the walls of a financial institution's branch office to making them instantly available in almost any neighborhood day or night. With an ATM card, a bank customer can go to any ATM machine, insert the ATM card into the card slot, enter a password and perform account inquiries, account balances, fund transfers, deposits and withdrawals.

At the beginning of 1995 the total of ATMs installed worldwide was approximately 483,000, a 14% increase on the previous year. Western Europe is the world's largest market for ATMs, accounting for just over 30% of the world total. Japan has 29% of the world's ATMs, the US 26% and Canada 4%. The total markets in Europe, Japan and the US grew by 10%, 4%, and 13% respectively. [5]

Even with this great success, ATMs are changing from a button driven, black and green screen to a touch-sensitive, interactive screen. In the past, ATMs have had three major components: 1) buttons that consumers use to inform the computer of their password and what they want to do, 2) a phone within the ATM booth so that consumers can call a customer service representative if they have inquiries, and 3) a slot for making deposits. These ATM systems are slowly being replaced with newer, interactive models. The buttons are replaced by a touch-sensitive screen allowing the consumer to see the options available on the screen and to touch the screen area for the service they want to do; the phone is replaced by a video capability allowing the consumer to see the customer representative when they touch the correct area on the screen requesting help—computer service with a smile; and the deposit slot is replaced by imaging capability enabling the consumer to place the check directly in the machine and immediately see the check on the screen (allowing them to prevent mistakes in typed amounts).

IMAGE PROCESSING

Image processing became popular in '90s and was a technological leap of the same magnitude as magnetic ink character recognition (MICR) in the '60s.[6] Even though image processing is currently being fine-tuned and hence not

Image processing is the process of capturing a paper document as a digital image and storing it on a computer.

used to its potential, many banks are offering limited forms of image processing as a service. Ideally it can save money by making duplicate storage of data unnecessary. *Image processing* is the process of capturing a paper document (such as a mortgage application or a check) as a digital image and storing it on a computer so that it can be processed electronically, rather than handling it physically. This technology eliminates most of the manual handling involved in many bank operations and is being further developed every day.

Image processing is used in banking in the following ways:

1. image statements
2. electronic file cabinets
3. check processing

IMAGE STATEMENTS

Image statements is the process of capturing a check or document as a digital image, storing it on a computer, printing multiple (12 to 18) reduced-size check images on a page, and sending customers these pages of reduced-size check images.

According to American Banker Association, sixteen percent (of the 330 banks in their survey) with assets of less than $500 million plan to move to image technology for account banking processes by the end of 1997, and 23% of the banks surveyed are using the technology to offer the image statement service.[7] Image statement services, provided by banks, give customers the option of receiving their monthly statements with the physical paper checks or receiving, (for a service fee) their monthly statements with images of their checks, and/or deposit, withdrawal, and transfer slips.

Image statements is the process of capturing a check or document a digital image, storing it on a computer, recycling the physical paper checks, printing multiple (12 to 18) reduced-size check images on a page, and sending customers these pages of reduced-size check images, instead of the physical paper checks, in their monthly statements. This lowers the weight, and thus, the cost of the mailing. However, banks are not only looking at check image statements as a way to generate fee income, and save money on postage, but also as a way to improve customer satisfaction.

Customers receiving monthly image statements with images of signed transactions show a reduced number of customer inquiries and increased customer satisfaction. In other words, customers will have the advantage of being able to see graphically (via scanned in images) all their transactions on a monthly basis, without the bulkiness of many small individual returned checks, on a few sheets of paper, and (if the bank offers the extra feature of including images of deposit, withdrawal and transfer transactions) without having to save all their transaction slips; thereby reducing customer inquiries and increasing customer convenience. Banks offer different types of image statements. Some banks offer monthly statements with reduced-size check images only, such as BankBoston. Others offer monthly statements with reduced-size check images and transaction images. The type of image statement service you receive depends on the products and service offered at your bank. However, regardless of the type of image statement service you use, they are all a great convenience to the customer.

ELECTRONIC FILE CABINETS

Bar coding is a pattern of vertical black lines of varying thickness and white background.

"Prior to implementing imaging programs, managing bank documents involved a labor-intensive process of opening the mail, microfilming each document, then sorting and delivering each one to the right department and processing agent."[8] With Electronic File Cabinets, banks are able to cut out all the extra employee time wasted in searching for documents. *Electronic File Cabinets* (EFC) is the process of combining imaging and bar coding to manage documents. "*Bar coding* is a pattern of vertical black lines of varying thickness and white background. The pattern defines a code by which the barcoded object is categorized."[9] EFC allows companies to share documents on a network by converting documents to images, and automatically indexing documents with a bar-code and then sorting them on the computer for easy retrieval.

In order to use EFC, the following process must occur: A bar code is appended to a document in a header sheet (a separate piece of paper which includes the bar code and identifies the different functions, such as making a folder, indexing, where to store the document and customer profiles). Then, the document is scanned and the computer takes care of the rest. Once scanned, the computer reads the bar code header sheet information (via bar code sensor devices as wands, or guns) and follows its instructions. Then, all the employees have to do is call up the document on their computer screen at their workstation when they need it. Banks using this technology are scanning approximately 23,000 documents per day.[10] Banks using the paper environment are indexing approximately 2,300 documents per day.[11] As you can see, EFC can be extremely beneficial to banks. These electronic images function the same way as paper documents do.

A mortgage application is a great example. In the manual paper environment, a person's mortgage file is literally a file folder containing all related mortgage documents, including the mortgage applications, credit file, etc. If a mortgage officer needs to review a customer's file, he/she must either be sent the file or go to the location of where the file is and physically pull the file from storage. With EFC, all mortgage documents are converted to images and the originals are recycled. Then, instead of using paper documents, the mortgage officers (or anyone involved in the mortgage application process within the bank) can pull up the customer's file on a computer screen and use the images to perform all necessary functions in processing a mortgage application or answering a customer inquiry. This technology, as in the paper environment, also allows the bank employee to add or delete information as needed to a file. As a matter of fact, an employee can access the image files when needed regardless of whether or not someone else is using the file or if they are in the bank or at another location. Electronic image documents allow more than one user to work on the document simultaneously, if necessary. Two employees can access and use the same document at the same time.

Another example would be customer service inquiries. When receiving a call (i.e. about a customer's loan status), customer service representatives would have to take their name and number down and then search through a microfilm library or paper files at a number of different locations for documentation before an inquiry could be addressed. Once the information was gathered, customer service representatives would have to make an additional call to the customer before resolution could occur and the customer service representative could respond to the inquiry.[12] With EFC, customer service representatives can give bank customers real-time information on the status of their business with the bank, regardless of the nature of the business, such as loan applications, billing disputes, credit card applications, etc.

Banks are employing EFC because it reduces personnel costs, eliminates unnecessary duplication, and reduces processing time and costs.

CHECK PROCESSING

In today's banking environment, many banks processing checks use the traditional technology: a labor-intensive movement of written checks from point to point. The traditional check collection process involves the following steps: The customer writes a paper check to purchase goods and services. The receiver of the check (the Payee) deposits the paper check into his/her bank account. A teller at the payee's bank receives the check and forwards it to the processing center. There the check is encoded with the MICR line. Then the check passes through a sorter and is sent to the customer's bank for payment. The customer's bank processes the physical paper check and returns it to the customer with the monthly banking account statement. Please note, that in some cases, the customer's bank recycles the physical paper check and includes reduced-sized images of the check in the monthly statement.

In this traditional technology, each check has to be handled up to fourteen times and about ten thousand of every million checks that go through sorters are rejected and have to be reprocessed manually.[13] This check collection process is extremely labor-intensive. Although it is not as slow as check processing without MICR, it is still slow enough to not meet customer's real-time demand on their accounts. For this reason, banks are exploring Electronic Check Presentment (ECP) and image processing to speed up the check collection process.

Electronic Check Presentment (ECP) is a process in which funds are exchanged via wire between the customer and the payee's banks, before the actual paper reaches the customer's bank. ECP involves the following steps: First, a payee's bank is presented with a check for deposit. Then, the payee's bank uses a check reader capable of reading handwriting to record the routing and other information from the check MICR line. Thirdly, the payee's bank wires that information to the bank on which the check is drawn. Then, the customer's bank takes the MICR information that was wired and processes the check. If the funds are available, the customer's bank sends an electronic message notifying the payee's bank that the check is bad. This technology is currently being used by some banks. However, since the physical paper check is sent after the MICR code lines are wired, this technology does not eliminate the transferring of checks from bank to bank.

Ideally, banks are searching for a way to immediately, upon receipt of the checks, recycle the paper checks and only send electronic images over the telephone lines, through a modem (A modem is a device allowing a user on a computer to call via telephone lines another user on another computer to communicate and share information). Thereby, terminating the paper chase ...

Image processing in relation to check processing is the process of using a camera-like device to capture a digital image of both sides of a check, storing it on a networked computer terminal, and sending these electronic images (via a modem) in lieu of the physical paper check for payment.

In addition to exploring ECP, banks are also exploring the image processing technology in the hopes to find an efficient way to do away with the paper trail. Image processing in relation to check processing is the process of using a camera-like device to capture a digital image of both sides of a check, storing it on a networked computer terminal, recycling the physical paper checks, and sending these electronic images (via a modem) in lieu of the physical paper check for payment. Network refers to two or more computers being connected together so that two or more people can look at a file and work on that file simultaneously or at different times.

Here is how it would work: The customer would write a paper check to purchase goods and services. The receiver of the check (the Payee) deposits the paper check into his/her bank account. A teller at the payee's bank receives the check and forwards it to the preparation center for sorting. There the check is sorted on a document processor equipped with 1) an image scanner to create a digitized image of the check to store on the computer and 2) a check reader to read handwritten and typed information on the checks (i.e. amount of check, routing and transit information, account number, etc.) to automatically enter into the bank's mainframe system. A mainframe is an early computer dinosaur system developed in 1960s. (Some mainframe systems are in use today, but the computer industry is trying to replace them with personal computer networks). Then, if the checks are successfully passed through the document processor and can be read by the sorter, the checks are sent through device called a power encoder that encodes the check information as check images are displayed on the computer screen. Once all the checks are scanned into the computer network system, the physical paper checks are recycled and the image of the check is transmitted to the paying bank for payment. The paying bank (customer's bank) then processes the check information almost instantaneously and returns to the customer with the monthly banking account statement reduced-sized images of the check. Therefore, in the future, image files will facilitate account entry, account and transit correction, proof, balancing and reconciliation—all performed without ever handling the check.[14] By the end of the decade, you will see this image check processing being used in most banks.

SMARTCARDS

SmartCard technology offers a wide range of products, such as credit, debit, ATM access, cash cards in five currencies, securities trading, insurance purchases, and related products. It also keeps store-visit records, customer demographics, frequent shopper points and is easy to use in different chains.[15] SmartCards is a new way to pay for everyday necessities without having to carry around a pocket full of change. Therefore, it is sometimes known as a multiple-service card or an electronic change purse, instead of a SmartCard.

Figure 8-1
Measuring SmartCard Opportunities:
Two Points of View

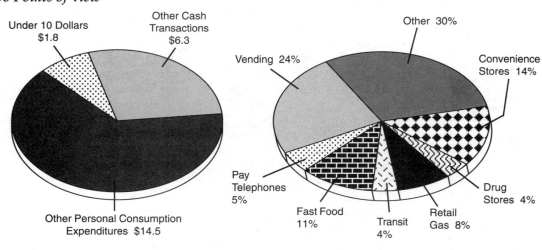

CONSUMER TRANSACTIONS
WORLDWIDE (IN TRILLIONS)

WHERE 198 BILLION SMALL-TICKET
PURCHASES OCCUR

American Banker, Thursday, October 6, 1994, page 14   Sources: Visa, MasterCard

The *SmartCard* is a plastic card with a microchip (instead of a magnetic strip as in credit cards) in which its general function is the processing of cashless payments within a credit limit defined by a bank without the on-line authorization (as needed in using credit cards). Using a SmartCard involves a bank customer being provided with a SmartCard (instead of an ATM card) for access to terminals, with a personal identification number. A bank customer can load up the SmartCard with money at the ATM machine, based on what he/she has in the bank account. Then, as explained previously, the bank customer can use the SmartCard for a wide range of products and services.

Europe started using SmartCards in 1995. By 1996 there was more than one card per adult in Europe. This means more than 300 million cards and 6,000 million annual transactions. Usage of cards is growing rather faster than the number of cards. The number of card payments has increased by over one billion transactions in just two years to an annual total of six billion card transactions. Debit cards predominate in Europe, in contrast to US world of credit cards.[16]

In the past, United States companies gave little thought to SmartCards. Then, in 1996, Visa International introduced the first SmartCard in the United States: Visa Cash. The Visa Cash Card is used instead of cash to make small purchases such as a cup of coffee, newspaper, pay phones, cinema tickets, or public transportation. There are two main types of VISA Cash cards: Disposable and Reloadable. Disposable cards are loaded with a pre-determined value. These cards typically come in denominations of local currency, such as $10. When the value of the card is used, the card is discarded and a new card may be purchased. These cards may be dispensed from machines which accept a variety of payment methods. Reloadable cards come without a predefined value. Cash value is reloaded onto the card at specialized terminals and ATMs. When the value is used up, you can load the card again. It's fast, convenient and easy.[17]

ELECTRONIC BANKING

Electronic banking means having the speed and convenience of a comprehensive range of banking services and financial data at your fingertips ... without ever having to leave your home or office.[18] Since the 1980s, electronic banking has been explored without much success. Now, after more than a decade, electronic banking has made an unstoppable comeback. Electronic banking is a new generation of around-the-clock financial services that you can access through a variety of devices such as personal computers, screen phones, touch-tone telephones, personal intelligent communicators and Internet access that can be located almost anywhere.[19]

PERSONAL COMPUTERS

Electronic Personal Computer banking is about convenience, reliability and security that will save the consumer time and expand their banking options 24 hours a day, 7 days a week, 365 days a year. With financial software featuring easy Windows-based tools (such as Quicken ® or Microsoft Money ®), you can use your PC to pay bills or make payments to anyone in the United States (without having to write a check or buy stamps); transfer funds between accounts (including credit card accounts); check balances; verify deposits and withdrawals; confirm that checks have cleared; receive a transaction history; place stop payments on checks; send a message to a Customer Service Representative; schedule regular, fixed-amount payments, such as a mortgage payment; review account activity for the past 30-45 days; and check interest rates on Cds and money market accounts right from your home or office.[20] This electronic banking power is available from many financial institutions and major financial software providers. Some examples of this PC software are HomeLink and PC Banking.

Using PCs is just as safe as using an ATM. A free telephone call gets you into the system. From there, you simply enter your Card number and password and start banking. Your password becomes encrypted when you enter it and is then transmitted through a separate network that only your bank's users can access. [21,22]

SCREEN PHONE

A *screen phone* is a powerful new tool that integrates the processing efficiency of a computer with the ease and convenience of a home telephone. A key feature of the device is its screen which uses ATM-like graphics to visually display service options and information. The screen is supported by a built-in microprocessor and keyboard. You use these features to select and access a choice of financial services, search an electronic telephone directory for a number and have it automatically dialed for you, and make purchases from retail catalog merchants. The screen phone offers the advantages of both off-line and on-line capabilities. When using a screen phone to pay bills, you enter and review your payment instructions without tying up your phone line or incurring high phone costs. Just stay off-line until you're ready to go and then press a button to exchange on-line data with your financial institution.[23]

TOUCH TONE TELEPHONES

Today, touch-tone telephones can be linked to Voice Response Units (VRUs) at financial institutions. These automated systems put a range of banking conveniences, such as electronic bill payment at your fingertips. VRU systems are less versatile than PC or screen phone technologies, but have evolved quite a bit in recent years.

Voice Recognition: Lets you bank by phone without having to use the keypad buttons. The VRU matches your voice responses on the phone with voice responses that you recorded when joining the service.

Voice confirmation: Lets you confirm your bill payment instructions by hearing them played back in your own pre-recorded voice.

Speech recognition: Lets you bank by phone without having to use telephone keypad buttons or pre-record your voice. The VRU "understands" the human voice.

These and other improvements are making the touch-tone telephone an increasingly easy, secure, and flexible way to do your banking from just about anywhere. [24]

PERSONAL INTELLIGENT COMMUNICATOR (PIC)

A PIC packs the capabilities of a personal computer, telephone, pager, fax machine, modem, calculator, datebook, notebook, and file cabinet into a portable, hand-held unit that fits into your pocket. PIC offers financial and communications convenience that is hard to beat. [25]

INTERNET ACCESS

As the Internet continues to spread in every direction around the world, more and more companies are coming on board with electronic banking offerings. Services are similar to those described in the Personal Computer section of this chapter, but free you from the need to obtain and install financial software. You simply go on-line to the company of your choice to obtain the services you need. Security is the challenge that goes hand in hand with this new global convenience. Companies such as Edify and Five Paces are working closely with financial institutions to create a secure on-line environment where your accounts are always protected when you use the Internet for banking purposes. Some examples of Internet Banking options (that at the end of 1996 were in pilot testing) are Internet Bill Pay, Fidelity Web Xpress[SM].[26,27]

Towards the end of 1996 there was over 200 different banks operating web sites, and this number is increasing rapidly. Around half of all the banks on the Internet are based in the US and Canada. This is where penetration of computers is the highest, and where many of the individuals and companies driving the expansion of the web are based. [28]

Banks are participating in the web by having a site which offers the company logo and perhaps a contact telephone number; information about themselves and their products; general financial advice, sometimes with a level of interactivity; information on a banks' non-bank activities, such as charity functions; selling financial products; and account services. A very small number of banks have begun to offer account transaction services on the Internet. This means that they are using the Internet to offer everyday transactions such as balance inquiry, transfer between accounts, bill payments and even 401(K) transactions.[29]

THE OUTLOOK FOR INFORMATION TECHNOLOGY IN BANKING

In order to meet the customer's increasing demands for easy access to real-time account information and speedy response time, banks have had to introduce new information technology tools for its back room operations (i.e. electronic file cabinets) and products and services (i.e. image statements, and SmartCards). So with all the great new technology accomplishments, where is information technology in banking headed?

The technology revolution is now moving into cyberspace: the World Wide Web, and "virtual" financial statements permitting instantaneous updating of financial statistics.[30] Internet options will expand dramatically to include electronic commerce, stock quotes, portfolio management, and many other financial services without requiring unique software for each service. Banks providing a full range of services via the Internet will increase to over 300 by the year 2006.[31]

By 2006, as bank PC connections make for cheap and efficient withdrawals and multimedia information kiosks provide interactive services, automated teller machines will become a thing of the past. Interactive television also is on the horizon, offering to bring a broad range of financial, shopping and information services into your home. When you need cash, for example, you may be able to download value onto a SmartCard simply by touching your television screen.[32] Each of these efforts is stretching technology to gain competitive advantage within the limits of service, security, cost and scalability.

CONCLUSION

In the information marketplace, data creates an appetite for more data. Complexity begets complexity. And providing data creates a natural incentive to extract more value from that data.[33] New technologies permit a company not only to streamline financial operations but also to exploit unused resources of information to attract new customers and sell more to existing customers.[34]

Banks alone will spend $19 billion on technology this year, according to Ernst & Young and the American Bankers Association. Close to half of all bank transactions are currently done outside the branch, and that percentage is expected to rise. So as geographical convenience ceases to matter and customers grow comfortable with PC banking and banking by phone, banks have found they must work hard to be the brand of choice. Accessed via the Internet, systems can offer clients a menu of services—including on-line account balances, E-mail connection to their broker, and bulletins of news and investments to consider.[35]

Although the Internet may change many areas of retail banking, one thing at least is likely to stay the same. The relationships that a bank has with its customers will remain of central importance to that banks' competitiveness and profitability.[36]

NOTES

1. "Banking Technology as a Competitive Weapon," http://www.cityscape.co.uk.

2. Hollis, Donald R., *The Bankers Magazine*, "Leveraging Information Technology Through Reliable Software." Boston, MA: Warren, Gorham & Lamont, 1994, p. 23–27.

3. Visa Home Page—http://www.visa.com.

4. Sellers, Rick, *Bank Management*, "Getting It Together in the Electronic Marketplace." Chicago, IL: Bank Administration Institute, 1994, p. 50–55.

5. "ATMs and Cash Dispensers 1997"—http://www.rbrldn.demon.co.uk.

6. Kekewich, Roy, *Canadian Banker*, "Imaging the Future." May–June 1991, pp. 6–10.

7. Ida, Jeanne, *American Banker*, "Smaller Banks for Imaging, ABA Finds." September 22, 1993, p. 21.

8. Cristoforo, Jerry, *Bankers Monthly*, "Document Tracking in the Electronic Filing Cabinet," New York: NY: Hanover Publishers Inc., January 1993, p. 22–23.

9. Ibid.

10. Ibid.

11. Ibid.

12. Ibid.

13. Kekewich, Roy, *Canadian Banker*, "Imaging the Future." May–June 1991, pp. 6–10.

14. Ibid.

15. Svigals, Jerome, *American Banker*, "Microchip Cards Offer New Uses, Require New Rules," Tuesday, January, 25, 1994, p. 14.

16. "Payment Cards in Europe,"—http://www.rbrldn.demon.co.uk

17. Visa Home Page—http://www.visa.com.
18. Standard Bank Home Page—http://www.sbic.co.za.
19. Visa Home Page—http://www.visa.com.
20. Citibank Home Page—http://www.citibank.com.
21. BayBank Home Page—http://www.baybank.com.
22. Bank of Boston Home Page—http://www.bkb.com.
23. Visa Home Page—http://www.visa.com.
24. Ibid.
25. Ibid.
26. Wells Fargo Personal Finance Home Page—http://wellsfargo.com.
27. Visa Home Page—http://www.visa.com.
28. "Banking in the Online World"—http://www.rbrldn.demon.co.uk.
29. Visa Home Page—http://www.visa.com.
30. "Finance's Info-Tech Revolution", Business Week, October 28, 1996, p. 129.
31. Infragence - Electronic Banking—http://www.infragence.com.
32. "Finance's Info-Tech Revolution," *Business Week*, October 28, 1996, p. 129.
33. Teitelman, Robert, Institutional Investor, "Inside the State Street Machine". Boston, MA, June 1994.
34. "Finance's Info-Tech Revolution," *Business Week*, October 28, 1996, p. 129.
35. "On the Cutting Edge," Business Week, October 28, 1996, pp. 13–141.
36. "Banking in the Online World"—http://www.rbrldn.demon.co.uk.

Quicken is a registered trademark of Intuit, Inc.

Microsoft and Windows are registered trademarks of Microsoft Corporation.

STUDY AND REVIEW QUESTIONS

1. Define information technology.
2. Discuss the impact of technology on the banking industry. Be sure to mention its product and services.
3. Define image processing. Compare and contrast the three types of image processing being used in banks.
4. Define ECP and its relationship to the check processing system.
5. Define and describe SmartCards and its role in the United States vs. Europe.
6. Describe electronic banking. Discuss each of the types of electronic banking being used.
7. Explain what the future holds for the banking industry in relation to information technology.

BIBLIOGRAPHY

"ATMs and Cash Dispensers 1997"—http://www.rbrldn.demon.co.uk.

"Banking in the Online World"—http://www.rbrldn.demon.co.uk.

"Banking Technology as a Competitive Weapon," http://www.cityscape.co.uk.

"Beyond Bean-Counting," *Business Week,* October 28, 1996, pp. 130–133.

"Finance's Info-Tech Revolution," *Business Week,* October 28, 1996, p. 129.

"On the Cutting Edge," *Business Week,* October 28, 1996, pp. 134–141.

"Payment Cards in Europe"—http://www.rbrldn.demon.co.uk.

"The Future of PrePayment Cards and Electronic Purses," January 1997—http://www.rbrldn.demon.co.uk.

"The Net Hits the Big Time," *Business Week,* October 28, 1996, pp. 142–144.

Bank of Boston Home Page—http://www.bkb.com.

BayBank Home Page—http://www.baybank.com.

Borowsky, Mark, *Bank Management*, "Terminating the Paper Chase." Chicago, IL: Faulkner & Gray, April 1993, pp. 22–25.

Borowsky, Mark, *Bank Management*, "Banks Are Betting on Electronic Present-ment." Chicago, IL: Faulkner & Gray, April 1993, pp. 26–27.

Citibank Home Page—http://www.citibank.com.

Cristoforo, Jerry, *Bankers Monthly*, "Document Tracking in the Electronic Fil-ing Cabinet," New York: NY: Hanover Publishers Inc., January 1993, p. 22–23.

Derfler, Frank J. and Les Freed, PC Computing, How Networks Work. Emeryville, CA: Ziff-Davis Press, 1993.

Fidelity Home Page—http://www.fidelity.com.

Hollis, Donald R., *The Bankers Magazine*, "Leveraging Information Technol-ogy Through Reliable Software." Boston, MA: Warren, Gorham & Lamont, 1994, p. 23–27.

Ida, Jeanne, *American Banker*, "Smaller Banks for Imaging, ABA Finds." Sep-tember 22, 1993, p. 21.

Infragence—Electronic Banking—http://www.infragence.com.

Kekewich, Roy, *Canadian Banker*, "Imaging the Future." May–June 1991, pp. 6–10.

Laudeman, Mark, *The Bankers Magazine,* "Technology's Role in Evaluating Business Borrowers," November–December 1994, pp. 35–39.

Murtaugh, Jeanne and Clifford Titus, *Financial Technology Review,* "Give Tech-nology a Chance," January/February 1994, p. 80.

Nekopulos, James M., *The Bankers Magazine,* "Mortgages in the Next Millen-nium," September-October 1994, pp. 22–23.

Radding, Alan, *Bank Management,* "Imaging Vendors Shape Processing." Chi-cago, IL: Faulkner & Gray, April 1993, pp. 28–33.

Reiman, Tyrus, *Canadian Banker,* "Technology at the Leading Edge," January–February 1991, pp. 24–30.

Sellers, Rick, *Bank Management,* "Getting It Together in the Electronic Market-place." Chicago, IL: Bank Administration Institute, 1994, p. 50–55.

Standard Bank Home Page—http://www.sbic.co.za.

State Street Documents, Marketing Services Division, September, 1996, p. 5.

Svigals, Jerome, *American Banker,* "Microchip Cards Offer New Uses, Require New Rules," Tuesday, January, 25, 1994, p. 14.

Teitelman, Robert, *Institutional Investor,* "Inside the State Street Machine." Boston, MA, June 1994.

Visa Home Page—http://www.visa.com.

Wells Fargo Personal Finance Home Page—http://wellsfargo.com.

White, Ron, *PC Computing,* How Computers Work. Emeryville CA: Ziff-Davis Press, 1993.

Wren, Peter, *Canadian Banker,* "Automation's Challenge to Letters of Credit," September-October 1991, pp. 14–18.

BANK INVESTMENTS AND
PROFITABILITY MANAGEMENT
Michael S. Tallo

INTRODUCTION

This chapter will discuss some of the various investment options available to a bank. Various types of investments such as stocks, bonds, municipal obligations, and the risk involved will be examined, along with some general investment strategies.

LEARNING OBJECTIVES

Upon completion of this chapter, students should have a better understanding of the following:

1. The investment process in the bank
2. The bond and stock markets
3. Asset/Liability Management
4. Balance Sheet and Income Statement Analysis

OVERVIEW

A bank may find itself with millions of dollars to work with each day. This cash may be used as tellers' cash, left in the vaults, or put to work through loans or various instruments in the investment field. Each bank must make these decisions every day in order to be profitable while satisfying depositor needs. Before a bank can invest or lend any money, it must address three areas: liquidity, safety, and income.

Liquidity

Liquidity is defined as the ability to convert an asset into cash. Some assets, such as stocks, Treasury obligations, and negotiable certificates of deposit are very liquid. There exist markets where an investor can sell these assets for cash in operation every day. Other assets, such as loans and buildings are not as liquid. *Safety* refers to either the probability of repayment, in the case of a loan, or the probability you will receive face value for assets such as stocks and bonds. Investments may be liquid, but there exists a probability that you will not receive face value due to a change in interest rates or other factors at work in the market. Income is a function of the risk involved. The riskier the investment or loan, the greater the return the investor should demand. Bonds with a longer term to maturity generally yield a higher return.

Liquidity is the first area of importance since a bank must be able to satisfy customer demands for withdrawals. Customers deposit their money with the expectation that it will be available to them when they need it. While it is highly unlikely that all customers will present themselves on any single day to withdraw their funds, banks can assume that some percentage will withdraw their funds, depending on the type of deposit or even some seasonal factor. Customers who have their funds in a time certificate will generally have to wait until the maturity date to withdraw the funds. Passbook customers can withdraw their funds at anytime, but seasonal factors such as Christmas or April 15th tax payments may place a higher withdrawal demand than other times of the year. Banks must keep some cash available to meet these demands and should monitor cash levels so that they are maintained at some minimum level. Currency represents a non-earning asset and as such generates no income. Maintaining some minimum-maximum currency level allows a bank to use its assets efficiently.

Credit demands also have an effect on the liquidity levels of a bank. Customers who have established a long relationship with the bank often have loan needs. They expect the bank to be able to lend them the necessary funds, provided they are a good credit risk. These requests are also a vital part of calculating adequate liquidity levels for a bank.

Liquidity can be divided into three categories: cash in vaults, bank balances at correspondent banks, and some short term investments. Cash on hand and in vaults represents a bank's first line of liquidity. Bank balances at correspondent banks or the Federal Reserve represent a second line of liquidity. It should be noted that while both cash and correspondent bank balances do not generate interest income, correspondent bank balances often generate income in terms of "soft dollars". These soft dollars can be used to offset correspondent charges for providing other services. The third line of liquidity would be those short term investments that can be sold or liquidated quickly at no loss to a bank. This third line of liquidity gives an institution both liquidity and income.

Safety

Safety is the second area that must be evaluated before an investment decision can be made. A bank must make safe investments in order to protect the depositors' funds. A bank that does not make safe investment decisions not only suffers a loss in terms of income and principal, but continued losses become public knowledge and can erode customers' confidence in the bank.

While safety is an important factor, it cannot be the overriding one. A bank that stresses safety often passes up many opportunities and can eventually be accused of not serving the public. Banks must minimize risk but should not avoid it completely. A bank must be adequately paid in terms of interest rate for the safety or credit risk it takes.

Income

Income is the third area of examination before an investment is made. Banks must generate income so that depositors can receive their interest, employees their pay, vendors their sums due, and stockholders their dividend. While banks must generate income, bankers cannot ignore safety or liquidity. The newspapers and magazines are full of stories that describe bankers who ignored safety when building large loan portfolios, only to see those loans turn into a non-performing status. Some of these banks never recover from those losses and are either acquired by the regulators or another bank.

When evaluating these alternatives it can be said that liquidity is the most important factor. Without sufficient liquidity a bank can quickly lose the customer's confidence either by being unable to satisfy withdrawal demands or loan requests. Once a bank has a sufficient liquidity base, it can then begin to invest funds in a safe manner to generate income.

Market Risk

When banks invest in the stock and bond market, they face market risk, as opposed to the credit risk incurred when lending funds. Market risk is evident in the stock market where the price of a stock can rise or decline dramatically overnight. One only has to remember the events of October 17, 1987 as an example of the risk involved. It should be noted that risk is not always negative. While risk is generally thought of as a reduction in value, there is always the probability, or risk, that the investment will increase in value.

Market risk is also evident when investing in bonds. Here the major risk is a change in interest rates. Bonds are a legal obligation of the government or a corporation as such, the holder is guaranteed principal and interest at maturity. Market risk is important should the holder want to sell the bond before maturity. If interest rates were to rise, the price or value of the bond will decline. Conversely, when interest rates decline, the relative market value of the bonds rise.

Interest Rates

A brief review of the theory of interest rates may be in order at this point. For the purpose of this discussion one should simply remember that the longer the term of the investment or loan, the higher the interest rate. The investor, the person buying the security, is assuming a risk that interest rates will rise which reduces the value of the investment. Thus, when the investment is made they require a fair return. The shorter the term of the investment, the smaller the risk since the investor has the opportunity to re-invest within a short period of time.

INVESTMENT ALTERNATIVES

Banks have two major areas into which they can invest funds, loans, or the stock and bond markets. Investment in the stock market though may be limited to certain institutions located in the New England States due to powers granted them by the various states, which were grandfathered to them in

1991. The basic function of a bank is to accumulate deposits from individuals and corporations, and then lend those funds to other individuals, businesses, and government. In fact, legislation has been passed, the Community Reinvestment Act, which requires banks to lend money back into the areas where deposits are generated. Given this as background, investments in the form of stocks and bonds often receive a low priority when management has limited funds to invest.

Investments can serve many purposes in a bank's overall asset/liability structure. The investment portfolio can be used as a source of liquidity by investing in short term obligations. In this fashion, money not needed for immediate use can generate income over a 30, 60 or 90 day term, and still be available to meet liquidity needs at the end of the term. Also, a bank may choose to invest in what is often referred to as "blue chip" stocks. Here the funds may generate some dividend income, portions of which may be tax exempt, while at the same time the bank is striving for long term appreciation. The portfolio can also be used to "lock in a spread". For example, assume a customer deposits $1,000,000 for 8 years. A bank may choose to invest in an 8 year investment and lock in a spread between interest expense on the deposit and the interest income on the investment. A loan may not provide the same security as the customer may choose to pay off the loan early and the bank may not be able to re-invest those funds at a favorable spread.

Let us now review some of the investment alternatives available to a bank. For the purposes of this text we have left out most of the financial calculations and concentrate on a basic understanding of the instrument and its use.

United States Treasury Obligations

Treasury obligations can be divided into three groups. Treasury bills which have a maturity of less than one year, Treasury notes which range from one to five years, and Treasury bonds which have maturity dates greater than five years.

Treasury bills generally have maturity dates of either 91 or 182 days, but can range up to one year. The 91 and 182 bills are sold at auction every Monday, unless the Federal Debt ceiling has been reached. Should the government reach the debt ceiling no further debt can be incurred by the Treasury until Congress increases the ceiling. This has occurred more than once during the 1980s. Treasury bills are sold at a discount. For example, you might pay $9,900 for a 91 day bill and receive $10,000 at maturity. The $100 difference represents your interest.

Banks often use Treasury bills as part of their asset/liability management strategy. Funds that are not needed immediately can be invested for a relatively short period of time and earn income.

Treasury notes are generally issued for two to five year terms but can be issued for a period of anywhere from one to five years. This investment could be used to offset some term deposit activity, again matching assets and liabilities. Treasury bonds represent long term borrowing by the government as these bonds have maturities ranging from 5 to 35 years. These bonds can be used as a long-term, fixed-income investment, or as a trading tool depending on the bank. Some bankers use these bonds as part of their trading portfolio, utilizing changes in interest rates to generate gains. The obvious risk here is what happens if the banker makes an error in forecasting rates. Large trading losses instead of gains would be incurred.

United States Agency Obligation

Closely related to U.S. Treasury obligations would be Federal Agency Obligations. While they are not direct obligations of the U.S. Government, they are closely related. Treasury obligations are explicitly guaranteed by the government as they have the power to tax or simply print currency to satisfy the obligation. Obligations issued by Federal Agencies do not share directly in those guarantees, but unofficially, the U.S. Government has stated that they would not allow these agencies to default. Because it is an unofficial guarantee, Agency obligations return a slightly higher yield than similar maturities of the Treasury. These agencies include the Federal Land Bank, the Federal Home Loan Bank, the Government National Mortgage Association, the Federal National Mortgage Association, the World Bank, and others. These government corporations were each established to assist certain segments of society. For example, the Federal Home Loan Bank, the Government National Mortgage Association and the Federal National Mortgage Association are all related to and involved with the housing and mortgage markets. The World Bank was established for the purpose of assisting in developing or reconstructing countries. The World Bank lends money to nations which are trying to develop their resources.

Advantages of Treasury and Agency Obligations

The major advantages to Treasury and Agency obligations would be their marketability, quality and stability. There is always a ready market in which investors can liquidate their holdings if necessary. The bond rating agencies, such as Moody's or Standard and Poor give government securities their highest rating. The government has the power to tax and print money, thus the investor is always guaranteed repayment, but no guarantee is given as to the purchasing power of the dollars they may receive.

Drawbacks of Treasury and Agency Obligations

The disadvantage of government securities is the risk of inflation. As rates rise, the income or rate of the bond is fixed, and the value of the bond declines. Again, the investor is guaranteed principal and interest at maturity, but may be sacrificing income by holding on to the bond. Should the investor sell the bond, a loss would be incurred.

Municipal Securities

Another investment alternative would be municipal securities. These are borrowings by state or local governments and agencies. They are generally a safe investment as only a few issues have defaulted in relation to the total municipal debt outstanding. These issues also generate income, in fact it is tax exempt income. Income derived from municipal securities is exempt from federal income taxes, and depending on the issue, may also be exempt at the state and local level. Thus, while the coupon rate may appear low, say 8.50% when compared to 11.50% for a similar term Treasury obligation, the tax exempt status would increase the yield. On the other hand, as Congress changes the tax laws of the nation, banks cannot deduct interest and dividends paid on a portion of its deposits if funds are invested in municipal securities. For example, a bank that has $10 million invested in municipal securities will lose the interest and dividend deduction of $10 million of deposits. There are a few securities issued by cities and town that are called "bank qualified" and are exempt from this rule. Thus, a bank that invests in bank qualified municipal securities will generate tax exempt income and preserve the ability to deduct the interest and dividends paid on deposits.

General obligation securities are issued by state, cities and towns. These obligations are backed by the investor's faith in the issuer. States, cities and towns have many ways to generate income through taxes and fees which help contribute to their credit rating. Of course, how the state or city manages its finances is also taken into consideration by the rating authorities.

Obligations are also issued on a district basis. School or park districts issue obligations and may rely on taxes or user fees to insure repayment. Other revenue bonds may be those issued to build tunnels, bridges, or water and sewer lines. Those who use the service will pay fees which are used to pay the obligations. Revenue bonds are not without risk though. Investors should analyze the project carefully to determine whether it will be a success. Bridges have been built using revenue bonds and consumers have then altered their travel plans to avoid the bridge. Thus the project does not generate the revenue expected and the bondholders may have to absorb the loss.

Corporate Bonds

A major source of funding for corporations in the United States would be bonds. The sale of bonds is cheaper than issuing additional stock, and bond interest is deductible under present tax laws.

A *bond* is a promise to pay a specific sum of money at a specific point in time at a certain rate of interest. The corporation issuing the bonds is borrowing money from the bondholders who base their investment decision on the corporation's credit rating. Firms such as Moodys or Standard and Poor issue their opinion of a firm's credit rating which has a direct impact on the company's ability to borrow and the rate they will have to pay. Those firms with a low rating, BB or less, would pay a higher rate of interest to borrow money compared to a firm rated A or AAA. The U.S. Government would have a rating of AAA.

Each bond issue would be accompanied by an indenture. This *indenture* is an agreement between the corporation and a trustee, usually a bank or a trust department, who represent the bondholders. This indenture would include authorization of the bond issue by the corporation, the interest rate, the maturity date, any property pledged by the corporation as security, and any other promises or commitments made by the company. Some bond indentures include a call feature which allows the corporation to redeem the bonds prior to maturity, often at a premium to the bondholder. This call feature could allow a company to redeem bonds which carry a high rate of interest and possibly replace them with new borrowings at a lower rate.

Bonds can be secured or unsecured. *Unsecured obligations* simply rely on the full faith and credit of the company. *Secured obligations* mean that the company has pledged some collateral to secure the bond. Mortgage bonds are secured by real estate, equipment trust bonds are secured by machinery, and collateral bonds could be secured by stocks or other bonds owned by the company. A mortgage bond secured by an office building is generally more attractive than one secured by an oil refinery. Should the issuer default, it is easier to sell the office building than the oil refinery.

Convertible bonds offer the bondholder an option to redeem their bonds for common stock. This conversion option is outlined in the indenture agreement and details the period when the conversion can be exercised and the price or ratio. Convertible bonds provide security in terms of principal and interest as well as the possibility of participating in capital appreciation.

A bond is a promise to pay a specific sum of money at a specific point in time at a certain rate of interest.

Convertible bonds offer the bondholder an option to redeem their bonds for common stock.

When analyzing various bonds for investment purposes, the following basic areas should be addressed:

1. What is the company's ability to repay?
2. What is the interest coverage? How many times does the company earn income sufficient to pay its bondholders their annual interest payment?
3. What is the company's prior history?
4. How large is the company? What are its competitive strengths and weaknesses?

Stocks

Another area of investment is the stock market. This area is available to a relatively few number of banks in the United States due to powers granted to them by the states in which they were originally incorporated. Banking legislation enacted in 1991 grandfathered these institutions, but does not allow other institutions to invest in these instruments.

Stocks represent an ownership position in the company and only guarantee the owner a share of the earnings and a claim to assets after all other creditors have been satisfied. The common stockholder does have voting rights and can vote on issues such as management, issuance of debt, issuance of additional stock, and other matters. Some stock may be issued without voting rights but it is not a common feature in the marketplace.

Preferred stock is a security which can exhibit certain features of both common stock and bonds. Dividends on preferred stock can be guaranteed, similar to interest payments on bonds. Preferred stock has a preferred claim over common stockholders in the event of a liquidation of the assets of the company. Dividend payments on preferred stock can be cumulative, meaning if the company does not pay the preferred dividend that amount will be added to any future dividend payments. Dividends to preferred stockholders must be current before any payments can be made to common stockholders. Preferred stock can also be participating. This means that after the common shareholder receives some set amount, the preferred shareholder will share in some additional dividends.

Dividends on preferred stock are usually expressed as a percentage of par value. *Par value* is the value the company has placed on the stock and has no relation to its market value. Preferred dividends of 7% on stock having a par value of $100 means the shareholder would receive a dividend of $7.00 per year.

Dividends are not always paid in the form of cash. Companies may declare stock dividends where shareholders receive additional shares of stock in lieu of or in addition to cash. Stock dividends are often used by small or growth companies where cash can be better utilized to purchase additional equipment or inventory. A 25 percent stock dividend would give each shareholder one additional share for each four shares owned. There is a technical difference between stock dividends and stock splits. A stock dividend reduces retained earnings and increases capital stock by the market value of the stock on the declaration date. Stock splits have no monetary effect on the balance sheet, other than reducing the book value of the shares.

Stocks represent an ownership position in the company and only guarantee the owner a share of the earnings and a claim to assets after all other creditors have been satisfied.

Preferred stock is a security which can exhibit certain features of both common stock and bonds. Dividends on preferred stock can be guaranteed, similar to interest payments on bonds. Preferred stock has a preferred claim over common stockholders in the event of a liquidation of the assets of the company.

Other Investments

Banks also invest liquid funds in other areas such as overnight federal funds, certificates of deposit, and term federal funds. *Federal funds* represent overnight borrowing between banks. These funds mature every day and the investor has the option to invest the funds for another day or redeem the investment and utilize the cash for other purposes. This vehicle allows the bank to have liquidity while at the same time earning interest income.

Certificates of deposit and *term federal funds* are another short term investment a bank may utilize. These instruments are offered with maturities ranging from 7 to 180 days. These investments are not insured and term federal funds are classified as a loan for regulatory purposes rather than an investment.

REGULATORY CONSIDERATIONS

The various regulators which monitor banks have regulations concerning investments and the maximum levels a bank may maintain. Depending on the bank charter obtained there may be limits regarding total investment in any one company or industry. For example, regulations may apply which limit a bank's investment in IBM to no more than 2 percent of surplus and further limit investment in computer-related companies to no more than 10 percent of surplus. These same restrictions also apply to loans to any one individual or related party. A bank must be aware of the regulatory limits and monitor the investment portfolio to insure they are followed.

ASSET/LIABILITY MANAGEMENT

A discussion of a bank's investment portfolio should include some analysis of asset/liability management. Asset/liability management is the basic process by which a bank examines its balance sheet and makes decisions concerning; the maturities of assets, the maturities and types of liabilities, a forecast of interest rates, and the overall effect of those factors on bank profitability.

Gap refers to the maturity or re-pricing opportunities for assets and liabilities.

One term used in asset/liability management is "gap." *Gap* refers to the maturity or re-pricing opportunities for assets and liabilities. A bank will add up the total dollar value of assets maturing or re-pricing in a particular time period, 30, 60, or 90 days, and compare that to the dollar value of liabilities maturing or re-pricing in the same time frame. The difference between the two is referred to as a gap. The results will have different meanings if interest rates are forecasted to be rising or falling. Banks may wish to be *asset sensitive*, that is having more assets mature or re-price if they believe rates are rising. Conversely, they would want to be *liability sensitive* if they forecast interest rates to fall.

Most banks are not perfectly matched as many asset/liability managers believe banks should assume some level of interest rate risk, rather than credit risk. Interest rate risk refers to the net increase or decrease in both income and market value of both assets and liabilities should interest rates rise and fall. Credit risk refers to the probability of repayment when making a lending decision. With all risks, interest rate risk must be measured and managed on a periodic basis.

The Federal Deposit Insurance Corporation Improvement Act of 1991 mandated that all regulatory agencies incorporate interest rate risk into the assessment of capital adequacy. Banks can acquire various assets and liabilities and the market value on these instruments can vary depending on the movement of interest rates in the economy. A sharp increase or decrease in rates could adversely effect the market value of a bank's assets or liabilities, which could translate into a cost to the various insurance funds should a bank have to be taken over by the regulators. Banks which assume more interest rate risk will have to retain more capital to protect the insurance funds.

Review of Financial Statements

A balance sheet of a bank is a snapshot of its assets and liabilities at a particular point in time. Assets represent what a bank owns and are usually divided into loans, cash, investments, and buildings. Liabilities represent what a bank owes to others and are generally divided into deposits, borrowings, and other liabilities. The difference between the two is referred to as capital or surplus and includes retained earnings, common stock, preferred stock, and additional paid in capital.

The income statement is a recap of activity over a particular time period. A fiscal year is any 12-month period and many banks have adopted a calendar year as their fiscal year. Income is derived from loans, investments, or fee income on deposit services. Operating expenses are comprised of salaries, benefits, computer services, occupancy costs, etc. Because banking is a service industry, salaries and benefits can comprise anywhere from 35–60% of an institution's operating expenses.

Ratio Analysis

Banking, as with any other industry, uses a number of ratios to measure profitability and financial health. While banking has its own terminology, it can be loosely translated into broad categories used in other industries. Sales in a retail firm is interest income for a bank. Cost of goods sold in industry becomes interest expense to a bank. Gross profit translates into interest margin.

Ratio analysis is used by regulators and analysts as a way to measure one bank's performance against the performance of other institutions. A bank that varies widely from the others in the industry may be a reason for additional analysis.

Balance Sheet Ratios

Loans/Assets. This represents a measure of the bank's business, what percentage of a bank's assets are invested in loans. This can be broken down further into variable or fixed rate loans.

Earning Assets/Assets. This reveals what percentage of a bank's assets are at work earning income. Assets such as cash or bank building are non-earning assets as they do not generate income. It is obvious that a bank would want this percentage to be as high as possible.

Capital/Assets. This is a measurement of a bank's overall strength. Banking regulators have a number of ways to measure or define capital. One measurement would be a straight calculation of capital/assets which currently has a minimum requirement of 4%. Assets can be measured or defined by their risk elements, and capital as a percentage of that number must be an 8% minimum. The higher the percentage, the healthier the institution.

Growth of capital and deposits. This ratio shows how the bank has grown from year to year and how well that growth was margined. It is not wise to have a large percentage growth in deposits or assets, without a corresponding growth in capital. Continued growth in that fashion over a number of years could find a bank with less than minimum regulatory capital requirements.

Liquidity. Liquidity is defined as the ability to convert assets into cash. Regulators measure an institution's liquidity to see how well it may be able to satisfy customer demands for withdrawals, loans, and general operating expenses.

Income Statement Ratios

Yield on Loans. This is calculated by dividing annual loan income by the average balance of the loan portfolio for the year. There are a number of ways to calculate average balance depending on the level of automation the bank has at its disposal. This yield can also be broken down between types of loans for further detail and analysis.

Yield on earning assets. This is determined by dividing income from earning assets, divided by the average balance of those assets. This ratio generally does not include service charge income.

Return on Assets. This is calculated by dividing annualized net income by total average assets. Often this ratio is calculated two ways, once before taxes and extraordinary items, and again after taxes and extraordinary items. This ratio is one of the major factors used when comparing a bank's performance against other banks. As a rule of thumb, a return of 1% on assets is generally viewed as a good year.

Return on Equity. This is calculated by dividing annualized net income by average stockholders equity. This ratio is important for a stockholder as the better the return on equity the greater the increase in the value of the stock.

Net Interest Margin. This is calculated by subtracting interest expense from interest income and dividing the result by average earning assets. This ratio reflects a bank's ability to withstand changes in interest rates and the ability to raise funds and invest them in higher yielding assets. A bank strives to have a high net interest margin.

Earnings Per Share. Earnings per share are calculated by dividing net income by the number of shares of stock issued and outstanding. Earnings per share is a barometer of how well a bank performs when compared to others. Shareholders want to see increased earnings from quarter to quarter which will effect market value of the stock. Stock analysts will dissect earnings per share in an attempt to predict where the company is heading in terms of long term profitability.

BIBLIOGRAPHY

Amling, Frederick, *Investments*, Third Edition, Prentice Hall, Inc. Englewood Cliffs, New Jersey, 1974.

Cohen, Jerome B., Edward D. Zinbarg, and Arthur Zeikel, *Investment Analysis and Portfolio Management*, Third Edition, Richard D. Irwin, Inc., Homewood, Ill. 1977.

Stigum, Marcia L. & Rene O. Branch, Jr., *Managing Bank Assets and Liabilities, Strategies for Risk Control and Profit*, Dow Jones-Irwin, Homewood, Illinois, 1983.

10

CONSUMER LENDING
Cheryl A. Gross

INTRODUCTION

This chapter consists of four sections:

1. Consumer Credit Analysis.
2. Types of Consumer Credit.
3. Consumer Credit Regulations.
4. Collections.

In the *Consumer Credit Analysis* section, the decision-making process is discussed. How do lenders decide whether or not to approve credit applications? What factors are taken into consideration?

In *Types of Consumer Credit,* the various types of credit products that banks offer to consumers are discussed. Which types are most popular and which are the least popular?

In *Consumer Credit Regulations* the four major federal consumer credit regulations; Truth in Lending, Fair Credit Reporting, Equal Credit Opportunity Act, and the Community Reinvestment Act are discussed. Although many aspects of banking have been deregulated, consumer credit is not one of them. Consumer credit is in fact one of the most heavily regulated areas of banking.

The first three sections discuss how banks lend money, the last section on *Collections* discusses how they get the money back from borrowers who have become either unwilling or unable to repay.

LEARNING OBJECTIVES

After reading this chapter, you should have an understanding of the following:

1. What factors do banks consider when analyzing applications for consumer credit?
2. Which factors are the most important? The least important? Why?

3. Which types of consumer loans are currently the most popular? The least popular? Why have home equity loans and credit cards become increasingly popular, while auto loans (from banks) and home improvement loans have declined in popularity?

4. What is meant by the term "indirect lending"?

5. What is credit scoring and how does it differ from judgmental credit analysis?

6. What do the four major consumer credit regulations require of lenders?

7. What are collections?

8. Should lenders expect to have delinquent accounts? If so, why?

9. What are the reasons for delinquencies?

10. What are the expenses associated with collections?

11. What is credit risk and market risk?

CONSUMER CREDIT ANALYSIS

Why do banks make loans? The answer is simple: to generate interest income. Unlike securities investments, which are made for both liquidity and income purposes, loans are not generally liquid. Loans are made utilizing depositors' money to generate earning assets for the Bank's portfolio. Since the bank is lending depositors' money, the potential for losing the money must be assessed. Every bank establishes credit guidelines to ensure that standards are applied to each loan applicant in the same manner. Standards are developed to be consistent with the amount of credit risk the bank is willing to assume. *Credit risk* is the probability of losing the depositors' money. The greater the probability of default, the higher the risk of the loan.

Credit risk is the probability of losing the depositors' money.

Credit Analysis is the process a lender uses to decide whether the applicant is worthy of the loan. Its purpose is to determine the ability of the prospective borrower to repay the debt and his willingness to do so.

Credit Analysis is the process a lender uses to decide whether the applicant is worthy of the loan.

Credit Analysis is often presented in terms of the C's of Credit. There can be anywhere from three to six elements. We will discuss four C's of Credit, the first two of which are the most important:

Capacity   Capital
Character   Collateral

Capacity—Capacity refers to the applicant's income relative to their debts and expenses. Debt to income parameters are established to minimize the risk of default. The greater the percentage of the borrower's income needed to pay their debts, the greater the probability that an unexpected expense will prevent timely payment. Additional factors which can effect the borrower's capacity are, employment and residence stability.

Character—Character is a very important consideration when analyzing an application. Character, as it relates to credit analysis, generally refers to the applicant's willingness and desire to repay obligations as demonstrated by their payment history.

Capital—Liquid assets which can easily be turned into cash; such as, savings, securities, or investments that could be relied upon to service the loan if income should decline or if one runs into unexpected expenses.

Collateral—Collateral is any tangible asset used to secure a loan. The collateral is used only to strengthen the loan. The loan is never made on the strength of the collateral alone, unless the individual is borrowing their own money such as in a passbook loan.

If capacity, character, capital and collateral are the important factors, how does a bank get the necessary information to enable it to analyze them?

1. *Applications*—What information is gathered in the application?

Employment	Capacity, Character
Income	Capacity
Debts, Expenses, Obligations	Capacity
Bank accounts	Capital
Home ownership	Character, Capital
Previous credit	Character

2. *Credit Reports*—What information is provided in the credit report? The credit report is a factual report, created internally by the bank or externally by a credit reporting agency. The report contains information about the applicant's current credit obligations, paid credit obligations and public records, such as, liens, attachments and bankruptcies. From the credit report, the bank is able to develop:

    — Quality, quantity and length of credit history.

    — Debt to income ratio.

    — The percentage of potential debt in use. Credit card balance versus credit card limit.

    — Number of recent credit inquiries and potential for additional debt.

3. *Loan Interview*—Loan interviews are completed when a consumer applies in person for a loan either by face to face interviews or in a telephone discussion between the applicant and the lender. The purpose of the interview is to gather information for the underwriting process, to clarify and develop the applicant's credit profile, to define and discuss the lenders' standards and requirements for the credit requested, while also providing the applicant with any required regulatory disclosures.

    Qualifications of interviewers vary from one lending institution to another, however certain general guidelines should be universal:

    a. An awareness and understanding of the state and federal regulations pertaining to lending.

    b. An awareness and understanding of the individual lending institution's lending policies.

    c. A sincere understanding and desire to help the applicant and make a good loan.

    d. An unbiased nature and manner when speaking to a customer.

    e. Discretion and integrity.

    Many times a loan interview can reveal some information about an applicant that will not be disclosed on an application. A qualified interviewer should listen carefully when the applicant speaks to acquire all the information needed to make a good loan.

    In conducting the interview, the interviewer should:

    a. Identify the credit need.

    b. Suggest products or services to meet the need.

    c. Present the features and benefits of the suggested products or services.

    d. Discuss the loan terms and conditions.

    e. Have the customer complete a loan application.

4. *Credit Decision*—Upon receipt of a completed application an analysis is performed to:

   a. Determine if the purpose is sound and realistic.

   b. Verify address, employment, income, savings, other assets and outstanding credit.

   c. Assess value of collateral.

   d. Evaluate applicant's credit history.

   e. Determine applicant's ability to pay.

   f. Determine a secondary source of repayment.

5. *Credit Investigation*—Information can be verified in a number of ways.

   a. *Internal checks*—An internal check involves reviewing the deposit and loan records of the Bank for balances, history and collateral value.

   b. *Direct check*—A direct check involves calling the references listed on the application.

   After completing all the steps and gathering all the pertinent information, the credit decision is made consistent with the credit risk the bank is willing to assume.

6. *Credit Problems*—We will discuss three different types of credit problem; too much credit, delinquent credit and no credit.

   There are times during the credit investigation when it is apparent that the individual has too much credit, the individual has had credit problems in the past or the individual has no credit. These situations do not necessarily mean that an individual is not credit worthy.

   a. Should an individual have too much credit (their debt to income ratio is high and granting the loan would be a greater credit risk than the bank wishes to assume), yet their credit is excellent, there may be several options to pursue:

      1. The outstanding credit could be combined (consolidated) to lower the individual's monthly payment.

   Example: Consider an individual who has a car loan and three credit cards on which they owe a total of $6876. Currently, they pay $473 per month. If you combine the balances and pay off the old bills, the new payment would be $228 for 36 months.

	Before		After	
	payment	balance	payment	balance
auto	323	3876		
cards	150	3000		
	$473	$6876	$228	$6876

      2. If the individual's situation cannot be improved, budget counseling can be provided by the bank or an independent non-profit organization such as Consumer Credit Counseling Services of America.

   b. If the applicant has had problems with his credit in the past, it does not necessarily prohibit one from ever getting credit again. It depends on the nature and the severity of the problem. Several issues should be explored.

1. Has the delinquency since been corrected?
2. How late were the payments?
3. How long ago was the delinquency?
4. What were the reasons?

If the problem has since been cleared up and the lender is satisfied as to the reasons behind it, such an applicant may very well be an excellent credit risk.

c. When an individual completely lacks a credit history, banks are reluctant to lend to them because they are an unknown quantity; there is no basis on which to make a determination of the applicant's credit "character." An individual can establish credit in the following ways:

1. *Guarantor/Co-Signer*—If this is the applicant's first loan, a parent or close relative may be willing to co-sign for them. A Co-signer is legally responsible for the debt, the individual guarantees if the borrower is unable or unwilling to make the payments, they will pay the debt. Lenders should use guarantors/co-signers carefully.

2. *Passbook Loan*—If the applicant has a savings or a Certificate of Deposit account, the bank may agree to lend up to a certain percentage of the balance (generally 80 percent to 90 percent), taking the passbook or Certificate of Deposit as collateral. In essence, the bank lends the individual their own money. After having paid off the secured loan in a satisfactory manner, that same bank may consider granting an unsecured loan.

3. *Department Store Credit Cards*—Department store credit cards are easier to obtain than bank loans. Department stores use credit cards to enhance sales. The more cardholders, the higher the volume of sales. If a customer has the store's credit card, they may be more likely to make a purchase. The stores make money both on selling the merchandise and on financing it. A department store, therefore, is willing to assume more risk then a bank which makes money only on the financing of the purchase.

4. *Automotive Finance Companies* have the same sales motive as Department Stores. They make money on both financing and selling the cars. Because they want to sell cars, they are willing to assume a greater risk. Many companies have special programs for first-time buyers. They may be willing to take losses on the financing end to increase the sales volume.

Judgmental Credit Analysis Versus Credit Scoring

There are two common ways to review credit applications. Judgmental credit analysis or using a credit scoring system. Using judgmental analysis, a loan officer reviews each and every application and reaches a credit decision based upon personal analysis (using the four C's discussed earlier), within the parameters of the bank's credit standards.

A credit scoring system is an automated credit approval process. In such a system, the applicant is given a score based upon various factors such as the level of income, the length of employment, the length of residence, and credit history. The higher the income, the greater the length of employment or residence, the better the credit history, the higher the credit score. To be approved for the credit, the applicant must score a minimum number of credit points. It must be emphasized that applicants can be scored only on the basis of objective, non-discriminatory criteria. A lender cannot score based upon such factors as sex, age, or location of residence.

Credit scoring is most likely to be used by high volume issuers of credit.

TYPES OF CONSUMER CREDIT INSTALLMENT AND REVOLVING CREDIT

Consumer credit is generally structured in one of two forms, installment (closed end) credit or revolving (open end) credit.

An installment loan has a specific periodic repayment schedule; for instance, 48 monthly payments @ $235.00 each. Once the loan is paid off, the borrower has to reapply if they wish to borrow again.

Revolving credit requires that a minimum periodic payment be made, either a certain percentage of the balance or a minimum dollar amount (such as "5% of the balance or $15, whichever is greater . . ."). The credit line can be used over and over again, without having to reapply.

SECURED AND UNSECURED CREDIT

Credit can also be granted on a secured or unsecured basis. A *secured loan* is a loan in which the lender either has a security interest in the item being financed (such as an auto or real estate) or has been given collateral (such as a passbook or a stock certificate) unrelated to the purpose of the loan itself. *Unsecured loans* (also called signature loans) are not secured or collateralized by any property, but are guaranteed only by the promise of the borrower to repay.

The cost (interest rate) of borrowing is determined by:

1. The amount of interest the bank is paying its depositors. Depositors' money is used to make loans.

2. The length of time the loan will be outstanding. Time increases both credit risk and market risk.

3. The value and quality of any collateral.

4. A premium for risk and profit.

5. A margin allocated for the expense to operate the bank.

As a general rule, the least risky loan is lending someone their own money (passbook loan). The most risky loan is an unsecured loan or line of credit.

TYPES OF CONSUMER LOANS

Mortgage (discussed in great detail in the following chapter)
Home Equity loans and Home Equity Lines of Credit
Home improvement loans
Auto loans
Credit cards
Check credit/overdraft protection
Personal loans (vacation, furniture, consolidation, etc.)
Student loans

Home Improvement Loans Versus Home Equity Loans

What is the difference between a home equity loan and a home improvement loan?

A *home equity loan* is secured by a second mortgage on the property; a home improvement loan may or may not be secured by a mortgage.

Home improvement loans are used for the specific purpose of home improvements. Borrowers, generally have to present estimates from the contractors doing the improvements. Interest may be tax deductible if the loan is secured by a mortgage.

An equity loan can be used for any purpose. Although the borrower's home is being used to secure the loan, the loan proceeds need not be used for the home. Loan proceeds can be used for anything, which helps to explain the popularity of equity loans.

> Loans secured by second mortgages are generally referred to as home equity loans.

It is important to note that loans secured by second mortgages are generally referred to as home equity loans. To further differentiate the installment type loan from the revolving credit type home equity loan, the loans are generally called Home Equity Loans and Home Equity Lines of Credit.

The following are reasons why home equity loans are popular:

1. Tax treatment—In certain situations, the interest paid is deductible for income tax purposes.

2. Loan proceeds can be used for any purpose.

3. Because they are secured by the borrower's home, the interest rate charged tends to be less than that on other types of loans. The rate may be tied directly to the prime rate. The prime rate is the rate that banks charge their best business customers.

4. Loan terms can be very flexible; they can be written either on an installment basis or on a revolving basis. Some can even be accessed by use of a credit card. In fact, some banks grant home equity loans which feature both a revolving credit option and a fixed term installment loan option.

Banks promote home equity loans for a number of reasons:

1. Home equity loans are low credit risk because they are secured by the borrower's home.

2. The market risk is also low because the interest rate is generally tied to the prime rate. The effect of tying the loan to prime causes the interest rate to move up and down at the same speed and in the same direction as the interest expense paid to depositors for the use of their money.

Home equity loans, however, may have significant disadvantages to the borrower, especially during periods of rising interest rates. Although the initial interest rates are likely to be lower than that those of other consumer loans, it is variable. If the prime rate increases, so will the rate on the equity loan (this can also cause the minimum monthly payment to increase considerably).

Home Equity Loans are secured by a mortgage on the borrower's home. If for any reason the individual defaults, the borrower stands to lose his home. Borrowers should be aware of and cautioned about the prudent use of the Home Equity Loan. Loans should be used to finance major purchases or expenses.(For example, autos, college tuition, home improvement.) They should not be used to finance nonessential or spur-of-the-moment purchases.

Auto Loans

While home equity loans have become increasingly popular, bank financed auto loans have declined in popularity. There are basically three reasons for this trend:

1. Automotive finance companies offer lower rates than banks to encourage sales.

2. Many consumers are using home equity loans to finance auto purchases to ensure the tax deductibility of interest paid.

3. Leasing an auto has become popular.

The first two factors have already been discussed. The most important factor why auto leasing has become popular is that the prices of autos have increased tremendously over the past five to ten years. By leasing an auto rather than owning it, the down payment can be avoided. The monthly lease payments are also lower than a monthly loan payment would have been. Leasing enables some individuals to "get more auto for the money."

Keep in mind that the individual is not purchasing the auto; they are only paying to use it over the period of the lease. The leasing company's name will be on the registration, not the lessee's name. At the end of the lease, the individual does not own the auto; it has to be returned to the lessor. In some types of leases the individual does have a purchase option at the end. However, when you add up the total of the lease payments and the purchase option, the total purchase price may end up being considerably larger than if the auto had been financed through a loan in the first place. If the individual's intention is to own the auto, it should be financed through a loan up front, not through a lease plus buyout option.

Leasing may be more advantageous for individuals who normally trade in their autos every few years and who do not put a great deal of mileage on them. Most leases have mileage limitations. If you exceed them, you may have to pay a penalty when the auto is turned in at the end of the lease. Also, if the auto is returned with greater than normal "wear and tear," you may be penalized.

Leasing may also be advantageous tax wise if the auto is used for business purposes.

Another current trend in auto lending (again, due to the increasing prices of autos) is the increasing length of the loans. It is not at all unusual today to see five-year auto loans (as opposed to the three- and four-year loans which were more prevalent in the past).

There are, however, three problems associated with increasing the term of the loan.

1. Market risk increases as the length of the loan increases. Remember, the interest rate on auto loans stays constant while the interest rate paid to depositors for use of their money may be changing.

2. Credit risk increases as time increases. As time increases, the potential that other factors, such as loss of job or change of residency may adversely effect the borrower's ability to repay increases.

3. The value of the collateral (auto) decreases over time.

Indirect Lending

Banks are also often involved in indirect auto lending. In the case of indirect lending, the auto dealer initially grants the loan directly to his customer. The bank then buys the loan from the dealer (also known as "buying the Paper").

Indirect lending does have several potential advantages to lenders. First, it is a method that can increase the bank's loan volume. In addition, much of the credit investigation and administrative work is performed by the dealers themselves. Depending on the specific agreement between the bank and the dealer, the dealer may have an obligation (called loan recourse) to take back all of or a portion of, the loans that go into default.

Banks generally become involved with indirect lending as part of a larger commercial relationship with the auto dealership. The process which auto dealers use to finance their inventory is a loan relationship called *floor planning.* Few dealers have the financial strength to purchase all of their inventory in cash from the manufacturer. Generally, the dealer's bank will finance his inventory when it arrives from the factory and will specify that the bank be repaid on an item-by-item basis as soon as the autos are sold.

The major disadvantage of indirect lending is that the bank may end up financing auto purchases that it would ordinarily decline. The value of the larger commercial floor planning relationship may create pressure on the lender to approve enough applications from the dealer involved to ensure that they will be able to keep the floor planning business.

Credit Cards

There are four major reasons credit cards are so popular among consumers today:

1. *Convenience*—Credit cards are readily accepted by millions of merchants nationwide. Some major department stores even accept bank cards along with their own cards. Carrying credit cards means that there is no need to carry around large sums of cash or a checkbook.

2. *Travel*—It is almost impossible to travel without a major credit card. Car rental agencies typically require a credit card before they will even reserve or rent an auto. Hotels typically ask for your credit card number if you want to make a guaranteed reservation over the phone.

3. *Changing Attitudes Toward Debt*—There is no longer any stigma attached to being in debt. Consumers are no longer willing to wait until they have enough savings before making purchases. Credit cards allow them to make the purchases now and pay later.

4. *Intensive Promotion*—Almost everyone has received many unsolicited offers in the mail for "Pre-Approved" MasterCard and/or VISA accounts. (Sometimes, the offers are worded as "invitations to apply." In these cases, the recipient has not been pre-approved, but the issuer is trying to motivate them to apply, using the very brief "express type" application.) Several lenders aggressively market their cards on a nationwide basis.

With the credit card market becoming increasingly saturated, card issuing banks are turning to two specific marketing techniques to encourage consumers to apply for and use their particular cards. These techniques are affinity group marketing and card enhancements.

An *affinity group* is any organization having a common bond or characteristic, such as labor unions, alumni groups, or charitable or professional organizations. Some lenders even market cards to the fans of the same professional sports team or to groups such as Elvis Presley fans.

The affinity card itself has the Group's logo right on its front to identify the cardholder as being a member. Furthermore, if the group is a charitable organization, the holder is likely to think about the organization whenever they use their card and will perhaps be more likely to make generous contribution to its next fundraising drive. In some cases, part of the annual fee is contributed to the sponsoring organization by the card issuer.

Card Enhancements are various special services that issuers add to their cards. Examples can be the following:

1.   insurance coverage (various types)

2.   credit card registration

3.   dining/shopping discounts

4.   car rental discount

5.   line of credit checks

6.   medical/legal assistance

7.   travel services, guaranteed hotel reservations

8.   cash back

Card enhancements are especially prevalent with Gold or Preferred credit cards. Such cards usually have more valuable enhancements than standard cards. For example, most gold cards cover the cost of the collision damage waiver on rental cars. If a cardholder is a frequent car renter, this feature could make up for the increased annual fees on such cards.

Just as important as the enhancements to many consumers is the prestige associated with such cards. Consumers often want gold cards so that they can impress friends and associates.

Many consumers think that in order to be granted a high line of credit, they must have a gold card. This is a mistaken impression. Cardholders can get a line of, for example $10,000, on a standard card (assuming, of course, that they qualify). A gold card, however, may have a higher minimum line (usually starting at $5,000).

Issuing banks promote gold cards heavily because the annual fees are usually higher than those on standard cards. And, because it usually takes a higher income to qualify for the gold cards, the bank's credit risk may be lower.

There are three sources of credit card earnings for banks:

1.   *Annual Fees*—Annual fees are assessed some cardholders. These fees can typically range from $10 to $30 on standard cards and from $25 to $75 on gold cards.

2.   *Finance Charges*—Finance charges are assessed on unpaid or revolving balances. Unless the balance is paid in full each and every month, by the cardholder 's due dates, the bank will charge interest on the balance (usually on the average monthly balance). The annual percentage rates (APR) typically range anywhere from 7% to 21%, depending on the particular issuer (and the state in which they are located). Some issuers, in fact, assess a finance charge even if the balance is paid in full each month.

3.   *Merchant Discounts*—When merchants deposit their credit card receipts at their bank, they do not receive credit for the full amount of the deposit. The bank charges a fee known as the merchant discount. This fee could range anywhere from 1% to 5%. If the discount is 2%, the merchant will only receive credit for 98% of the deposit.

Rather than debiting each and every credit card deposit, many banks debit the account once monthly for the total discount due during the period.

The amount of the discount fee assessed to the merchant is determined by two factors, the average number of charge tickets included in the merchant's daily deposit and the average ticket amount. A merchant, such as a discount drugstore, that deposits a large number of tickets and has a low average ticket amount, will end up being charged a higher discount than would a travel agent, that likely deposits a fewer number of tickets and has a high average sale amount.

A bank that chooses to concentrate on attracting participating merchants will earn a greater percentage of its credit card income from the merchant discounts than a bank that chooses to concentrate on attracting individual cardholders. Whether a bank earns more from annual fees than from finance charges depends upon both its pricing structure and the paying habits of its cardholders.

Rates on credit cards are generally among the highest of any consumer credit product. There are several reasons for this:

1. Credit cards are usually unsecured and revolving, reflecting multiple high risk factors:

    a. Market risk—credit cards are lines of credit which continually revolve. As time increases, the probability increases that the interest expense the bank pays their depositors' for use of their money will fluctuate and increase.

    b. Credit risk—As time increases, the greater the likelihood that other factors may adversely affect the borrower's ability to repay.

    c. The instrument is unsecured. Unsecured credit is riskier than secured credit.

2. There is a high incidence of fraud associated with credit cards, the costs of which are largely borne by the issuers (and passed on to the cardholders in the form of higher rates).

3. Credit card processing is expensive. Handling the individual charge slips, printing the monthly statements, processing and embossing the cards, and responding to consumer complaints and inquiries requires a considerably larger staff than do other credit products. As a result, many banks are now outsourcing credit card processing.

Overdraft Protection, Credit Reserve, Reserve Credit

These forms of credit consist of an unsecured line of credit commonly attached to a depositor's checking account that can be accessed by writing a check. They are used to cover unintended overdrafts or used as a revolving line of credit. With this type of account, the customer can make themselves a loan whenever they need it (up to their assigned credit line) by writing a check. Interest rates are typically higher, reflecting the same risk characteristics as a credit card.

This type of account has specific benefits for both the bank and the customer. The bank is spared the time and expense of handling insufficient funds checks. Rather than having to return the checks, they are charged against the customer's line of credit. The customer is protected form accidentally overdrawing their account, thereby avoiding overdraft charges and potential embarrassment.

Personal Loans

Personal loans are granted for any number of legitimate purposes. One crucial point to keep in mind is that personal loans are not "personal" in the sense that the lender does not have a right or an obligation to determine the purpose of the loan.

Personal loans are typically unsecured and made at a fixed interest rate for a fixed length of time. This allows for a level monthly payment throughout the term of the loan.

Student Loans

There are three major categories of student loans. They are:

1. *Government insured and Government subsidized student loans*—Government insured and subsidized student loans are granted at below market rates for the sole purpose of financing the student's education. The interest on these loans is paid by the government while the student is in school and during the first six months after graduation (after which time, the loan has to be put on a repayment basis). If the student leaves school before graduation, they must begin repayment within six months of having left school.

    The student generally has up to ten years to amortize (pay down) the loan, depending upon the initial balance. The interest on the loan is borne by the student while in repayment.

    These loans are need based and intended to assist low to moderate income families and students. As such, the interest paid to the lender is subsidized by the government. This subsidy takes two forms.

    a. The government pays the interest expense while the student is in school.

    b. The government compensates the lender for market risk by reimbursing the lender the difference between the contract rate and the market rate. The market rate is determined by the rate paid on the 91 day Treasury Bill plus 2.70%. In addition, these loans are insured against credit risk. Students generally have no credit history on which to make a loan decision. The government, therefore, guarantees that the loan will be repaid as an inducement for the lender to grant the loan.

2. *Government insured, Unsubsidized student loans*—these loans resemble a Government insured subsidized loan in all respects except:

    a. There is no needs test, therefore, everyone is eligible

    b. The student must pay the interest on the loan while they are in school.

3. *Privately insured student loans*—These loans are generally made to the undergraduate students' parents or to graduate students individually. The credit risk and market risk are borne by the lender. The guarantee agency, however, insures against default for a fee based on the lenders default record. Interest is charged at the variable market rate and interest is paid by the parents while the student is in school. Graduate students may defer payment of interest until they graduate or until they leave school.

CONSUMER CREDIT REGULATIONS

Truth in Lending

A *grace period* is the length of time before interest accrues. Grace periods are not mandatory but must be disclosed if used.

Truth in lending "requires creditors to give you certain basic information about the cost of credit."[1] Its goal "is to let consumers know exactly what the cost is and to let them make comparisons more readily."[2] "The charges must be stated in a uniform way."[3] In the case of an installment loan, the consumer must be told the finance charge and the annual percentage rate (APR). Both of these items "must be displayed prominently" on all loan documents.

The *finance charge* is the total dollar amount the customer pays to use credit. The credit actually includes interest and any other fees, such as insurance premiums.

The *annual percentage rate* is the "relative cost of credit on a yearly basis."[4]

In the case of revolving credit, the consumer must be told the method by which the finance charge is calculated (be it adjusted balance, previous balance, average daily balance) and the length of the grace period, if any. A *grace period* is the length of time before interest accrues. Grace periods are not mandatory but must be disclosed if used.

Truth in lending also regulates credit advertising. Certain trigger terms, such as interest rate, require an APR disclosure.

In addition Truth in Lending requires, that anytime (except at the time of purchase) a borrower's home is used as security and a mortgage is recorded, the borrower be given a right of recession. The *right of recession* refers to a three business day period, (after the loan documents have been signed) during which the borrower has the right to cancel the loan at no cost or penalty to themselves. As a result, the bank is obligated to the loan the day the documents are signed but the borrower does not become obligated until after the recession period. The recession period is intended to allow the borrower to think about the implications of using their home as security.

Fair Credit Reporting Act

The goal of this act is "to protect consumers against the circulation of incorrect or obsolete credit information. Also it ensures that credit reporting agencies adopt fair procedures for maintaining, obtaining and giving out credit information."[5]

You will recall from the credit analysis discussion that credit reports contain information about the applicant's current credit obligations, paid obligations and public records. As a result, if the credit report contains inaccurate or obsolete information the credit applicant might be unfairly denied credit.

The Fair Credit Reporting Act gives consumers certain rights that they may exercise if they have been denied credit based upon information provided by a credit report. Consumers must be told the name and address of the Consumer Reporting Agency involved in the credit denial(the principal credit reporting agencies nationwide are TRW, Trans Union and Equi Fax).

The credit reporting agency must tell the consumer "the nature, substance and sources of the information."[6] (The agencies, however, generally will send the consumer an exact copy of his report.) The information must be provided to the consumer free of charge.

In some instances, the borrower will disagree with the information contained in the credit report. If the information is incorrect the credit reporting agency has an obligation to correct the report. In the event of an unresolvable dispute between a consumer and the credit reporting agency, the consumer has the right to have "his version of the dispute placed in the file."[7]

Credit reports may not be pulled by anyone who does not have "a legitimate business need for the information."[8] In other words, the applicant's credit report can only be pulled if he has applied for credit or if he currently owes a balance to the credit grantor (or has a revolving line available).

Equal Credit Opportunity Act (ECOA)

The Equal Credit Opportunity Act "assures that all credit applicants will be considered on the basis of their actual qualifications for credit and not turned away because of personal characteristics."[9]

It is expressly illegal for a creditor to discriminate against anyone "based on age, sex, marital status, race, color, religion, national origin, or if you receive any type of public assistance or income, such as veterans' benefits, welfare or social security, or exercise any rights under the Consumer Protection Act."[10]

A credit applicant must be notified within thirty days of the completion of the application whether or not the application has been approved. If the lender needs more than thirty days, the consumer must be informed within thirty days that such additional time will be necessary and the reason for the delay (such as a backlog of credit applications during a particular month).

If a credit request is denied, the denial it must be given in writing and explain the specific reasons for the denial of credit.

Community Reinvestment Act (CRA)

This act requires that banks service the credit needs of their community. It requires lenders to ascertain the credit needs of the market area they serve. Banks must adopt a community reinvestment statement which includes a map defining their service area and describing the types of credit they offer. CRA notices must also be posted in the lobby of each office.

CRA activities represent an excellent marketing opportunity and good basic bank business. Banks attempt to consistently analyze their market and provide products which fill the needs of that market. CRA focuses the market analysis and product development efforts on the low to moderate income areas of the bank's community.

> CRA activities represent an excellent marketing opportunity and good basic bank business. CRA focuses the market analysis and product development efforts on the low to moderate income areas of the bank's community.

COLLECTIONS

Loan *collections* is the process used by lenders to convince, encourage, and motivate those borrowers who are past due on their loans to bring them up to date.

Collections are especially significant because of the expense involved with overdue loans. The expenses are:

1. No interest is collected, therefore, there is no income on the asset.
2. Depositors are still paid for the use of their money.
3. The normal expenses associated with a loan must still be paid (the cost of billing, staff and overhead).
4. Additional collection expenses of notices, phone calls and legal action are incurred.
5. Finally, the loan may become a loss resulting in the entire unpaid balance becoming an expense.

Lenders are expected to incur some delinquencies. If a lender has no delinquencies, it may mean that their credit criteria is too strict and that they are declining a lot of good loans. All banks are expected to have some delinquencies; the important point is that they should be a small percentage of the lender's total loan portfolio and they should be dealt with immediately and effectively.

Collections are carried out by oral and written communications. The task is to find out why the borrower is late and find a solution to enable them to bring the loan up to date.

The first collection effort normally is a reminder letter a few days after the missed due date. It may be computer generated and may be a form letter signed by a collector.

If the initial efforts produce no response, there are several ways to proceed, depending on the particular situation. The idea is to reinforce the concept that it is the customer's obligation to pay the lender.

Once the delinquency has gone beyond the reminder stage, the next steps are a combination of oral and written communication. At this point, a collector may play the role of a financial advisor or counselor; their job is to hear the customer out and see if anything can be done to help them. For example, can a reasonable payment plan be worked out which will allow the borrower to gradually bring the account up to date?

The three most common reasons for loan delinquencies are marital problems, unemployment, and illness/health related problems. These are not issues that borrowers are anxious to talk about, nor is another common reason, financial irresponsibility.

Ultimately, if the borrower and the bank cannot resolve the delinquency, the bank may repossess (take back) the collateral and/or pursue legal action to collect the unpaid obligation.

Skip Tracing

Collections occasionally involves trying to locate people who do not want to be found. This process is known as skip tracing. There are many sources that can be used to attempt to locate "skips":

1. Calling the references listed on the credit application.

2. Calling the last known employer.

3. Pulling new credit reports to check for recent inquiries.

4. Asking the Post Office to notify the bank of a change in address.

5. Using private investigators.

Charge-Off

When a delinquent account becomes uncollectible, it is proper to remove it from the Lenders books as an earning asset. This process is known as "charging off a loan." If a loan is classified as a "charge-off," it is no longer included in the bank's total assets. It has been written off against an account known as "reserve against loan losses."

Conclusion

Consumer credit analysis is the process by which lenders judge the credit worthiness of prospective loan applicants. The factors taken into consideration are commonly referred to as the "C's" of credit; character, capacity, capital, and collateral.

There are two types of risk in every loan:

1. Credit risk; which is the potential that the loan will not be repaid.

2. Market risk; which is the risk that the cost of interest paid to depositors (to lend their money) will increase relative to the interest income.

Home equity loans and credit cards are among the most popular consumer credit products available today. Equity loans are favored because of their tax treatment, flexibility, convenience, low initial rates, and heavy promotion. Credit cards are popular for their convenience and wide acceptability.

Consumer credit is among the most heavily regulated areas of banking today. The four major federal consumer credit regulations are Truth in Lending, Fair Credit Reporting, the Equal Credit Opportunity Act, and the Community Reinvestment Act.

Truth in Lending involves certain disclosure that must be made concerning the cost of credit. Fair Credit Reporting regulates the circulation of consumer credit information. It protects consumers against the reporting of incorrect data and gives them certain rights in the event that they have been denied credit based upon such a report. The Equal Credit Opportunity Act specifically prohibits discrimination of any type whatsoever in the granting of consumer credit. The Community Reinvestment Act requires banks to serve the credit needs of their community.

Collections can be described as the process which lenders use to convince, encourage, and motivate delinquent debtors to bring their accounts up to date. It is performed through written and oral communications. One cannot possibly hope to convince the debtor to pay unless one communicates with them. Collections are especially significant because of the expense involved in servicing overdue loans.

NOTES

1. The Board of Governors of the Federal Reserve System, *Consumer Handbook of Credit Protection Laws*, p. 3.

2. Federal Deposit Insurance Corporation, *Truth in Lending . . . What It Means to You.*

3. Ibid.

4. The Board of Governors of the Federal Reserve System, *Consumer Handbook to Credit Protection Laws*, p. 4.

5. Federal Deposit Insurance Corporation, Office of Compliance Programs, *Fair Credit Reporting Act . . . Your Rights.*

6. Ibid.

7. Ibid.

8. Ibid.

9. The Board of Governors of the Federal Reserve System, *Consumer Handbook to Credit Protection Laws*, p. 10.

10. Ibid.

STUDY AND REVIEW QUESTIONS

1. Why is collateral the least important of the 4C's of credit?

2. Explain how overdraft protection works.

3. Explain the difference between finance charge and annual percentage rate.

4. Your customer is planning to put an addition on their home. They are unfamiliar with the types of loan programs available to them and ask for your help. What would you advise and why?

5. Of all the various loan products outlined in Chapter 10, which is considered the most risky and why?

6. Explain Credit Risk and Market Risk.

7. Why are collections significant?

8. What types of questions can be answered in a credit report about a credit applicant?

9. How do you get credit when you have had no previous credit history?

10. What are the various types of consumer loans that banks make?

11. What are the major reasons that make credit cards popular among consumers?

12. What are the sources of earnings in a bank credit card program?

13. What are the common factors that cause loan delinquency?

BIBLIOGRAPHY

Board of Governors of the Federal Reserve System, *Consumer Handbook to Credit Protection Laws*.

Federal Deposit Insurance Corporation, Office of Compliance Programs, *Fair Credit Reporting Act . . . Your Rights*.

The Federal Reserve Bank of Philadelphia, *How the Equal Opportunity Act Affects You*.

The Federal Reserve Bank of Philadelphia, *How to Use and Establish Credit*.

The Federal Reserve Bank of Philadelphia, *Your Credit Rating*.

The Federal Reserve Bank of Chicago, *Credit Guide*.

Federal Deposit Insurance Corporation, Office of Consumer Affairs, *Equal Credit Opportunity and Women . . . Your Rights*.

Federal Deposit Insurance Corporation, Office of Consumer and Compliance Programs, *Consumer Information . . . For Your Protection*.

Federal Deposit Insurance Corporation, *Truth in Lending . . . What It Means to You*.

Federal Deposit Insurance Corporation, *Equal Credit Opportunity and Age . . . Your Rights*.

Federal Deposit Insurance Corporation, *Truth in Lending . . . What It Means to You*.

11

Mortgage Lending
Donald R. Washburn

Mortgage: a legal document by which real property is pledged as security for the repayment of a loan.

Introduction

Historically the majority of home mortgage loans were made by thrift institutions; savings banks, cooperative banks and saving & loan associations. Since mortgage loans are long-term loans, they needed to be funded by less volatile types of deposits (savings deposits) and the role of home financing in the past had been left to the thrift institutions.

Commercial banks, with deposits consisting mainly of more volatile demand and short term deposits, were reluctant to commit these deposits to long-term investments or long-term loans and therefore concentrated on serving the short-term investment or loan needs of the commercial or business sector.

In the current banking environment all types of depository institutions including the commercial banks, the thrift institutions and the credit unions, are competing to serve the home mortgage needs of the nation.

There are several reasons for this change in lending strategy.

First, the types of deposits held by commercial banks have changed from a majority of demand deposits to a majority of savings and time deposits. This change in deposit mix allowed commercial banks to safely consider participating in home mortgage financing.

Second, the introduction of the adjustable-rate mortgage (ARM) provided depository institutions with a mechanism to protect the profitability of the long-term mortgage loan against the changing cost of the institution's deposits which fund the loans. Looking back to the interest rate environment of the

In the current banking environment all types of depository institutions including the commercial banks, the thrift institutions and the credit unions, are competing to serve the home mortgage needs of the nation.

153

early 1980s, the prime lending rate reached 21% and bank certificate of deposit rates reached the high teens. Institutions with large portfolios of fixed-rate mortgage loans, with interest rates mostly below 9%, were negatively impacted with these long-term loans providing earnings to the institution which were less than the cost of deposits which funded them. Adjustable rate mortgages, which allow institutions to periodically adjust the rate of interest on the mortgage loan, provides institutions a mechanism to protect the margin between their cost of funds and the interest rate received for the loans.

And last, the development of the secondary mortgage market provided mortgage lenders the opportunity to sell their long-term mortgage loans, both fixed-rate and adjustable-rate , to investors willing to take on the interest rate risk and market risk of the long-term mortgage not acceptable to the depository institution.

In this chapter we will review mortgage lending, the secondary mortgage market, the types of mortgages available to borrowers, the mortgage application process as well as the major laws & regulations that impact mortgage lending.

LEARNING OBJECTIVES

After reading this chapter, you should have an understanding of the following:

1. The secondary mortgage market and how it has impacted mortgage lending.

2. The basic types of mortgage loans and their major features.

3. How to qualify individuals for mortgage loans.

4. How the mortgage loan application process works; what impediments need to be cleared for approval and what costs are borne by the borrower.

5. What laws and regulations impact the mortgage lending process.

THE SECONDARY MORTGAGE MARKET

The secondary mortgage market consists of organizations that purchase newly originated mortgage loans from originators and then package and resell the loans to investors as mortgage backed securities (MBS).

The major organizations that facilitate secondary mortgage market activities are:

1. The Federal National Mortgage Association (FNMA), known as "Fannie Mae."

2. The Federal Home Loan Mortgage Corporation (FHLMC), known as "Freddie Mac."

Both of these organizations buy mortgage loans from banks and mortgage companies, assemble groups of similar mortgages into packages or pools and resell them to investors as mortgage backed securities (MBS). Investors in the securities may be individuals, corporations, pension funds and in many cases, banks.

The secondary mortgage market allows banks to offer a wide variety of home mortgages to their customers and communities while providing the bank a method to avoid the interest rate risks and the market risks of investing deposit funds in certain home mortgages.

In addition, the secondary mortgage market allows banks that may not have sufficient loanable funds to continue to make additional mortgages. As banks sell the mortgages that they have originated, they receive the funds back from the secondary mortgage market organizations that have purchased them. This allows the originating bank to make additional mortgage loans to its customers and communities. This process creates a continuous supply of loanable funds for home mortgages.

The secondary mortgage market, however, requires that banks apply very specific loan and underwriting standards to the loans originated for sale into the secondary mortgage market. If the standards, called guidelines, aren't strictly adhered to, the markets won't purchase the mortgage loan and the originator will be required to hold the loan in its own portfolio, a consequence that may not be desirable to the originating organization.

Banks cannot afford to operate under vague loan and underwriting standards because of enhanced bank regulatory oversight and the need to prepare loans so as to be investment quality and saleable in the secondary markets.

The secondary mortgage market plays such a large role in the home mortgage market that, in general, a new type of mortgage loan may not be successful until the secondary mortgage market is willing to purchase it. An example of this was the introduction of the convertible mortgage; an adjustable-rate mortgage that can be converted to a fixed-rate mortgage during its term. The convertible mortgage did not become widely available until the secondary mortgage market approved it for purchase.

COMMON TYPES OF HOME MORTGAGES

The following is a list of home mortgage loans and their features which are commonly originated for bank loan portfolios and secondary mortgage market sales:

Fixed-rate Mortgage Loans

15 Year Term
20 Year Term
30 Year Term

Adjustable-rate Mortgage Loans (ARM)

1 Year Adjustments
3 Year Adjustments
5 Year Adjustments

There are also various hybrids and variations of the standard mortgage loans:

Convertible Mortgage Loan
5 or 7 Year Two-step Mortgage Loan
15 or 30 Year Biweekly Payment Mortgage Loan
5/1, 7/1 or 10/1 Adjustable-rate Mortgage Loan
5 Year or 7 Year Balloon Mortgage Loan

Fixed-rate mortgage loans carry a constant rate of interest over the term of the loan.

Adjustable-rate mortgage loans carry a rate of interest that may change during the term of the loan.

Fixed-rate mortgage loans, as the name implies, carry a constant rate of interest over the term of the loan.

Adjustable-rate mortgage loans carry a rate of interest that may change during the term of the loan.

If the interest rate of an ARM can change during the term of the loan, why would someone want the uncertainty of the adjustable-rate mortgage over the certainty of the fixed-rate mortgage?

The initial rate of interest charged on an ARM is generally lower than the rates of interest available on fixed-rate loans. The lower rates of interest available with the ARM are made possible because the borrower is taking much of the risk of future interest rate increases onto themselves, relieving the lender of much of the interest rate risk. ARM borrowers are therefore compensated for this risk taking by enjoying lower initial interest rates as compared to the then current fixed rates. Within ARMs, some interest rates are lower than others. Generally, the shorter the adjustment period, the lower the initial rate. For example, a 1 year ARM will have a lower initial rate than a 3 year ARM, which will have a lower initial rate than a 5 year ARM.

The ARM borrower can also get "more for their money" with the ARM because of the lower initial interest rate. They will be able to afford a larger loan amount, providing them the opportunity to buy a more expensive home or provide a smaller down payment to buy a home. The lower initial interest rate translates directly to a lower monthly loan payment.

The disadvantage of the ARM is the possibility that higher future interest rates will cause the loan rate to rise, which will cause the monthly payment to also rise. But, on the other hand, if interest rates at the time of adjustment are down relative to the previous adjustment period, the ARM borrower will get the benefit of even lower interest rates and lower monthly loan payments following the adjustments.

Common features of an ARM are the **index,** the **margin** and the periodic and lifetime **interest rate caps.**

The **index** is the rate to which the ARM rate is tied; changes in the index at time of adjustment will cause a change, up or down, in the ARM rate. ARMs are generally tied to a U.S. Treasury securities index.

A **margin** is an amount which is added to the index at adjustment time to calculate the adjusted interest rate. Margins may vary from lender to lender if the ARM is being originated for the lenders portfolio, but are fairly standard if the ARM is originated for sale into the secondary mortgage market.

Periodic and lifetime **interest rate caps** are also typical features of an ARM. Caps are limits placed on how much the interest rate can change at each adjustment (period cap) or over the life of the loan (lifetime cap). An ARM can have both, one, or no caps. Any caps and their limitations may have an impact on the ARMs initial rate and the margin added to the index at adjustment time because a cap will limit the interest rate risk of the borrower and shift some of that risk back to the lender.

Convertible mortgages are a hybrid of an ARM and a fixed-rate mortgage. A convertible starts off as 1 year ARM and contains an option, on a one time basis, to convert to a fixed rate loan during a specific limited period in the future. The converted interest rate will then be a current fixed rate of interest plus a reasonable margin. The conversion to a fixed rate is strictly optional on the part of the borrower. The mortgage loan documents contain all the specific details for the conversion and must be disclosed to the loan applicant at the time the loan application is made to the lender.

Two-step mortgages combine a fixed-rate mortgage with a one time interest rate adjustment. A two-step starts off with a rate of interest fixed for either the first 5 or 7 years that is normally lower than the current fixed rate mortgage rates. The interest rate is then adjusted once after the initial period to a fixed rate for the remaining term of the 30 year loan based on a predetermined fixed-rate loan index plus a reasonable margin. The adjusted rate is not optional and the mechanism for change will be contained in the mortgage loan documents and must be disclosed to the loan applicant at the time application is made to the lender.

Biweekly mortgages are loans that call for the periodic payments to be made every two weeks versus the conventional monthly payment. The two-week payment is half of the normal once a month payment and will ultimately save the borrower in total finance charges paid on the loan and accelerate the period of time the loan takes to pay in full.

5/1, 7/1 and 10/1 ARMs are hybrid adjustable-rate mortgages that combine a longer initial interest rate period with the 1 year adjustable-rate mortgage loan.

Balloon mortgage loans are fixed rate mortgage loans that do not completely amortize by the maturity or final due date of the loan. As a result the borrower must pay off the remaining unpaid loan balance with a lump-sum payment or else refinance the unpaid loan balance into a new loan.

MORTGAGE POINTS

The mortgage origination process has many costs associated with it. The loan applicant normally (but not always) pays for such origination expenses as the cost of the appraisal, cost of the credit report and the costs for the legal and closing work. The loan originating facility incurs other expenses associated with taking the application such as the expense of processing the application and preparing the loan for delivery to the bank's loan portfolio or for sale into the secondary mortgage market. Mortgage lenders for many years have recouped their costs or provided themselves with additional income by charging points (also known as origination fees or loan discounts). A point is equal to 1% of the mortgage loan amount. For example, in a $100,000 loan, a 1 point charge equals $1,000 and a 2 point charge equals $2,000. Points are considered a pre-paid finance charge for the purpose of computing the total finance charges and annual percentage rate (APR) in the Truth-in-Lending disclosures required to be given in home mortgage transactions.

THE QUALIFICATION PROCESS

The secondary mortgage market has developed a set of income ratios that are used to determine the maximum loan amounts that different levels of income will support.

By applying the income ratios, a lender can determine the maximum affordable mortgage loan amount for any prospective borrower.

Qualifying is the process a lender uses to determine if a prospective mortgage loan borrower has sufficient income to service the mortgage loan desired. The secondary mortgage market has developed a set of income ratios that are used to determine the maximum loan amounts that different levels of income will support. Whether mortgage loans are originated for the lenders own portfolio or to be sold into the secondary mortgage market, these income ratios are widely used by mortgage lenders.

By applying the income ratios, a lender can determine the maximum affordable mortgage loan amount for most prospective borrowers. The ratios determine both the maximum monthly housing expense payment and the total monthly long-term debt payments that the borrower can afford.

Total monthly long-term debt is the combined total of the monthly housing expense payment and all other monthly payment obligations which will continue for at least the next ten months. These obligations may include payments for auto loans, student loans, credit cards and any other contractual or legal obligation. In the case of credit cards or revolving credit accounts, the minimum monthly payments are used in calculating the payments total.

The first ratio or the housing expense ratio is the relationship between the borrowers gross monthly income and the total monthly housing expense. The monthly housing expense payment for ratio purposes is made up of the following components:

1. Loan principal

2. Loan interest

3. Real estate taxes

4.   Property hazard insurance

5.   Private mortgage insurance (PMI)

The last three components take the form of escrow payments. Escrow payments, sometimes called reserves, are funds held in an account by the lender to assure future payment for such recurring items as real estate taxes, hazard insurance and in some cases private mortgage insurance.

Real estate taxes must be paid by the borrower. As a condition of the mortgage loan the lender requires that the borrower pay taxes as they come due. In some circumstances mortgage lenders will escrow the real estate taxes and pay them to the city or town when they are due.

Property hazard insurance provides the mortgage borrower protection against loss because of damage or destruction of the property. Mortgage lenders, as a condition of granting the loan, require that the structures on the mortgaged real estate be insured against damage or destruction. In some circumstances mortgage lenders will escrow the property insurance premiums and pay the premium to the insurance company when they are due.

Private mortgage insurance (PMI) is normally required by mortgage lenders when the relationship of the mortgage loan and the value of the mortgaged property is greater than 80%. PMI insures the lender against losses that may occur in a mortgage loan because of default and the value of the property does not satisfy the loan and the foreclosure expenses. The PMI premiums are normally paid by the borrower as part of their mortgage payment. PMI premiums increase with higher loan-to-value ratios and premiums on ARMs are higher than on fixed-rate loans. PMI companies consider ARMs to have a higher risk of default than fixed-rate mortgages because of the potential interest rate (and monthly loan payment) increases during the initial years of the loan.

In calculating the first ratio, or housing expense ratio, the total monthly housing expense is divided by the prospective borrowers gross monthly income. The result of the calculation should be a ratio not exceeding 28%. It can be noted that some mortgage lenders and the secondary mortgage market will accept a first ratio, or housing expense ratio, of more than 28% under certain circumstances.

The second ratio, or the total monthly long-term debt ratio, measures the total amount of all the prospective borrowers monthly obligations to their gross monthly income. Most lenders and the secondary mortgage market want this ratio to be no more than 36%.

Let's look at the following example of ratio calculations:

Bill Smith's gross monthly income	$2,500
Mary Smith's gross monthly income	$2,750
Combined gross monthly income	$5,250

What is the maximum monthly housing expense payment the Smith's qualify for?

Calculation: .28 (28%) x $5,250 = $1,470

What is the maximum amount of total monthly obligations?

Calculation: .36 (36%) x $5,250 = $1,890

With the results of the ratio calculations a lender can calculate a maximum affordable mortgage loan amount.

> Private mortgage insurance (PMI) is normally required by mortgage lenders when the relationship of the mortgage loan and the value of the mortgaged property is greater than 80%.

Let's continue with the Smith's calculations:

Estimated real estate taxes	$150	($1,800 annually)
Estimated property insurance	$ 50	($ 600 annually)
Estimated PMI	$ 0	($ 0 annually)
Total escrows per month	$200	

Maximum housing expense payment at 28%	$1,470
Less: escrows per month	$ 200
Housing expense payment available for loan principal & interest payment	$1,270

Using a 30 year fixed-rate loan at 9% per annum, the Smith's can afford a mortgage loan of $157,000 based on the first ratio.

Before we conclude the calculation, we must also test the second ratio to determine that the Smith's fall within the 36% overall limitation.

The Smith's also owe on a:

Auto Loan	$ 250 per month
Student Loan	$ 50 per month
Credit cards	$ 50 per month
Total other debt payments	$ 350 per month

Total housing expense payment	$1,470
Total other debt payments	$ 350
Total long-term debt payments	$1,820

The above second ratio calculation indicates that the Smith's can afford up to $1,890 of monthly long-term debt payments. In this example therefore, the Smith's should be able to qualify for the $157,000 mortgage and still be within the second ratio limit.

APPLICATION PROCESSING AND APPROVAL

The mortgage lender's sequences for processing and approving mortgage loans may differ from lender to lender. The following steps are normally contained in a lender's process:

1. The loan applicant completes the mortgage application and pays any required application and/or rate lock fees.

2. The lender will prepare and provide to the applicant any required regulatory disclosures.

3. The lender investigates the applicants credit performance normally by acquiring a credit report from a credit reporting agency. If the credit report reveals current or previous delinquent payments or liens, attachments and bankruptcies, the applicant may be required to explain the cause of the problem and the current status of the problem. Recent delinquencies and unresolved past credit problems may cause the applicant's request to be declined.

4. Verifications of the applicants income, employment, deposits and loans are typically made in writing. The secondary mortgage market requires that certain standards be met in the verification of the applicant's statements.

Mortgage lenders want to be assured that applicants are not borrowing the down payment (if loan is for a home purchase) unless already disclosed by the applicants and that the applicants have the resources to make required down payments, to pay the closing costs and have reserves available to service the loan if they temporarily lose their main source of income.

5. An appraisal determining the market value of the real estate is conducted by either the lenders staff appraiser or by an independent fee appraiser. Secondary mortgage market rules and bank regulatory standards on the form and content of the appraisal and the qualifications of the appraiser are very strict and produce high quality opinions of value.

    The appraisal report and its opinion of value become very critical in loan requests where there are low down payments or high loan-to-value situations. Loan underwriters, PMI companies and secondary mortgage markets become more sensitive to all the underwriting factors when the property appraises for substantially less than its selling price or produces a high (90% or more) loan-to-value ratio.

6. Mortgage loans that need private mortgage insurance coverage (loan-to-value greater than 80%) are submitted to the PMI company for their underwriting. The PMI underwriters will carefully review the applicant's payment ratios, credit history and the appraisal results, and if their standards (similar to secondary mortgage market standards) are met, an approval for PMI coverage will be issued by the company.

7. The lender will review a completed mortgage loan application for adherence to the lender's loan standards and secondary mortgage market standards (if loan is to be sold into the secondary mortgage market) and decide to approve or decline the loan request. If the loan request is approved the lender will issue a loan commitment letter detailing the terms of the loan and the conditions that must be met to close the loan. If the loan request is denied, the lender must notify the applicant of the denial and provide the applicant with the specific reasons for denial.

8. Following the approval and the issuance of the loan commitment letter, the lender will prepare to close the loan. Most lenders will retain the services of an experienced real estate attorney to prepare the loan for closing. The closing attorney will prepare to close the loan by obtaining a title search of the real estate, arranging for the issuance of a title insurance policy and preparing documents necessary to perfect the lenders lien or mortgage on the property. The closing attorney will also normally attend the loan closing and represent the bank in the execution of all the loan documents.

Mortgage Processing and Closing Costs

Processing a mortgage loan for a commitment and preparing the loan to close involves some very complex specialized tasks and documents. There are some significant costs incurred for performing these tasks and preparing the documents. Most mortgage lenders do not build the recovery of these costs into the loan itself. Therefore, it is customary that the mortgage loan borrower be required to pay for many of the processing and closing costs.

Following is a sample of costs that are normally paid by the mortgage borrower:

1. Appraisal fee

2. Credit report fee

3. Points or origination fee

4. PMI insurance premium (if required) for first year

5. Closing attorneys fee

6. Title insurance policy premium

7. Plot plan or mortgage survey cost

8. Municipal lien certificate fee

9. Mortgage recording fee

LAWS AND REGULATIONS THAT IMPACT MORTGAGE LENDING

In the prior chapter on Consumer Loans we discussed a number of laws and regulations that impact the lending function of a bank; the Truth-in-Lending Act, the Fair Credit Reporting Act, The Equal Credit Opportunity Act and the Community Reinvestment Act. Mortgage lenders are also required to comply with the following additional laws:

> The Fair Housing Act
>
> The Home Mortgage Disclosure Act
>
> The Real Estate Settlement Procedures Act

The Fair Housing Act (FHA)—A 1968 civil rights law, the Fair Housing Act prohibits discrimination in the sale or rental of a dwelling on the basis of race, color, religion, handicap, sex, familial status, or national origin. Under the Fair Housing Act, it is unlawful for any person who engages in the business of making or purchasing residential real estate loans, or in the selling, brokering, or appraising of residential real property, to discriminate on the basis of the factors listed above.

The Home Mortgage Disclosure Act (HMDA)—Enacted by Congress in 1975 and amended during the period 1988 to 1996, the Home Mortgage Disclosure Act (Regulation C) is intended to provide the public with loan data that can be used to determine whether financial institutions are serving the housing needs of their communities, to assist public officials in distributing public sector investments, and to assist in identifying possible discriminatory lending patterns. Financial institutions are required by Regulation C, which implements HMDA, to report data regarding loan applications, as well as information concerning their loan originations and purchases. HMDA requires most lenders to report the race, sex, and income of mortgage applicants and borrowers.

The Real Estate Settlement Procedures Act (RESPA)—Enacted by Congress in 1974 and amended during the period 1992 to 1996, the Real Estate Settlement Procedures Act (Regulation X) requires that consumers be provided, in a timely manner, specified information on the nature and cost of settlement of (closing) a real estate loan transaction. RESPA contains certain disclosure requirements and restrictions for settlements of residential real estate loans.

Fair Lending

The Equal Credit Opportunity Act, the Fair Housing Act, the Home Mortgage Disclosure Act and the Community Reinvestment Act are commonly known as the fair-lending laws. We have previously discussed each of these laws and their relationship to discrimination in lending. Recently there has been an increased focus on fair-lending compliance by bank regulatory agencies and the U.S. Justice Department. The federal financial institutions supervisory agencies have issued guidelines or "suggested fair lending activities" which they deem appropriate for financial institutions to use in meeting their fair-lending obligations. The following is the list of those suggested fair lending activities:

1. Use of an internal second review system for consumer, mortgage and small business loan applications that would otherwise be denied.

2. Enhanced employee training that engenders greater sensitivity by financial institution management, and employees, to racial and cultural differences in our society.

3. Training of loan application processors to assure that any assistance provided to applicants in how to best qualify for credit is provided consistently to all loan applicants.

4. Efforts to ensure that all persons inquiring about credit are provided equivalent information and encouragement.

5. Use of flexible underwriting and appraisal standards that preserve safety and soundness criteria while responding to special factors in low- and moderate-income and minority communities.

6. Efforts to encourage equal employment opportunity at all levels throughout the institution, including lending, credit review, platform and other key positions related to credit applications and decisions.

7. Affirmative marketing and call programs designed to assure minority consumers, Realtors, and business owners that credit is available on an equitable basis; marketing may involve sustained advertising programs covering publications and electronic media that are targeted to minority audiences.

8. Ongoing outreach programs that provide the institution with useful information about the minority community, its resources, credit needs and business opportunities.

9. Participation on multi-lender Mortgage Review Boards which provide second reviews of applications rejected by participating lenders.

10. Participation in public or private subsidy or guarantee programs that would provide financing on an affordable basis in targeted neighborhoods and communities.

11. Use of commissions or other monetary or nonmonetary incentives for loan officers to seek and make safe and sound consumer and small business loans in minority communities.

Fair lending objectives must be a part of every depository institutions daily routines. "Fair lending is good business. Access to credit, free from considerations of race or national origin, is essential to the economic health of both lenders and borrowers."[1] "Fair lending benefits not only the institution's bottom line, but also the individual, society and the economy. Institutions that turn away potentially creditworthy customers, deny themselves the opportunity to establish relationships with new customers and generate new revenues. By identifying more creditworthy individuals, including those living in low- and moderate-income communities, the industry improves the quality of life in all neighborhoods."[2]

CONCLUSION

The secondary mortgage market has dramatically impacted the home mortgage lending business. It has allowed many lenders, who are reluctant to make long-term loans, to actively participate in this type of lending. Additionally, the introduction of the adjustable-rate mortgage in the early 1980s attracted more mortgage lenders because the lender was no longer faced with the risk of rising interest rates while holding onto low yielding long-term loans.

The secondary mortgage market and enhanced regulatory oversight have brought well defined underwriting standards to the home mortgage industry. Income, credit and appraisal standards have been almost universally adopted by mortgage lenders who originate loans for their own portfolio and for secondary mortgage market sales.

Mortgage lenders also have additional laws and regulations that impact the home loan business. The Fair Housing Act, the Home Mortgage Disclosure Act and the Real Estate Settlement Procedures Act impact the way home lenders go about their business.

Fair lending is good business and all home lenders must take careful steps to ensure that their practices and processes do not unlawfully discriminate and all groups are provided equal access to credit.

NOTES

1. The federal financial supervisory agencies, Fair lending letter to all banks and thrifts (Washington D.C., May 27, 1993).

2. The Federal Reserve Bank of Boston, *Closing the Gap: A Guide to Equal Opportunity Lending* (Boston, MA, 1993) p. 5.

3. Alan R. Morse Jr.—Massachusetts Commissioner of Banks, cover letter accompanying release of Administrative Bulletin 5–10 entitled *Community Reinvestment and Fair Lending Policy* (Boston, MA, August 31, 1993).

CHAPTER SUMMARY

The mortgage loan is one of the more important loan products that a bank offers to their communities today.

In today's mortgage lending environment, the Secondary Mortgage Market plays a significant role in providing competitive and varied mortgage loans to the mortgage borrower and liquidity to the banks that originate mortgage loans for sale into the Secondary Mortgage Market.

Most mortgage loans fall into two categories, fixed rate loans and adjustable rate loans. From these two types many variations have been developed providing flexibility to both lenders and borrowers.

As in any type of loan arrangement, a process of qualifying loan applicants is employed. The Secondary Mortgage Market has standardized the qualifying process for mortgage loans originated for sale to investors and their guidelines are well developed and strictly enforced. Many mortgage lenders have adopted these guidelines for their own portfolio loans.

Mortgage lending is subject to additional consumer lending laws that require lenders to provide disclosures concerning the borrowers cost of obtaining mortgage credit and to provide unbiased access to credit to all members of the banks community.

Once the exclusive product of savings banks and S&L's, mortgage loans are now also a competitive product of commercial banks, credit unions and mortgage companies.

STUDY AND REVIEW QUESTIONS

1. Discuss the steps that must be completed when processing a mortgage application.

2. You are a mortgage officer in the bank and have been asked to qualify the following potential mortgage applicants:

    a. Using the Qualifying Income Ratios discussed in the text, calculate the maximum mortgage payment and the maximum total long-term debt payment for the following cases:

	Case A	Case B
Gross Monthly Income	$2,500	$4,000
Maximum Housing Expense Payment	$_____	$_____
Maximum Total Long-term Debt	$_____	$_____

    b. Using the Work Sheet, the Payment Tables below, and the results of the Qualifying Income calculations above, find the maximum mortgage amount that Cases A and B would qualify for if they intended on applying for a 30 Year Fixed Rate loan at the rate of 10% per year:

Additional Facts:	Case A	Case B
Monthly Tax Escrow	$100	$125
Monthly Insurance Premium	$ 25	$ 30
Monthly PMI	$ 0	$ 0
Other Long-term Monthly Payments	$200	$200

Work Sheet

	Case A	Case B
Maximum Housing Expense Payment (from above 2.a.)	$_____	$_____
less: Monthly Tax Escrow	$_____	$_____
less: Monthly Insurance Premium	$_____	$_____
Equals: Maximum Monthly Principal & Interest Payment	$_____	$_____
From the 10% Payment Table below, how much mortgage does A & B each qualify for?	$_____	$_____

3. What would happen to the above results if we made the following fact changes:

    a. a 30 Year variable-rate loan were available at a 9% interest rate?

    Loan Amount   Case A = $_____   Case B = $_____

    b. the maximum terms of the fixed-rate, 10% loan and the variable-rate, 9% loan were only 15 years?

    Fixed-rate: Case A = $_____   Case B = $_____
    Variable-rate: Case A = $_____   Case B = $_____

    c. the Other Long-term Monthly Payments were $250 in Case A and $400 in Case B?

    Case A: P&I payment = $_____   Loan Amount = $_____
    Case B: P&I payment = $_____   Loan Amount = $_____

Payment Tables
Monthly Payment Necessary to Amortize a Loan

9% Interest Rate		Loan	10% Interest Rate	
15 Years	**30 Years**	**Amount**	**15 Years**	**30 Years**
$ 10.15	$ 8.05	$ 1,000	$ 10.75	$ 8.78
$ 20.29	$ 16.21	$ 2,000	$ 21.30	$ 17.56
$ 30.43	$ 24.14	$ 3,000	$ 32.24	$ 26.33
$ 40.58	$ 32.19	$ 4,000	$ 42.99	$ 35.11
$ 50.72	$ 40.24	$ 5,000	$ 53.74	$ 43.88
$ 60.86	$ 48.28	$ 6,000	$ 64.48	$ 52.66
$ 71.00	$ 56.33	$ 7,000	$ 75.23	$ 61.44
$ 81.15	$ 64.37	$ 8,000	$ 85.97	$ 70.21
$ 91.29	$ 72.42	$ 9,000	$ 96.72	$ 78.99
$ 101.43	$ 80.47	$ 10,000	$ 107.47	$ 87.78
$ 202.88	$ 160.93	$ 20,000	$ 214.93	$ 175.52
$ 304.28	$ 251.39	$ 30,000	$ 322.39	$ 263.28
$ 405.71	$ 321.85	$ 40,000	$ 429.85	$ 351.03
$ 507.15	$ 402.32	$ 50,000	$ 537.31	$ 438.79
$ 608.56	$ 582.78	$ 60,000	$ 644.77	$ 526.55
$ 709.99	$ 563.24	$ 70,000	$ 752.33	$ 614.31
$ 811.42	$ 643.70	$ 80,000	$ 859.69	$ 702.06
$ 912.84	$ 724.17	$ 90,000	$ 967.15	$ 789.82
$ 1014.27	$ 804.83	$ 100,000	$ 1074.61	$ 877.58

BIBLIOGRAPHY

Single Family Seller/Servicer Guide. Federal Home Loan Mortgage Corporation.

Fair Lending Compliance. Day, Berry & Howard Banking Law Update. Fall 1993.

Massachusetts Division of Banks. *Consumer Guide to Obtaining a Home Mortgage.*

The Federal Reserve Bank of Boston. *Closing the Gap: A Guide to Equal Opportunity Lending.* 1993.

U.S. Department of Housing and Urban Development. Settlement Costs. A HUD Guide for Homebuyers.

Allan R. Morse, Jr., Massachusetts Commissioner of Banks. Cover letter accompanying release of *Administrative Bulletin 5–10 "Community Reinvestment and Fair Lending Policy."* August 31, 1993.

Massachusetts Division of Banks. *Administrative Bulletin 5–10, "Community Reinvestment and Fair Lending Policy."*

The federal financial institutions supervisory agencies. Fair lending letter to all banks and thrifts. May 27, 1993.

12

COMMERCIAL LENDING
Lawrence J. Sands
Patricia D. Urbano

INTRODUCTION

A commercial bank is a financial intermediary. Unlike companies which manufacture goods or distribute a product, a commercial bank is primarily a *service* organization, as was the discussed in the first chapter. As an *intermediary*, the bank acts as a middleman between depositors and borrowers. Depositors can be either consumers, commercial businesses, governments, or other banks. These four groups use the bank's *deposit* services, such as checking and savings accounts, money market accounts, and certificates of deposit. Likewise, the same four groups at various times use the bank's *credit* services. Individuals, businesses, governments, and other banks borrow, or receive credit, from commercial banks.

As you have already learned, individuals borrow from banks in the form of *consumer* loans, credit cards, and home mortgages. The U.S. Government borrows from commercial banks in the form of Treasury Bills, Notes and Bonds, which commercial banks buy from the U.S. Treasury. Banks borrow from other banks in the form of Federal Funds Transfers. Businesses borrow from banks in the form of *commercial* loans. Our focus in this chapter will be to:

1. Identify the purpose of commercial lending.
2. Review the various legal entities that use commercial loans.
3. Analyze the commercial loan application process.
4. Explore the various components involved in making a decision on a commercial loan.
5. Discuss the necessary elements in closing a commercial loan.
6. Understand the importance of good loan administration.
7. Study the changing environment affecting commercial lenders.

LEARNING OBJECTIVES

After reading this chapter, you should have an understanding of the following:

1. The reasons that banks make commercial loans.
2. The different legal entities that use commercial loans.
3. The various components of the commercial loan application process.
4. The factors considered in the commercial credit decision.
5. The required documentation for closing a commercial loan.
6. The importance of the loan administration function.
7. The changes commercial lenders are making to remain competitive.

PURPOSE OF COMMERCIAL LENDING

Commercial lending serves two primary purposes for a bank. First: Making a commercial loan may generate a profit for the bank, and second: the business loan product is essential for many companies and therefore is an important piece of the array of products and services that banks offer their customers. There are three components of the *yield*, or return that banks earn on commercial loans: *Interest Rate, Fees and Deposit Balances.*

A bank performing its duty as a financial intermediary handles deposits from all areas of the economy, including consumers, businesses, governments, and other banks. A commercial bank attracts deposits from these customers either by paying interest or providing payment services. It is the deposit balances that are used to fund the commercial loan demand from the customers and prospects of the bank.

> The difference between the *Cost of Funds* and the *interest rate* the bank charges its customer is known as the *spread*.

The profitable bank is able to lend out its deposit balances at a rate of interest that is higher than the rate of interest it pays to its deposit customers. The difference between the *Cost of Funds* and the *interest rate* the bank charges its customer is known as the *spread*. Spread, or gross profit on the loan must cover the cost of making and servicing the loan. Included in this expense are overhead factors such as salaries, utilities, rent and a provision that some percentage of the overall loan portfolio will never be repaid (allowance for bad debts). The other two components of the yield also support the expenses that are incurred in making and servicing the commercial loan portfolio.

> A *liability* is any account on a company's books that the company owes.

Because the commercial bank has an obligation to give back the depositors' money when requested (either on demand or at the maturity of a time deposit), the bank accounts for these deposits as a liability on its balance sheet. A *liability* is any account on a company's books that the company owes. Other examples of liabilities are bills that must be paid or rent that is due. Remember—a bank is obligated to give back that money to its depositors; so in effect the bank is borrowing the deposits from consumers, businesses, the U.S. Government, and other banks. The bank is paying the depositors an interest rate, and promises to give back the deposit when asked.

> A loan is a *receivable* because the bank plans on receiving repayment. *Equity*, or *Net Worth* is the difference between Total Assets and Total Liabilities and is a representation of the worth of the company.

When a bank makes a loan or extends credit, it creates an asset account. An *asset* is simply any amount on a company's books for which it will receive payment, or anything that the company owns. A bank expects to get repaid on its loans; therefore, a loan is a *receivable* because the bank plans on receiving repayment. *Equity*, or *Net Worth* is the difference between Total Assets and Total Liabilities and is a representation of the worth of the company. In summary, deposits are liabilities because a bank is obligated to pay back that money; a liability is money the bank owes to others. Loans are assets because a bank is expecting to be repaid by others.

A Bank's Balance Sheet

Assets				Liabilities
Cash	5	8		Deposits
Loans	4	8		Total Liabilities
Furniture & Fixtures	2	3		Net Worth
Total Assets	11	11		Total Liabilities & Equity

The fundamental process of taking in deposits at lower interest rates and lending the money at higher rates is a commercial bank's major source of profit. As a financial intermediary, the bank is a middleman and services both the depositors and borrowers.

BUSINESS ENTITIES THAT BORROW FROM COMMERCIAL BANKS

There are many types of legal entities that borrow from banks. As outlined in the chapter on consumer debt, individuals borrow from a bank. In the commercial lending department a bank does business with legal entities that fall under the following categories:

Proprietorship—An entity owned by an individual and usually operated under a d/b/a (doing business as) title. For example, John Smith opens a business as John Smith d/b/a Smith's Bake Shop. There is no legal difference between John Smith and his business, Smith's Bake Shop. A proprietorship is the least expensive and most common form of business entity. The risk to the proprietor is that he or she has unlimited personal liability. The proprietorship itself has a limited life, in that when the owner dies, the business entity also ceases to exist.

Partnership—A legal entity in which two or more individuals join together. Usually operated under a d/b/a, a partnership is governed by a partnership agreement that details the rights and responsibilities of each of the partners. Partners are joint and severally liable; that is each is responsible for all of the partnership's debts. The partnership is a very common form of business ownership. Unless specifically provided in the partnership agreement, this form of business enterprise also has a limited life. To the extent that upon the death of the partners, the business ceases operation.

Corporation—A legal entity formed by investors known as stockholders. This form of business, however, has an unlimited life. The most expensive of the entities to establish, a corporation provides the investors with a measure of protection. The stockholders' liability is limited to the amount of their initial investment. In order to document a loan to a corporation, one must have documentation that empowers someone to act on behalf of the corporation. Corporations usually register their names with the state in which they operate in order to protect their trademarks.

The *personal guarantee* is a legal promise by the owner to accept responsibility for the corporation's debts if it does not meet its obligations. There are two forms of guarantees, *unlimited* and *limited*.

As we learned in partnerships and proprietorships, the individuals involved in those two entities have unlimited liability. In a corporation the owner's liability is limited to the amount of their investment. In order to ensure the cooperation and assistance of the management in a corporation, the bank may require the personal guarantee of the corporation's debt. The *personal guarantee* is a legal promise by the owner to accept responsibility for the corporation's debts if it does not meet its obligations. There are two forms of guarantees, *unlimited* and *limited*. An unlimited guarantee provides the bank protection up to any amount the business owes the bank. A limited guarantee puts a cap on the exposure at a certain dollar amount. For example, a person may be required to guarantee up to a certain dollar amount (say $100,000).

TYPES OF COMMERCIAL LOANS

All commercial loans can be categorized according to some basic characteristics, such as the length of the loan, the type of collateral or security, and the general purpose of the loan. Most commercial loans are *secured,* that is, some form of collateral is pledged to ensure repayment. Some loans are *unsecured,* that is no collateral is pledged. The need for collateral is negotiable and is based on the bank's comfort with the company's ability to repay.

The following chart gives a general outline of the various types of commercial loans:

Loan Type	Purpose	Secured By	Usual Terms	Other Provisions
Line of Credit	To support working capital	Accounts Receivable & inventory	Demand, reviewed annually	Must cycle out of debt for 60 days
Line of Credit	Overdraft protection	All assets	Demand, reviewed annually	
Term Loan	To purchase equipment or vehicle	Equipment or vehicle	3 to 5 years matching the useful life of equipment	
Term Loan	To finance leasehold improve-ments	All assets of the company	3 to 5 years	
Term Loan	To buy a new business	All assets of the company	5 to 10 years	Covenants which are tied to projections
Commercial Mortgage	To purchase or refinance land or building	Land or building	15 to 25 years	
Commercial	To finance capital improve-ments	Building in which improve-ments are made	10 to 20 years	

Lines of Credit

Payable upon demand, lines of credit have no specific maturity date. The borrower makes periodic, usually monthly, interest payments. Principal may be repaid at any time. Lines of credit are usually used to finance short term (less than one year) purposes such as the supplementing of the company's own working capital. For example, the company may need assistance in financing short term needs of paying its weekly payroll when receivables collection may take three weeks on average. Lines of Credit are usually secured by the assets that relate directly to the primary source of repayment, such as accounts receivable and inventory.

Term Loans

Payable in installments with a specific maturity date, term loans are commonly used to finance assets with a useful life of longer than one year. Machinery, equipment, and vehicles are common assets that can be financed by term loans. The term of the loan usually matches the useful life of the asset being financed.

Banks usually require that term loans contain certain *covenants*. A covenant is an agreement between the Borrower and the Lender that certain expectations will be met. For example, the Borrower covenants that it will be profitable or that it will generate sufficient cash flow to meet its debt obligations. Unlike a line of credit that is reviewed annually by the Bank, a term loan represents a longer commitment; in exchange for that commitment to lend long term, the Bank expects that certain covenants will be honored.

Loan covenants and all other details of a term loan are explained in a document called a *Loan Agreement.* This document is a tool used by the Bank to minimize its risk in lending for a longer period of time.

Commercial Mortgages

A commercial mortgage is a specific kind of term loan that is secured by real estate. Since real estate has a longer life than most equipment and vehicles, it usually carries a longer term of up to twenty-five years. Loans that are secured by real estate are usually classified differently from term loans for many reasons. In recent years, bank regulators have closely scrutinized bank real estate portfolios in order to verify that loan to value ratios remain conservative and to be sure that banks were not investing in excessively speculative real estate.

THE COMMERCIAL LOAN APPROVAL PROCESS

While each different bank has its own specific policies and procedures to follow in granting commercial loans, there are basic steps that loan officers everywhere employ in order to underwrite loans to their commercial customers.

The Application Process

The first step in the loan approval process is the submission of a loan application by the prospective borrower. The borrower often sets up an appointment with the loan officer at the bank, or quite often, the loan officer chooses to visit the prospective borrower at his or her place of business. Very often, a visit to the premises of the business reveals much more than what is written on the application: the neatness of the facility, the morale of the work force, and the level of sophistication of the company's product or service can only be observed through a site visit. The application outlines facts about the company, including: address; tax payer identification number; and credit references that help the lender perform a credit check on the business as well as on the principals. Basic questions on the application concerning why the borrower needs the money, how much, and for how long, provides the basis for a dialog between the banker and the borrower to gain a mutual understanding of how the proposed credit facility will fulfill the borrower's need for financing and what makes sense for a repayment schedule.

Accompanying the application are the company's historical financial statement, which are prepared by an independent accountant and which serve to outline the company's financial history for the past three years. Financial statements include a *Balance Sheet*, an *Income Statement*, and a *Statement of Cash Flows* for each of the three years. A Balance Sheet provides a snapshot of one particular day in the life of the company and details the nature of the company's assets and offsetting liabilities. The Income Statement, on the other hand, is the summary of twelve months operations. It shows the total amount of revenues generated, the corresponding expenses incurred, and the resulting profit or loss. The Statement of Cash Flows converts both the Income Statement and Balance Sheet from the *Accrual* method of accounting to the *Cash Basis* of accounting. Accrual statements recognize income when earned and expenses when incurred while Cash Basis statements recognize income when it is received and expenses when they are paid. Personal income tax returns are an example of a financial report completed on a Cash Basis. The Statement of Cash Flows is the most precise method of measuring the company's ability to support ongoing operations and to repay its debt and fixed obligations.

Another key piece of information that the loan officer receives in the application process is a Personal Financial Statement. Since the owner of the company is usually requested to personally guarantee the loan, an understanding of the owner's personal financials is essential for the lender.

With all of the above information in hand, the lender is ready to move to the second stage of the loan approval process, which can be called the *decision making step*.

Decision Making Step

The lender makes the credit decision based not only upon the financial information provided in the application process, but also based upon his or her impressions of management's ability to lead the company into its next growth stage, the integrity and experience of key decision makers, and an assessment of management's willingness to work with the lender in an ongoing relationship. Summarized as *character*, these attributes far outweigh other components that comprise the decision making process. In other words, without a mutual trust and understanding, the basic underwriting standards of the commercial lender are compromised.

In addition to character, the company's ability to repay the loan, often called *capacity*, is closely scrutinized. A close analysis of the company's historical cash flow will help the lender to understand the level of ongoing and reliable cash flow that is available for debt service. The lender will analyze the stability of earnings, the ability of the company to weather bad times, and the stability of the industry in which the company operates.

The company's assets, or *collateral*, provides a key to understanding the level of risk of the loan. Since most loans to small and mid-sized companies are secured, the quality of the assets is very important. As explained earlier, many lines of credit are secured by Accounts Receivable and Inventory.

If the accounts receivable are to well-known, reputable firms who have a history of paying their bills on time, the quality of the receivables is considered to be very good because the receivables are said to hold their value in liquidation. Inventory that is not limited to a specialized, one purpose use but rather which has a generic value to many end buyers also is excellent collateral because it retains its value in a liquidation scenario.

Fixed assets, such as machinery and vehicles, as well as real estate, are other forms of collateral that a lender may consider as a mean of securing a commercial loan.

Finally, the overall strength of the company, or its *capital base*, enters into the decision making process. The company's capital base comes into existence in a combination of ways including the original investment the owner makes into the company, the retention of past profits in the company, and additions of capital injected into the company by the owner or other stockholders.

The lender often relies on outside information to support his or her loan decision. For example, in a loan secured by commercial real estate, the lender commissions an appraisal, which helps establish an unbiased value for the property in question. Furthermore, the lender commissions an environmental study, often called a *21-E* report to determine whether or not the property is reasonably free of hazardous waste.

CLOSING THE LOAN

Once the loan is approved by either the loan officer or the bank's appropriate loan committee, the loan must be documented, or closed. The borrowers usually go to the bank for the closing, or to a designated attorney's office if the loan is large or complicated. Most loans that involve real estate are also closed by attorneys because such loans involve the recording of liens that are most often completed by attorneys.

The *Note* signed by the Borrower, is "I promise to pay."

The *Note* is the most important document signed at the closing. Although the note may consist of several pages, its basic message, which is signed by the Borrower, is "I promise to pay." The specifics of the interest rate, the length of the note, and other pertinent details are also found in the Note.

If the loan is secured by collateral, the Borrower also signs a *Security Agreement* and *UCC Filings* that make a matter of public record the lien holder and the asset that is pledged. If the collateral is real estate, the security agreement is specifically called a *Mortgage*. The mortgage is also part of public record and serves to notify any interested party that the real estate in question is encumbered with a lien.

Another very important document is the *Personal Guarantee* signed by the owner or principal of the business. While not every loan requires a personal guarantee, it is commonplace to have the guarantees of individuals who own a closely held company. The guarantee implies a level of cooperation from the owner/principal that further enhances the loan's quality.

In any term loan, the Bank often requires a *Loan Agreement*, which, as the name implies, spells out the long term agreement between the Borrower and the Lender. The lender often outlines the *covenants* that the Borrower is required to meet on an annual or quarterly basis in order to stay in compliance with the terms of the Loan Agreement. Covenants include very general requirements such as maintaining insurance on all assets as well as very specific requirements, such as the company's debt to net worth ratio must remain below 2:1.

LOAN SERVICING

Once the loan is booked, it must be systematically reviewed in order to insure that the loan continues to meet the Bank's credit standards. For example, a system must be in place to insure the receipt of yearly corporate and personal financial statements, to verify that insurance on the assets does not lapse, and to test that covenants have been met.

Following upon existing loans and insuring ongoing compliance to the Bank's underwriting standards is often called "managing a portfolio," and is an equally important part of a lender's job as booking new loans.

CHANGING ENVIRONMENT

Increased competition has caused banks to reevaluate the methods used to receive, decision, book and service commercial loans. With additional competition from commercial banks, community banks and non-bank lenders' bankers have been faced with eroding spreads. This has brought about the need to streamline the entire commercial lending process. The cost of booking a commercial loan is relatively stable, whether the loan is $10,000 or $10,000,000.

The 80/20 rule applies to commercial loans: 80% of the loans account only 20% of the dollar volume causing many banks to have a different approval process for the high volume/low dollar section of the market. The trend is for banks to treat the smaller business loans more like consumer credit. A streamlined application process, standardized documentation, and exception management are a few of the tools banks are implementing. Many banks are using *credit scoring*, a computerized loan decisioning program, as a tool to expedite the review process. This program analyzes the information provided by a potential borrower and rates the likelihood that the subject will be able to repay the loan based on several pre-determined criteria. This assists lenders in making a cursory analysis of the information provided and eliminating the obvious approvals and obvious declinations. This provides more time for the lenders to spend on the loans that need more analysis. By providing standardized documentation lenders are able to offer a more competitively priced product on a timely basis. Exception management is where bankers monitor a pool of amortizing loans. As long as the loans remain current, they receive little attention. If the loan becomes overdue, reaches a maturity date or trips any of several "red flags" they receive immediate attention from a lender. This management by exception frees up lenders from servicing demands, thereby allowing the lender to make more decisions on new loan requests. The loan servicer only gives attention to the small percentage of loans that have an exception, thus substantially increasing the number of loans assigned to these lenders.

The Community Reinvestment Act (CRA) is a federal government mandate to banks to provide a complete array of products and services to all areas of the community. This requirement is now reviewed as part of the examination process that banks undergo on a regular basis. A substandard CRA record may be grounds for a bank to be denied charter requests for opening new branches or not obtaining approval for acquisitions until improvements are made.

The changing environment has forced banks to be innovative in product development and aggressive in marketing their products and services. As the trend toward mergers and consolidations continue into the next millennium banks must anticipate the changing needs of their customers and meet those needs by producing new products.

STUDY AND REVIEW QUESTIONS

1. What factors are considered when commercial loans are priced?
2. Identify and discuss the elements considered by a loan officer when reviewing a commercial loan request.
3. Discuss the elements that make up the profit a bank generates on a commercial loan.
4. What is risk and how does it impact a banks' decision making process on commercial loans.

Commercial Loan Process Flow Chart

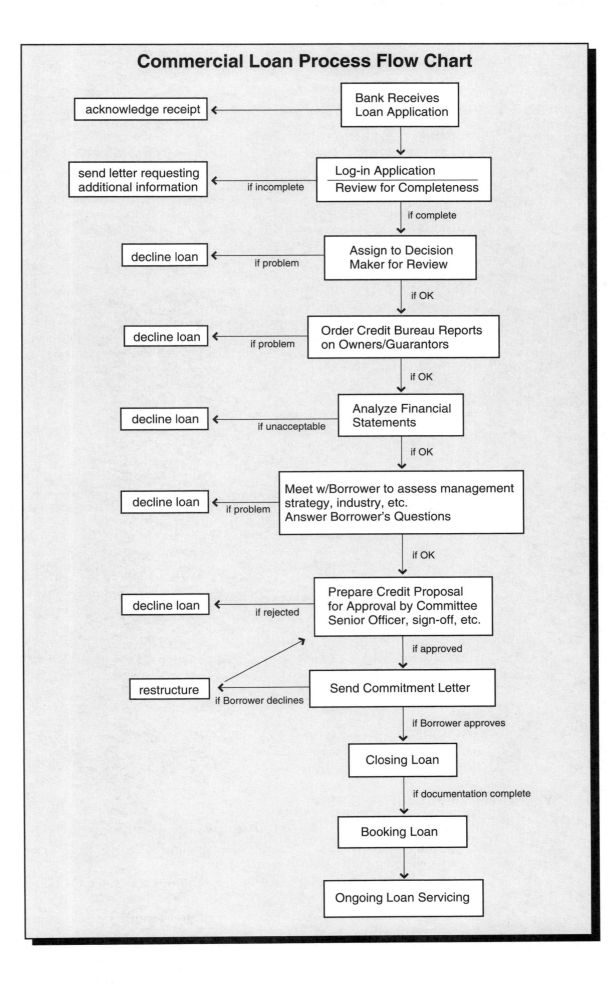

13

COMMERCIAL CASH MANAGEMENT SERVICES
David Splaine

INTRODUCTION

Cash management is performed by every organization in the country. The level of sophistication of each organization or person's cash management varies widely based on their level of understanding and requirements. *Cash management* is simply the science, or some would say the art, of minimizing one's holding of static cash.

This minimization is accomplished through a variety of methods, including disbursement and collection management and the use of information about one's cash. This chapter will focus on both the tools and the techniques of cash management for these three methods of minimization.

LEARNING OBJECTIVES

After reading this chapter, you should have an understanding of the following:

1. What is meant by cash management?

2. What is the goal of cash management?

3. Which factors influence the management of a company's cash position?

4. What is meant by the term *float*?

5. Describe the different types of float.

6. What are lockbox services?

7. Describe how deposit concentration works.

8. What tools can a cash manager use in disbursement management?

9. What various methods can be used to access information on cash balances from banks?

10. How can controlled disbursement improve cash management?

OVERVIEW

The ideal cash management system employs specific banking services in support of corporate objectives to achieve the goal of efficient use of corporate cash.

Every business uses some type of cash management system. The degree of sophistication, however, often varies widely, even among related companies of similar size. Sometimes these variances are the result of procedures that are not keeping pace with the growth and expansion of the company. In other instances, these gaps result from the absence of any formal planning.

In designing or refining any cash management system, four basic general objectives should be considered:

1. The system should maintain productive use of funds in the corporation's cash pool. Uncollected receivables and idle balances provide no benefits. The system should reduce or eliminate them wherever practical.

2. The system should minimize operating costs of the cash management system. The system should return more in benefits than it costs to run.

3. The system should minimize management involvement in day-to-day system operation. Valuable management time is geared to more productive tasks.

4. To compensate banks appropriately for cash management, the system should be designed so that banks are compensated fairly for the services they provide for the company.

Virtually all aspects of cash management are concerned with the concept of float. Therefore a thorough understanding of float is necessary to effectively evaluate the major components of a cash management system.

FLOAT

Float is the status of funds that are in the process of being collected. All cash management aims to reduce and minimize the six basic kinds of float.

The term *float* refers to the status of funds in the process of collection. Companies experience float from the time a sale is made until the account receives collected funds on their customer's check. For purposes of measurement and analysis, float can be broken into six categories:

1. *Invoicing Float*—Funds tied up in billing receivables. This float is largely under the company's internal control and can be reduced through more efficient clerical procedures.

2. *Mail Float*—Funds tied up from the time the customer mails the payment until the check is received. Bank services are available to reduce mail float.

3. *Processing Float*—Funds tied up in sorting and recording before the checks are deposited.

4. *Availability Float*—Funds tied up from the time the check is deposited until available funds are credited to the account. This float is totally influenced by the efficiency of the company's bank and check clearing system.

5. *Disbursing Float*—Funds available in the company's bank account until their payment check clears.

6. *Information Float*—Funds sit idly in the company's account until they receive notice of the account activity.[1]

Banks provide a variety of services to commercial customers to meet the four objectives of cash management and reduce float. These services are divided into three categories: Collection Management, Disbursement Management, and Information Management.

Collection management is designed to accelerate cash collection and concentration. Through the controlled, efficient disbursement of funds, *Disbursement management* maintains the highest level of available cash for as long as possible. *Information management* allows the company's financial manager timely, accurate, and useful information through his bank account.

While a highly sophisticated cash management system may include many different techniques of cash management, the following sections summarize several of the major tools in each category.

Collection management aims to speed up cash collection. Disbursment management tries to keep the highest possible levels of cash available. Information management aims to keep companies up to date on the status of their cash.

COLLECTION MANAGEMENT

Lockbox

To control float, a bank may operate a *lockbox* at the post office for a company, hence speeding up the posting of payments.

Funds that have not been collected are of no real value to corporate customers. Through lockbox cash management services, today's cash manager can depend on fast, efficient collection and crediting of incoming remittances. Companies benefit through control over mail, processing and availability of float and banks offering these services benefit from fee income and increased non-interest bearing deposit dollars.

The concept of a lockbox service is simple: The bank, acting on the company's behalf, rents a post office box or several boxes in the company's name at a post office with the best mail time for the company. Bank messengers intercept the company's mail, and it is delivered directly to the bank. The mail is then opened, sorted, copied, and deposits are made directly to the company's account.

Usually the mail is picked up by the bank continuously throughout the day. The bank works cooperatively with the Postal Service to determine the best pickup times.

The lockbox service is divided into two groups that are determined by the volume of checks.

Wholesale lockbox receipts typically involve high-dollar, low-volume remittances. In this type of arrangement, receipts are often handled by hand by highly trained staff. Float is extremely important in wholesale lockbox due to the size of the checks being deposited and the related cost of slow collections.

Retail lockbox is designed for organizations with a high volume of remittances. In this situation, the timely and accurate posting and crediting of the customer's account is important for both the bank and the customer-organization. The bank usually works with the organization to design a remittance slip to be mailed by the customer with his/her check that will be read and processed by high-speed automatic equipment. Each document is scanned and verified, data is captured, and a detailed audit trail is created.

The company will often require some type of computer tape transmission or consolidation from information captured in retail lockbox. Many banks can provide companies with this information in a standard format on either tape or in hard copy.

Companies such as large retailers, non-profit fundraising organizations, gas stations and credit card operations are large users of retail lockbox.[2]

Deposit Concentration

As pointed out earlier, concentrating cash as quickly and efficiently as possible is one of the cornerstones of cash management. Due to a variety of reasons, many companies collect their funds on a broad, decentralized basis. Deposit Concentration Services are designed to provide rapid, economical cash concentration and detailed, timely, and usable deposit information.

Companies with multiple cash concentration points such as gas outlets, grocery chains, retail stores, cinemas, multiple lockbox sites. However, to efficiently utilize cash at the corporate level, managers may desire to concentrate these deposits into on account. **Deposit Concentration** can be accomplished by consolidating balances of branch sites and/or banks or deposit into a concentration bank.

Generally, daily deposit amounts are reported by the corporate branch via telephone, fax or terminal to the concentration bank. The concentration bank maintains file information pertaining to their customers' depository bank relationships. When the deposit information from the field is reported, this information is accessed and a preauthorized transfer is initiated by the concentration bank. These are two common methods for making these transfers: Depository Transfer check (DTC's) or Electronic Funds Transfer (EFT).

The concentration bank maintains file information pertaining to their customers' depository bank relationships. When the deposit information from the field is reported, this information is accessed and a preauthorized transfer is initiated by the concentration bank. There are two common methods for making these transfers: Depository Transfer Checks (DTC's) or Electronic Funds Transfer (EFT).

Depository Transfer Checks (DTC's)

Depository transfer checks (*DTC's*) and *Electronic funds transfers* (EFT's) transmit deposit information quickly to a *concentrating bank* or the ACH (Automated Clearing House).

DTC's are non-negotiable paper instruments that require no corporate signature and that transfer funds from a corporation's account at one bank to an account at another bank at minimal cost. DTC's are payable only to the bank of deposit for credit to a company's specific account.

Electronic Funds Transfer (EFT)

Concentration can also be handled electronically, eliminating the need to create and clear a paper check. Once the deposit is reported to the concentration bank, the transfer occurs through the Automated Clearing House (ACH), providing next day availability.

DISBURSEMENT MANAGEMENT

Zero Balance Accounting

A consolidated account can be divided into *sub-accounts* that are kept at zero-balance until just-in-time for account transfers.

The *Zero Balance Account* is an account owned by a corporate customer in which the balance is always maintained at zero. When corporate checks are presented to the bank for payment, the bank automatically transfers funds from another account, which may be an investment account or line of credit.

This system is designed to centralize disbursement made by branch offices, operating divisions, subsidiaries, or payable categories and allows for accurate control of cash and minimizes the monitoring of these specific accounts.

Another form of zero balance account works in the reverse of the above noted. Specifically, excess deposited corporate funds, upon which no checks have been presented is swept into another account usually an investment account to earn interest. When checks are presented and the balance becomes negative, funds are transferred into the account.

Zero balance accounts allow for corporate control of account balances resulting in increased income.

Payroll Services

Banks often perform a company's *payroll services*, meeting the criteria of labor-intensity, repetitiveness, and confidentiality through the use of computers.

One of the first cash management products introduced by banks was payroll services. Preparing the payroll is perhaps one of the most inefficient uses of a corporate treasurer's time. Banks recognized the nature of payroll—repetitive, confidential and labor intensive—made it a prime candidate for computer applications. With this profile and the disbursement of cash involved, banks began offering a variety of payroll products.

Banks now prepare, distribute, and handle a variety of payroll checks and records. Typically, the bank creates a payroll master file with basic employee data provided by the company. The company's payroll staff then provides the bank with data such as employee hours worked and other variables (salary adjustments, terminations, and new employees) each pay period.

The bank's computer calculates the net pay, taxes, and a variety of other deductions customized by the company's requirements. Usually, checks and detailed statements are delivered to the company within forty-eight hours of receipt of the payroll information.

This arrangement also includes a direct deposit feature. Under this feature an employee has the option of having partial or net wages deposited directly into a personal bank account at virtually every bank in the United States. To use direct deposit, the employee's bank must be capable of accepting National Automated Clearing House credits. Employees also receive a printed statement of earnings and deductions for their records.

Controlled Disbursements

Banks help companies control *disbursements* by keeping companies informed of their cash positions and borrowing needs on a daily basis.

The management of funds disbursement is a critical function of the corporate treasurer. The uncertainty associated with incoming check presentment can cause a company to be under-invested or to borrow funds unnecessarily.

A controlled disbursement account will permit a company to know its cash position early enough in the day to make critical same-day investment or borrowing decisions—an absolute necessity for cash managers. Control created by the system enables a company to fund accounts only as checks are presented for payment.

One or more demand deposit accounts, depending on a company's needs, are opened at one of a holding corporation banks. Multiple payables accounts can be used individually for various disbursement categories or on a consolidated basis through a zero balance accounting system. Because of the flow of funds through the check clearing network, additional disbursement float can often be realized from this system. This translates to investment dollars or reduced borrowings for the corporation.

Each of the holding corporation banks receives a single daily Federal Reserve presentment that is intercepted and reported to corporate treasurers on a timely basis. A Fed presentment represents periodic daily deliveries by the Federal Reserve Bank of checks drawn on the bank. By noon, disbursement requirements are known, facilitating daily investment or borrowing decisions.

A special services group then proceeds to fund the controlled disbursement account(s) based on the company's instructions—from a master account via wire transfer or from investment maturities.

The controlled disbursement process is summarized in Figure 13-1. Steps 1-6 represent the check issuance on the clearing process. That is, corporate headquarters issues a check (Step 1) to make check payments (Step 2) to vendors (3). These checks are deposited in the vendor's bank (4) and make their way through the banking check collection system (5) and ultimately to the company's controlled disbursement account within the bank's holding company (6).

At that point, the company is informed through terminal reporting or telephone (8) of the clearing totals for the day (7) that will be charged against the company's account that day. At that point, the decision to adjust the company's checking account level can be made by the treasurer.

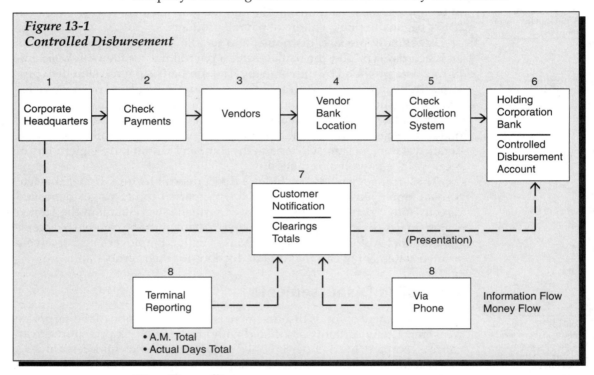

Figure 13-1
Controlled Disbursement

The Benefits

Resulting from increased disbursement float, funds are available for investment or debt reduction for as long as possible.

By funding only those checks presented for payment each day, the time required for monitoring forecasting and analyzing disbursements is substantially reduced.

The guesswork of forecasting daily disbursement requirements is eliminated, providing the cash manager the ability to make faster and more accurate daily investment, borrowing, or other corporate finance decisions.

Payable Through Drafts

A company may choose to pay its trade obligations in a number of ways—checks, wires, preauthorized debits. Payable Through Draft is another method that allows a corporation to review actual disbursement items before the items are finally paid. The payable through draft combines the features of a draft and a check and, for certain kinds of expenditures, it can greatly improve cash control.

A *payable through draft* is drawn on the issuing corporation, rather than its bank.

A payable through draft is drawn on the issuing corporation rather than on the corporation's bank. While it is treated just like a check in a bank's transit collection process, the bank separates, lists, totals, and delivers the drafts to the company each day. The corporation reviews the drafts for authorization or return.

Because the company is authorizing the payment after the item has been presented, it is not necessary to have a signature on file with the bank. This feature permits the draft to be created by the bank's customers, suppliers, salesmen, branch, or plant managers, using their company's account fund at the bank. Efficiency and audit control over a variety of payables can be maintained at a corporate level, at the same time allowing for local, regional, or divisional autonomy.

Benefits of Payable Through Drafts

Sales Expenses—Payable through drafts have been used as an effective means of reimbursing territorial salesmen for their expenses. This system minimizes the paperwork exchange, provides prompt payment, and leaves the company in a position to review the items presented each day.

Vendor Payments—Some companies have reduced clerical cost by using the payable through draft service to permit small vendors to draw their own payments. Because a high percentage of checks issued for payables are for small amounts, the paperwork cost per dollar disbursed is high. By including a payable through draft with a purchase order, the vendor can "pay" himself at a large savings in clerical cost to the issuer.

Insurance Adjustments—Frequently, insurance companies use payable through drafts to settle claims as soon as local adjusters and policyholders have agreed to settlement figures.

Figure 2 summarizes the collection process for a payable through draft. Up to bank notification, this process is similar to that which a regular check makes. Unlike a check, when a draft is presented to the bank, it in turn notifies the issuing corporation and forwards the draft to the corporation for approval.

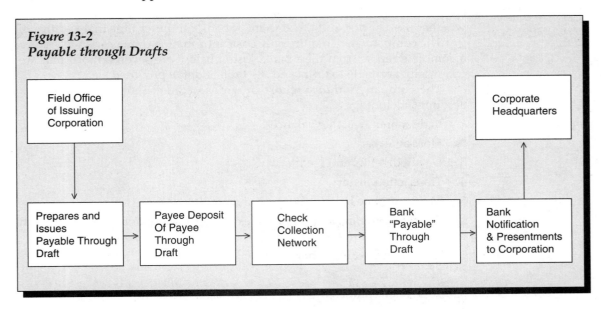

Figure 13-2
Payable through Drafts

Funds Control

Excess balances are minimized because the draft account need not be funded until the payable through drafts are presented for payment. Local and/or imprint accounts can be eliminated.

Administrative Control

Corporate headquarters can authorize payable through drafts initiated by salesmen, vendors, and so forth, while retaining full control over final payment of those drafts.

Division or field office personnel can make a local payment (to make an advantageous purchase, for example) without having their signatures on file at the bank.

Cost Effectiveness

High-volume payers find that the payable through draft costs much less than a check. The bank does not examine or file these items (the customer does), and this savings can be passed on in lower costs.

Information Management

Collection and Disbursement management are two important parts of a complete cash management program. The third part of the puzzle is information management. While the first two arrangements move the cash within the banking system, the third serves as the window for information to the corporation.

In the early 1970s, Chemical Bank introduced ChemLink, a trademarked computer information system for corporate treasurers. At the time of introduction, the costs of such a system only allowed the largest of companies to utilize the information effectively. As with virtually all computer products, the costs quickly were reduced and an advanced version of this system is used by a wide variety of companies at a relatively low cost.

Computerized access to a company's account information allows the treasurer to manage the cash better.

The information that is available to officers within the bank is available to corporate treasurers through this computer link. Companies are typically charged by the bank for the amount of information normally requested, whether used or not, and the amount of bank computer time that is utilized.

The company may require only basic information or may wish to receive a complete report from their bank. Listed below are seven options that are commonly available to users and the type of detail provided.

The company *balance report* provides detailed information on bank accounts, including:

1.   Ledger and available balances,
2.   Float analysis,
3.   Detailed debits and credits,
4.   Transaction history,
5.   Month-to-date balances, debits, and credits.

Other bank balance report provides balance information for accounts with other banks, including:

1.   Ledger and available balances,
2.   Float analysis,
3.   Total debits and credits,
4.   Balance history.

Money market report provides current interest rate quotations on thirteen different investments, updated three times daily.

Foreign exchange report provides current daily exchange rates for selected currencies, including:

1. interbank buy/sell quotes for key currencies.

2. spot, 30-, 60-, 90-, and 180-day rates.

Deposit concentration report provides information on all transactions and receipts concentrated the prior day, including:

1. daily summary data.

2. division or unit location breakdowns.

3. transaction dates and amounts.

Funds transfer report allows the company to transfer funds, repetitive and non-repetitive, from a corporation's house account to any account at another bank specified by the company. Transaction confirmations are available through this module.

Messages, also an interactive module, enables companies to transmit information and communicate directly with their bank.[4]

Investment Management

A company may have designed a cash management system to keep cash balances to a minimum and use excess balances either to reduce borrowings or increase investments. Many banks offer a target loan balance or sweep arrangement to facilitate this goal. The basic operating issues for each of these arrangements is the same.

The bank establishes a base balance for the corporate account or accounts. The base balance must be large enough to support ongoing activities with the bank—including account maintenance, a credit line, and the price of the investment service.

Corporate account balances in excess of the base amount are calculated daily and invested in acceptable securities or used to reduce loan balances. Advises detailing all activities are mailed directly to the company.[5]

A *sweeps* account "clears" a company's basic excess cash balance from its account on a daily basis to invest in securities, etc.

CONCLUSION

Cash management services are offered to meet the needs of corporations to speed collection of payments and to manage excess funds. Today banking involves a worldwide market, involving more than deposits, lending and processing payments; namely the expedient, efficient management of corporate funds dealing in an international arena.

The major cash management services offered are categorized as collection management, disbursement management and investment management and include lockbox, deposit concentration, zero balance accounting, payroll, and through drafts all augmented through the availability of instantaneous computerized account information and investment options for excess cash.

Banks benefit by offering cash management services by generating fee income and increased non-interest bearing deposit growth.

NOTES

1. First National Bank of Chicago, *Cash Management Techniques*, Chicago, Illinois.
2. Shawmut Bank N.A., *Corporate Services*, Boston, Massachusetts.
3. *Ibid*.
4. *Ibid*.
5. *Ibid*.

STUDY AND REVIEW QUESTIONS

1. What are the two major reasons why banks offer cash management services?
2. Distinguish between wholesale and retail lockbox.
3. What advantages does a lockbox service offer a corporation?
4. List the advantages of zero balance accounting to a corporation.
5. Explain how a payroll service operates.

EXERCISES

1. Interview the appropriate person in your organization and determine the types of cash management services offered by your bank.
2. Discuss how a local utility company uses lockbox services to their advantage.
3. Determine how information management is utilized by your bank in making decisions.
4. Discuss the importance of cash management services in a global economy.

BIBLIOGRAPHY

Bank Administration Institute, *An Analysis of Float in the Commercial Banking Industry*, 1982.

Bank Administration Institute, *Contemporary Issues in Cash Management*, 1983.

Bank Administration Magazine, Bank Administration Institute, Rolling Meadows, Illinois.

Cash Management Techniques, First National Bank of Chicago, Chicago, Illinois.

Corporate Cash Flow Magazine, Communication Channels, Atlanta, Georgia.

Corporate Services, Shawmut Bank N.A., Boston, MA.

Fabazzi, Frank J., *Corporate Cash Management—Techniques and Analysis*, Homewood, Illinois—Dow—Jones—Irwin, 1985.

14

Bank Marketing
Joseph P. Madaio

Introduction

Perhaps no single part of the banking business has changed so dramatically as the marketing function. Changes in the regulatory environment, as well as advances in technology, have fostered not only new services, but new distribution systems for existing services. Social and economic differences in banking consumers have caused us to be more precise regarding our customers' wants and needs. Intense competition from an expanded financial services industry has translated into a need for a more effective and efficient marketing effort. These factors are just some of the reasons for marketing's transition from "an art to a science" in the industry of banking.

Gone are the days when bank marketing, if it existed at all, was principally a public relations role. Marketing, out of necessity, has evolved as a sophisticated function in its own right. Marketing is now an integrated part of the business of banking. Successful marketing is critical to the bank's overall survival, today more than ever.

Learning Objectives

After reading this chapter, you should have an understanding of:

1. The activities which make up a sound marketing program,
2. The role of research in aiding the decision-making process and reducing risk,
3. How bank products fit into the overall marketing mix,
4. The importance of advertising and promotion in bringing customers into the bank,

5. Why sales and sales management have gained prominence in banking,

6. Corporate communications—both internal and external,

7. The blending of marketing activities to drive the marketing program.

MARKETING MANAGEMENT

Today marketing pervades all aspects of the organization in the banking industry. Most banks have either a specified individual or a department dedicated to marketing. However, you might find the approach to be uniquely different from one institution to another. Thus, we will discuss marketing as a process, with specific attention to the activities which make up that process.

The responsibility of marketing is the implementation of an annual marketing plan consistent with the framework of the organization's overall goals and objectives. Specifically, marketing encompasses the elements of product, price, place, promotion and, in a growing number of banks, people.

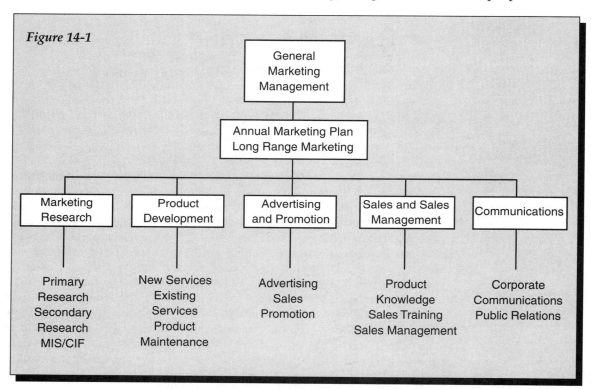

Figure 14-1

MARKETING RESEARCH

"Knowledge is power" is an old adage that is certainly true when it comes to marketing research. What we know about our own bank, customers and our competitors becomes the foundation for the marketing planning process. Who are our customers? What services do they use? Why do they bank with us? Answers to these questions and others are the basis for the process to begin.

A simple and workable definition of marketing research is the acquisition and use of information that can be input to the marketing management undertaking.

Marketing research tells a bank what it needs to know about the needs and wants of its customers.

It is important to note that research is an ongoing activity which is useful at any point in marketing planning, not just at the beginning. Information at any stage reduces the risk in decision-making. Generally speaking, marketing research can be categorized as primary research and secondary research.

Primary Research refers to data gathered as part of an original study, i. e. research that is done by or for the bank itself.

Secondary Research is the use of information from existing sources, i.e. analysis of data compiled by someone other than the bank and possibly for another purpose.

Primary data collection is specific to obtaining an answer to a question. Simple observations or complex studies may be used to collect such information. Examples of these techniques are:

1. *Professional Shoppers* are trained specialists who inquire about and apply for services to measure sales and service activities through personal contact with bank personnel.

2. *Mail, Telephone or Personal Interviews* are well planned and executed surveys designed to find specific answers from a targeted group. Surveys can determine such things as levels of customer satisfaction, advertising awareness, market share, why people come to the bank or why they leave.

3. *Focus Groups* are small representative groups whose in-depth comments and reactions will help structure such things as new product ideas, advertising campaigns or, in some cases, marketing strategy based on their general attitudes regarding the bank.

It is important to note that marketing research is a sophisticated process in itself. One needs to be concerned with the best survey method, sample design and data collection materials to be confident that the results are reliable and applicable to the market at large.

Two of the best examples of *secondary data* come from the United States Government and the Federal Deposit Insurance Corporation (FDIC). Every ten years the government conducts the U. S. Census which presents us with a wealth of information regarding age, sex, income, marital status, employment, etc. by geographic areas. While the census is done primarily to determine representation in the House of Representatives, it is the basis for any and all data reporting on the population at large. Incidentally, this type of data is called *demographics*.

Yearly, the FDIC reports the addresses of branches of all member banks along with deposit data. This information can be used to determine market share of individual branches.

In a contemporary banking environment, a new tool has emerged to assist in the process of data analysis. The *Marketing Information System* (MIS) utilizes the data collected as part of the daily operation to a marketing advantage. As an integrated part of the bank's data base, an MIS can determine activity at both branch and account level which may assist in staffing and pricing decisions.

The most useful aspect of an MIS is the creation of a *Central Information File* (CIF) which lists all account relationships by customer and/or by household. This allows for a more efficient promotional effort. For example, this eliminates the possibility of promoting a specific service to an individual customer or household who may already have it with you. It also presents the opportunity to target specific products to customers who may have these services with other institutions.

Today, many banks are merging CIF data with secondary sources of information. This allows a comparison of the bank's demographics to the general population of the marketplace it serves. The bank now has the ability

---

Primary research gathers data from an original source.

Secondary research gathers data from primary research sources.

The U.S. government and the FDIC are excellent secondary data sources.

The *MIS* (Marketing Information System) is a computerized collection of data from a bank's own daily operations, which is then stored in a *CIF* (central information file).

to identify consumers who may be more inclined to using specific bank services.

PRODUCT DEVELOPMENT

Bank *products* must meet a market need.

Ideas for products in the past have not always been rooted in customer need. Product development has been driven more often by the ability to offer a service than by consumers' wants. Some of today's core banking products: NOW accounts, credit cards, automated teller machines; in fact, needed to initially find markets in which to be accepted. Technology and government regulation have also played major roles in product development as evidenced by telephone and home banking, money market accounts and home equity lines of credit. However, bringing any product to market assumes some satisfactory level of customer approval and requires a progression of steps:

1. *Product Definition*—A detailed description of the planned offering and the potential market needs to be established.

2. *Internal Capabilities*—Legal, compliance and operational issues need to be dealt with as specifications take shape.

3. *Distribution* (Place)—A strategy of how the product will get to the customer must be determined. In banking, our retail outlet is our branch network. But, today we also get the product to the customer via mail, telephone, various forms of electronic banking, automated teller machines and (even house calls!)

4. *Price*—A detailed pricing analysis will consider the costs to the bank, profit margin, competitive pricing of the same or similar products and the bank's overall pricing policy. Options for pricing in banking can consist of rates, fees, balances and requirements for attached services.

5. *Promotion*—How the product will be brought to the attention of potential customers is the last step in the process.

Each step in this process represents a point where the product idea can be accepted or rejected. However, products that successfully make it through the analysis require one additional test—How will the new offering affect existing products currently available to the customers? Many times a new service presents an opportunity to eliminate an existing service, as often the new service poses a better alternative to the consumer. These issues must also be carefully weighed before the new product introduction.

Product Maintenance monitors product progress after introduction.

Once the product is introduced, it will continue to be monitored. This phase is simply called Product Maintenance. Each of the products in the bank's portfolio will be at varying stages of the product life cycle: introduction, growth, maturity or decline. Situations present themselves to modify, enhance and even eliminate existing products. All products should be monitored as part of an on-going product strategy.

ADVERTISING AND SALES PROMOTION

Any discussion of advertising and sales promotion in banking gives you an idea of just how much marketing has changed. Greater portions of promotional budgets are being spent on targeted approaches as opposed to mass media. The "rifle" is replacing the "shotgun" in an effort to get more "bang for the buck."

Although not mutually exclusive, most advertising is mass media and most sales promotion is targeted to some extent. In broad terms, advertising is used to bring consumers into the bank and sales promotion is used to make them customers.

Advertising brings customers into a bank; *sales promotion* sells them a product.

Advertising is a paid message carried by some form of media (television, radio, newspaper, outdoor and so on) which attempts to persuade the viewer to take some action desired by the sponsor.

Planning for advertising involves a number of key components:

1. Budget—determines how much money to spend.

2. Creative Strategy—determines the message.

3. Media Strategy—determines the appropriate communication channels.

A complement to advertising, Sales Promotion, refers to a number of applications that stimulate a consumer to make a purchasing decision. Each promotional undertaking requires a planning process similar to advertising.

Some successful sales promotions used in banking include: statement stuffers, newsletters, direct mail and telephone solicitations, account premiums, employee incentives, seminars, shows and exhibits.

PERSONAL SELLING AND SALES MANAGEMENT

To this point, we have discussed activities and processes related to the organization of marketing. Here we will begin to address people issues. Personal Selling involves one-on-one direct communication between the banks sales representative and the prospective customer. While selling is a much more accepted role for the banker, sales management is still evolving.

Personal selling has been part of the business of banking for some time. In the commercial and municipal areas of the bank a form of sales is prevalent due to the nature of those products and markets. However, selling to retail customers, or personal consumers, is a more recent phenomenon. Recognition of sales as a force with this market comes about as a result of:

1. the competitive nature of the financial services business beyond banking, requires us to take advantage of any sales opportunity,

2. the role of the banker as a highly respected financial advisor, leading to the banker as a consultative sales person, and

3. the realization that the more services a customer has with the bank, the more likely they are to remain a customer.

A comprehensive sales management program begins with training, and two types are required:

A good bank salesperson needs to know the *product* and *how to sell*.

1. *Product Training* deals with the features and benefits of the product, pricing, processing and operational procedures.

2. *Sales Training* converts the benefits orientation of the product training into a sale by identifying what the customer needs.

Beyond the training phase, management of sales also addresses goal setting, staff motivation, sales tracking and recognizing good performers. Strategically, sales management will involve protecting and enhancing the customer base in addition to new accounts solicitation.

CORPORATE COMMUNICATIONS

We've talked about communications related to products and/or customers as we discussed advertising, sales promotion and sales management. Communications related to general information about the bank is referred to as *corporate communications* and *public relations*. The banks public can be defined in terms of internal and external groups. Employees, customers and shareholders constitute the former; the investment community, the community at large and the government, the latter.

Much of the responsibility for corporate communications is done, as a matter of course, by the financial function with quarterly and annual reports and other financial disclosures. Other efforts usually impart information to employees, customers and the general public and incorporate participation in or organization of community events and activities.

Public relations is the management of non-advertising, unpaid use of the media to present the bank in a positive light. Some opportunities for public relations might be officer promotions, product introductions or publicity of community events.

Public relations is unpaid advertising favorable to the bank.

MARKET SEGMENTATION

Markets can be *segmented* by population, customer type, etc.

Although not previously mentioned, *market segmentation* is an emerging element that cuts across a number of marketing activities previously discussed. Segmentation recognizes a specific user of banking services and then tailors precise marketing strategies to attract this group. To be segmented a group must be measurable, of some substance and be accessible. Segmentation criteria can be by location, population characteristics, product use, customer type and life-style to name but a few.

Some successful examples of segmentation in banking are the senior and affluent consumer markets and the small and middle markets on the commercial side. A given market segmentation strategy will have a profound effect on related strategies. Marketing to seniors requires specific product planning, advertising and promotional activities. Their product orientation, for example, is toward services for those with accumulated wealth who want to protect it. Saving and investment services interest them most. They would not be predisposed to lending services.

THE FUTURE IS NOW

Technology creates new avenues of distribution.

With technological improvements happening every day, banking is not immunized. Consumers can now "access" the bank in ways never before possible. Today, you will find banks offering "home banking" via personal computers, and access to banking products and services is available over the *Internet*. Automated Teller Machines are capable of speaking foreign languages and supplying customers with statements of their account activity. Debit Cards allow direct access to checking balances and are being used at retail establishments eliminating the need to write checks at all.

These are just several examples of how automation is changing the financial services industry and every other business for that matter. Much of what we know as "traditional banking" is becoming obsolete as we move into the twenty-first century. As a result, marketing has needed to keep up by becoming more "cutting edge" and creating such things as "web sites," for example, in order to reach potential customers in new and different ways.

CONCLUSION

Marketing in a bank is a complex process. The individual activities that make up marketing, when blended together, can help with the overall success of the institution. Marketing is not however, a frivolous function and subsequently demands the same understanding, dedication and attention of any other management function. There is quite a bit more to it than is presented on these few pages. Hopefully, what is provided here is a general overview to encourage you to find out more about bank marketing.

STUDY AND REVIEW QUESTIONS

1. Market segments are defined as consumer groups identified by their demographic or psychographic profiles, their wants or needs, or their response to advertising and promotional activities. Discuss specific examples of how banks have been successful in implementing products or services for specific market segments.

2. Advertising is a paid message carried by some form of media which attempts to persuade the viewer to take some action desired by the sponsor. Choose several newspaper/magazine advertisements for financial services to discuss in class.

3. A good bank salesperson needs to know both the product and how to sell. Give several examples of customer's needs and wants and match with appropriate products.

BIBLIOGRAPHY

Bethany S. Brown, "Bank Marketing," *Fundamentals of Banking*, (Needham Heights, Massachusetts: Ginn Press, 1989).

Neal E. Hunt, James A. Scurlock, *Marketing Handbook—Branch Banking Series*, (Washington, D.C.: American Bankers Association , 1990).

Robert J. McMahon, *Bank Marketing Handbook*, (Boston, Massachusetts: Bankers Publishing Company, 1986).

Mary Ann Pezzullo, *Marketing for Bankers*, (Washington D. C.: American Bankers Association, 1982).

15

TRUST SERVICES
David Pimenta

INTRODUCTION

The Trust Department is the area of banking that provides financial services for a fee to individuals and other entities. These services include the administration of trusts, estates, guardianships, and conservatorships and the management of agencies. Customers for these services include individuals, corporations, charitable institutions, and governmental units.

Traditionally, there has been a complete separation of trust departments and commercial departments within banking institutions. Commercial departments make their profits by lending money on terms that are most advantageous to the bank. Profits are made on the difference between the amount paid by the bank on its deposit or the price paid by the bank to borrow money and the amount of interest it charges when it lends money to others.

A trust department makes its profits by the fees charged for its services. Trust departments have a fiduciary relationship with its customers, which means that the bank has a duty to act in the best interests of the clients on issues within the terms of the relationship. Basically, they must ensure that they invest on terms that are most advantageous to the client. This concept of fiduciary relationship is the basis of trust department services.

This chapter examines how the trust department services the financial needs of individuals and institutions and describes the variety of products available to fill these needs.

LEARNING OBJECTIVES

After reading this chapter, you should have an understanding of the following:

1. Definition of trusts and agencies.

2.   Services to individuals.

3.   Services to corporate and institutional customers.

WHAT ARE TRUSTS?

Trusts have five basic necessities.

A *trust* is a legal relationship based on reliability, confidence, good faith, and fairness by which one party (the trustee) assumes legal ownership of property and manages the property for the benefit of another party (the beneficiary) in accordance with the terms of a written instrument. The five major elements of a trust are as follows:

1.   *Trustor*—The trustor is the individual or other entity who has created the trust. Other terms for this person are settlor, grantor, or creator.

2.   *Trustees*—The trustee is the individual or institution holding legal title to the trust property. If there is more than one trustee, they are known as co-trustees. The duties of a trustee are as follows:

    a.   Invest and manage the trust property in accordance with the Prudent Man Rule

    b.   Comply with the terms of the instrument in the distribution and payout of the trust income and property.

    c.   Account to the donor and/or beneficiaries for all transactions that occur in the trust

    d.   Exercise discretion in accordance with the criterion set forth in the instrument to determine who should receive trust income or principal.

    e.   Prepare and file trust income tax returns and supply tax information to the beneficiaries.

    f.   Provide the custody, safekeeping and record keeping duties necessary for trust property.

3.   *Beneficiary*—The beneficiary is the person or persons who have the right to enjoy the benefits of the property that is the subject of the trust. They are said to have equitable title to the property in the trust. Types of beneficiaries include:

    Income Beneficiaries—Those who receive the income produced by the trust.

    Principal Beneficiaries—Those who may receive part or all of the principal of the trust during the period that the trust is in existence.

    Remainderpersons—Those who will receive the property in the trust when it terminates.

4.   *Property*—Property must be held in the trust in order to make it valid. This property is also known as the trust res. Examples of property that are the subject of a trust include stocks, bonds, cash, real estate or personal property.

5.   *Trust Agreement or Instrument*—The trust agreement is the written document that creates the trust. It states specifically who the trustee is and who is to have beneficial interest. The instrument sets forth the guidelines by which the trustee will administer the trust. It states who is to receive money from the trust, the criteria by which money can be paid, and when the trust will be distributed and to whom the trust will be distributed.

All trusts fall into one of two categories:

Living trusts are created during a grantor's lifetime, and may be revocable or irrevocable.

1. *Living Trusts* or *Inter Vivos Trusts*—These are trusts created during a person's lifetime. Living Trusts provide professional management of assets to a person while they are living. They can also provide protection against the need for a guardian if the donor becomes incapacitated. Living Trusts avoid probate and the donor has the opportunity to test the trustees' performance. There are two kinds of Living Trusts:

   a. *Revocable Living Trusts*—A revocable trust is one that is set up by the donor whereby he or she retains the right to revoke, amend or terminate the trust at any time. At the death of the donor, the trust becomes irrevocable and can no longer be changed.

   b. *Irrevocable Trusts*—an irrevocable trust is the opposite of the revocable trust and cannot be revoked, amended, or terminated once it is established and funded. Irrevocable trusts may provide tax savings to the donor.

Testamentary trusts are trusts under the will of the decedent.

2. *Testamentary Trusts*—These are trusts created by the terms of a person's will. They are created only upon the trustor's death and therefor do not provide any lifetime benefits to the trustor. Investment management is provided for the beneficiaries and the donor retains control over his or her assets after death through the terms of the trust.

WHAT IS AN AGENCY?

An *agent* acts for a *principal*, but has no legal rights to the property which is the subject to the agency.

An agency may appear to be very similar to a trust, and the duties of the agent may be very similar to those of a trustee. An *agency* is established when a person (the principal) authorizes another person (the agent) to act on behalf and subject to the control of the principal. An agency is a contractual relationship and is therefore established by a letter of instructions or agency agreement. There are several distinctions between an agency relationship and a trust.

1. A *trustee* always has legal title to the trust property. An agent does not have title to the property of his principal, but merely has certain powers with respect to it.

2. An *agent* is always subject to the control of the principal, but a trustee is not subject to the control of either the beneficiary or the trustor. Of course, if the trust is revocable, the trustor does have some control over the trustee in that he can revoke the trust at any time; but for the most part, a trustee will not be subject to the control of the trustor or the beneficiary except to the extent that he must comply with the terms of the trust instrument and can be held liable if he does not do so.

3. An agent's authority is limited to that specifically granted to him by the principal. A trustee is presumed to have broader powers. Except as limited or reserved by the trustor or by law, a trustee is considered to have all powers necessary or appropriate to carry out his duties under the trust.

4. An agent acting within the scope of his authority, and who has disclosed the fact that he is acting as an agent for another, incurs no personal liability. His principal alone is liable on any contract or debts incurred by the agent. A trustee is personally liable to third persons for his acts. He cannot subject the beneficiary to such liability.

5. An agency terminates on the death of either the principal or agent. The agency can also be terminated at any time by either the principal or the agent. A trust, on the other hand, generally does not end upon the death

of the trustor. Also, the death of a trustee will not terminate a trust in most cases, as the instrument will provide for a successor trustee to take his or her place.

6. As an agency terminates at the death of the principal or the agent, the property comprising the agency will be subject to probate.

SERVICES TO INDIVIDUALS

Trusts have evolved slowly from English common law over a period of several hundred years. In the United States, the demand for managing the assets for heirs came as a result of the nation's change from an agricultural economy to a manufacturing and industrial economy.

With the onset of an industrial society, wealth was concentrated less and less in agriculture and more and more in stocks and bonds of the companies that were transforming the economy. Financiers and industrialists did not wish to pass their vast fortunes directly to their heirs but wanted to ensure that the fortune would be well-managed and passed to future generations. In the mid-nineteenth century, U. S. Trust Company of New York was chartered as the first institution whose sole function was to provide fiduciary services. Trust institutions and departments have continued to grow as the need for more sophisticated financial planning, investment services, estate planning, and estate settlement have also grown.

Trusts are designed to meet the financial management and confidential needs of the beneficiaries.

Trust department services are designed to meet the needs and requirements of its customers. Some of the needs of the customers include investment services and management of property. Customers may also have the need for privacy; they do not want the extent of their finances made public. In many cases, customers want to control the distribution of their wealth after their death. They may want to ensure that children from a prior marriage are taken care of or that an unsophisticated spouse who is not familiar with handling financial affairs is given protection or assistance. The donor may also want protection for a child who is a spendthrift and wants the control of a trustee to limit the child's access to money. Other needs include tax minimization, recordkeeping, safekeeping of assets, as well as financial protection from the customer's own possible incapacity.

Administration of Trusts

A *living trust* is not subject to probate.

A trust is a confidential relationship. Therefore, it meets a customer's need for privacy. While a testamentary trust is subject to the jurisdiction of the probate court and is therefore a matter of public record, a living trust is not subject to the probate court and therefore ensures privacy. By setting up a living trust, the donor also obtains professional investment services and property management. The trustee, in investing the assets for the donor in a trust agreement, is guided by the Prudent Man Rule, which was a landmark opinion established by the Massachusetts Supreme Judicial Court in Harvard College vs. Amory (1830). The ruling in this case stated that: "All that can be required of a trustee to invest is that he shall conduct himself faithfully and exercise a sound discretion. He is to observe how men of prudence, discretion, and intelligence manage their own affairs, not in regard to speculation, but in regard to the permanent disposition of their funds, considering the probable income, as well as the safety of capital, to be invested. "The rule is a rule of fiduciary conduct, not of performance. If a fiduciary has conducted himself properly, then the fact that the assets of the trust may have declined in value will not, in and of itself, be grounds for liability. In making investment decisions, the trustee should take into consideration the objectives or goals of the trust i.e. college tuition, retirement, medical care etc. The trustee should review the time frame to meet that goal and should consider the risk tolerance of the client.

One of the greatest challenges of a trustee in investing the assets of the trust is to balance the needs of the current income beneficiaries, who will be looking for maximum income, with the needs of the remaindermen (the individuals who will eventually receive the principal of the trust) who no doubt will be looking for maximum growth. The trustees have a fiduciary duty to both sets of beneficiaries. It is this balance between the needs of the income beneficiaries and the wishes of the remaindermen that make investing trust funds both interesting and difficult.

Incapacity Hedge

A living trust can also help alleviate the concerns of a donor about what will become of the management of that property should the donor become incapacitated. Once the trust is established, it continues beyond the incapacity of the trustor and can pay out income to him as well as pay his bills and other expenses.

Under the terms of some living trusts, the donor retains the right to direct the investments. In this situation, the trustor is looking for the bank to provide safekeeping of assets, recordkeeping, and an accounting of all transactions that occur. Generally, the instrument provides that if the trustor becomes incapacitated or is otherwise unable to manage his affairs, the trustee will step in and manage the investments. A living trust also provides the donor with the opportunity to work with the trustee during his lifetime. In this way, the trustor can assess the quality of the services provided by the trustee prior to his death. If the donor is not pleased with the quality of the service, he can revoke the trust if he has reserved this right.

Irrevocability

A sprinkle or spray trust gives the trustee the power to determine the distribution of trust benefits.

Upon the death of a trustor, the trust becomes irrevocable. Income and/or principal of the trust will be paid out and distributed by the trustee in accordance with the terms of the trust instrument. Many trusts provide that the trustee will have discretion to determine who will receive money and in what proportion. This kind of trust is known as a *sprinkle trust* or *spray trust* that gives the right to the trustee to spray or sprinkle income and/or principal to any number of beneficiaries. Criteria such as health, maintenance, support, and education are generally given to aid the trustee in his decision making of how to distribute the money. The advantage of this type of trust is that the trustee can direct money to those beneficiaries who have the greatest financial need. Because the trustee is impartial, all decisions are based solely on the needs of the beneficiaries and are not subject to favoritism.

A wide variety of trusts are available; many are designed to fill a specific purpose. Some trusts are designed to accumulate income for a period of years—for instance, until the intended beneficiaries reach a certain age—and then distribution is made to them. Other trusts are established for a short term to provide support for elderly parents or for the college education of children. At the end of the period, the property returns to the trustor. Another type of trust is a life insurance trust that is set up to receive the proceeds of life insurance policies upon the death of the donor. The trustee collects these proceeds and invests the funds to provide for the beneficiaries.

Trusts can also provide tax savings for the trustor in some cases. This can be true for income taxes as well as estate taxes. A trust can be used to ensure that available credits and deducations are fully utilized.

In summary, some of the advantages of trusts are protection of beneficiaries, controlled distribution of property, privacy, prudent investment management of assets, and flexibility.

William Jones is married with two children. It is his second marriage and his children are from his first marriage. He has considerable wealth that he inherited as well as received from the sale of his business. As he is now retired, he wants to enjoy himself and travel. He is concerned because there is a history of Alzheimer's disease in his family and as he has always handled the family finances, his wife is rather unsophisticated in this area. His children are in their late twenties and his youngest has a learning disability which has affected his ability to be employed.

After meeting with his attorney and personal banker, Mr. Jones sets up a living revocable trust with the bank that had served him well when he was in business. The bank as trustee takes title to his property and manages the assets for him. Under the terms of the trust instrument, the trustees must pay the income to Mr. Jones or for his benefit for his lifetime. Trust principal cannot also be used for his care. Upon Mr. Jones' death or incompetence, the trustees have the discretion to pay income and principal among the group which includes his wife and two children.

As a result, Mr. Jones can enjoy his retirement knowing that his needs are being met. His property is being professionally managed and his expenses can be paid by the trust if he is unable to do so. If he becomes incompetent, the trustees can see to his needs without the appointment of a guardian. When he dies, he can be assured that the trust assets will be fairly allocated among his wife and children according to their relative needs. The trustees can pay his wife's expenses and advise her on financial matters. The trustees will review the needs of the children and provide financial assistance from the trust when necessary. The trust can also protect funds from the beneficiaries' creditors.

ADMINISTRATION OF AGENCIES

Four basic types of agency accounts are administered by bank trust departments:

> The four kinds of agency accounts are *custody, investment management, agent fiduciary,* and *guardianship.*

1. *Custody Account*—A custody account is an agency account in which the bank performs three functions. First, the bank will have safekeeping of all securities held in the custody account. Second, the bank will receive all income and disburse all monies at the direction of the customer. Third, the bank will render accounts or periodic reports to the customer concerning the account activity and listing the securities held in the account. The bank as custodian does not give investment advice, but merely completes investment transactions in accordance with the direction of the principal.

2. *Investment Management Account*—An investment management account is also an agency in which the bank has safekeeping of the securities, receives and disburses all income, and accounts for or periodically reports to the principal regarding the account activities and the assets held. These functions are the same as those in the custody account. However, in addition to these duties, the trust department has a responsibility to supervise the investment of the accounts. Depending upon the agreement, the trust department as agent may have full discretion to change the investments of the investment management account or may make

recommendations to the principal, who must approve all transactions before they are executed.

3. *Agent Fiduciary Accounts*—An agent fiduciary account is one under which the bank performs services for another fiduciary, such as an executor, administrator, or trustee. The agency agreement will establish the extent of the services to be provided by the agent. The agreement may require full investment services or may just require basic custodial duties.

4. *Guardianship Accounts*—A guardianship account is established to professionally manage and protect the assets of a person who is mentally incapable of handling his/her affairs or the assets of a minor. The duties of the financial guardian are very similar to the duties of a trustee, in that the guardian must protect the assets of the minor or ward as well as give periodic accounting of the guardian's activities. A guardianship is subject to the review of the probate court that appoints the guardian.

In summary, agencies fill the need that a person may have for the safekeeping of assets as well as recordkeeping. In some cases, it does fulfill the need that a person may have for investment services. It does not provide privacy, as the agent must disclose that he is acting in the capacity of an agent and not as a principal. Agency accounts cannot be used to control the distribution of wealth after a person's death because the agency ends upon the death of the principal. Agencies do not provide financial protection to the principal from his possible incapacity.

SETTLEMENT OF ESTATES

Due to its expertise in this area, bank trust departments often are called upon to settle a person's estate. When the bank has been named in the decedent's will, the bank is executor of the will. If the person has died intestate (without a will), or in the case where the named executor does not wish to serve, then the bank is appointed administrator or personal representative by the court to settle the estate. The bank may also serve as agent for an executor where the named executor is an individual who does not have the expertise to settle the estate and wishes to hire the bank as his or her agent.

> Persons who die leaving a valid will die *testate*, and without such a will, *intestate*.

Two terms that should be remembered in the discussion of estates are *testate* versus *intestate*. An individual who dies leaving a valid will has died testate; an individual dying without a will is said to have died intestate.

Probate

> *Probate* (from the Latin "to prove") determines the validity of a will.

The first step in settling an estate is to probate the will. The term probate means proof. The will is probated to prove that it is valid and was intended by the decedent to dispose of his or her estate. The will is filed in the probate court and notice is given to all interested parties as well as published in a local newspaper. The will is then a matter of public record, and anyone may review its contents in the probate court. The probate process also affords others to object to the will if they can prove fraud, undue influence or that the testator was incompetent at the time he or she wrote the will. The process provides protection for the testator and his or her heirs.

A will is a written instrument executed in accordance with certain formalities to take effect upon death; through it a person directs the disposition of his or her probate property. The will does not control the disposition of non-probate property such as joint property which goes to the joint owner by operation of law upon the death of the other joint owner, life insurance proceeds, and living trust assets which distribute according to the terms of the trust agreement. The requirements of a valid will are that:

1. It must be in writing

2. The person writing must have been over eighteen years of age.

3. The person writing the will was competent and of sound mind.

4. The will is signed by the person who wrote the will in the presence of two disinterested witnesses.

A valid will must be written by a person 18 years of age or older, of sound mind, and signed in the presence of two disinterested witnesses.

Settlement Steps

Once the will has been probated and the executor appointed, certain steps must be taken in the settlement of the estate. The first step is the gathering and securing of all assets in the name of the decedent. These assets include bank accounts, stocks, bonds, tangible personal property, real estate, life insurance policies, and any business interests. The executor must then appraise the assets to determine the date of death value. Once the executor has appraised the assets, he then prepares an inventory that is filed in the probate court.

An executor must secure the estate's assets and settle all debts, expenses, and taxes.

The next step is to develop a budget and pay any valid claims against the estate. It is the executor's duty to pay all valid bills that were outstanding at the time of the decedent's death. In addition, the executor must pay the expenses of the last illness, the administrative costs of settling the estate, and the costs of the funeral. Often there is insufficient cash to satisfy all these claims, and the personal representative must sell enough assets to raise the necessary money. The personal representative must determine which assets are to be sold first, the timing of such sales, and is under obligation to secure the best deal possible for the estate.

The next step is the tax filing stage. The executor is responsible for the preparation and filing of all applicable estate, income, and inheritance tax forms. Any taxes owed must also be paid to the state and federal government.

A Final Accounting

Once all taxes have been settled, the executor must make a final accounting to the probate court of all of the activity in the estate and distribute the assets in the estate in accordance with the terms of the decedent's will. If the person died intestate, the state law will direct how the assets are to be distributed. Timing for the settling of an estate may be as short as one year and, in some cases where the estate is complex, as long as four to five years.

In summary, the settlement of an estate is a complex area requiring legal and financial expertise. Expert planning before a person's death and also during the period of settlement of the estate can help to minimize taxes as well as to facilitate the final distribution of the estate's assets.

TRUST DEPARTMENT ORGANIZATION

The organization of a trust department varies greatly from one banking institution to another. It is not the purpose of this chapter to go into the many organizational charts which could be used in one institution or another, but rather to give an example to assist the reader in understanding both the complexity of the trust business and the organization of that business within a commercial bank.

A typical trust department is headed by a trust department executive, who is answerable to the president of the bank and the board of directors. Beneath the department executive, the trust business might be broken into four sections:

1. *Business Development*—This area is responsible for bringing new personal and institutional accounts into the institution.

2. *Administration*—This section would be responsible for the day-to-day administration of personal trust, estates, agencies, employee benefit trusts, and corporate trusts. The administrators are also responsible for tax and estate planning for their customers and must ensure compliance with the terms of the trust instrument. They are responsible for the gathering of material necessary to exercising proper discretion. The question of who is to receive funds from the trust involves determining the instrument provisions, the value of the trust, remainder interests, life styles of the beneficiaries, their future anticipated needs as well as tax considerations and what would the donor have done in the same situation.

3. *Investments*—This area would be responsible for research and all investment decisions in accounts over which the bank has investment supervision.

4. *Support Services*—Sections considered support services might include accounting, income collection, real estate, tax, and all other security processing and operational activities.

REGULATION OF TRUST DEPARTMENTS

In order to operate a trust department, a bank must receive a separate permit or charter from the state banking commission. The comptroller of the currency is authorized to grant national banks the right to provide fiduciary services such as trust management, estate settlement and guardianships or conservatorships. The authority to supervise the exercise of trust powers of national banks is in the comptroller of the currency which conducts periodic audits of the trust departments. In addition, the trust department must comply with regulations and examinations by the state banking authority, the Federal Reserve, Federal Deposit Insurance Corporation and the Securities and Exchange Commission.

SERVICES TO INSTITUTIONAL CUSTOMERS

Everything discussed in this chapter up to this point has been geared towards the services of individual or personal trust customers. This section will deal with how a commercial bank's trust department may serve corporate and large institutional customers.

Trust departments also may manage corporate benefit plans—a fast-growing field.

Commercial bank trust departments may also serve as trustee or agent for employee benefit plans. Managing employee benefit trusts is one of the fastest growing and most lucrative areas for trust departments. Employee benefit trusts began in the nineteenth century, but during World War II became increasingly important as a result of the wage freeze imposed by the government. Benefits became a more important factor in attracting and retaining employees. The growth in the union movement coupled with tax breaks given to corporations for the funding of pensions fostered this growth.

In 1974, ERISA (Employee Retirement Income Security Act) was passed and required corporations to create separate funds for pension payments rather than make these payments out of corporate assets. The act also defined fiduciary standards, funding requirements, reporting and disclosure procedures, participation and vesting schedules among other areas. The complexity of many of these regulations forced corporations to seek out professional managers rather than managing the plans in house. Although all of these plans are commonly called retirement plans, several different employee benefit trusts include profit sharing plans, 401(k) plans, pension plans, employee stock option plans, and thrift and saving plan trusts.

An employee benefit trust is established by determining the following:

1. *The Plan*—The employee benefit details specifically the rules and regulations governing the employee benefit plan. It is designed to meet the specific needs of the corporation and its employees. The plan includes such things as eligibility requirements, benefits to be paid, retirement age, vesting schedules, and basic administrative duties.

2. *The Trustee*—The plan will name the trustee of the employee benefit trust. The trustee must ensure compliance with the terms of the employee benefit plan. The trustee has a fiduciary responsibility to the beneficiaries of the trust and not the corporation.

3. *The Trust*—Just as a trust agreement is necessary for a personal trust, an employee benefit trust agreement must be drawn by the corporation's attorney. It will define the investment and administrative duties of the trustee.

4. *Employee Acceptance Form*—Any employee who participates in the plan must sign an employee acceptance form that shows he accepts the terms of the plan as presented.

5. *Board and Stockholder Approval*—The plan must be accepted by the board of directors of the corporation.

6. *Disclosure*—The corporation must disclose the plan and trust agreement to all participants and all regulatory bodies.

In administering benefit trust, the bank, as mentioned earlier, can serve as trustee or agent. In the case where the bank is serving strictly as agent, it is fulfilling its role in a bookkeeping and accounting function only. When the bank serves as trustee, the trust department has taken on the additional responsibilities of asset management.

The Employee Retirement Income Security Act sets forth the fiduciary standards with which a trustee of an employee benefit trust must comply. The following are the primary duties of a trustee:

A bank employee benefit trust department must work for the benefit of the trust's beneficiaries and consult with company management on investment strategy.

1. To manage the property for the benefit of the employees and their beneficiaries.

2. To work with the management of the company in planning and implementing investment strategy.

The trustee must receive, hold, invest, and reinvest the assets of the trust. The trustee is held to the Prudent Man Rule, and ERISA requires diversification of assets in order to minimize risk. The trustee must act solely in the interest of the participants and beneficiaries and must avoid any conflicts of interest such as investing solely in stock of the corporation that established the plan. The trustee must consider the cash that will be needed to pay out benefits and provide the needed liquidity to meet these payments.

The trustee is also required to provide annual reports, supplemental reports, and asset valuation reports to all of the plan participants, beneficiaries, the Departments of Labor and Treasury, the Internal Revenue Service, and the corporation.

In summary, the management of employee benefit trusts is a growing area for commercial bank trust departments. Trust departments have the necessary experience to satisfy the complex reporting and administrative requirements of ERISA and the investment expertise to satisfy its fiduciary requirements.

Corporate Trust

A bank's corporate trust department may administer a company's *stock* services or *bond* services (paying bond holder of record, etc.).

Corporations raise funds in two primary ways: the issuing of stock and the raising of debt capital or bonds. A commercial bank trust department can serve a corporation in both areas, as shown by the following:

1. *Issuance of Stock*—The trust department would serve the corporate customer in the following ways:
   a. as transfer agent—transferring the ownership of stock from one owner to another.
   b. as proxies—sending out any voting information to the stockholders and receiving and recording the responses.
   c. providing custody and safekeeping of unissued securities.
   d. destroying cancelled certificates.
   e. ensuring that shareholder inquiries are answered in accordance with the Security and Exchange Commission requirements as to providing replacement certificates for lost securities.
   f. maintaining an adequate supply of certificates.
2. *Raising Debt Capital/Bonds*—The trust department may also assist corporations when they raise money by issuing bonds. The bank will serve in the following capacity:
   a. Bond register—Keeping the records of ownership.
   b. Paying agent—The bank will pay the bond holders.
   c. Record and bookkeeping functions—The activities of a corporate trust department are governed by federal and state regulations. These include the Securities Act of 1933, the Glass-Steagall Act, the Securities Exchange Act of 1934, the Trust Indenture Act of 1939, and Articles 8 and 9 of the Uniform Commercial Code.

Trustee for Charitable Organizations

Banks may also administer the trust of charitable and/or not-for-profit organizations.

Bank trust departments may also serve as trustee or agent for large charitable organizations. As these charities take in money for their charitable purposes, they increasingly turn to commercial bank trust departments for active management of their investments and/or as agent in a bookkeeping and accounting capacity. One of the advantages for a charity for using bank trust departments is the opportunity to participate in the bank's pooled or common trust funds. This function allows the charity to effectively manage small contributions from their donors. There are several types of charitable vehicles:

A *community* *foundation* provides a large number of possible services.

1. ***Community Foundations***—Community foundations provide a wide range of services to a community and offer along with these services the flexibility of how the gift is to be used. The dominant advantage of a community foundation is that it allows an individual to fund a charitable activity of his/her choosing and have it efficiently managed as part of a larger organization. For example, an individual may wish to establish a charitable foundation of perhaps $10,000 to carry out a charitable endeavor of his/her choosing. However, management fees and costs of investment services on a $10,000 foundation would prohibit this fund from being run on its own. Therefore, an individual may merge this foundation with a large community foundation to achieve an efficient management of the smaller sum of money. The bank, as trustee, is responsible for the safeguarding, investing, managing, and accounting of the funds in the foundation.

Charitable remainder trusts pay non-charitable beneficiaries for a period of time, usually until their death, at which time the remainder of the funds goes to a charitable beneficiary.

2. ***Charitable Remainder Trusts***—Charitable remainder trusts are trusts created with a non-charitable beneficiary having a right to receive payment from the trust for a period of time, and remainder interest passes to a charitable organization qualified under Section 107(c) of the Internal Revenue Code.

   There are two types of charitable remainder trusts:

   a. ***Charitable Remainder Unitrust***—A charitable remainder trust—with the amount of payment to the non-charitable beneficiary for life or a term up to twenty years—is prescribed as a fixed percentage (not less than 5 percent) of the fair market value of the trust assets, valued annually, to be paid not less often than annually. The trustee is responsible for the annual valuation of the trust assets and the computation of the amount that will be paid to the non-charitable beneficiary during the year. The trustee is also responsible for the management of the assets in the trust to ensure a stream of income sufficient to meet the payout requirement. In addition, the trustee must invest for growth as it has a fiduciary responsibility to the charitable remainder.

   b. ***Charitable Remainder Annuity Trust***—A charitable remainder annuity trust is similar to a unitrust in that an amount of money is paid annually to a non-charitable beneficiary for a term up to twenty years or the beneficiary's life.

      In a charitable remainder annuity trust, the amount of the statutory payment is determined at the time the trust is initially set up. Once the amount of the annual payout is determined, it remains the same for the period of the trust. The trustee does not have to value the trust annually, but must ensure that adequate income is produced to meet the necessary payout to the noncharitable beneficiary.

3. Charitable Lead Trusts—A charitable lead trust is the mirror image of a charitable remainder trust. The income is paid to a charity for a number of years with the remainder interest going to a non-charity. The income paid to the charity must be in the form of an annuity or a fixed percentage of the market value of the trust. These trusts may be for a period of more than 20 years and the income payout can be for less than 5% of the fair market value. This trust is a popular option when the donor has adequate current income but may need additional funds in the future.

In summary, commercial bank trust departments can serve in two essential capacities regarding the charitable community. The first is as an investment advisor and the second is acting as agent. The bank's role as investment advisor and/or agent is similar to that of its role in regard to individuals. The trustee is held to the same degree of fiduciary responsibility and prudency.

CONCLUSION

Bank trust departments are no longer just "sleepy depositories," but dynamic entities.

Bank trust departments differ from other areas of commercial banking because of the nature of their fiduciary responsibility to their customers. A fiduciary is under an obligation to act in the best interests of the beneficiaries of the trust regardless of whether it conflicts with the best interests of the bank in general. For years, bank trust departments have been stereotyped as sleepy repositories for old money. These same departments are now marketing themselves aggressively to new clientele, both corporate and individual, with new and innovative products designed to meet the needs of this new clientele. Trust departments have also increased the number of services offered in order to meet the full financial needs of the customers. A trust department typically can provide clients with recordkeeping, bill paying, and tax preparation services in addition to money management. The bank, in effect, can act as a private banker in addition to providing traditional bank services.

By providing services to both individuals and corporations, the trust department assists the commercial bank by providing a full range of banking services for customers, and customers are not required to use multiple banks to provide for their full financial needs.

STUDY AND REVIEW QUESTIONS

1. Describe the five major elements of a trust.
2. What steps would you take to determine the validity of a will?
3. Describe what type of will would best suit your current situation and why.

APPENDIX I

DEPOSIT INSURANCE

INTRODUCTION

One of the major advantages that banks are able to offer their customers is that, contrary to other types of investments, bank deposits, subject to certain limitations, are *insured* against possible loss.

In this section, the workings of the four deposit insurance funds relevant to Massachusetts banking institutions are discussed.

LEARNING OBJECTIVES

After reading this section, you should understand the following:

1. The various deposit insurance funds and the types of financial institutions for which they provide coverage.

2. The relative strength of the funds.

3. The workings of FDIC coverage.

TYPES OF DEPOSIT INSURANCE

There are four types of banking institutions in Massachusetts—commercial banks, savings banks (mutual and stock), cooperative banks (mutual and stock) and savings and loan associations. Each of these has a different type or combination of deposit insurance coverage.

Commercial banks	FDIC (BIF)
Savings banks	FDIC (BIF) and DIFM
Cooperative banks	FDIC (BIF) and SIF
Savings & Loan associations	FDIC (SAIF)

The two FDIC funds represent the dissolution in 1987 of the Federal Savings and Loan Insurance Corporation (FSLIC). The Bank Insurance Fund (BIF) represents the FDIC insurance coverage afforded commercial banks and savings banks since the inceptions of the Federal Deposit Insurance Corporation in 1933. The Savings Association Insurance Fund (SAIF) is the former FSLIC insurance fund brought under FDIC administration. Although membership in a federal deposit insurance agency is optional for state-chartered banks that aren't members of the Federal Reserve System, virtually all Massachusetts commercial banks and savings banks obtained federal insurance, and, since the 1980s, *all* Massachusetts financial institutions have joined a federal deposit insurance agency (BIF or SAIF).

FDIC coverage is limited to $100,000 per "title." These limits are discussed at length later in this section.

The two state insurance funds—the Deposit Insurance Fund of Massachusetts (DIFM) and Savings Insurance Fund (SIF) represent separate insurance funds created in 1934 for what were two very different types of financial institutions. These funds provide coverage for funds not insured by the FDIC. So deposits in Massachusetts savings banks and cooperative banks insured by these two funds are covered in full.

FDIC Insurance Coverage Limits

Bank customers often inquire as to the limits of FDIC insurance coverage. Because of the way that the Federal Deposit Insurance Act is crafted, a simple explanation of this coverage is impossible. Banks attempt to provide the basic information on this coverage, often by providing copies of brochures developed by the FDIC. However, explaining the more complicated aspects of coverage is a matter best left to the FDIC itself. This is especially true because misstating the amount of coverage to a customer's detriment could be not only a federal offense, but also the genesis of a civil suit for damages.

At its most basic level, FDIC coverage is limited to $100,000 per depositor. A depositor receives separate insurance for accounts held in different capacities. For example, a depositor's individual accounts are first added together to determine the total balance, and the first $100,000 is insured. (A sole proprietor's business account is added together with his personal accounts, regardless of how they are titled. The coverage is based on actual ownership, rather than the name carried on a bank's books.)

A separate $100,000 coverage is provided for a depositor's interest in joint accounts. For joint accounts, the process is multi-stepped.

First, all accounts with the same combination of joint owners are added together. The excess over $100,000 in this group total is uninsured. Next, each joint account is assumed to be divided as to ownership equally (unless it is plain on the books of the bank that another allocation is required), regardless of who actually placed the funds in the account. Then, each joint owner's portion of all joint accounts is aggregated with others of his joint account balances, and insured to $100,000.

For example, assume that account (1), owned jointly by A and B, holds $75,000. Account (2), owned by A and C, holds $80,000. Account (3), owned by C and D, holds $50,000. Account (4), owned by B and A, holds $30,000. Finally, account (5), owned by A individually, holds $95,000.

The first step is to identify any individually-owned accounts. Account (5) is owned only by A, and is fully insured to $95,000.

Next, we find joint accounts with identical ownership. Accounts (1) and (4) are owned by the same combination (note that the order of the names makes no difference), and add to $105,000. That makes $5,000 of that account uninsured. The remaining $100,000 is assumed to belong equally to *A* and *B*.

A holds $50,000 in the combined accounts (1) and (4), plus $40,000 in account (2). His insured interest in joint accounts, then, is $90,000.

B holds $50,000 in combined accounts (1) and (4), and this is *B*'s insured interest in joint accounts.

C holds $40,000 in account (2) and $25,000 in account (3), for a total of $65,000.

D holds $25,000 in account (3), fully insured.

Another separate line of insurance is provided for revocable trust accounts, sometimes referred to as "Totten" trusts. If deposited by an individual with the intention that the funds will go to the named beneficiary upon the owner's death ("in trust for," "pay on death," etc.), and the beneficiary is the owner's spouse, child(ren) or grandchild(ren), the funds will be insured for up to $100,000 in the aggregate for each named beneficiary, separate from any other accounts of the owner(s) or beneficiary(ies). In these cases, the deposit account may carry insurance of more than $100,000 total, depending on the number of beneficiaries and owners.

For example, an account jointly owned by husband and wife, in trust for four named children of the husband and wife, could be insured for up to $800,000, since there is separate insurance for each of the joint owners with respect to each named beneficiary. Put another way, each combination of owner and beneficiary gets a separate $100,000 limit.

Note, however, that the relationships cannot go backward. A child cannot have a separately insured Totten trust account benefiting his parent or grandparent. (Although the account would be a valid Totten trust, it would not obtain insurance separate from the child's individual accounts in the same bank.)

Also, while a spouse can have a separately insured revocable trust account with his/her spouse as beneficiary, a joint account in the form "Spouse *A* and Spouse *B* i/t/f Spouse *B* and Spouse *A*" would be treated as a normal joint account of Spouse *A* and Spouse *B*.

Separate insurance is also available for an individual's total retirement accounts in the same institution. All forms of retirement accounts with the same beneficial owner are added together and a single $100,000 insurance limit imposed on that owner's beneficial interests.

CURRENT TRENDS

Although Congress is suggesting that depositors be limited to a single $100,000 amount regardless of the number of banks involved, most observers feel such a plan would be unworkable. Congress' musings on this subject came about when the insurance funds were heavily under-capitalized, and were designed to limit the exposure of the funds during bank failures. With a stronger banking system in the mid 1990s and more adequate insurance fund capitalization, Congress may not have the political will to make such an unpopular move.

APPENDIX II

LIFE INSURANCE

INTRODUCTION

In this section, what life insurance is all about is discussed. Why is it purchased? What are its purposes? What types are available?

This section will then look at Massachusetts Savings Bank Life Insurance (SBLI) and compare it to commercial life insurance coverage.

LEARNING OBJECTIVES

After reading this section, you should have an understanding of the following:

1. Why is life insurance purchased?

2. What are the two major types of life insurance and how do they differ from each other? What are the advantages and disadvantages of both?

3. What group is generally underinsured today and why?

4. How does Massachusetts SBLI differ from commercial life insurance? What are its advantages and disadvantages? Who is eligible to purchase it?

WHAT IS LIFE INSURANCE?

First, why do people purchase life insurance? What does it do for them?

Many people view life insurance as something one purchases to cover one's burial expenses, but there is much more to life insurance than that.

Life insurance is
designed to care for
one's dependents after
one's death.

Life Insurance is purchased to "take care of one's dependents" after one's demise. Its purpose is to take care of the expenses one's income covered while one was alive. For instance, one's mortgage, personal loans, children's tuition, and so forth. Life insurance is bought so that one's family will not suffer financially after one's death, so that they will be able to take care of themselves, so that they will not lose the house. As for how much life insurance

213

one should carry, there are several points of view. Ideally, the family should be able to pay off all their debt and to be able to cover their everyday expenses for about two years after one's death. This can easily come to quite a large sum.

One generally purchases or increases one's life insurance when one's financial responsibilities increase—with marriage, children, or the purchase of a home.

TYPES OF LIFE INSURANCE

There are two generic types of life insurance, whole life and term. What are the differences?

Whole life insurance is *level-premium* insurance throughout one's life.

Whole Life is characterized by a level premium throughout the insured's life. While one is young, the premiums are greater than the actual cost of the insurance. This extra amount, often referred to as the "savings element," is used to cover the actual cost of one's insurance as one gets older. In other words, by charging a greater amount than is necessary during one's early years, the premium is able to remain the same as one gets older.

The amount of the level premium is determined by one's age at the time the insurance is originally purchased. Because life insurance (similar to most forms of insurance) is risk-based, the greater the perceived risk, the greater the cost. Obviously, as one's age increases, the risk of one's death increases. Thus, the level at which the whole life premium will be fixed will be determined by one's age at the time the insurance is originally purchased. The younger one is at this point, the lower the level premium.

If whole life is the type of coverage one desires, there is much to be said for purchasing it when one is young. If whole life is purchased, for example, at age 21, the premium will remain fixed at a lower level than if it was purchased at age 30.

Whole life insurance has a *cash value* against which you may borrow.

Whole life has what is known as a cash value, which (due to the savings element) increases over the years. Generally, one can borrow against the cash value of the policy. Any loan balance outstanding at death would be deducted from the proceeds.

Figure Appendix II-1

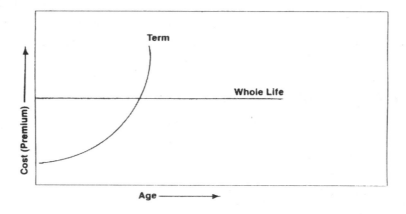

Term life insurance carries an ever-increasing premium as one ages. There is *no* savings element.

Term life is characterized by an increasing premium as the age of the insured increases. Term life is pure insurance; there is no savings element whatsoever; likewise, there is no cash value. One therefore cannot borrow against it. The premium reflects the true cost of one's coverage as one gets older and older. When one is young, term insurance is substantially less expensive than whole life. However, as one gets older and older, the premium steadily increases until it becomes significantly higher than whole life.

Term insurance needs to be renewed every few years (the policies are generally written for lengths of between one and five years). At each renewal, the premium will increase, reflecting one's increased age. One major disadvantage of term insurance is that at a certain age (generally between 65 and 70), the policy expires; that is, it can no longer be renewed, at any price.

Which type of insurance is better? It depends on your own personal situation. Because of its initial lower cost, many young people purchase term insurance. Considering today's cost of living, along with the typical six-figure mortgage balance, people find that it is generally necessary to purchase a rather large amount of insurance if one truly wants to take care of one's family. So much, in fact, that most people certainly could not afford to purchase such an amount as whole life.

Given this problem, term has become quite popular today. Term does have the disadvantage of steadily rising premiums as one gets older. However, when one gets older, one's financial responsibilities decline, the mortgage gets paid off, and the children graduate from college. As these responsibilities decline, so does one's need for life insurance. One can then decrease the amount of his coverage. While one's premiums will in fact increase as one gets older (under term insurance), once a certain stage in your life is passed, one's need for life insurance will decline. However, if one has chosen to purchase term, because of its affordability or whatever other reason, it should be kept in mind, as was mentioned earlier, that the coverage will expire once a certain age is reached. For this reason, it is generally prudent to purchase an appropriate amount of whole life along with the term. (By "appropriate" is meant whatever level one feels is necessary to meet his needs upon the expiration of the term.)

Today, *women* tend to be under-insured.

Generally speaking, what group is extremely undercovered today? **Women!** Men have traditionally been the breadwinners, the ones who earned the family income. Women have been entering the workforce in great numbers. In many cases, but certainly not all, it has become necessary for both the husband and the wife to work in order to support the family. Rising home prices have certainly played a role in this process. The wife's income is just as critical as the husband's, but very often only the husband has sufficient life insurance.

MASSACHUSETTS SAVINGS BANK LIFE INSURANCE

Massachusetts Savings Bank Life Insurance (SBLI) can be bought only at mutual savings banks.

Massachusetts SBLI was established in 1907. Its purpose was to enable "working people" to purchase affordable life insurance. There are no commissions involved; the bank employees who sell SBLI receive no commissions whatsoever. Generally speaking, when one purchases life insurance from a commercial company, a good portion of one's initial premiums cover the salesman's commission.

You can only purchase Massachusetts SBLI at Mutual Savings Banks. (Only three states have SBLI systems—Massachusetts, New York, and Connecticut).

Mutual Savings Banks in Massachusetts generally fall into two classifications as far as SBLI is concerned: those banks who actually issue the policies are known as *issuing banks;* those who do not issue policies themselves, but who act as middlemen between their customers and the issuing banks are known as *agency banks.*

Issuing banks actually originate SBLI policies, while *agency banks* only sell policies as middlemen.

Who can purchase Massachusetts SBLI? Only those who either live or work in Massachusetts. Full-time students residing in Massachusetts are also eligible. If one moves out of Massachusetts (or is no longer employed within the state) one can keep any SBLI already in force, but cannot purchase any additional SBLI coverage.

The maximum coverage per individual was limited until very recently by the number of mutual savings banks actually issuing policies, the limit being $1,000 per such bank. As an example, there are currently about 58 issuing mutual savings banks; under the old regulations, the maximum coverage would have been $58,000. However, just recently the limit was raised to $250,000 per individual. (It is no longer tied to the number of issuing banks but is still well below the amount available from commercial insurance companies, which remains SBLI's major weakness.) However, one can easily get around this weakness by purchasing one's first $250,000 from SBLI and then going to a commercial company for any additional coverage.

CONCLUSION

Life insurance, contrary to what many may think, is much more than simply funeral insurance. Its major purpose is to give one the "peace of mind" that one's dependents will be taken care of after one's death; that they will be financially secure.

There are two major generic types of life insurance, whole life and term, each having specific advantages and disadvantages.

In Massachusetts (and two other states) Mutual Savings Banks are able to offer SBLI. Due to the absence of sales commissions, SBLI can be offered at a substantially lower price than commercial life insurance policies.

GLOSSARY

abstract of title   A condensed history of the title to a designated parcel of land; an actual file containing excerpts from all documents pertaining to the title, and stating all liens, charges or encumbrances affecting the title.

accelerated amortization   The restructuring of an existing mortgage loan for the purpose of shortening the originally agreed upon loan term by increasing the monthly payments.

accelerated cost recovery system (ACRS)   A set of depreciation rules that allows the cost of certain assets held for business or investment to be recovered over a predetermined period, usually shorter than the useful life of the asset or the period the asset is used to produce income. These rules are authorized by the Economic Recovery Tax Act of 1981 and affect real and personal property placed in service after December 31, 1980. ACRS was modified slightly by the Tax Equity and Fiscal Responsibility Act of 1982.

accelerated depreciation   The method of computing depreciation whereby the depreciation charges are higher in the first years of an asset's life than in succeeding years.

acceleration clause   A clause of a legal contract that states the lender's right to demand full payment of the debt in the event of a default. It may appear on a promissory note, mortgage instrument or security agreement.

access deposit account   A type of deposit account in which funds are accessible to the account holder by check, telephone order, debit card or a similar device. NOW accounts are a type of access deposit account.

accident and health insurance   A type of insurance that provides monthly benefits to the insured. The benefits are paid for a prescribed period of time if the insured loses income because of an accident or illness.

accommodation check   A check or draft drawn by an institution either on itself or on its account at another institution, signed by an authorized officer and payable to a third party designated by the individual requesting the check. It serves many of the purposes of a money order and is also called a bank check. *See also* check.

account hold   A warning placed on a deposit, loan or other account to indicate the need for special handling.

accounting   The process of systematically identifying, measuring and communicating economic information and presenting this information in periodic, interpretative financial statements and reports.

accounting equation   The basic equation of double-entry accounting that reflects the relationship of assets, liabilities and net worth (i.e., reserves + stockholders' equity + retained earnings). In its simplest form it may be expressed: Assets = Liabilities + Net Worth.

accounting processes   The classification of accounts, accounting records, forms, procedures and controls through which changes in asset, liability, reserves, capital, income and expense account transactions are generally recorded and controlled.

accrual basis accounting   A method of accounting whereby income and expense items are recognized and recorded when income is earned and expense is incurred, regardless of cash receipt or payment. *See also* cash basis accounting.

accrue   The action of increasing or accumulating. It is used in accounting in regard to depreciation, expense, income, interest and other factors.

accrued interest   The interest that has been earned but not received.

ACH   *See* automated clearinghouse.

acquisition credit   *See* origination fee.

acquisition loan   A loan for the purpose of purchasing raw (bare) land.

ACRS   *See* accelerated cost recovery system.

actual cash value   The replacement cost of real estate at current market value, minus the sum equal to financial depreciation, technological obsolescence and location deterioration.

add-on interest   The interest on a loan that is computed by determining the interest charge for the term of the loan and adding that charge to the principal of the loan. The borrower signs a note for principal plus interest, although only principal is disbursed to the borrower.

adjustable rate mortgage (ARM)   A type of alternative mortgage loan program in which, by regulation, the interest rate may be adjusted without interest rate limits, and payments may be adjusted as frequently as each month. (Each individual contract, however, may stipulate interest rate limits and frequency of payment adjustments.) The principal loan balance or term of the loan also may be adjusted to reflect the rate change. The purpose of the program is to allow mortgage interest rates to fluctuate with market conditions.

adjusted gross income   The gross income less the total allowable adjustments for federal income tax purposes.

adjustment period   The time period between one interest rate change and the next for an adjustable rate mortgage.

advance   A loan; more specifically, a loan made by a Federal Home Loan Bank to a member institution.

adverse action   A denial of credit to an applicant.

Advertising Division, Inc.   An advertising agency, affiliated with the United States League of Savings Institutions, that specializes in the creation of advertising and promotional materials for savings institutions.

aggregate demand   An expression of how much output consumers, businesses and governments want to buy at given levels of prices.

agreed order   A statement in the reaffirmation agreement that represents a court order; it is signed by the court, the lending institution's attorney and the borrower's attorney. It provides that the institution can repossess the property, that the right of redemption no longer exists and that all interim payments belong to the institution.

air space   A two- or three-dimensional space located above ground level. All condominium apartments above the first floor are located in, and represent title to, air space.

allowable contributions   A maximum dollar amount a participant can contribute to an IRA during a taxable year. Contributions are deemed allowable if they meet specific rules concerning their composition and timing. The rules governing allowable contributions differ among the various types of IRAs. *See also* excess contribution.

allowable distributions   The distributions from IRAs between ages 59H and 70H, in any amount; or, after age 70H either (a) in full or according to payout schedules, or (b) as a consequence of the participant's death or disability. *See also* lump-sum distribution; period certain.

amenity   An advantage that adds to the attractiveness of and the pleasure received from a piece of real estate, such as beautiful scenery, the nearness of good public transportation, tennis courts or a swimming pool.

The American League of Financial Institutions   A trade organization of minority savings institutions that is affiliated with the U.S. League of Savings Institutions but maintains a separate membership and a separate board of directors.

amortization   The repayment of a debt in a specified number of equal periodic installments that include a portion of principal and accrued interest. Most home mortgage loans are fully amortized. *See also* direct reduction .

annual percentage rate (APR)   A measure of the cost of credit, expressed as a yearly rate, that relates the amount and timing of value received by the consumer to the amount and timing of payments made. The APR includes the quoted interest rate plus certain service charges and other finance charges associated with the loan.

annual report   A summary, prepared yearly, of a business' financial condition and major accomplishments. Copies of this informational report are distributed to interested parties such as stockholders, managers and customers.

annuity   A guarantee, often made by a life insurance company, to provide an annual income paid over the lifetime of a person or persons.

annuity certain   The benefits from an annuity contract that are paid over a guaranteed period of time, whether or not the annuitant is living, as in five-year certain or ten-year certain.

appraisal   An estimate of the worth of a piece of property; especially, an estimate of the market value of a piece of real estate by a professional having knowledge of real estate prices and markets. Usually obtained for mortgage underwriting purposes.

appraised equity capital   The difference between the book value and market value of certain savings institution assets, such as land improvements.

appreciation   The increase in value of a material item, especially an increase in market value of real estate.

APR   *See* annual percentage rate.

ARM   *See* adjustable rate mortgage.

articles of incorporation   A document issued by a government giving a corporation the legal right to do business.

assessment   1. An estimate of the value of a piece of real property for the purpose of levying taxes; also called assessed valuation. 2. A charge against real property for some local improvement, such as a sewer repair or street paving; also called a special assessment.

asset and liability mix   The relationship of total asset value to outstanding debt in an investment portfolio. *See also* net worth.

asset reserves   The funds set aside by a depository institution against transaction account and other short-term deposit balances. Asset reserve requirements are set by the Federal Reserve Bank.

assets   A quality or an item of value; what a business owns and what is owed to the business.

assignment   The written transfer of some or all ownership rights to real or personal property from one party to another; the transfer may be actual or conditional upon the performance or nonperformance of specified acts by either party to the contract.

assignment of rents   A legal document that assigns all rents and income from a property to the mortgagee if a mortgagor defaults.

assumable loan   A loan contract that allows for the transfer of the liability from the original borrower to a new owner of the mortgaged property; the ability of a mortgage loan to be taken over by a new borrower.

assumption   The transfer of liability on an existing mortgage loan contract from the original borrower to a new owner of the mortgaged property.

assumption statement   A statement, drawn up by the financial institution when the assumption of an existing loan is under consideration, showing the current status of the loan account, as well as general information about the amount and due date of the monthly payment and insurance coverage.

ATM   *See* automated teller machine.

attachment   A seizure of defendant's property by court order as security for any judgment the plaintiff may recover in a legal action.

attachment of security interest   The acquisition of the secured party's rights in the collateral. In a secured transaction, attachment makes the security interest enforceable against the borrower.

attorney-in-fact   An attorney-in-fact is a depositor-owner's agent.

audit   An official examination of account records, policies and procedures of an institution to determine fair presentation of financial statements and/or effectiveness of policies and procedures on operating efficiency. May include confirmation of account balances with customers, evaluation of internal controls and testing the accuracy of transactions recording.

automated clearinghouse (ACH)   An organization formed by financial institutions using a computer-based facility to settle automatic payment and deposit transactions among financial institutions in a given geographic area. *See also* clearinghouse.

automated teller machine (ATM)   A device that is similar to a cash dispenser in purpose and operation. However, an ATM performs a full range of transactions, usually including deposits of funds and transfers.

automatic deposit plan   A plan whereby customers arrange for checks, such as Social Security payments or payroll checks, to be sent directly for deposit to their accounts.

automatic guarantee   A provision of the Veterans Administration under which it will guarantee without prior approval a mortgage loan made by a supervised lender.

bad debt reserve   *See* reserve for bad debts.

balance sheet   A financial statement that reports the types and amounts of assets, liabilities and net worth of an entity as of a certain date.

balloon mortgage   A mortgage with periodic installments of principal and interest or interest only; installment payments do not fully amortize the loan. The unpaid principal is due in a lump sum at the end of the term.

bank draft   An order for the payment of money that is drawn by a commercial bank on its account with an out-of-town bank.

Bank Protection Act of 1968   A federal law authorizing the Federal Home Loan Bank Board (FHLBB) to set minimum security standards for all of its member savings institutions.

bankers' acceptance   A promissory note that is drawn by a corporation to pay for merchandise and on which payment at maturity is guaranteed on the bank's credit standing. It is generally used in foreign trade when buyers and sellers are unfamiliar with one another's financial condition and therefore require a guarantee of payment by a third party known to have a good credit standing.

Banking Act of 1933   The first major banking legislation of the Roosevelt administration. It created the Federal Deposit Insurance Corporation and provided for insurance of deposits at member banks, regulated the operation of banks, limited branch banking and effected other important changes in banking law. Many of its provisions subsequently were amended. Also known as the Glass-Steagall Act.

bankruptcy   The legal process in which a person declares his or her inability to pay debts, any available assets are liquidated and the proceeds are distributed among creditors.

base rate   The rate of interest that a bank from time to time will publish as its base lending rate.

basis points   An investment term that refers to hundredths of 1% yield. Thus, "50 basis points" higher yield is equal to 1/2% higher yield for a particular investment.

basis price   The price of a security expressed as yield or percentage of return on the investment.

batch processing   A data-processing technique in which a number of similar data or transactions are collected over a period of time and batched for processing as a group.

bear market   A condition of a stock market characterized by a selling trend and declining prices.

bearer bond   *See* coupon bond.

bearer check   A check payable to cash or to the bearer rather than to a specific party.

bellwether stocks   The major stocks, such as IBM and AT&T, that are consistently accurate in reflecting current trends in the market.

benchmark reserves   The reserve funds, representing a specified percentage of deposits, that all members of the Federal Savings and Loan Insurance Corporation (FSLIC) must hold.

beneficiary   The person designated to receive the benefits accruing from the funds in a trust account or an insurance policy.

beta   A measure of the investment risk of a particular security. A beta of one is equal to the market average. A beta of less than or greater than one indicates that a stock has reached less than or greater than the market average.

binder   A written statement binding two parties to an agreement until a formal contract can be executed. A binder is used to secure insurance for a mortgage until a complete policy is issued.

blank endorsement   An endorsement consisting only of the endorser's signature written by hand or stamped; designation of the next titleholder and restrictions on the subsequent use of the negotiable instrument are not stated. *See also* conditional endorsement; endorsement; restrictive endorsement; special endorsement.

blanket mortgage loan   A loan made to developers or contractors who have purchased a single tract of land for the purpose of dividing it into smaller parcels for sale or development.

blue chip stock   The common stock of large, fairly stable companies that have shown consistent earnings and, usually, have long-term growth potential.

board of directors   The governing body of an institution; responsible for the direction of policies and for reviewing the objectives and procedures of the organization.

bond   An evidence of a debt; the issuer of the bond usually is obligated to pay the bondholder a fixed sum at a stated future date and to pay interest at a specified rate during the life of the bond. Bonds may be issued by corporations, the federal government, and state and local governments.

bond discount   The difference between the purchase price and par value of a bond when the par value exceeds the purchase price.

bond premium   The difference between the purchase price and par value of a bond when the par value is less than the purchase price.

bond rating   *See* rating.

book value   The value of a business as a whole; comparable to its net worth on a balance sheet.

bookkeeping   The recording and posting of transactions and the maintenance of account records reflecting the financial transactions and activities of an institution.

borrower's acceptance   A signed statement from the mortgagor, used in construction lending, stating that all work contracted for is in place and of acceptable quality; that is, the contractor has, to the borrower's satisfaction, fully and equitably discharged his or her obligation under the terms of the contract.

branch office   An additional office, physically separate from the main office of a savings institution but subject to the main office's direction and control, at which deposits or withdrawals and loan payments may be made.

breakeven analysis   A mathematical process used to determine the level of sales or production at which the total costs and total revenue of a business are equal.

broker   A person who acts as an agent for others in selling or buying securities, real estate, insurance, or other services or products.

brokered funds   The savings deposits, in the form of certificates of deposit, that are placed in an institution by a broker acting on behalf of an investor. Fees and commissions are paid to the broker by the savings institution.

budget   A plan for future expenditures and investments over a specified period of time, taking into account projected income and management objectives, as well as the institution's general asset, liability, capital and reserve positions.

building and loan association   *See* savings institution.

building code   A set of municipal or state regulations that states the requirements for the construction, maintenance and occupancy of buildings intended to provide for the safety, health and welfare of the public.

bull market   A condition of a stock market characterized by increased buying and rising prices.

buydown   A mortgage agreement in which the lender pledges to make a below-market-rate loan to a borrower in exchange for an interest rate subsidy. The subsidy is provided by a third party, such as a real estate developer.

buy on margin   The purchase of securities using only a specified fraction of the purchase price. The remainder of the funds needed for the purchase is provided by credit extended by the broker to the buyer.

bylaws   The regulations that an institution makes for its own management. In the case of federal institutions, the form and content of the bylaws are prescribed by federal regulatory agencies.

call option   The option to buy a given amount of a commodity at a specified price during a specified period of time. *See also* put option.

calling officer   A financial institution employee who is responsible for going outside the institution to seek and develop new customer affiliations and to maintain current customer affiliations with the institution.

canceled check   A check that has been paid by the financial institution on which it was drawn. It is stamped "paid" on the day it is paid and charged to the drawer's account.

cap   *See* payment cap.

capacity A borrower's financial ability to repay a loan according to scheduled payments. It is determined by calculating an applicant's total income minus total expenses, usually on a monthly basis.

capital The money and other property owned by a person or corporation, used in the conduct of business.

capitalization   1. The process of adding uncollected earned interest to the loan balance. Interest is recorded on the date it is earned whether or not it is collected. Some states prohibit the use of interest capitalization. 2. A method for estimating the present value of future income. 3. The total value of owners' investments in a business.

capitalization rate   The rate of return in appraising, represented by net rental income compared to the market value of a property. It is expressed as *a* percentage. Could be compared to the comparable rate of return on other kinds of investments of similar risk.

capital gain or capital loss   The profit or loss resulting from the sale or exchange of real estate, securities or other capital assets.

capital market   A financial market for long-term debt obligations and equity securities.

capital stock   *See* stock.

capital stock institution   *See* stock institution.

carrying charges   The part of the finance cost that is charged by most creditors to cover costs incurred by loaning money or extending credit. Billing fees, administrative expenses and bad debt losses are examples.

cash   An accounting term that includes cash drawer money, vault cash, petty cash, and demand deposits in commercial banks or regional Federal Home Loan Banks.

cash basis accounting   A method of accounting in which income and expense items are recognized and recorded when cash is received or disbursed. *See also* accrual basis accounting.

cash dispenser   A self-service device installed by financial institutions to permit customers to withdraw cash at times when branch facilities are closed and at places other than branch facilities. The customer usually activates the machine with a magnetically encoded plastic card, identifies himself or herself with a secret code, and indicates the type of withdrawal and the amount by using push buttons on the keyboard.

cash equivalent   A term referring to instruments that are easily converted into cash, such as receivables, U.S. Government Securities, short-term commercial paper, and short-term municipal and corporate bonds and notes.

cash flow statement   An accounting statement which combines the cash income from the Income Statement with the changes in the Balance Sheet accounts to arrive at the actual cash generated by the company over a given period of time.

cash journals   The records of original entry that contain a chronological listing of all cash transactions of a firm. One record is kept for cash receipts and another for cash disbursements. *See also* records of original entry.

cash market   The market for commodities or securities in which delivery occurs immediately; also called the spot market.

cashier's check   A check drawn by a bank on itself, signed by a cashier or other authorized bank officer and payable to a third party named by the customer making the withdrawal.

certificate account   A savings account evidenced by a certificate which, if held for a fixed or minimum term, will receive a fixed or variable rate of return greater than a regular savings account.

certificate of compliance   A written statement issued by government agencies requesting a customer's financial records; it certifies that the agency complied with the requirements of the Right to Financial Privacy Act to gain access to the records.

certificate of deposit   *See* certificate account.

certificate of title   The evidence of ownership for an automobile or recreational vehicle. It gives a description of the property and lists any liens against it.

certified check   A check that guarantees the following: (1) the signature of the drawer is genuine and (2) sufficient funds are on deposit for its payment. The amount certified is set aside by the financial institution for the express purpose of paying the check, and the financial institution is obligated to pay the check when payment is requested.

certified financial planner   A designation offered by the College for Financial Planning to individuals who complete a financial curriculum, qualifying examination and term of experience in the financial services business. Certified financial planners provide personal financial planning for the individual.

certified public accountant (CPA)   A designation given to accountants who have passed a qualifying examination and met certain educational and public accounting experiences as set forth by the state licensing authority. CPAs generally are licensed independent accountants who offer professional services to businesses or individuals for a fee.

Chapter 7 bankruptcy   A type of bankruptcy in which the debtor's assets are liquidated and distributed among creditors. Also called straight bankruptcy.

Chapter 11 bankruptcy   A type of bankruptcy in which a borrower's assets are distributed to creditors according to a plan constructed by the borrower or creditors and in which creditors classify their claims in the way most beneficial to them.

Chapter 13 bankruptcy   A type of bankruptcy in which a debtor proposes a method for partially or wholly repaying debts while retaining use of the assets.

chart of accounts   A listing of the accounts to use in the course of business and a listing of the account numbers to be used in conjunction with account titles.

charter   The legal authorization, granted by the federal government or a state government, for a savings institution or other corporation to do business.

chattel mortgage   A mortgage on personal property, such as an automobile or furniture, given as security for the payment of an obligation.

check   A written unconditional order to a drawee institution to pay out a definite sum of money from the maker's account. *See also* accommodation check; cashier's check; traveler's check.

check collection system   The network of banks, clearinghouses and Federal Reserve Banks with check processing facilities that routes a check from the financial institution where it is first deposited to the financial institution on which it is drawn and, in the process, causes funds to be transferred from the payer's account to the payee's account.

check credit   A line of credit on which customers can write checks to access a preapproved loan amount. *See also* overdraft protection.

check truncation   The process of microfilming customers' paid checks or drafts in which the microfilm is the official record of the transaction. The official record is retained by the customer's institution, and canceled checks and drafts are not returned to account holders.

checking account   *See* demand deposit; NOW account.

classification of accounts   A list of general ledger accounts that provides for the systematic groupings of similar accounts. The classification consists of six major account groups: asset, liability, reserve, capital, income and expense accounts.

clearinghouse   An organization of financial institutions formed to exchange and settle for checks drawn on each other. *See also* automated clearinghouse.

Clifford trust   An irrevocable trust account, usually established for the purpose of reducing the amount of the grantor's income tax without materially increasing that of the beneficiary. To qualify as a tax-savings device under the Internal Revenue Code, the term of the trust must be longer than 10 years, and the trustee must be an independent party (not the grantor or grantor's spouse) who is not subservient to the grantor.

closed-end credit   A type of credit whereby the specific amount of credit to be extended, length of time for repayment and payment amounts are determined before purchase.

closed-end investment company   An investment company that has a fixed number of shares outstanding, with no continuous offering or redemption of shares. The company invests its funds in securities, other corporations or governmental bodies.

closing costs   The expenses that are paid by a buyer and seller for the purchase, sale or financing of a property. These include loan fees, title fees, appraisal fees and others.

club account   A deposit account characterized by small, fixed, weekly or biweekly deposits, a short term and a definite goal for saving. Examples are Christmas club accounts and vacation club accounts.

CMO   *See* collateralized mortgage obligation.

CMSA   *See* consolidated metropolitan statistical area.

collateral   An item, of tangible or intangible value, that is owned or being purchased and that is used to secure promise of future payments. Examples are an automobile, real estate, deposit account or negotiable instrument. A lender can repossess collateral if the loan is not repaid.

collateral loan   A loan for which the borrower has pledged certain property as security for the payment of an obligation.

collateral pledge   The agreement under which a third party pledges a deposit account or other property as additional security for the lender's mortgage secured advance of funds to a borrower.

collateralized mortgage obligation (CMO)   A mortgage-backed security that passes borrower payments into a trusteed pool from which principal and interest are paid to security holders class by class, with one class completely paid off before any principal is repaid to the next greater maturity class. *See also* real estate mortgage investment conduit.

collection   The actions taken by a lender to contact delinquent borrowers to establish the lender's firm position in dealing with delinquency and to relay a sense of urgency to the borrowers about submitting the past due amount.

combination loans   The loans made on unimproved real estate, development loans, and loans on other improved real estate that are combined with permanent financing loans or are made to borrowers who have secured permanent financing from other lenders.

commercial bank   A privately owned and operated financial institution chartered by a state or federal agency for the purposes of facilitating commerce, providing a safe repository for deposited funds, facilitating the transfer of those funds by check and extending credit.

commercial loan   A loan for the purpose of financing inventory or operating expenses of a business.

commercial mortgage loan   A loan secured by real estate. The real estate is used for business purposes or to generate income. Also known as income property loan.

commercial paper   An unsecured promissory note issued by a corporation at a discount from face value; it is to be redeemed in a short period of time, usually 90 days. Exempt from SEC registration when maturity is under 270 days.

commission   The compensation paid to a person for transacting some business or doing a service.

commitment   An agreement between a lender and a borrower to loan money at a future date, provided specified conditions are met.

commitment fee   The payment made by a potential borrower to a potential lender for the lender's promise to lend money at a specified future date.

commitment letter   A letter from the lender to the borrower stating that the loan application has been approved for a specific amount, term and rate and listing the conditions under which the loan funds will be disbursed.

commodities futures   The contracts for future delivery of economic goods, such as agricultural and mining products or securities, at a predetermined price; these contracts are traded on commodities exchanges. *See also* financial futures.

common law   The body of law developed in England primarily from judicial decisions based on custom and precedent, unwritten in statute or code, and constituting the basis of the English legal system and of the system in all of the United States except Louisiana.

common stock   The shares of a corporation, representing proportionate ownership or equity, that give the holder an unlimited interest in the corporation's earnings and assets after prior claims have been met. *See also* stock.

Community Reinvestment Act of 1977 (CRA)   The federal legislation that requires financial institutions to delineate their communities and to explain how they serve their communities' credit needs. Institutions must, among other procedures, prepare a CRA statement, display a CRA notice and maintain a public comment file.

compensating balance   The demand deposit or other noninterest-bearing deposit made to a financial institution by a business to obtain credit.

compound interest   The interest that accrues when earnings for a specified period are added to principal, so that interest for the following period is computed on the principal plus accumulated interest.

condemnation   The legal process for taking private property for public use, under the right of eminent domain, with just compensation to the owner.

conditional endorsement   A type of restrictive endorsement on a negotiable instrument that designates both the next titleholder and conditions to the endorser's liability.

condominium   A system of direct ownership of a single unit in a multiunit structure. The individual holds legal title to his or her unit and owns the common areas of the structure and the land jointly with other owners. The owners may sell their unit to anyone; the owners pay individual property taxes and may claim tax exemptions just as they would if they owned a free standing single-family home.

conduit   **1.** A type of rollover IRA for use by individuals who want to roll over all or any portion of a lump-sum distribution from one retirement plan to another. **2.** A firm that issues mortgage-backed securities based on mortgage loans it purchases from a number of lenders.

conforming mortgage loan   A mortgage loan that conforms to regulatory limits such as loan-to-value ratio, term and other characteristics.

consolidated metropolitan statistical area (CMSA)   A geographic unit composed of two or more adjacent standard metropolitan statistical areas having a combined population of 1 million or more, with close social and economic links. Formerly known as standard consolidated statistical areas.

consolidated obligation   The debt securities that are issued by a Federal Home Loan Bank and consolidated into larger issues for the capital markets .

construction loan   A short-term loan for financing the cost of construction. The lender makes payouts to the builder at periodic intervals as the work progresses.

construction loan agreement   A written agreement between a lender and a builder or borrower with respect to a construction loan. The agreement defines the amount of funds for construction, describes permitted uses of the funds and the payout procedure, and provides for completion of construction in accordance with approved plans and specifications.

consumer bank   *See* nonbank bank.

consumer credit   The credit extended to a natural person for personal, family or household purposes.

consumer credit classified as a loss   The closed-end consumer credit accounts delinquent 120 days or more and the open-end consumer credit accounts delinquent 180 days or more, according to FSLIC regulations.

Consumer Credit Protection Act   *See* Truth-in-Lending Act.

consumer loan   A secured or unsecured loan to a natural person for personal, family or household purposes; consumer credit can be open- or closed-end credit but does not include credit extended in connection with credit cards and loans in the nature of overdraft protection.

consumer price index (CPI)   A statistical device calculated by the Bureau of Labor Statistics, U.S. Department of Labor. The index is used to measure changes in the cost of living for consumers.

consummation   A term, defined under Regulation Z, meaning the actual time that a contractual relationship is created between borrower and lender, irrespective of the time of performance of a particular transaction. Depending upon the state law of contracts governing a particular institution, consummation may occur at the time a loan is closed, at the time a lender accepts (as distinct from receives) a borrower's loan application or at the time a firm commitment is given to make a loan.

continuous compounding   A term that refers to compounding over the smallest time interval possible and that yields the highest effective interest rate.

contract   A binding agreement between two or more persons or parties. Contracts are carefully spelled out and watched over by government regulators.

contract for deed   A written agreement between the seller and buyer of a piece of property, whereby the buyer receives title to the property only after making a determined number of monthly payments; also called an installment contract or land contract.

contributory IRA   A type of Individual Retirement Account established by individuals who set aside all or a portion of their yearly compensation; also called a regular or individual IRA.

controller   A chief financial operations officer of an institution. The controller is responsible for supervising the operations of the accounting department and preparing its financial reports, reporting to management and evaluating the financial position of the institution for management.

conventional loan   A mortgage loan made by a savings institution without FHA insurance or VA guarantee; called a conventional loan because it conforms to accepted standards, modified within legal bounds by mutual consent of the borrower and the lender.

conversion   A term in the financial service business that refers to a change of ownership from mutual to stock (or vice versa) or a change of charter from state to federal (or vice versa).

conversion clause   A provision, in some adjustable rate loans, that allows the borrower to change from an adjustable to a fixed-rate loan at a specified time during the term of the loan.

convertible   The term used for a bond or preferred stock that, under specified conditions, may be exchanged for common stock or another security, usually of the same corporation.

cooperative   A system of indirect ownership of a single unit in a multiunit structure. The individual owns shares in a nonprofit corporation that holds title to the building; the corporation, in turn, gives the owner a long-term proprietary lease on the unit.

co-operative bank   The legal name used in Massachusetts, and sometimes in New Hampshire, Rhode Island and Vermont, for a state-chartered savings association.

corporation   A form of business organization legally binding a group of individuals to act as one entity, carrying on one or more related enterprises and having the powers, rights and privileges of an individual; the corporation continues to exist regardless of changes in its membership or ownership.

correspondent bank   A financial institution that provides one or more services for another institution in return for the maintenance of deposit balances and/or fees. Typical services are check handling for out-of-area checks, trust services and technical services.

cosigner   An individual or entity that signs a legal document on an equal basis with the signer. On a promissory note, all cosigners are individually and jointly liable for repayment of the full debt.

cost accounting   The process of collecting and summarizing the operational revenue and expense items of a firm and analyzing their behavior to facilitate internal decision making and performance appraisal.

cost approach to value   An approximation of the market value of improved real estate measured as reproduction cost or replacement cost.

cost of funds   The amount that a bank pays for its money, which it then lends to a borrower. The difference between the interest rate which a bank charges the borrower and the cost of funds is called the *spread*.

cost of living   The amount of money necessary to pay taxes and to purchase goods and services related to a given standard of living. Unlike the consumer price index, the cost of living takes into account changes in buying patterns and tastes.

Counter-cyclical Industry   An industry which rises and falls in the opposite direction of the economy as a whole.

countersignature   An additional signature given to attest the authenticity of an instrument.

coupon bond   A debt obligation on which the bondholder collects interest regularly by clipping attached coupons as they mature and presenting them for payment to the bond issuer. Beginning in 1983, no bonds issued with maturities of more than one year will come in bearer form. *See also* registered bond.

coupon book   A set of payment cards or computer cards that the borrower returns to the institution one at a time with regular loan repayments or with deposits for savings accounts such as a club account.

covenant   A constraint in a loan agreement that sets forth certain requirements as to what the borrower will and will not do.

CPA   *See* certified public accountant.

CPI   *See* consumer price index.

CRA   *See* Community Reinvestment Act of 1977.

creative financing   A type of financing other than traditional fixed-rate, fixed-term financing.

credit   1. The exchange of goods or services on the promise of future payment. *See also* consumer credit. 2. An accounting term that refers to the right-hand side of an account record in which the amounts are entered in a double-entry system of bookkeeping.

credit analysis   A determination of the risk inherent in making a loan or extending credit to a particular person or business, including consideration of the loan applicant's income, expenses, past use of credit and general ability to manage financial affairs.

credit bureau   An agency that collects and distributes credit-history information on individuals and businesses.

credit card   A plastic card that can be used by the cardholder to make purchases or obtain cash advances utilizing a line of credit made available to the cardholder by the card-issuing financial institution.

credit life insurance   A type of insurance on the life of a borrower that pays off a specified debt if the borrower dies.

credit rating   A professional estimate of the financial position and integrity of a person or company, based on present financial condition, past credit history and other relevant factors.

credit risk   The degree of loan repayment uncertainty or risk that the institution assumes in advancing funds to a borrower; it is based upon credit information obtained.

credit union   A cooperative organization chartered by a state government or the federal government for the purpose of collecting deposits from members and making loans to members at a low interest rate.

creditor   An individual or business to whom money or something of value is owed.

cross-selling   The process of offering additional services to a customer who already is using one or more services; e.g., explaining the advantages of a telephone transfer account to a customer making a deposit to a regular savings account.

Crown loan   An interest-free loan, usually used among family members for the purposes of eliminating gift taxes, reducing estate taxes and reducing the family's overall income tax liability.

cumulative dividends   A feature of preferred stock that requires all preferred dividends in arrears (dividends not paid to stockholders for previous periods) to be paid before any common dividends are paid.

cumulative voting plan   A management policy of a stock corporation wherein the total number of votes a stockholder can exercise is determined by multiplying the number of shares owned by the number of directors to be elected.

currency   Coins or paper money used as a medium of exchange.

current asset   An asset expected to be converted into cash within 12 months.

current liability   A liability scheduled to be paid within the next 12 months.

current ratio   An indicator used in analyzing a firm's liquidity position; it is computed by dividing current assets by current liabilities.

current yield   The annual income divided by the current price of the security; annual return.

custodial gift   A gift to a minor child from an adult who retains control over the gift, or grants such control to another adult, until the child reaches maturity and legally can accept responsibility for the gift.

custodial IRA   An IRA in which a fiduciary relationship is created. Laws and regulations on Individual Retirement Accounts view most custodians as having all of the powers and responsibilities of a trustee. Under state law, there may be some technical legal distinctions relating to the powers of custodians as compared to trustees, but this is a matter for legal experts. Federal law does not distinguish between custodial and trusteed IRAs. *See also* trust.

Cyclical Industry   An industry which rises and falls in concert with the economy as a whole.

D and O insurance   The insurance that protects directors and officers of financial institutions from liability due to errors and omissions committed while acting on behalf of the institution.

dealer   A person or business entity that acts as a middleman to facilitate the distribution of consumer goods from the manufacturer to the public. The dealer buys merchandise from the manufacturer and sells it to the consumer for a profit.

dealer paper   The retail installment contracts purchased by a financial institution for a price negotiated with a dealer. The transfer of the contract from dealer to institution is evidenced by execution of the assignment section of the contract.

dealer reserve   The portion of dealer income held by the institution as protection against the possibility that dealers might default on their obligations as spelled out in the dealer's agreement.

debenture   A corporate bond that is backed only by the general credit and strength of the issuing corporation.

debit   A charge to a customer's access account or a charge against a customer's deposit account. Also, in accounting, a debit refers to an entry on the left-hand side of an account record in which amounts are recorded in a double-entry system of bookkeeping.

debit card   A plastic card designed to give a customer access to funds in his or her deposit account to obtain cash or effect a transfer of funds.

debt to income ratio   The ratio that expresses the relationship of the sum of the applicant's monthly credit obligations to his or her monthly income.

debtor   A person who owes money or something else of value.

decedent   A deceased person, ordinarily used with respect to one who has died recently. A deposit account held in the name of an executor or administrator of a deceased person's estate is called a decedent estate account.

declaration of condominium ownership   A complex legal document, with appropriate addenda, that provides for qualifying a multiunit property for condominium development and sale in accordance with a state's condominium act (law).

declining balance depreciation method   A systematic conversion of an asset's cost into a periodic expense whereby a fixed percentage rate is applied to the decreasing book value of the asset.

deed   A written agreement in proper legal form that transfers ownership of land from one party to another. *See also* quit claim deed; warranty deed.

deed absolute   *See* deed given to secure a debt.

deed given to secure a debt   A form of mortgage in which title to the property is handed over to the lender by the borrower as security for the repayment of a debt; also called a deed absolute.

deed in lieu of foreclosure   A transfer of title to real property from a delinquent mortgagor to the mortgagee, given to satisfy the balance due on the defaulted loan.

deed of trust   A legal document, used in some states, that conveys title to real estate to a disinterested third party, who holds title until the owner of the property has repaid the debt; accomplishes essentially the same purpose as a regular mortgage. *See also* trust indenture.

default   The failure to do what is required by law or by the terms of a contract.

deferred expense   An expense paid for in one accounting period but whose recognition is delayed to subsequent accounting periods, such as a prepaid insurance premium.

deferred income   The income received during one accounting period but earned in a subsequent period or periods, such as advance collection of interest on a loan.

deficiency judgment   A legal judgment given when the property securing a debt is insufficient to satisfy the remaining debt.

deflation   An economic condition in which the purchasing power of the dollar increases; a reduction in the general level of prices. *See also* inflation.

delinquency rates   The percentage of overdue loans in relation to the total amount of loans outstanding.

demand deposit   An account that is withdrawable by check at the demand of the depositor; also called a checking account.

demand loans   Loans which have no specific maturity date, but on which repayments can be technically demanded by the bank at any time. In reality, the lender may have difficulty enforcing the demand function of the loan, unless he has reasonable certainty that the riskiness of the loan has increased substantially from the time when the loan was originally made.

demography   The study of characteristics of human-populations, such as age, sex, level of education and employment.

denomination   The value or size of a series of coins or paper money.

de novo institution   A new institution.

Department of Housing and Urban Development (HUD)   The cabinet department of the federal government responsible for federal housing programs and urban affairs; it governs FHA and GNMA operations.

deposit   The placement of funds in an account at a financial institution subject to terms agreed upon by the depositor and the institution.

deposit account   The funds placed in an account that can be withdrawn only by the owner(s) or a duly authorized agent, or on the owner's nontransferable order; sometimes called a savings deposit or share account. A deposit account represents a binding contract between depositor and depository. *See also* individual entries, such as certificate account; individual account; joint tenancy account; etc.

deposit account contract   The contractual relationship encompassing all of the terms and conditions to which the customer and the savings institution are subject when the customer opens a deposit account; usually contained, in part, in the signature card.

Depository Institutions Act of 1982   A major federal law, also known as the Garn-St Germain Act, that touched on a range of activities for commercial banks, thrifts and credit unions. Major provisions include expanded lending powers for depository institutions, new investment authorities, noncash capital assistance for qualified financial institutions, and a requirement that federal financial regulators develop a "money market" account for banks and thrifts.

Depository Institutions Deregulation and Monetary Control Act of 1980   A major federal law affecting all depository institutions. Among the important provisions of the law were an orderly phaseout of regulated maximum interest rates on accounts in depository institutions; an increase on FSLIC and FDIC insurance for individually owned deposit accounts; and nationwide authorization of NOW accounts. The law expanded the influence of the Federal Reserve System on all financial institutions by changing reserve requirements on certain accounts and expanding access to certain Federal Reserve Services to all depository institutions. Provisions specifically affecting federal savings institutions included increased authorization to make consumer loans and authorization to engage in credit card operations.

depreciation   The decline in the dollar value of an asset over time and through use. For tax purposes, the dollar amount of annual depreciation may be computed differently from the actual decline in value.

development loan   A loan made for the purpose of preparing raw land for the construction of buildings. Preparation may include grading and installation of utilities and roadways.

direct reduction   The application of loan repayments directly to loan principal. *See also* amortization.

direct transfer   The moving of IRA funds from one IRA trustee directly to another IRA trustee, with no check made payable to the IRA participant. The direct transfer is not subject to any time or frequency restrictions.

disclosure statements   The information required by government regulations to be given to a borrower prior to consummation of a loan.

discount   The difference between the selling price and the par (face) value of a bond. A bond selling at a discount sells for less than its par value.

discount broker   A stockbroker or brokerage house that processes the purchase or sale of securities at a discount from the customary broker commission. Generally, the discount broker does not provide market advice.

discount certificates   The certificates of deposit offered at an issue price that is less than the stated maturity value. The difference between the issue price (amount invested) and the stated redemption value of the account at maturity is called the original issue discount. Savings institutions can offer discount certificates on any time deposit that the institution offers.

discount interest   A type of interest that is determined by calculating the total amount of interest for the loan and subtracting it from the principal loan amount. The borrower receives the net loan amount (the difference between the principal loan amount and interest amount) but agrees to repay the principal loan amount.

discount rate   The interest rate charged by the Federal Reserve Banks on loans to their member banks.

discounted interest   A deduction from principal for finance charges at the time a loan is made. The remaining amount is repaid through installment payments

discounted price   The price of a security (usually a bond) that sells at less than its face value. The security accrues interest until it reaches its face value at maturity.

discounting   The advance deduction of interest from the principal amount of a loan, so that the borrower receives the principal amount less the interest due over the term of the loan, but repays the full principal amount; suitable only for short-term loans.

disintermediation   The process by which individuals build up their holdings of market instruments, such as U.S. government and agency issues, stocks and bonds, and slow down additions to their deposit accounts at financial institutions. *See also* financial intermediary.

dividend   The portion of a corporation's profits paid to each stockholder as a return on the stockholder's investment.

doing business statutes   The state laws that define the licensing and other conditions under which a corporation, or other entity licensed by another state or the federal government, may conduct business in a state.

domicile   The place where a person has his or her true, fixed, permanent home and principal establishment and to which, whenever he or she is absent, he or she has the intention of returning. The term is not synonymous with residence; a person may have several residences but only one domicile.

dormant account   A deposit account on which no transaction (except the crediting of earnings) has occurred for a specified number of years. At the end of the specified time period, funds in the account escheat to the state.

double entry   A method of bookkeeping in which there are two entries for each transaction, one as a debit and the other as a credit. The entries check and balance each other.

draft   An order for the payment of money, drawn by one person or organization on another; a bill of exchange payable on demand. *See also* bank draft; sight draft.

draw   The release of a portion of the construction loan proceeds according to the schedule of payments in the loan agreement; also called advance, disbursement, payout or take down.

drawee   The bank on which a check is drawn.

drawer   The party who issues an order, draft, check or bill of exchange.

due-on-sale clause   A mortgage clause that demands payment of the entire loan balance upon sale or other transfer of the real estate securing the loan.

earnings   *See* interest.

earnings per share (EPS)   The total after-tax earnings of a corporation divided by the total number of its shares outstanding.

easement   An interest in land granted by the landowner for the benefit of another, entitling its holder to specific limited uses or privileges, such as the right to construct and maintain a roadway across the property or the right to construct pipelines under or powerlines over the land. Party wall easements, which share a common foundation, are commonplace in town house and condominium apartments.

ECOA   *See* Equal Credit Opportunity Act.

economic life   The length of time over which a piece of property may be put to profitable use. Usually, less than the physical life.

economic obsolescence   The loss of property value caused by environmental factors outside the property itself, such as a change in zoning laws.

economic rent   The amount of rental a property likely would command in the open market if it were vacant and available for rent.

education loan   An advance of funds made to a student for the financing of a college or vocational education. Various programs are funded through federal or state agencies or private organizations.

effective interest rate   The actual return one receives on an investment. *See also* effective yield.

effective yield   The actual rate of return to the investor. *See also* effective interest rate.

EFTS   *See* electronic funds transfer system.

electronic funds transfer system (EFTS)   A system whereby financial information is transferred from the deposit account of the payer to the deposit account of the payee. The payment message may be executed instantaneously, as in a purchase transaction at the retail point-of-sale terminal, or it may be executed on a batch basis, as in the daily distribution of transactions by the automated clearinghouse to member financial institutions.

eminent domain   The right of a government to obtain ownership of private property for public use such as a street or park; compensation is made to the owner.

Employees   Retirement Income Security Act of 1974 (ERISA). A federal law that established minimum federal levels of acceptability for private pension plans.

encumbrance   A claim or liability attached to real property, such as a mortgage or unpaid taxes. *See also* lien.

endorsee   The person or entity to whom a bill of exchange, promissory note, check or other negotiable instrument is endorsed.

endorsement   A signature written by hand or stamped on the back of a negotiable instrument whereby the ownership thereof is assigned or transferred to another. *See also* blank endorsement; restrictive endorsement; special endorsement.

endorser   The person or entity that endorses a negotiable instrument.

EPS   *See* earnings per share.

Equal Credit Opportunity Act (ECOA)   A federal law that makes it illegal for creditors to discriminate against any applicant on the basis of sex, marital status, race, color, religion, national origin, receipt of public assistance benefits or the borrower's good faith exercise of rights under the Consumer Credit Protection Act.

equitable right of redemption   A privilege granted by states to borrowers allowing a certain amount of time before the foreclosure sale during which borrowers can pay the outstanding loan balance and recover the property. *See also* redemption period; statutory right of redemption.

equity   The owner's interest in a property. In its simplest form it may be expressed: Equity = Assets - Liabilities.

equity line of credit   An open-end loan that is secured by the borrower's ownership interest in real property and that may be made for a variety of purposes. *See also* line of credit.

equity loan   A loan that uses the borrower's equity in real property as security. An equity loan, which may be made for a variety of purposes, is also known as a second or junior mortgage loan.

ERISA   *See* Employee Retirement Income Security Act of 1974.

errors and omissions insurance   A form of insurance coverage that protects the financial institution against liability in the event that it fails to procure or maintain agreed-upon insurance coverage for a borrower.

escalator clause   A provision for rental increases during the term based on an index beyond the control of the lessor or lessee.

escheat   The reversion of property ownership to the state if the intestate and without heirs.

escrow   A written agreement among three or more persons, under which documents or property being transferred from one person to another is placed with the third person as custodian; the transfer is completed only upon the fulfillment of certain specified conditions.

escrow account   An account held by the financial institution in which a borrower pays monthly installment payments for property taxes, insurance and special assessments, and from which the lender disburses these sums as they become due. Also called reserve, impoundment or trust account.

escrow closing   A kind of loan closing in which an escrow agent (a disinterested third party) accepts the loan funds and mortgage from the lender, the downpayment from the buyer and the deed from the seller.

estate   The ownership rights that a person has to lands or other property; the term also denotes the property itself. *See also* leasehold estate.

estate planning   The orderly process of planning assets, bequests and estate disposition for such purposes as insuring liquidity, providing for family needs, and avoiding forced sales and unnecessary taxes.

estates of deceased   Executors or court-appointed administrators of the *estates of deceased* persons may settle such estate obligations and report to the court all matters relevant to the estate.

examiner   An individual engaged by the federal or state supervisory authorities to examine the operations of the savings institutions within their jurisdiction.

exception   An item that may not be covered by title insurance because it limits in some way the owner's rights to his or her property; exceptions may include easements, liens and deed restrictions.

exception items   The checks or negotiable orders of withdrawal, received by the drawee institution, that cannot be paid for one reason or another.

excess contribution   An amount greater than the Individual Retirement Account participant's annual allowable contribution. An excess contribution is subject to a 6% penalty imposed on the participant by the Internal Revenue Service. *See also* allowable contributions.

exculpatory clause   A clause in a trust instrument relieving the trustee of liability for any act performed in good faith under the trust instrument.

executor/executrix   The individual appointed in a will and approved by a probate court to administer the disposition of an estate according to directions in the will.

expenses   The disbursements of the firm; the cost of goods sold or services rendered during a given time period.

face value   The value of a bond at which it can be redeemed at maturity. Same as its "redemption value." Face value also is called *par value* in bonds; the term should not be confused with the par value of stocks.

factoring   A financing method used in commercial lending whereby the firm sells its accounts receivable to a financial institution.

Fair Credit Billing Act   The federal legislation, enacted and made part of the Consumer Protection Act in 1974, that is designed to provide consumers with the opportunity to question amounts billed to them by creditors. The debtor can question the accuracy of the billing statement by writing to the creditor within 60 days of receiving the statement. Between the time that the auditor receives the letter from the debtor and responds accordingly, the debtor is not required to submit payment for the disputed amount.

Fair Credit Reporting Act   The 1971 federal law designed to protect consumers from inaccurate credit information. The Act lists the rights of consumers with regard to both credit grantors and consumer-credit reporting agencies.

Fair Debt Collection Practices Act   A part of the federal Consumer Credit Protection Act, effective in 1978, designed to cover primarily independent debt collectors and third parties who collect debts for others, and to protect consumers from a variety of unfair, abusive and deceptive debt collection practices.

fair lending practices regulations   The FHLBB regulations that pertain to the application and appraisal practices of federal institutions. The regulations prohibit the use of discriminatory appraisals and require the preparation of written loan underwriting standards, the collection of monitoring information and the maintenance of loan application registers. *See also* loan underwriting standards.

Fannie Mae   *See* Federal National Mortgage Association.

Farmers Home Administration (FmHA)   An agency of the federal government that makes, participates in and insures loans for the construction and purchase of homes in rural communities.

FASB   *See* Financial Accounting Standards Board.

FDIC   *See* Federal Deposit Insurance Corporation.

Federal Deposit Insurance Corporation (FDIC)   An instrumentality of the federal government that insures deposit accounts in member commercial banks, bank holding companies and mutual savings banks.

Federal Home Loan Bank   One of the 12 regional banks of the Federal Home Loan Bank System that provides credit to member savings institutions, savings banks and life insurance companies.

Federal Home Loan Bank Board (FHLBB)   An independent agency in the executive branch of the federal government that governs the Federal Home Loan Bank System, the Federal Savings and Loan Insurance Corporation and the Federal Home Loan Mortgage Corporation, and charters and regulates federal savings institutions.

Federal Home Loan Bank System   A federally established system made up of the Federal Home Loan Bank Board; the 12 regional Federal Home Loan Banks; and member savings associations, savings banks and life insurance companies. The fundamental purpose of the system is to serve as a central credit facility for member institutions.

Federal Home Loan Mortgage Corporation (FHLMC)   A secondary market facility of the Federal Home Loan Bank System that buys and sells conventional, FHA and VA loans, and participating interests in blocks of such loans; commonly called the Mortgage Corporation or Freddie Mac.

Federal Housing Administration (FHA)   A government agency within the Department of Housing and Urban Development that administers many programs for housing loans made under its auspices with private funds, including mortgage insurance for lenders and rent or interest assistance for low-income tenants and mortgagors.

Federal Insurance Contribution Act (FICA) A federal act that combined Social Security, old age, survivors, disability and hospital insurance tax into a single tax. Details and coverage are changed frequently by Congress.

federal insurance reserve A general loss reserve required to be established by a federal savings institution under the rules and regulations of the Federal Savings and Loan Insurance Corporation.

Federal National Mortgage Association (FNMA) A government sponsored but privately owned secondary mortgage market corporation that buys and sells mortgage-backed securities and FHA, VA and conventional loans; commonly called Fannie Mae.

federal reserve note The paper currency placed in circulation by the Federal Reserve Banks and issued in denominations ranging from $1 to $100.

Federal Reserve System The group made up of the Federal Reserve Board, the 12 district Federal Reserve Banks and nationally chartered commercial banks. The Federal Reserve System serves as a credit facility for member commercial banks and controls the nation's money supply by regulating its requirements on reserves.

federal savings institution A specialized financial institution chartered and regulated by the Federal Home Loan Bank Board.

Federal Savings and Loan Insurance Corporation (FSLIC) An instrumentality of the federal government that insures deposit accounts in federally chartered savings associations, federally chartered savings banks and state-chartered savings associations that belong to the Federal Home Loan Bank System.

fee simple estate A type of real estate ownership in which the owner is entitled to all of the rights and privileges, and accountable for the responsibilities incident to his or her property.

FHA *See* Federal Housing Administration.

FHA Title I Loan A loan for the purpose of home improvement. It is insured for 90% of loss by the Federal Housing Administration if the borrower does not repay.

FHLBB *See* Federal Home Loan Bank Board.

FHLMC *See* Federal Home Loan Mortgage Corporation.

FICA *See* Federal Insurance Contribution Act.

fiduciary A person or corporation with the responsibility of holding or controlling property for another.

fiduciary account A deposit account containing funds owned by one individual but administered for that individual's benefit by another individual who is legally appointed as conservator, trustee, agent or other fiduciary.

FIFO An acronym for first in, first out. In savings terminology, a method of determining deposit account earnings. Earnings are computed on the balance of the deposit account at the beginning of the earnings period, plus additions received during the period, minus withdrawals that are charged against the earliest amount in the account. In accounting, a system of inventory evaluations. *See also* LIFO.

FIMA *See* Financial Institutions Marketing Association.

finance charges The sum of all charges payable directly or indirectly by the borrower and imposed directly by the creditor as an incident or condition of the extension of credit. Finance charges must be included on truth-in-lending disclosures and described as the total dollar amount the consumer pays for the use of credit.

Financial Accounting Standards Board (FASB) An independent, seven member board that is influential in the development of accounting standards in the private sector.

financial futures The contracts based on financial instruments (treasury securities, certificates of deposit and others) whose prices fluctuate with changes in interest rates. Financial futures represent a firm commitment to buy or sell a specific financial instrument at a specified time and at a price established in a central, regulated marketplace. *See also* commodities futures.

financial institution A corporation chartered for the purpose of dealing primarily with money, such as deposits, investments and loans, rather than in goods or other services.

Financial Institutions Marketing Association (FIMA) A professional organization affiliated with the United States League of Savings Institutions and dedicated to the better marketing of savings institution services. Formerly called the Savings Institutions Marketing Society of America.

financial intermediary A financial institution that accepts money from savers and investors and uses those funds to make loans and other investments in its own name; includes savings associations, mutual savings banks, commercial banks, life insurance companies, credit unions and investment companies. *See also* disintermediation; intermediation.

financial leverage The use of borrowed funds in an effort to increase the return on equity. *See also* operating leverage.

Financial Managers Society, Inc.   An organization affiliated with the United States League of Savings Institutions and devoted to the professional training and advancement of operations and financial executives, such as controllers, accountants, internal auditors and data processing managers of savings institutions.

financial ratios   The measures of the operating results and financial condition of a business that relate one item on the balance sheet (or income statement) with another. Financial ratios are used to assess a firm's past and present condition.

financial statements   The reports that represent a summary of a firm's accounting data and reflect the firm's financial condition. The four basic financial statements are the balance sheet, income statement, statement of retained earnings and statement of changes in financial position.

financing statement   A document, filed at a designated public office, that serves as public notice to third parties that a lender has established security interest in collateral.

fiscal policy   The federal government taxation and financial activities, largely in the hands of the President and Congress. *See also* monetary policy.

fixed annuity   The guaranteed income, received at regular intervals, for which the basic amount of each payment has been fixed in advance; minor variations may occur with interest rate changes.

fixed assets   The tangible assets, such as office buildings, furniture, fixtures and equipment, that are used in the operation of a business, that have a relatively long life and that are not intended to be sold in the normal process of the business.

fixed income investment   A type of investment in which the dividend, interest or rental income is fixed contractually.

fixed-rate mortgage   The term commonly used to describe a mortgage loan with a constant interest rate and payment throughout the life of the loan. The periodic payments of principal and interest made by the borrower during the term of the loan result in the mortgage loan being paid in full at maturity.

flexible payment mortgage (FPM)   An alternative mortgage loan program in which the borrower pays only interest on the loan for up to five years. After this period, payments are increased to include principal and interest to amortize the loan over the remaining term.

float   The time that elapses between the day a check is issued and the day it is presented to the drawee institution for the funds to be transferred.

floor plan   An architectural drawing of the length and width of a building and the arrangement of rooms illustrated in a horizontal section taken at some distance above the floor. The plan shows walls, windows, doors and other architectural features. Mechanical floor plans show heating, cooling and plumbing equipment and lines; electrical floor plans show lighting fixtures, electrical equipment and convenience outlets, as well as switches and sometimes circuits.

floor planning   The loans made to finance dealers' inventory purchases.

flowchart   A diagram showing a logical sequence of operations or actions. Symbols and interconnecting lines are used to represent the function to be performed and to indicate when it is to be performed.

FmHA   *See* Farmers Home Administration.

FNMA   *See* Federal National Mortgage Association.

forbearance   The act by the lender of refraining from taking legal action on a mortgage that is delinquent, usually contingent upon the borrower's performing certain agreed-upon actions.

foreclosure   The legal action that bars a defaulted mortgagor's right to redeem the mortgaged property. This action is brought about to satisfy the outstanding balance on a mortgage loan; usually, it results in the secured property being sold at public auction.

foreclosure by court action   A legal procedure in which the lender files suit against the defaulting borrower, and the court issues a decree establishing a debt and arranges for public sale of the property by a court officer.

foreclosure under power of sale   A legal procedure, permissible in some states, in which the institution exercises a right, expressed in the loan documents, to take over the property of the defaulting borrower without court action and offer it at public sale to the highest bidder.

forgery   The false making or altering of any written instrument with intent to defraud.

forward commitment contract   An agreement between buyers and sellers of loans to purchase or sell loans at a specified future date according to terms outlined in the agreement.

401K   A tax-deferred savings plan that allows employees to contribute up to a specified percentage of their salaries into one or more employer-selected plans. Employee contributions are made with pretax dollars, which are not reported for income-tax purposes. Employers usually match employee contributions in a specified way. Also called a salary reduction plan.

FPM   *See* flexible payment mortgage.

Freddie Mac   *See* Federal Home Loan Mortgage Corporation.

FSLIC   See Federal Savings and Loan Insurance Corporation.

full faith and credit bond   See general obligation bond.

fully amortizing loan   A loan in which the principal and interest will be repaid fully through regular installments by the time the loan matures.

future advances clause   A clause in a mortgage instrument that allows a lender to advance additional funds without executing a new mortgage instrument.

future value   The amount to which a sum of money earning compound interest will grow by a certain date.

futures contract   A binding agreement that specifies that on a certain date and at a certain place, a minimum grade of a standardized quantity of commodities or securities is to be delivered and paid for in full; contracts are traded only on the exchange which issued them.

futures exchange   A membership organization, like the stock exchange, that provides a place where its members can trade commodities or securities for future delivery in a controlled, orderly manner.

futures market   The market in which futures contracts are bought and sold on many basic fibers, foodstuffs, metals, currencies and financial instruments.

GAAP   *See* generally accepted accounting principles.

gap management   The attempt to bring the dollar difference between rate sensitive assets and rate-sensitive liabilities to zero or as close to zero as possible.

Garn-St Germain Act   *See* Depository Institutions Act of 1982.

general ledger   A record or legend that shows increases and decreases for each asset, liability, reserve, capital, income and expense account. Each individual account is called a general ledger account.

general obligation bond   A bond formally sanctioned by either the voting public or its legislature. The governmental promise to repay the principal and pay interest is constitutionally guaranteed by virtue of the government's right to tax the population. *See also* revenue bond.

general reserves   The funds set aside for the sole purpose of covering possible losses. Includes the Federal Insurance Reserve, Reserve for Contingencies and any reserve "locked up" for losses.

generally accepted accounting principles (GAAP)   The accounting theory and procedures adopted by the accounting profession to facilitate uniformity and understanding in preparing financial statements.

Ginnie Mae   *See* Government National Mortgage Association.

Glass-Steagall Act   *See* Banking Act of 1933.

GNP   *See* gross national product.

good faith estimate   A disclosure required under the Real Estate Settlement Procedures Act (RESPA) that must be given to all mortgage loan applicants at application time. The disclosure is an estimate of all settlement charges likely to be incurred at closing.

goodwill   An intangible asset derived from a business' favorable reputation, advantageous location or other characteristic. *See also* intangible asset.

Government National Mortgage Association (GNMA)   A government corporation, supervised by the Department of Housing and Urban Development, that provides special assistance for the purchase of certain FHA and VA mortgages and guarantees securities backed by pools of mortgage loans; commonly called Ginnie Mae.

grace period   A specified period after the regular due date of a loan payment during which no collection procedures are begun and no late charge or other penalty is assessed. Payments submitted within the grace period generally do not adversely affect the borrower's permanent credit history.

grace period provision   A clause in a promissory note stating that a borrower who has prepaid a loan may at any time skip payments until the loan balance equals the amount it would have been if the borrower had not prepaid.

grantor   The person who makes a settlement or creates a trust of property; also called a settlor.

gross income   All income that is not legally exempt from tax.

gross national product (GNP)   The total market value of all goods and services produced by a nation in a specified period of time.

gross operating income   An accounting term that includes income received from the ordinary operation of the business before deducting expenses of operation.

guarantor   The individual or entity that guarantees to repay a debt if the borrower defaults.

hazard insurance   A form of insurance coverage for real estate that includes protection against loss from fire, certain natural causes, vandalism and malicious mischief.

hedge   A way to protect oneself against a possible investment loss by making a counterbalancing transaction.

highest and best use   An appraisal concept that considers all the possible, permissible and profitable uses of a property site to estimate the use that will provide the owner with the highest net return on the investment, consistent with the existing neighboring land uses.

hold   A notation made on an account record to show that a specific amount of money temporarily is withheld from the available balance. A hold may be placed on a checking account or regular deposit account to show a certain amount is not available to the owner or to show that the account requires special handling.

holder-in-due-course rule   1. A rule, contained in the Uniform Commercial Code, which originally stated that subsequent purchases of a promissory note are not subject to any claims regarding the initial transaction. This rule was amended in 1976 by the Federal Trade Commission to require all subsequent holders of a note to be subject to claims against the seller. 2. A rule, contained in the Uniform Commercial Code, that pertains to NOW draft and check negotiability. If a check or NOW draft is negotiated to a third party who has no particular knowledge of the prior transaction, that third party takes the check or NOW draft free and clear of any defenses existing between the original parties—drawer (e.g., consumer) and payee (e.g., merchant). The innocent third party has a right to receive payment for the check, even though the drawer is dissatisfied with the payee's merchandise.

holding company   A corporation that owns stock of another corporation and, in most cases, has a voting control over that corporation.

home   A residential structure containing one, two, three or four dwelling units, as defined in government statistics.

home equity loan   *See* junior lien.

home financing   The providing of funds, secured by a mortgage, for the purchase or construction or improvement of a residential structure containing one, two, three or four dwelling units.

home improvement loan   An advance of funds, usually not secured by a mortgage and usually short-term, made to a property owner for the upgrading of residential property, such as maintenance and repair, additions and alterations or replacement of equipment or structural elements.

Home Mortgage Disclosure Act   The federal law enacted in 1975 requiring the disclosure of mortgage loan data by depository institutions that are located in metropolitan statistical areas and that make federally related mortgage loans. Those institutions subject to the Act are required to disclose to the public aggregate mortgage loan data in terms of number of loans and total dollar amounts with respect to all mortgage loans that they originate and purchase each year.

homeowner's insurance   A broad form of real estate insurance coverage that combines hazard insurance with personal liability protection and other items.

Home Owners' Loan Act   The federal legislation enacted in 1933 that provided emergency relief to homeowners through creation of the Home Owners' Loan Corporation to refinance or purchase existing home mortgages. The Act also authorized the creation of federally chartered and supervised savings associations.

homestead association   The name used by some state-chartered savings institutions in the state of Louisiana.

household   The persons residing in a discrete housing unit with access to either the outside or a public area; called a family when members are related by blood or law.

Housing and Urban Development Act   The federal legislation enacted in 1968 that gave federal associations the authority to invest in mobile home and home equipment loans. The law also expanded the authority of federal associations to issue a wide variety of savings plans, notes, bonds and debentures.

HUD   *See* Department of Housing and Urban Development.

implied warranty   An unwritten assurance that a product is fit for consumption. Under the 1976 amendments to the Uniform Commercial Code, the lender assumes the role of the seller in being responsible for the implied warranty. *See also* holder-in-due-course rule.

improved real estate   The real estate on which there is a structure (or structures) to be used for home or business purposes or both.

improvement lien   *See* special assessment.

income approach to value   The process of estimating the market value of a property by comparing the net rental income the property would produce over its remaining effective life with the yields on other kinds of investments with comparable risks.

income property loan   *See* commercial mortgage loan.

income statement   The financial statement that contains a summary of a business' financial operations for a particular period. It shows the net profit or loss for a period by stating the company's revenues and expenses.

independent audit   An examination of financial statements conducted by an "independent" CPA according to generally accepted auditing standards (GAAS) for the purpose of expressing an opinion on their fair presentation in accordance with generally accepted accounting principles (GAAP).

index   A numerical figure used in economics that describes relative changes in some quantity; e.g., the consumer price index. Adjustable mortgage loan interest rates often vary from period to period based on the movement of a specified index.

index of leading economic indicators   A composite of 12 economic measurements compiled by the Commerce Department to aid in predicting likely changes in the economy as a whole.

indirect loan   A loan originated by a dealer, retailer or seller of goods and services to finance the purchase of those goods and services and transferred to a third party. The loan is an indirect loan between the party to whom it is transferred and the borrower.

indirect origination   The purchase of a ready-made loan from a source other than a regular lender (such as a subdivision contractor or a mobile home or home improvement dealer), usually as part of an ongoing business relationship between the financial institution and the seller. *See also* loan origination.

individual account   1. A type of account ownership in which the account is owned and controlled by one individual. 2. A term used to describe account ownership by a natural person or persons as distinguished from ownership by a corporation or other legal entity.

Individual Retirement Account (IRA)   A tax-deferred, trusteed deposit account into which certain eligible individuals contribute funds for retirement up to annual contribution limits. Approved vehicles for IRAs include deposit accounts and certificates at financial institutions, insurance annuities, mutual fund offerings and certain self-managed securities accounts at stock brokerage firms.

inflation   An economic condition in which the purchasing power of the dollar decreases; a rise in the general level of prices. *See also* deflation.

inheritance tax waiver   A release, signed by the appropriate state taxing official, relinquishing any claim of the state to the assets of an estate, or a portion thereof, under consideration.

installment credit plan   A repayment plan in which payments are scheduled at regular intervals; e.g., monthly, quarterly or semiannually, and must be continued until the full amount of the loan is satisfied. It allows consumers to obtain or enjoy the benefits of goods and services while paying for them in small amounts over a specified period of time.

installment debt   *See* installment credit plan.

Institute of Financial Education   A national educational organization affiliated with the United States League of Savings Institutions and dedicated to increasing the professional skills of savings institution personnel through classroom courses, correspondence study, executive training programs, seminars, workshops, clinics and other methods. Formerly called the American Savings and Loan Institute.

insufficient funds   A term used to indicate that the drawer's deposit balance is less than the amount of a check presented for payment. Also known as not sufficient funds, abbreviated NSF.

insurance   The indemnification against loss from a specific hazard or peril.

insurance fund   The FDIC or FSLIC funds reserved to offset any claims made by depositors of defaulted member institutions.

insured institution   An institution whose deposit accounts are insured by the Federal Savings and Loan Insurance Corporation, the Federal Deposit Insurance Corporation or some other governmental account-insuring agency.

intangible asset   An item, owned by a business entity, that has value but no physical characteristics; for example, patents, copyrights and goodwill. *See also* goodwill.

interest   1. A financial institution's periodic payments to savers for the use of their funds; also called dividends or earnings in reference to deposit accounts. 2. The payments a borrower makes to a financial institution for the use of its loan funds.

interest rate risk   The risk related to the chance of a change in the market value of a fixed-income investment because of an increase in the general market level of interest rates.

interim loan   A short-term mortgage loan, often for the construction of a building.

intermediation   The investment process by which savers and investors place funds in financial institutions in the form of deposit accounts, and the financial institutions in turn use the funds to make loans and other market investments. *See also* financial intermediary.

internal auditing   An examination of accounting and administrative (policies and procedures) records to determine accuracy of reporting systems and efficiency in operations. Internal auditing usually is conducted by an employee of the firm and is not a substitute for the independent audit.

internal control   The plan of organization and all of the coordinate methods and measures adopted within a business to safeguard its assets, check the accuracy and reliability of its accounting data, promote operational efficiency and encourage adherence to prescribed managerial policies.

intestate   The term that describes an estate left by a decedent who did not draw up a will specifying how his or her estate should be distributed.

investment   An outlay of a sum of money with the expectation that a profit or income will be realized.

investment banker   An individual who serves as a liaison between businesses that need capital and investors with funds to invest by underwriting security issues and providing other services for the issuing company and investors.

investment company   A company that invests pooled funds of shareholders in securities of other organizations. Examples are mutual funds and closed-end funds.

IRA   *See* Individual Retirement Account.

IRA transfer   The transfer of IRA funds from one trustee/custodian to another trustee/custodian without any payout of funds to the participant. Because IRA transfers are direct transactions between trustees/custodians, the IRA law views such transfers as separate and distinct from either distributions or rollovers. *See also* rollover IRA.

irrevocable trust   A trust in which the grantor does not reserve the right to annul the trust agreement.

joint ownership   A general term used to describe ownership by two or more parties; also called multiple ownership.

joint tenancy   A type of ownership by two or more parties who share equal rights in and control of property, with the survivor or survivors continuing to hold all such rights on the death of one or more of the tenants.

joint venture   A tax-advantaged entity, usually of a limited duration, that is formed by two or more companies to raise investment capital.

journalizing   The recording of transactions in five steps: (1) the date; (2) the account to be debited and the amount; (3) the account to be credited and the amount; (4) the explanation; and (5) the cross-reference to the general ledger.

journal voucher   A source document that provides written authorization for a financial transaction. Commonly used for disbursements from the petty cash account.

judgment lien   A charge against the real or personal property of a debtor as a result of a final ruling by a judicial court. Judgment liens give creditors a security interest in a debtor's property and can include the right to acquire and retain possession of the property until the debt is satisfied.

jumbo certificate   A market-rate certificate savings account consisting of $100,000 or more.

junior lien   A lien subsequent, or second in line, to the claims of the holder of a prior lien.

junk bond   A low-grade, high-risk bond with a high stated yield; rated BB or under in Standard & Poor's; Baa in Moody's. *See also* rating.

Keogh plan   A tax-deferred, trusteed savings plan that allows self-employed individuals, or those who own their own unincorporated businesses, to accumulate funds for retirement. Employers who establish a Keogh plan for themselves must make the benefit available to qualified employees.

land development loan   An advance of funds, secured by a mortgage, for the purpose of making, installing or constructing those improvements necessary to produce construction-ready building sites from raw land.

land planning   The design procedure of laying out streets, building lots and other elements for the improvement of a subdivision or other land area. The process includes site evaluation, determination, allocation and location of specific uses of land, incorporating considerations such as typography, access and circulation, vehicular and pedestrian traffic, amenities and other site improvements and uses.

land trust   A trust in which all assets consist of real property holdings.

late charge   A penalty imposed by the lender for delinquent repayments, as specified in the debt instrument.

lease   A contract by which the possession and use of real estate or equipment is conveyed by the owner to another under conditions specified in the contract. Especially in real estate, the term of and conditions of an agreement to occupy and use an apartment, office or other improvement.

leasehold estate   A kind of real estate possession in which the holder does not have title to the land but rents it under a written lease from the owner. *See also* estate.

leeway period   The period of time during which IRAs may be established or IRA contributions may be made, applying retroactively to the preceding taxable year. The leeway period for IRAs extends to April 15. *See also* taxable year.

legal tender   The coin or paper currency required by law to be accepted in payment of obligations.

lending policy   An institution's statement of its basic lending philosophy, including standards, guidelines and limitations that are to be observed and adhered to in the decision-making process.

leniency clause   A clause, in a promissory note, that spells out a financial institution's willingness to adjust loan payments temporarily if a borrower is experiencing severe financial difficulties through no personal fault.

lessee   A person or business that is granted use and possession of property in return for rent. In real estate transactions, the lessee is known as the tenant.

lessor   An owner of property who allows another to use it in return for rent.

leverage   The strategy of using borrowed money in an attempt to get a higher rate of return. This strategy succeeds when the interest rate on the loan is lower than the rate of return on the investment.

liabilities   The amount that one entity or person owes to others; for example, deposit accounts.

liability insurance   A type of insurance that protects the insured against claims of negligence.

lien   A claim that one person, or organization, has upon the specific property of another as security for the payment of a debt or charge. *See also* encumbrance.

lien holder   A person who holds a mortgage or has a legal claim on the specific property of another person as security for a debt. *See also* junior lien.

lien theory   A theory of real estate law which holds that a mortgage conveys to the mortgagee a claim to, or lien on, the mortgaged property.

lien waiver   A document signed by a supplier and subcontractor stating that the firm has been paid for its work and waiving its right to file a claim against the property.

life insurance company   A type of financial intermediary through which people invest in the company's policy and in turn are guaranteed payment to designated beneficiaries at the time of the policyholder's death. People also may choose to invest in a policy to build up cash savings.

LIFO   An acronym for last in first out. In savings terminology, a method of determining deposit account earnings that deducts any withdrawals during an earnings period from the last additions to the account prior to the withdrawal. Also, an accounting method for evaluating inventory. *See also* FIFO.

life-line banking   A banking service that benefits low-income customers by providing no-cost or low-cost services and minimum balance requirements on accounts.

line of credit   A preestablished borrowing limit set forth by a lending institution and assigned to an individual or business based on creditworthiness. A line of credit is used with open-end loans that allow borrowers to charge a number of purchases against an account, eliminating the need to reapply for credit prior to individual purchases. *See also* equity line of credit.

liquid assets   The total funds held in the form of: (1) cash; (2) demand deposits; (3) time and savings deposits; and (4) investments capable of being quickly converted into cash without significant loss, either through sale or through scheduled return of principal over a short term.

liquidation   The process of converting assets into cash and discharging liabilities.

liquidity   A measure of the ability of a business, individual or institution to convert assets to cash without significant loss at a particular point in time.

liquidity risk   The threat of not being able to liquidate an investment conveniently and at a reasonable price.

living trust   A trust that transfers control of funds or property from a grantor to a trustee who distributes the income according to the terms of the trust agreement; known as a living trust because it is operative during the lifetime of the grantor.

load fund   A class of mutual fund in which a sales commission is charged when a purchaser buys shares. *See also* no load fund.

loan   A sum of money advanced to individuals, businesses, government units or others, to be repaid with or without interest as set forth in the accompanying bond, note or other evidence of indebtedness.

loan application   A written or oral request for an extension of credit, which is made in accordance with procedures established by a lender (creditor) for the type of credit requested. Also, the form on which pertinent data about the request are recorded.

loan application register   A register that lists all loan applications taken by a lending institution. Under the Fair Lending Practices Regulations, as amended in 1980, regulated institutions must keep separate registers for mortgage loans, mobile home loans, home improvement loans and equipment loans. Information to be entered in the register includes property location and data, applicant information, loan terms and loan disposition.

loan agreement   Document which the borrower signs that outlines the covenants which, if broken, allow the bank to accelerate or make demand on a term loan.

loan closing   The process that brings a loan into legal existence, including the signing of all loan documents, their delivery to the appropriate parties and the disbursing of at least some of the loan proceeds.

loan fee   The initial service charge to the borrower for placing a loan on the records of an institution; also called a loan origination fee, premium or initial servicing fee.

loan information sheet   A listing of loans being offered for sale in secondary market transactions, showing principal balance, term, loan-to-value ratio and other items.

loan origination   The steps taken by a lending institution up to the time a loan is placed on its books, including solicitation of applications, application processing and loan closing. *See also* indirect origination.

loan origination fee   A one-time charge based on the amount of a loan and paid at settlement. The fee is usually paid by buyers, but may be assumed by a seller.

loan participation agreement   A contract, in secondary market transactions, under which the seller agrees to supply, and the buyer agrees to purchase, interests in blocks of loans at a future date; the agreement sets forth the conditions for individual transactions, and the rights and responsibilities of both parties. *See also* participation.

loan policy   The written guidelines detailing the methods and procedures for accomplishing a financial institution's goals and objectives. It details the types of loans an institution makes, the employees who may take loan applications for the institution and the procedures for accepting and processing an application.

loan portfolio   The total of all the loans that a financial institution, or other lender, holds at a given time.

loan proceeds   The net amount of funds that a financial institution disburses at the direction of a borrower and that the borrower thereafter owes.

loan processing   The steps taken by an institution from the time a loan application is received to the time it is approved, including taking an application, credit investigation, evaluation of the loan terms and other steps.

loan servicing   The steps taken to maintain a loan, from the time it is made until the last payment is received and the loan instruments are canceled. Steps may include billing the borrower, collecting payments and escrowing real estate tax and fire and casualty insurance payments.

loan settlement statement   A document, prepared for and presented to the borrower at a loan clos-

ing, showing all disbursements to be made from the loan proceeds.

loan terms   The loan amount, interest rate and length of time granted for repayment of the loan.

loan-to-value ratio   The ratio, usually expressed as a percentage, that the principal amount of a mortgage loan bears to the mortgaged property's appraised value, as "an 80% loan" or "a 95% loan limit."

loan underwriting   The process of determining the risks inherent in a particular loan and establishing suitable terms and conditions for the loan.

loans in process   General ledger account from which loan funds usually are disbursed.

loan underwriting standards   A written summary of a financial institution's lending policies and procedures; it also may cover the types of loan programs that the institution offers. The underwriting standards must be made available to members of the public upon request. *See also* fair lending practices regulations.

loan workout   The plan of action initiated by the lender that involves taking steps with the borrower to resolve a problem loan.

location information   The information defined by the Fair Debt Collection Practices Act to protect borrowers' financial privacy. The Act limits the amount of information that loan collectors can obtain from third parties when trying to find a borrower. For example, a collector cannot obtain the address of the borrower's place of residence or the borrower's place of employment from a third party.

lock box   A post office box to which customers mail payments to an institution. Payments are picked up for processing by either the institution itself or another institution that has contracted to provide these processing services.

long-term asset   An asset whose economic life is expected to exceed one business cycle, normally greater than one year.

long-term debt   A debt that is due after more than one year.

lump-sum distribution   The withdrawal of an individual's pension benefits or retirement savings in the form of a single payment or lump sum. All, or any part, of a lump-sum distribution can be used to establish a rollover IRA. *See also* allowable distributions.

magnetic ink character recognition (MICR)   The electronic reading of machine-legible characters printed in magnetic ink, such as those appearing on checks.

manufactured home   A dwelling that is wholly or partly built in a factory and then delivered whole, or in parts, to the site where it is assembled.

manufactured home loan   A loan to an individual for the purchase of a manufactured home, secured by the lender's claim on the home. The most common type of manufactured home is the mobile home.

margin   1. The difference between the interest rates charged on loans and the rate that the institution pays to raise lending funds. Also known as spread. 2. The percentage of the purchase price of a security that must be put up in cash.

market data approach to value   The method used in appraising to determine the market value of a property by comparing the property being appraised to similar properties recently sold. Comparisons are made regarding such qualities as the price paid, financing arrangements and physical attributes.

market research   The process of planning, gathering, analyzing and interpreting the facts about a market; about the product or service being marketed; and about the past, present and potential customers for that product or service.

market segments   Consumer groups identified by their demographic or psychographic profiles, their wants or needs, or their response to advertising and promotional activities.

market value   The highest monetary price a property can be expected to bring if the following conditions are present: (1) buyer and seller are normally motivated and free of undue pressure, (2) both are well-informed or well-advised and act prudently in their best interests; (3) reasonable time is allowed to test the property on the open market; (4) payment is made in cash or financed at terms usual for both the location and type of property. Market value also contemplates the sale's consummation and passing of full title from seller to buyer.

marketable securities   Those securities that have available a ready, active market.

marketing concept   The assumption that an organization, by determining and understanding what its customers want and need, will learn what to produce.

marketing mix   The combination of the product or service offered by an institution, and its pricing, distribution, packaging and promotion.

master plan insurance   A form of coverage that insures a financial institution against loss resulting from certain types of damage to a security property, whether or not the borrower maintains any coverage.

maturity   1. The period of time for which credit, an insurance contract, or a mortgage loan is written. 2. The dates on which certain types of investments may be redeemed at face value. 3. The amount of time one must wait before realizing the rate of return expected when the investment was made.

maturity amount   The value of an investment at the end of its economic life.

mechanic's lien   A lien, created by statute in most states, in favor of persons who have performed work or furnished material used in the construction of a building or other improvement; also called a materialmen's lien.

members   The group of savers and borrowers in a mutual savings association who elect directors, amend the bylaws, approve any basic corporate change of policy or organization and, in general, possess most of the rights of ownership that stockholders have in a stock corporation.

merger   A business consolidation in which two or more corporations create a new corporation by unifying their capital, liabilities and assets.

metropolitan statistical area (MSA)   A geographic unit composed of one or more counties around a central city, or urbanized area, with 50,000 or more inhabitants. Contiguous counties are included if they have close social and economic links with the area's population nucleus. Formerly known as standard metropolitan statistical areas (SMSAs).

MICR   *See* magnetic ink character recognition.

mobile home   *See* manufactured home.

modification agreement   An agreement between a lender and borrower that alters permanently one or more of the terms—interest rate, number of years allowed for repayment, monthly payment amount and the like—of an existing mortgage loan.

monetary policy   The government regulation of the supply of money and credit; usually assigned to the Federal Reserve Board. *See also* fiscal policy.

money   A generally accepted medium of exchange, measure of value or means of payment.

money laundering   The transfer of illegally obtained funds between accounts in different financial institutions to obscure the origin of the funds. Penalties to financial institutions engaged in these activities are outlined in the Bank Secrecy Act.

money market   The common term for the mechanism whereby loanable funds are traded in the form of short-term debt securities.

money market deposit account   A savings account, offered by financial institutions, that is designed to be directly equivalent to and competitive with money market mutual funds. Although a minimum initial deposit is required, the account has no interest rate ceiling on balances above the minimum initial deposit. There is no regulated minimum term.

money market fund   A mutual fund that invests in short-term obligations only, such as commercial paper or Treasury bills. The yields on these investments fluctuate due to varying interest rates and the continuously changing investment portfolios.

money order   An order purchased from a financial institution, the U.S. Postal Service or a commercial company to pay a sum of money specified by the purchaser to a party named by the purchaser. Because the funds being transferred in this way have already been paid to the firm or government body issuing the order, anyone who cashes the order after properly identifying the payee is sure of reimbursement; thus, a money order is easily converted to cash anywhere in the nation.

mortgage   A legal document by which real property is pledged as security for the repayment of a loan. The pledge ends when the debt is discharged.

mortgage-backed security   A bond-type investment security representing an undivided interest in a pool of mortgages.

mortgage banker   An individual or corporation that deals in mortgage loans by originating the loans and then selling them to investors, with servicing retained by the seller-banker for the life of a loan in exchange for a fee.

mortgage bond   A bond that is secured by real property.

mortgage-equity analysis   A method of estimating value by dividing the investment in a property into its mortgage and equity components and capitalizing.

mortgage life insurance   An insurance policy on the life of a borrower that repays an outstanding mortgage debt upon death of the insured.

mortgage pool   A number of mortgages combined and issued as a single security by financial institutions. Repayments from the pool are used to pay off the security.

mortgagee   The institution, group or individual that lends money on the security of pledged real estate; commonly called the lender.

mortgagor   The owner of real estate who pledges property as security for the repayment of a debt; commonly called the borrower.

MSA   *See* metropolitan statistical area.

multifamily   A structure defined in government statistics as containing more than four dwelling units; or, sometimes, used to describe a unit itself.

municipal bond   The obligation of a state or local government agency to repay with interest a sum of money borrowed for municipal purposes, such as the building of low-income housing, improving streets or building bridges. Commonly called municipals.

Mutual fund   A financial corporation that invests funds obtained from the sale of shares of its own stock in the securities of other corporations. Dividends paid to shareholders are based on the earnings of the securities, minus expenses. Also called an open-end investment company.

Mutual institution   A savings institution that issues no capital stock, but is owned and controlled solely by its savers and borrowers, who are called members. Members do not share in profits, because a mutual institution operates in such a way that it makes no "profit," but members exercise other ownership rights.

mutual savings bank   A financial institution incorporated for the purposes of: (1) providing a safe place for individuals to save and (2) investing those savings in mortgage loans, stocks, bonds and other securities.

National Council of Savings Institutions (NCSI)   A trade organization that resulted from a merger between the National Savings and Loan League and the National Association of Mutual Savings Banks.

National Flood Insurance Program   A program that provides flood insurance at affordable rates through a federal subsidy. In return for this subsidy, communities in designated flood hazard areas must administer local measures that aid in flood prevention.

nationwide loan   A mortgage loan secured by property located outside an institution's normal lending territory but within the United States or its territories and possessions. An institution may invest in, sell, purchase or participate in these loans.

NCSI   *See* National Council of Savings Institutions.

negative amortization   A mortgage repayment plan in which the borrower makes less-than-interest-only payments on the amount of money borrowed during part of the payment term. Unpaid interest is accrued on the outstanding loan balance, causing the loan balance to increase instead of decrease.

negotiable   A term meaning assignable or transferable, in lieu of money, in the ordinary course of business.

negotiable instrument   A written order or promise to transfer money from one party to another by delivery or by endorsement and delivery, and without formal assignment; when the transfer has been made, the receiving party has full legal title. A negotiable instrument ordinarily is in the form of a check, draft or bill of exchange, promissory note or acceptance.

negotiable investment   An investment that can be sold.

net income   The difference between the revenues earned and the expenses incurred by a corporation in a given period.

net savings inflow   The change in an institution's savings account balances over a given period, determined by subtracting withdrawals during the period; also called net savings gain or net savings receipts. When interest credited to accounts during the period is excluded, the resulting figure customarily is referred to as net new savings.

net worth   The sum of all reserve accounts (except specific or valuation reserves), retained earnings, permanent stock, mutual capital certificates, securities that constitute permanent equity capital in accordance with generally accepted accounting principles, and any other nonwithdrawable accounts of an insured institution. Generally, the net worth of an individual or business is the difference between total assets and total liabilities. *See also* asset and liability mix.

no load fund   A class of mutual fund in which no load fee (sales commission) is charged when a purchaser buys shares. *See also* load fund.

non-amortized loan   A loan in which the periodic payments are sufficient to cover only the interest due; the principal is not reduced.

non-bank bank   A financial service institution that either accepts demand deposits or makes commercial loans, but does not do both. Also known as a consumer bank.

Non-cyclical Industry: An industry which remains unaffected by the changes in the overall economy.

non-filing insurance   A type of insurance that insures the institution against a loss that results from unintentional errors or omissions in the filing or recording of a security interest.

non-operating expense   The expenses resulting from nonrecurring financial transactions that do not result from the regular and ordinary operations of a firm (e.g., expense of maintaining real estate owned or a loss from the sale of real estate owned).

non-operating revenue   The revenue derived from nonrecurring financial transactions that do not result from the regular or ordinary operations of a firm (e.g., profit on the sale of real estate owned).

no-par stock   A stock issued with no face value.

notary public   A public officer authorized to attest to the signing of documents (such as deeds or mortgages) requiring certification. The person signs and affixes a seal to the document.

note   *See* promissory note.

notice account   A deposit account on which the customer agrees to give the institution a specified notice before making a withdrawal. As long as the customer gives the agreed notice, the funds earn a higher interest rate than that paid on other regular accounts; insufficient notice for a withdrawal may incur a penalty.

novation   The substitution of a new obligation for an old one between the same or different parties.

NOW account   A savings account from which the account holder can withdraw funds by writing a negotiable order of withdrawal (NOW) payable to a third party. Interest may be paid on the NOW accounts. *See also* NOW account drafts.

NOW account drafts   The negotiable instruments written on a NOW account to make third-party payments. May also be referred to as a check. *See also* NOW account.

NSF   *See* insufficient funds.

odd lot   A block of shares smaller than a round lot (a multiple of 100) and usually traded at one time.

offsite improvements   The improvements, in land development, that are off the development site, such as roads and utility services to the site, and that enhance the value of the development.

onsite improvements   The improvements within the boundaries of a land development, such as streets, sidewalks and utility services, that increase the value of the development.

on-us checks   The term used by a financial institution to refer to checks drawn on itself. A check is considered an on-us check when it is cashed over the counter by the payer bank.

open-end credit   An available (open) line of credit up to a predetermined amount (dollar credit limit). Consumers can draw against their line of credit without making specific arrangements for each purchase. Consumers also can make payments that most closely reflect their financial capabilities at a particular time. As the loan balance is reduced, the available credit increases to the predetermined limit. The line of credit remains available until either the borrower or lender cancels it.

operating expense   A charge incurred as a result of the customary savings and lending business of an institution, excluding interest on borrowed money, interest paid to savers and taxes. Major operating expense items are compensation and related costs, office occupancy, fixtures and equipment, advertising, federal insurance premiums, and professional and supervisory fees.

open-end investment company   *See* mutual fund.

operating income   The receipts arising from the customary savings and lending business of an institution; sometimes called gross operating income. Major operating income items are interest on loans and other investments, and loan fees and charges.

operating leverage   The degree to which fixed costs comprise a firm's total costs. *See also* financial leverage.

operations analysis   A system of analyzing specific savings institution operations in order to establish norms, appraise efficiency, improve operations and reduce costs.

origination fee   A consideration (fee), other than the average interest provided by the loan contract, received by an institution for or in connection with the acquisition, making, refinancing or modification of a loan, plus an consideration received for making a loan commitment, whether or not an actual loan follows such commitment. Institutions treat a portion of the consideration as immediate income and the excess over limits established by the FSLIC as deferred income. Acquisition credits sometimes are referred to as loan origination fees.

outstanding check   A check that has not yet been presented for payment to the financial institution on which it was drawn.

overdraft   A draft or check written for an amount that exceeds the balance in a customer's account.

overdraft protection   A line of credit on which customers can write checks for an amount over and above the balance in their checking accounts. *See also* check credit.

overimprovement   The condition of a property, in appraising, wherein the value of the site plus the cost of the building's improvements have considerably more value than most of the nearby sites.

over-the-counter (OTC)   A means of trading shares of a company not listed on an organized stock exchange.

ownership   The state of holding a lawful claim or title to property.

par value   1. A value that has been assigned to a share of stock by the corporate charter. This value has nothing to do with the market value of the share. 2. The value of a bond at maturity. *See also* face value.

partial release   An institution's relinquishment of its claim to some part of the real property that secures a mortgage loan.

partially amortizing loan   A loan in which the periodic payments cover all of the interest due,

but only part of the principal; a sizable balance remains when the loan matures.

participation   1. The partial ownership interest in a mortgage or package of mortgages. 2. The origination, by two or more lenders, of a single (often large) mortgage loan. *See also* loan participation agreement.

participation loan   A loan made or owned by more than one lender; the joint investors share profits and losses in proportion to their ownership shares.

partnership   A form of business organization in which two or more persons join in a commercial or business enterprise, sharing profits and risks as they have contractually agreed. No stock is issued, and the partnership exists only as long as all partners stay in the business; a change of partner necessitates the formation of a new partnership.

passbook   The evidence of ownership of a savings account; the customer's record of transactions on the account, such as deposits, withdrawals and earnings received.

passbook account   *See* regular savings account.

passbook loan   *See* savings account loan.

pass-through security   A security representing an interest in a pool of mortgages in which mortgage repayments are passed through to the security-holder.

payee   The party to whom a check is payable.

payer   The person who pays, or is to make payment of, a check.

payment cap   A restriction placed upon the extent to which the monthly payment can change during the term of an adjustable rate mortgage loan or from one adjustment period to another.

payoff   The complete repayment of loan principal, interest and any other sums due; payoff occurs either over the full term of the loan or through prepayments.

payoff statement   A formal statement prepared when a loan payoff is contemplated, showing the current status of the loan account, all sums due and the daily rate of interest. Also called a letter of demand.

payout   The disbursement of loan funds to a borrower. In construction lending, the incremental disbursement of loan funds contingent upon the completion of a specified portion of a structure, such as a foundation, roof, etc.

payroll savings plan   An arrangement whereby an employee authorizes his or her employer to deduct specified wages or salary each pay period and to forward that amount to a financial institution for deposit in the employee's savings account.

p/e ratio   *See* price-earnings ratio.

penalty clause   1. A clause in a promissory note specifying a penalty for late payments. 2. A clause in a savings certificate specifying a penalty for premature withdrawal from such an account.

pension fund   A fund set up to collect regular premiums from individuals and their employers, invest those funds safely and profitably, and pay out a monthly income when an individual reaches retirement age.

period certain   A predetermined amount of time during which a participant receives allowable distributions from an IRA. A period certain may be any length of time so long as the period is less than the participant's life expectancy. *See also* allowable distributions.

period of redemption   The length of time during which a defaulted mortgagor may reclaim the title and possession of his or her property by paying the debt secured by the property.

permanent insurance   A form of life insurance incorporating a savings or investment feature. The full death benefit will continue to remain in force when the policy matures, without the necessity for any further premium payment, as compared with term insurance, which lapses upon nonpayment of the premium.

permanent lender   A lender that provides long-term financing for projects after construction has been completed.

permanent loan   A long-term loan or mortgage that is fully amortized and extended for a period of not less than 10 years.

personal check   A check drawn on a depository institution by an individual against that individual's own funds.

personal identification number (PIN)   A secret number or code used by an account holder to authorize a transaction or obtain information regarding that person's account. The PIN may be used in conjunction with a plastic card to insure that the person activating an automatic device with a plastic card is the individual to whom the card was issued.

personal loan   An unsecured loan usually made for the purpose of debt consolidation, vacation or the purchase of durable goods.

personal property   The movable items that a person owns, either tangible, such as furniture and other merchandise, or intangible, such as stocks and bonds.

personal savings   The balance remaining after deducting expenditures for goods and services from the after-tax income of individuals and families.

personal selling   The face-to-face contact between a financial institution employee and a prospective customer for the purpose of establishing an account relationship.

Phoenix institution   A savings institution comprising failing or insolvent institutions as a result of FSLIC-arranged mergers. Phoenix alludes to the mythical bird that consumed itself by fire and was reborn from its own ashes.

physical deterioration   The loss of property value due to the actual decay of the physical components of real estate.

PIN *See* personal identification number.

planned unit development (PUD)   A land development project planned as an entity; building units are generally grouped into clusters, allowing an appreciable amount of land for open space. Generally more than one housing type or land use is included, and the project is generally subjected to various types of review and approval by the controlling governmental unit.

point   An amount equal to 1% of the principal amount of an investment or note. Points are a one-time charge assessed by the lender to increase the yield on the mortgage loan to a competitive position with other types of investments.

pooling of interest method   A method of accounting used when combining two or more institutions in which assets, liabilities and net worth of the combined institutions are recorded at their book value. Adjustments are made when institutions use different accounting methods for recording assets and liabilities.

portfolio   A list, or grouping, of the income-earnings assets of an individual or a financial institution.

point-of-sale, place-of-business (POS or POB)   The retail firm where an electronic funds transfer system (EFTS) computer terminal is located.

postal money order   An instrument, like a check, sold by United States post offices for payment of a specified sum of money to the individual or firm designated by the purchaser.

posting   The process of transferring journal entries to the general ledger.

power of attorney   A document that authorizes one person to legally act in place of another person under specified conditions for specific purposes.

power of sale clause   A clause in a mortgage document that gives the institution the right to sell the property at a public auction without a prior court judgment.

preauthorized payment   A system established by written agreement whereby a financial institution is authorized by the customer to debit his or her checking account for a monthly loan payment. The institution is instructed to honor such debits, whether paper check, magnetic tape or punch card. *See also* Transmatic®.

preferred stock   A stock yielding a fixed-dollar income. The stockholder has a claim to earnings and assets before the holder of common stock, but after the claim of bonds. *See also* stock.

premium   1. A product given free or sold at a fraction of its real price; offered as an inducement to the public to open or add to a deposit account. 2. The price paid for a contract of insurance. 3. A fee charged for the granting of a loan. 4. The amount above the face value of an investment.

prepayment clause   A clause in a promissory note stipulating the amount a borrower may pay ahead of schedule without penalty, as well as the penalty for larger prepayments.

present value   A representation of the current value of a sum that is to be received at some time in the future.

price-earnings (p/e) ratio   A ratio often used by investors to determine the value of a stock. The ratio is the market value of a share divided by its earnings for the previous year.

prime rate   The interest rate charged by leading banks for loans to their most secure customers.

principal   The amount of money borrowed, as distinguished from interest or charges.

principal balance   The portion of the loan amount not repaid, exclusive of interest and any other charges.

private mortgage insurance   An insurance policy, offered by a private company, that protects a lender against loss up to policy limits (customarily 20% to 25% of the loan amount) on a defaulted mortgage loan. Its use usually is limited to loans with a high loan-to-value ratio; the borrower pays the premiums.

probate   The process of admitting a will to record, resolving questions that arise in estate administration and approving the accounts of an executor or of an administrator. Also, an order of court judging a will to be valid and ordering it to be recorded.

pro forma statements   The projected income statement and balance sheet for some specified future period.

pro rata   A Latin term meaning in proportion to; e.g., the amount charged to each homeowner to cover the cost of a special assessment.

profit and loss statement   *See* statement of operations; income statement.

profit center accounting   A method that identifies for each operating function its contribution to the profit of the institution as a whole.

promissory note   A written promise to pay a stipulated sum of money to a specified party under conditions mutually agreed upon. Also called a note, installment note, promise or bond.

property   A piece of real estate; or, generally, something owned or possessed.

property and casualty insurance   A type of insurance that provides for the replacement of or compensation for lost, stolen, damaged or destroyed property.

property assessment   The valuation of real property for tax purposes.

proprietorship   An entity owned by an individual and operated under a d/b/a (doing business as) title. The individual is 100% personally responsible for all debts incurred.

prospectus   A document detailing investment objectives and other important characteristics of a security, and the key characteristics of the issuer, including its management and financial position. Under SEC regulations, the prospectus (1) must contain the no-approval clause, stating that the SEC has not approved or disapproved of the issue; and (2) must be provided to all prospective investors.

proxy   1. The authority or power to act for another. 2. A document giving such authority. 3. The person authorized to act for another.

public unit account   A deposit account that contains the funds of a state, county, municipality or other government unit.

PUD   See planned unit development.

purchase method of accounting   A method of accounting used in institution mergers whereby the assets and liabilities of the acquired institution are recorded at their fair value. The direct acquisition costs are included in the cost of the acquired institution. Goodwill is recorded for the excess of cost over identifiable assets minus liabilities. As of the acquisition date, the acquired institution's net worth is eliminated.

option   The option to sell a given amount of a commodity at a specified price during a specified period of time. *See also* call option.

qualified opinion   The second paragraph in an independent auditor's report, which states that the financial statements present fairly the financial position of a firm according to generally accepted accounting principles applied on a basis consistent with that of the previous year *except* for a particular matter.

qualified pension plan   A classification given by the Internal Revenue Service to a retirement or profit-sharing plan that meets certain requirements; also known as Section 401(a) plan. This classification means only that the plan qualifies for favorable tax treatment.

qualified retirement plan   A private retirement plan that meets Internal Revenue Service guidelines and regulations and offers tax advantages to businesses and individuals.

quit claim deed   A deed by which the owner of real estate conveys to another whatever title or interest he or she has to a property, but which makes no representation that the property is free from encumbrances except those created by the owner. *See also* deed.

rate of return   The measure of profitability of an investment expressed as a percentage rate of gain or loss per year on the amount invested. Also known as return on investment. *See also* yield.

rating   A formal opinion in securities trading given by an outside professional service on the credit reputation of a bond issuer and the investment quality of its securities. This opinion is expressed in letter values (AAA, Baa-l, etc.).

real accounts   The accounts—asset, liability, reserve and capital—whose balances are not canceled out at the end of an accounting period but are carried over to the next period. These accounts appear on the post-closing trial balance and the statement of condition (balance sheet). Sometimes called permanent accounts.

real assets   The tangible assets, in contrast to financial assets or securities. Included are real estate, land, gold, coins, stamps, art and antiques.

real estate   A parcel of land and any buildings or other objects permanently affixed to it. Same as real property in some states.

real estate mortgage investment conduit (REMIC)   A residential and commercial security vehicle, made possible by the Tax Reform Act of 1986, that allows issuers to sell mortgages outright while offering investors multiple classes of securities from which to choose. The vehicle offers issuers both balance sheet and tax advantages. *See also* collateralized mortgage obligation.

real estate investment trust (REIT)   An unincorporated trust or association, managed by one or more trustees for the benefit of a number of beneficiaries, that invests in real estate such as office buildings, apartment houses and shopping centers.

real estate owned (REO)   The real estate owned by a lending institution as the result of default on the part of a borrower.

Real Estate Settlement Procedures Act (RESPA)   A federal law, enacted in 1974 and subsequently amended, that requires lenders to provide home mortgage borrowers with information of known or estimated settlement costs. *See also* good faith estimate; Uniform Settlement Statement; Regulation Z.

real property   An area of land and any buildings or other objects that are permanently affixed to it.

real time   A term that pertains to the processing of information or transactions as they actually occur.

recession   A period of reduced economic activity during which the level of unemployment rises, the means of production becomes increasingly idle and general prosperity lags.

reconciliation   The process of analyzing the cause of differences between two related records. The most frequent use in accounting is bank statement reconciliation during which statements from depository banks are analyzed and compared with the institution's cash account.

records of original entry   The general journal and special journals (e.g., cash receipts and disbursements journals) that list and serve as written records of the firm's transactions in chronological order. All transactions are analyzed and recorded in one of these journals before being posted in the general ledger account. *See also* cash journals.

recourse   The right to demand payment from the maker or endorser of a negotiable instrument.

redemption of accounts   The power of a mutual savings institution to buy back the savings accounts of its members by paying their full withdrawal value.

redemption period   *See* period of redemption.

redemption right   A defaulted mortgagor's right to redeem his or her property after default and court judgment, both before and after sale of the property. *See also* equitable right of redemption; statutory right of redemption.

red herring   A preliminary prospectus used by companies during the term between the Securities Exchange Commission authorization of a security and the date on which the issuer is authorized to sell.

redlining   The refusal of a business to extend credit to, lend to, insure, or otherwise assume some financial risk involving a piece of real property or place of business located in a high-risk geographical area, most often a declining inner-city neighborhood; alternatively, fees for financial services in a redlined area may be set prohibitively high.

refinancing   The repayment of a debt from the proceeds of a new loan using the same property as security.

registered bond   A bond on which the company automatically mails interest payments to the bond's owner. The bond also is registered in the name of the owner by the issuing company. *See also* coupon bond.

registered investment advisor A person who is registered with the Securities and Exchange Commission and who provides advice on a fee basis regarding the purchase or sale of securities.

registered representative An individual who handles the buying and selling of securities for customers and who is licensed through the National Association of Securities Dealers and sponsored by a broker-dealer.

regular mortgage The legal document used in most states to pledge real estate as security for the repayment of a debt. Also known in some states as a deed of trust.

regular savings account A savings account that typically requires a low minimum balance, no minimum term, no specified minimum deposit, and no notice or penalty for withdrawals. Also called passbook account.

Regulation J The Federal Reserve regulation that specifies the rules under which the Fed will accept, clear and settle for items collected through the Federal Reserve System.

Regulation Q A 1933 Federal Reserve Board ruling that made commercial banks subject to rate controls for interest on savings accounts.

Regulation Z The title of the Federal Reserve Board's regulations implementing the Consumer Credit Protection Act for all lenders. *See also* Truth-in-Lending Act; Real Estate Settlement Procedures Act.

rehabilitation loan A loan to finance substantial alteration, repair or improvement of primary residential property.

reinstatement A complete resolution of a mortgage delinquency by the borrower, thus restoring the loan to current status.

REIT *See* real estate investment trust.

release The discharge of property from a mortgage lien; a written statement that an obligation has been satisfied.

release deed *See* satisfaction of mortgage.

REMIC *See* real estate mortgage investment conduit.

REO *See* real estate owned.

reorganization The distribution of borrowers' assets to creditors, according to a plan constructed by the borrowers or creditors, in which creditors classify their claims in a way most beneficial to them. Also called Chapter 11 bankruptcy.

replacement cost The current cost of producing, on a site, similar (but not identical) improvements possessing equal utility with the original improvements. *See also* reproduction cost.

repossession A remedy available to lenders whereby personal property used as security for a delinquent debt is acquired and disposed of

for the purpose of repaying the loan in whole or in part.

reproduction cost The current cost of duplicating the improvements on a site with identical (or effectively identical) materials. *See also* replacement cost.

repurchase agreement 1. An agreement between a financial institution and a customer where the institution sells a portion of a government security it owns, agrees to pay a specified interest rate and to repurchase that security, plus accrued interest, at a specified time. (Such investments are not insured by the FSLIC or FDIC.) Commonly called a repo. 2. An agreement used in consumer lending to establish the indirect lender's right to seek loan repayment from the dealer if conditions set forth in the retail installment contract are not met. The dealer refers to merchants who originate the retail installment contract with the buyer of the merchandise.

required reserves A specified amount of cash in a financial institution's own vault or claims on cash on deposit with other financial institutions, the minimum amount of which is prescribed by the institution's regulatory agency or agencies. The purpose of requiring a minimum amount of reserves is to maintain the ability to pay liabilities in cash.

rescission Rescission by the owner-depositor is the cancellation of power of attorney.

reserve for bad debts A reserve account to which bad debt losses are charged. Under federal tax laws, savings institutions are allowed to build up such reserves by making tax-deductible allocations of earnings according to a specified formula.

reserves The portion of earnings set aside to take care of any possible losses in the conduct of business; especially funds that represent a specified percentage of savings deposits and that all members of the Federal Savings and Loan Insurance Corporation (FSLIC) must hold to cover potential losses on loans or other investments.

residence *See* domicile.

residential mortgage loan A loan secured by real estate of one- to four family dwellings.

RESPA *See* Real Estate Settlement Procedures Act.

restrictive endorsement An endorsement that limits the negotiability of an instrument or contains a definite condition as to payment. It purports to preclude the endorsee from making any further transfer of the instrument. *See also* blank endorsement; endorsement.

retail banking The banking services offered to the general public, including consumers and small businesses.

retail open charge credit   The credit extended to borrowers to acquire goods with the promise to pay the retailer in full usually within a 30-day period. The consumer usually pays no additional fees for the privilege of the delayed payment.

retail revolving credit   A credit purchase in which a customer is permitted to purchase goods or services by agreeing to make full payment for them within 25 to 30 days, or a monthly payment in which an interest charge for the privilege of using this type of credit is added.

retained earnings   The corporate profits that are neither paid out in cash dividends nor used to increase capital stock but are reinvested in the company.

retirement bond   A bond issued by the United States government as part of an individual retirement savings program, also known as a Qualified Retirement Bond. *See also* retirement savings programs.

retirement savings programs   A general term relating to the three programs created by the Employee Retirement Income Security Act of 1974 (ERISA): IRAs, retirement annuities and retirement bonds.

return on average assets   A ratio used to measure the efficiency with which a business entity uses its assets. Return on average assets is expressed as a ratio:

$$\frac{net\ income}{average\ total\ assets}$$

(net of loans in process if a lending institution)

The higher the ratio (greater the return), the greater the efficiency.

return on - average equity   A ratio used to measure a business entity's effectiveness in investing its net worth. Return on average equity is expressed as a ratio:

return on average equity   The higher the ratio (greater the return), the more effective the investment. Return on average equity is expressed as a ratio:

$$\frac{net\ income}{average\ equity}$$

The higher the ratio (greater the return), the more effective the investment.

return on investment   *See* rate of return.

revenue bond   A bond backed only by the revenue of the facility constructed with the funds it raised, such as an airport or turnpike. *See also* general obligation bond.

revenues   The earnings of a firm; the dollar amount received for goods sold or services rendered during a given time period.

revocable trust   A trust in which the grantor reserves the right to annul the trust; if this is done, the trust property reverts back to the grantor. See *also* trust account.

right of foreclosure   The right of the lending institution to take over property and close out the mortgagor's interest in it if the mortgagor violates the provisions of the mortgage or note.

right of rescission   The right of consumers to cancel any credit transaction in which the collateral used to secure the transaction is their principal place of residence. The cancellation must occur within three business days from whichever of the following events occurs last: (1) the date of the transaction; or (2) the date on which the truth-in-lending disclosures are received; or (3) the date on which the notice of the right to cancel is received.

right of setoff   The right of the creditor to commence judicial proceedings against a borrower, sell repossessed collateral or use other assets of the borrower to satisfy payment of the debt.

risk   The probability of loss, or the degree of uncertainty, associated with the return on an investment.

risk/reward trade-off   The decision which the loan officer makes when trying to balance the riskiness of the loan against the compensation his bank will receive from the borrower.

robbery   The taking by force, or the attempt to take by force, property, money or other things of value belonging to, or in the possession of, a person or a business.

rollover   A distribution of the funds from a qualified retirement plan to a participant for the establishment of another qualified retirement savings plan.

rollover IRA   A type of IRA that allows employees who receive a lump-sum distribution from a qualified plan, upon leaving an employer or upon termination of an employer's qualified plan, to deposit all or any portion of the funds in an IRA. *See also* IRA transfer.

round lot   A block of shares, usually in multiples of 100, for trading on the exchanges.

routing and transit numbers   The identification numbers that appear on each check or draft designating the institution and its location for purposes of facilitating the check-collection process.

Rule of 72   A method used to estimate the number of years required for compounding to double the original investment. Calculated by dividing 72 by the interest rate earned on an investment.

Rule of 78s   A method of recognizing add-on interest by using predetermined factors to calculate the portion of total interest earned for the period. A declining ratio is applied to a fixed-loan amount to determine interest earned for the period. Also known as sum-of-the-digits method.

rules of the class   The terms and conditions, established by the savings institution's board of directors and included in the savings account contract, that are applicable to each deposit account classification, such as time and amount of deposit, rate of interest, penalty provisions and the account designation.

SAF Systems and Forms   An affiliate corporation of the U.S. League of Savings Institutions that develops and supplies operations materials and management systems to financial enterprises.

safe deposit box   A space in a vault that is rented to an individual for the safekeeping of valuables.

sale leaseback   An agreement under which a seller deeds real property to a buyer for a consideration and the buyer then leases the property back to the seller, usually on a long-term basis.

sale and servicing agreement   A contract, in secondary market transactions, under which the seller-servicer agrees to supply, and the buyer to purchase, loans from time to time; the contract sets forth the conditions for individual transactions, and the rights and responsibilities of both parties.

Sallie Mae   *See* Student Loan Marketing Association.

satisfaction of mortgage   A recordable instrument prepared by the lender that evidences payment in full of the mortgage debt. Also known as a release deed.

savings account   Savings accounts bear interest without specific maturity dates. There are no ceilings on such interest.

savings account loan   A loan secured by the pledging of savings funds on deposit with the institution.

Savings and Loan Foundation   A nonprofit corporation that sponsors national advertising programs to increase public knowledge and acceptance of the services of FSLIC-insured savings institutions.

savings association   A financial intermediary that accepts savings from the public and invests those savings mainly in residential mortgage loans; always a corporation, it may be either a mutual or capital stock institution and may be either state-chartered or federally chartered. Also called a savings and loan association, co-operative bank, homestead society, or building and loan association. In this *Glossary,* savings associations are among those businesses referred to as savings institutions.

savings certificate   The evidence of ownership of a savings account that typically represents a fixed amount of funds deposited for a fixed term.

Savings Institution Management Sciences, Inc.   A corporation, affiliated with the United States League of Savings Institutions, that develops and sells management science services related to the collection, processing and maintenance of information and data of all kinds.

scheduled items   An FSLIC regulatory category in which every insured institution is required to include the total amount of its slow loans (including slow consumer credit loans), real estate owned as a result of foreclosure, and real estate sold on contract or financed at a loan-to-value ratio greater than normally permitted. The scheduled items' computation reflects the soundness of an institution's portfolio and affects an institution's investment authority.

seasoned loan   A loan that has been on the institution's books long enough to demonstrate the borrower's intent to repay the debt.

second mortgage   *See* junior lien.

secondary market   The market through which investments originally sold in the primary market are bought and sold by subsequent owners and purchasers, either over-the-counter or through an exchange.

secondary mortgage market   A market in which mortgage whole loans and interests in blocks of mortgages are bought, sold and traded to other lenders, government agencies or investors.

secured loan   A loan for which the borrower pledges collateral that will be forfeited to the lender in case of default on the loan.

Securities and Exchange Commission (SEC)   A federal commission that has broad regulatory responsibilities over the securities markets, the self-regulatory organizations within the securities industry and persons conducting a business in securities.

Securities Investor Protection Corporation (SIPC)   A nonprofit brokerage community corporation created by an act of Congress to promote investor confidence in the nation's securities markets. It provides protection against theft and loss of securities held only in a brokerage account. The SIPC does not protect against bad investment decisions, bond coupons that were not clipped by mistake or lost interest. Protection is $500,000 per customer of which no more than $100,000 can be used for cash claims.

securities market   A mechanism for the buying and selling of securities between investors; examples are the over-the-counter markets, New York Stock Exchange and American Stock Exchange.

securitization   The pooling of similar loans in a package, which is then sold as a tradable security. The pooling of loans acts as collateral for the securities.

security   1. An evidence of debt or of property (such as a bond or stock certificate). 2. An item given as a pledge of repayment. 3. The steps taken by a business to safeguard its offices against theft or vandalism.

security agreement   The section of a note, or a separate document, that represents a transfer of property from a borrower to a creditor, given in fulfillment or satisfaction of a debt. In general, a security agreement identifies the creditor and borrower and contains a description of the collateral. In addition, the terms and conditions of the agreement and any special provisions required by state or federal statutes are listed.

security interest   An interest in collateral that secures payment or performance of an obligation.

SEP   *See* Simplified Employee Pension Plan.

Series EE Bond   An interest-bearing certificate of debt issued at discount by the United States Treasury and sold in denominations of from $50 to $1,000. The bond is redeemable at face value upon maturity. This bond replaced the Series E Bond in 1980. *See also* United States Savings Bond.

Series HH Bond   An interest-bearing certificate of debt issued at par value by the United States Treasury and sold in denominations of $500, $1,000 and $5,000. The owner receives a series of interest payments during the life of the bond. This bond replaced the Series H Bond in 1980. *See also* United States Savings Bond.

service bureau   A business that rents computer time or sells data processing services to users.

service corporation   A corporation, owned by one or more savings institutions, that performs services and engages in certain activities for its owners, such as originating, holding, selling and servicing mortgages; performing appraisal, brokerage, clerical, escrow, research and other services; and acquiring, developing or renovating, and holding real estate for investment purposes.

servicing   *See* loan servicing.

servicing contract   A document, in secondary market transactions, that details servicing requirements and legally binds the servicing institution to carry out the requirements.

settlement statement   *See* loan settlement statement.

settling   The process of balancing the accepted in-clearing drafts and the return items that an institution receives and making the payment within the check collection system.

settlor   A person who makes a settlement or creates a trust of property; also called a grantor.

sight draft   A customer's order to a financial institution holding his or her funds to pay all or part of them to another institution in which the customer holds an account; also called a customer draft.

signature card   A form, executed by a depositor when the depositor opens an account, establishing the type of account ownership and setting forth some of the basic terms of the account.

simple interest   A method of calculating interest in which the amount of the interest is computed on the principal balance of a loan or deposit account for each given period.

Simplified Employee Pension (SEP) Plan   A plan used by an employer to make contributions toward an employee's retirement income. The employer makes contributions, up to annual contribution limits, directly to an Individual Retirement Account set up by an employee with a savings institution, insurance company or other qualified financial institution.

single premium life   A type of permanent life insurance that can be paid for in one payment. The cash value is usually higher and the death benefit lower than in conventional annual premium policies.

site value   The worth of land without improvements, as if vacant.

skiptracing   A process in which collectors try to uncover information to help them locate missing debtors and collect repayment.

slow loan   An FSLIC regulatory category in which every insured savings institution is required to list its delinquent loans. The regulations spell out what constitutes a slow loan in terms of the loan's age and length of delinquency.

Small Business Administration (SBA)   A federal government agency that makes, guarantees and purchases participations in loans to wholesale, retail, service and manufacturing businesses.

SMSA   *See* metropolitan statistical area.

sold loan   A mortgage loan that has been sold to an investor but still is serviced by the seller.

source document   A financial institution's original written record of a transaction, showing a description of the transaction and authority for making the transaction. Source documents are executed by customers, employees or officers, depending on the type of transaction involved.

sources and uses of funds statement   The financial statement that shows the cash flow between balance sheet accounts during a reporting period.

special assessment   A claim against a property that arises when the cost of a major improvement, such as street lighting, is distributed among the benefited properties; also called an improvement lien. Failure to pay any installment of the assessment may result in foreclosure by the political entity that levied it.

special endorsement   An endorsement that transfers title to a negotiable instrument to a party specified in the endorsement. *See also* blank endorsement; endorsement.

speculate   The action of making an investment, despite great uncertainty, in the hope of realizing a substantial return.

split-rate account   A special classification on which earnings are paid at more than one rate.

spousal IRA   A type of contributory IRA that enables a working spouse to establish an IRA for his or her nonworking spouse. Spousal IRAs were created by the Tax Reform Act of 1976.

spread   The difference between the return on investments and the cost of funds. *See also* margin.

stale-dated check   A check payable on demand that is uncashed for an unreasonable length of time after its issue.

standard consolidated statistical area (SCSA)   *See* consolidated metropolitan statistical area.

standard metropolitan statistical area (SMSA)   *See* metropolitan statistical area.

standby commitment   A promise to loan funds at specific terms in the future if, at that time, the borrower still wants the loan.

statement of changes in financial position   A financial statement that outlines the sources and uses of funds and explains changes in cash or working capital of a firm.

statement of condition   *See* balance sheet.

statement of operations   A financial statement that reports an institution's income and expenses over a specified period.

statement of retained earnings   The financial statement of a stock institution that contains a report on the beginning balance of retained earnings, the net income and the withdrawals of the period, and the resulting ending balance of retained earnings. For mutual institutions, this statement is usually called a statement of general reserves.

statement savings   A system of reporting on the status of an account. The statement is mailed to the customer at specified periods, and contains a record of any account action—deposits, withdrawals, interest payments, etc.—that has taken place during that period.

statutory right of redemption   A defaulted borrower's right, in certain states, to redeem his or her property for a specified period of time after a foreclosure sale, by paying off the debts in default. *See also* equitable right of redemption; redemption right.

stock   A certificate in evidence of a shareholder's proportionate ownership of a corporation. The owner may have voting rights and rights to any dividends declared by the board of directors. Also called guaranty stock. *See also* common stock; preferred stock.

stock institution   A savings institution organized as a capital stock corporation, with investors providing operating capital by purchasing an ownership interest in the institution, represented by shares of stock. Their stock holdings entitle them to virtually the same rights as stockholders in any other corporation, including a share of the profits.

stock dividend   The distribution of shares of stock in direct proportion to the number of shares originally held by the stockholders of a corporation.

stockholder   A person who owns part of a corporation as represented by the shares held.

stop-payment order   An order by the customer instructing the financial institution to refuse payment of a specific draft or check.

straight-line depreciation method   A systematic conversion of an asset's cost into a periodic expense whereby an equal allocation of original cost is expensed each period of an asset's useful life.

Student Loan Marketing Association (SLMA)   A government-sponsored corporation chartered by Congress to market loans made under the federally sponsored Guaranteed Student Loan Program by financial and education institutions, state agencies and other organizations. It provides a source of funds and a secondary market for government-guaranteed student loans. Also known as Sallie Mae.

subordination clause   A mortgage clause that makes other debts or rights in the real estate secondary to the mortgage.

sum-of-the-years' digits depreciation method   A systematic conversion of an asset's cost into a periodic expense whereby a declining percentage rate is applied to the fixed, depreciable cost of the asset.

Super NOW   A variation of the NOW account. The Super NOW account has a higher minimum balance and interest rate than NOW accounts.

supervisory authority   The official or officials authorized by law to see that financial institutions are operated in conformity with the charter, statutes, regulations and bylaws governing their operation.

surrender of collateral statement   The statement in a loan contract that gives the lending institution the right to secure personal property without a court order.

survey   A scaled plan drawing that shows the exact dimensions and boundaries of a property, including lot lines and placement of improvements on the property, as well as any easements, rights-of-way or other pertinent information. A survey looks much like a map of the property.

sweep   An arrangement linking an account that pays low interest or no interest (Account A) with an account that pays higher interest (Account B). When the balance in Account A exceeds a specified amount, excess funds are swept into Account B. Conversely, if the balance in Account A falls below a specified amount, money is pulled back into it from Account B.

syndicate   A temporary association of two or more persons formed to carry out some specific business venture. One example is the formation of a syndicate to develop large-scale real estate projects.

system security   The protection of information-system hardware, software and data from unacceptable risks. System security guards against unauthorized access to information and systems and protects the accuracy of the organization's information.

systems analysis   1. A detailed examination of the components and requirements of an existing system, such as an organization or a data-processing system. 2. A detailed examination of the information needs of an organization, the characteristics and components of present information systems, and the data-processing requirements of proposed information systems.

tax deductions   The expenditures, as allowed by the IRS, that reduce the amount of taxable income; for example, medical expenses, charitable donations and interest paid.

tax-deferred annuity   An investment vehicle in which pretax dollars are invested by an individual to provide a future stream of income to the individual for a definite period of time, or for life. Federal income tax on pretax dollars and interest earned are postponed; generally used for retirement purposes.

tax-deferred income   The income upon which tax liability originates (is established) but income tax payment on this income amount is postponed.

tax-deferred investment   An investment on which the payment of income tax owed is postponed until a later time, usually when a person is in a lower tax bracket.

tax-exempt   An investment that is not subject to federal and/or state income tax.

tax identification number (TIN)   The number used to identify an individual or entity for federal income tax purposes.

tax lien   A government claim against real property for unpaid taxes.

taxable year   The yearly period used as the basis of federal income tax calculations; also known as the tax year. *See also* leeway period.

tax-sheltered income   The total amount of tax-deferred and tax-exempt income earned in a given taxable year. The result is reduced tax liability in the particular taxable year.

tax sheltering   A legal means of postponing or reducing the amount of tax due.

tenancy by the entirety   A form of ownership by husband and wife, recognized in certain states, in which the rights of the deceased spouse automatically pass to the survivor.

tenancy in common   A form of ownership in which two or more parties own property, but in which each owns a separate interest; when one owner dies, that owner's share passes to his or her heirs, not to the remaining owner(s). In tenancy in common account ownership, signatures of all owners are necessary for withdrawal.

tenant   A person or business that has the temporary use and right of occupation of real property owned by another.

term   The time period granted for repayment of a loan.

term deposit   *See* time deposit.

term life insurance   A type of life insurance that provides only a death benefit to be paid to a designated beneficiary upon the insurer's death. In general, there is no cash value feature, and coverage terminates at the end of the specified term.

term loan   A loan with a maturity of usually three to five years during which interest is paid but the principal is not reduced. The entire principal is due and payable at the end of its term.

testamentary account   The funds owned and controlled by an individual and invested in a revocable trust account, tentative or Totten Trust account, payable-on-death account or similar account evidencing the intention that funds will be paid to a named party at the owner's death.

third-party sponsored IRA   A trust created by an employer for the exclusive benefit of his or her employees or their beneficiaries or by an association of employees for the exclusive benefit of its members or their beneficiaries and treated as an Individual Retirement Account.

thrift institution   A financial intermediary that promotes thrift by providing customers with savings deposit facilities; for example, savings associations, savings banks and credit unions.

tiered-rate account   A special classification on which earnings may be paid at different rates depending upon the balance.

time deposit   A deposit of funds in a savings institution that may be withdrawn under stated conditions as to the time or notice required; also called term deposit.

time share ownership   A form of ownership of real property. Title to a resort or vacation home is divided among many different owners. Each owner acquires the right to occupy the property during a specified portion of each year.

time-sharing   A data-processing operation in which a computer is shared by several users working at separate terminals at the same time.

TIN   *See* tax identification number

title   The ownership right to property including the right to possession. *See also* abstract of title.

title insurance   The insurance which protects the lender and the homeowner against loss resulting from any defects in the title or claims against a property that were not uncovered in the title search and that are not specifically listed as exemptions to the coverage on the title insurance policy.

Title I   The section of the National Housing Act of 1934 that authorizes the Federal Housing Administration to insure home improvement and mobile home loans.

title report   A written statement by a title company of the condition of title to a particular piece of real estate as of a certain date.

title search   A review of public records to disclose any claims or defects in the current owner's title to real estate.

Title II   The section of the National Housing Act of 1934 that covers all basic residential mortgage insurance programs of the Federal Housing Administration.

tolerance range   An accurate calculation of the annual percentage rate (APR) to within ranges prescribed by federal regulations. Depending on the transaction type, the APR must be within either 1/8 or 1/4 of 1% of the figures computed by the federal examiner.

Totten Trust   A revocable trust account established without a written trust agreement.

town house   A low-rise, single-family dwelling attached to two or more similar dwellings separated by party walls and having separate entrances.

transaction   An event that causes some change in the assets, liabilities or net worth of a business.

transaction account   A deposit account that permits payments to be made directly to a third party on the depositor's negotiable or non-negotiable order. Examples are NOW accounts, checking accounts and third-party payment accounts.

transit number   An identifying code number devised by the American Bankers Association and assigned to each financial institution in the check-clearing system. Each number has two parts, separated by a hyphen. The first part is a code identifying the geographic location of the paying institution; the second part is a code identifying the institution itself.

Transmatic®   The trade name of a franchised, preauthorized payment system for savings institutions that was developed and is offered by SAF Systems and Forms.

traveler's check   An order, over the signature of the issuing company, to pay on demand the amount shown by the denomination of the check. Traveler's checks may be cashed almost anywhere in the world and are insured against loss, theft and destruction. *See also* check.

Treasury bill   A short-term Treasury obligation issued at a discount under competitive bidding, with a maturity of up to one year. It is issued payable to the bearer only, and is not sold in amounts of less than $10,000.

Treasury bond   A federal government obligation, ordinarily payable to the bearer, that is issued at par, with maturities of more than five years and interest payable semiannually.

Treasury certificate   A United States security usually issued at par, with a specified rate of interest and a maturity of one year or less; issued payable to the bearer and not sold in amounts of less than $1,000.

Treasury note   An obligation of the United States, usually issued payable to the bearer, with a fixed maturity of not less than one year or more than 10 years; issued at par, with a specified semiannual interest return.

truncation   *See* check truncation.

trust   A completed transfer of ownership of a piece of property by the owner (grantor) to another (the trustee) for the immediate or eventual benefit of a third person (the beneficiary). *See also* custodial IRA.

trust account   1. A deposit account, established under a trust arrangement, that contains funds administered by a trustee for the benefit of another person or persons. 2. An escrow account. *See also* irrevocable trust; revocable trust.

trust agreement   A written agreement under which a grantor transfers legal ownership of property to another person or entity for the benefit of a third person subject to the various incidents of a trust.

trustee   The legal title holder and controller of funds in a trust account established for the benefit of another according to a trust agreement.

trust fund   A financial arrangement in which financial resources are placed in the custody of an individual (trustee) by someone (grantor) for the benefit of another person (beneficiary). One person may fill more than one role, depending on the type of trust.

trust indenture   *See* deed of trust.

Truth-in-Lending Act   The popular name for the Consumer Credit Protection Act of 1968 and its provisions that require lenders to make certain disclosures of financing costs to the borrower at specified times in the loan application process. See *also* Regulation

turnkey program   A United States Department of Housing and Urban Development program for public housing whereby, under contract to a local housing authority, a private developer builds public housing with private loan funds and, upon completion of the project, turns over to the housing authority the keys to the property.

203(b) loan   A home mortgage loan insured by the Federal Housing Administration under Section 203(b) of the National Housing Act of 193.

uncollected funds   The funds that have been deposited in an account from a check that has not yet been paid by the drawee bank.

underwriting   The process, in mortgage lending, of determining the risks inherent in a particular loan and establishing suitable loan terms and conditions.

unearned interest   The interest on a loan that has already been collected but has not yet been earned because the principal has not been outstanding long enough.

Uniform Commercial Code   A body of business-related laws dealing with sale of goods, their transportation and delivery, financing, storage and final payment.

Uniform Gift to Minors Act   An act that sets forth provisions for giving a minor an intangible gift (e.g., bank accounts, stocks or bonds), that results in income shifting with an adult serving as custodian. The custodian (e.g., parent) has direct control over the gift and can sell and reinvest proceeds from the gift for the minor with the minor recognizing any gain and/or annual income that results. The minor's income from the gift cannot be combined with the custodian's property (e.g., parents using part of the child's income to purchase a car for the parents).

Uniform Settlement Statement   The Department of Housing and Urban Development form that lists all charges imposed on the borrower and the seller in connection with a home mortgage loan settlement. The Real Estate Settlement Procedures Act requires that the lender make the Statement available to the buyer and seller at the time of settlement. *See also* Real Estate Settlement Procedures Act.

Uniform Transfer to Minors Account   A Uniform Transfer to Minors Account cedes property or gifts to persons under 21 years of age. An intermediary custodian usually controls the account until majority age is reached.

unit investment trust   A classification of investment company issuing redeemable securities sold in units that represent the undivided interest in a group of securities, such as mortgages or municipal bonds.

United States League Financial Services, Inc.   An affiliate of the United States League of Savings Institutions that provides financial services, other than insurance, to savings institutions.

United States League Investment Services, Inc.   wholly owned subsidiary of the United States League of Savings Institutions that provides research, development, sponsorship, marketing and promotion of investment services to the savings institution business.

United States League of Savings Institutions   A national trade organization of savings institutions working for its members and the public interest by supporting the promotion of thrift; encouraging private investment in the purchase of homes; developing safe, efficient operating methods for member institutions; and working to improve the statutes and regulations affecting the savings business.

United States League Services, Inc.   A wholly owned subsidiary of the United States League of Savings Institutions that provides insurance programs to League members and, through those institutions, to their loan and savings clientele.

United States Savings Bond   The interest-bearing certificate of debt issued by the United States Treasury. It is nontransferable, noncallable, registered, redeemable at specified redemption values, variable as to time or maturity and fully taxable. *See also* Series EE Bond; Series HH Bond.

universal life   A form of permanent life insurance in which the death benefit may be adjusted up or down and premium payments may vary from year to year.

unqualified opinion   The second paragraph in an independent auditor's report that states that the financial statements present fairly the financial position of a firm according to generally accepted accounting principles applied on a basis consistent with that of the previous year.

unsecured credit   The credit extended on the borrower's promise to repay and for which collateral is not required. It is usually extended to consumers possessing a good credit reputation.

usury   An amount of interest, charged for the use of money, that is more than allowed by law.

VA   *See* Veterans Administration.

valuation   An estimated value of real property.

value   The dollar amount placed on collateral that indicates the price for which it can be realistically sold.

variable rate certificate   A certificate account with an interest rate that fluctuates during the deposit term according to a predetermined schedule and formula index.

vesting   The process by which an employee's rights to retirement benefits become nonforfeitable. Most pension or profit-sharing plans allow for vesting to take place in stages, according to a predetermined formula and over a set period of time. In contrast, IRA contributions are vested fully and immediately on a participant's behalf.

Veterans Administration (VA)   A government agency that aids veterans of the U.S. armed forces in various ways; its housing assistance takes the form of a guarantee to the financial institution on loans with low downpayments to qualified veterans.

voluntary association account   A deposit account held by a nonincorporated group, such as a club, baseball team, church, civic group or charity; otherwise, generally similar to a corporation account.

voucher payment plan   A method of construction loan payouts in which the contractor or borrower completes lender forms requesting each payout when a particular, prespecified stage of construction is reached.

wage assignment   A written agreement between a borrower and a financial institution, which states that upon default, the institution has the right to obtain a specific portion of the borrower's wages from a specific employer without notice or hearing. The FHLBB prohibits this type of clause in consumer loans and certain equity loans made by Federal Home Loan Bank System members. The wage assignment differs from wage garnishments in that garnishments require a court judgment, whereas assignments do not.

wage garnishment   A legal proceeding whereby a financial institution seeks a court order to obtain debt repayment from a third party (employer) who owes money (wages) to a borrower.

warranty deed   A deed in which the seller warrants that the title to the real estate is good, merchantable and without defects.

whole loan   A mortgage loan sold in its entirety by the original lender to an investor. When a whole loan is sold, all of the contractual rights and responsibilities of the original lender pass to the investor.

wholesale banking   The function of providing bank services, loan security and loans to large corporate customers.

withdrawal form   A source document and authorization for withdrawals from a savings account used by the customers and kept by the savings institution for its records.

withdrawal ratio   The ratio of withdrawals expressed as a percentage of gross savings receipts for a given period of time.

with full recourse   A term in a written agreement, used in lending, that gives the buyer in a sale or other transaction the right to full reimbursement from the seller for any losses resulting from the loans or other items purchased.

withholding   The amount deducted from gross wages or other taxable income at the time of receipt.

without recourse   A term in a written agreement, used in lending, that abrogates the right of the buyer, in a sale or other transaction, to reimbursement from the seller for any subsequent losses resulting from the loans or other items purchased.

with partial recourse   A term in a written agreement, used in lending, that gives the buyer in a sale or other transaction the right to reimbursement for an agreed-upon portion of any losses resulting from the loans or other items purchased.

wraparound mortgage   A mortgage loan that secures a debt that includes the balance due on an existing senior mortgage loan and an additional amount advanced by the wraparound lender. The wraparound lender thereafter makes the amortizing payments on the senior mortgage.

write-off   The accounting procedure of removing an amount from the asset category of a balance sheet and recording it as an expense item on the income statement; this type of adjustment is necessary when an institution takes a loss, as in the sale of real estate owned.

yield   The return on an investment, expressed as a percentage of the market price or, where the investment is owned, of the price paid for it originally. *See also* effective yield; rate of return.

yield curve   A line or curve that graphically represents the relationship between interest rates of securities having equal qualities but different maturities.

yield interest rate   The actual rate of return an investor receives on an investment.

yield to maturity   A yield concept designed to give the investor the average annual yield on a security. This calculation is based on the interest rate, price and length of time to maturity; and takes into account any bond premium or discount.

zero-coupon bond   A corporate debt issue containing a promise to pay face value at a designated future date, usually 10 years hence. Interest accrues and is taxable, but not paid until redemption. It is sold at a substantial discount, but does not include the coupons that provide regular prematurity interest rates on conventional issues.

zoning ordinance   A community law designed to classify and regulate land use, in order to protect the health, welfare and safety of people in the community.

Index